HIPPOCRATES' WO

In ancient Greece, gynaecology originated in the myth of the first woman Pandora, whose beautiful appearance was seen to cover her dangerous 'insides'.

Hippocrates' Woman demonstrates how ancient Greek healers read the signs offered by their patients' bodies, arguing that medicine was based on ideas about women and their bodies found in myth and ritual. Helen King deploys a wide range of comparative materials from the social sciences to discuss religious healing, chronic pain, and the creation of a powerful self-image by aspiring healers. She outlines how nursing and midwifery have tried to create their own versions of the ancient Greek past to give themselves greater status, and presents a detailed account of how doctors twisted ancient Greek texts into ways of controlling women's behaviour. Finally, she analyses how later medicine, by diagnosing 'hysteria' and by recommending practices such as clitoridectomy, gave its decisions authority by claiming ancient Greek origins which never existed.

Hippocrates' Woman provides a controversial, provocative and stimulating insight into the origins of gynaecology and the influence of the early study of medical texts on later medical practices and theories up until the Victorian era.

Helen King is a Wellcome Trust Research fellow and Lecturer in the Departments of Classics and History at the University of Reading. Her wide range of publications on women and medicine includes *Hysteria Beyond Freud* (1993).

Praise for Helen King

'Once Upon a Text: Hysteria from Hippocrates',
in *Hysteria Beyond Freud*, ed. Sander Gilman, Helen King, Roy Porter,
George Rousseau and Elaine Showalter
(Berkeley, University of California Press, 1993)

The definitive analysis of the historical construction of the 'disease'
of hysteria/uterine suffocation
Medieval Feminist Newsletter

Helen King has delivered a tour de force on the classical period . . .
a triumph of original scholarship
Times Literary Supplement

The opening essay, 'Once Upon a Text: Hysteria from Hippocrates' by
the English Classicist Helen King, is a scholarly and analytic tour
de force and one of the most exciting revisionist analyses
I have recently read.
Bulletin of the History of Medicine

HIPPOCRATES' WOMAN

Reading the female body in Ancient Greece

Helen King

Routledge
Taylor & Francis Group
LONDON AND NEW YORK

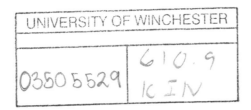

First published 1998
by Routledge
2 Park Square, Milton Park, Abingdon, Oxon OX14 4RN

Simultaneously published in the USA and Canada
by Routledge
270 Madison Ave, New York, NY 10016

Routledge is an imprint of the Taylor & Francis Group, an informa business

Typeset in Garamond by Keystroke, Jacaranda Lodge, Wolverhampton

British Library Cataloguing in Publication Data
A catalogue record for this book is available from the British Library

Library of Congress Cataloguing in Publication Data
King, Helen.
Hippocrates' woman : reading the female body in ancient Greece / Helen King.
p. cm.
Includes bibliographical references and index.
ISBN 0–415–13894–9 HB. — ISBN 0–415–13895–7 PB
1. Gynecology—Greece—History. 2. Medicine, Greek and Roman. 3. Gynecology—Greek influences. 4. Women—Greece—History. 5. Body, Human—Social aspects—Greece—History. I. Title.
RG59.K56 1998
618.1′00938—dc21 98–3728
CIP

ISBN 10: 0-415-13894-9 (hbk)
ISBN 10: 0-415-13895-7 (pbk)

ISBN 13: 978-0-415-13894-9 (hbk)
ISBN 13: 978-0-415-13895-6 (pbk)

TO MY PARENTS

CONTENTS

ACKNOWLEDGEMENTS

Much of the material used in this book has been presented to a variety of seminar audiences; some has been previously published, often in places which are not easily accessible, and appears here in a revised form. The Introduction and first two chapters have not been previously published; sections of Chapter 2 develop ideas first explored in '"We tried to draw down the blood but she died": women and death in Hippocratic medicine', Classical Association AGM, Oxford, 1992 and 'Diagnosing the future', Institute of Classical Studies, January 1991. Chapter 3 is a revised version of 'The daughter of Leonides: reading the Hippocratic corpus' in *History as Text* (ed. A. Cameron; Duckworth, 1989, 13–32), which derived from a seminar series at the Institute of Classical Studies.

I first became interested in the Hippocratic treatise *On the Diseases of Virgins* after hearing Mary Lefkowitz speak on it at the Institute of Classical Studies, London while I was a student. Chapters 4 and 10 use this text as their starting point. Chapter 4 develops 'Bound to bleed: Artemis and Greek women', published in *Images of Women in Antiquity* (ed. Averil Cameron and Amelie Kuhrt; London, Croom Helm, 1983; reprinted 1993, 109–27), and 'Sacrificial blood: the role of the *amnion* in Hippocratic gynecology', *Helios* 13(2) (1987) = *Rescuing Creusa* (ed. M.B. Skinner; Texas Tech University Press, 117–26). 'Bound to bleed' was based on the first seminar paper I ever gave, delivered at the ICS on 5 November 1981. My work was stimulated by attending J.-P. Vernant's lectures at the Collège de France in spring 1981, and subsequently benefited from comments from Geoffrey Lloyd, Jan Bremmer and Vivian Nutton.

Chapter 5 is a version of 'Comparative perspectives on medicine and religion in the ancient world', published in *Religion, Health and Suffering* (ed. Roy Porter and John Hinnells; London: Kegan Paul, 1998), reprinted here with permission. Chapter 6 uses some material first published as 'The early anodynes: pain in the ancient world' in *The Management of Pain: the historical perspective* (ed. Ronald D. Mann; Carnforth, Lancs and Park Ridge, NJ: Parthenon Press, 1988, 51–62), which is reprinted with permission. Another version of this chapter is scheduled to appear in *Constructions of the Classical*

Body (ed. Jim Porter; University of Michigan Press, forthcoming), and is reprinted with permission.

Chapter 7 has not previously been published. An early version was presented to the ICI Staff Seminar in Runcorn, and shorter versions were presented at the American Philological Society in San Diego, 1995, and the History Department, University of York in November 1997.

Chapter 8 is an updated version of a paper originally written for a seminar on nursing and anthropology in Oxford, published as 'Using the past: nursing and the medical profession in ancient Greece' in *Anthropology and Nursing: cross-cultural and historical perspectives* (ed. Pat Holden and Jenny Littlewood; London: Routledge, 1991, 7–24). I first studied some of the material developed in Chapter 9 from a very different angle in 'Agnodike and the profession of medicine', *Proceedings of the Cambridge Philological Society* 32 (1986), 53–77, but the argument of this chapter derives from a paper delivered at the invitation of Larissa Bonfante at the Onassis Hellenic Foundation, New York in 1995.

A version of Chapter 10 was published in the *International Journal of the Classical Tradition* 2 (1996), 372–87, and was based on papers given at the Third Meeting of the International Society for the Classical Tradition, Boston University, 8–12 March 1995, at the universities of Leeds, Bristol and Birmingham and at the Wellcome Unit for the History of Medicine, Oxford. In particular I would like to thank Irvine Loudon for his encouragement when an earlier version was presented at the Wellcome Institute, London in 1987, and Vivian Nutton for his invaluable comments on the present version. Its completion as an article was made possible by the British Academy Research Leave Scheme.

A longer version of Chapter 11 was published in *Hysteria Beyond Freud*, written with Sander Gilman, Roy Porter, George S. Rousseau and Elaine Showalter (University of California Press, 1993), 3–90. Sections were presented to the Pybus Club (Newcastle, 1985), the Classical Association Triennial Meeting (Oxford, 1988), a conference organised by the Wellcome Institute for the History of Medicine (London, 1990) and the Liverpool Medical History Society/Society for the History of Science (Liverpool, 1991). The previously published version had the benefit of the comments of Monica Green and Mark Micale.

This book would never have reached completion without the opportunities provided by funding from the Wellcome Trust University Award Scheme from June 1996 onwards, and I would like to thank the Trust, and especially David Allen, with Michael Biddiss and Tessa Rajak of the University of Reading for making this award possible. Over the many years in which I have been working on it without these opportunities, I have been very fortunate in my friends in the profession, whose support has been much appreciated and who have offered me welcome opportunities to discuss my work with a wide range of audiences. In particular I would like to thank Gillian Clark, Nancy

Demand, Pat Easterling, Monica Green, Ann Ellis Hanson, David Harley, Lesley Dean-Jones, Geoffrey Lloyd, Nicole Loraux, Hilary Marland, Catherine and Robin Osborne, Roy Porter, Wesley Smith, Heinrich von Staden and Andrew Wear. Of those who have kept my mind on the target by regularly asking me when 'the book' would be coming out, my thanks to John Elford, Sally Humphreys, John McGurk, Fergus Millar and of course Vivian Nutton.

In carrying out the research for this book, I have been privileged to work in excellent libraries; in particular, the Institute of Classical Studies, the Wellcome Institute in London, the Cole Collection at the University of Reading and the unique ambience of the Fondation Hardt in Geneva. I have also been able to rely throughout on the encouragement of my parents, and the enthusiasm of my students at Liverpool and Reading. The advice and help on matters medical of Anita Davies, Jerry Hobdy, Rebecca James and the late Simon Stewart have been invaluable.

Ann Ellis Hanson and Vivian Nutton have been outstanding in their support over the years, and have surpassed themselves in commenting on the whole manuscript, which has benefited enormously from their constructive criticism. Responsibility for those errors of fact or interpretation which remain rests firmly in my hands. Richard Stoneman has been involved in various versions of this project since 1985, and must be almost as delighted as I am that this manuscript has been completed. I would also like to thank Beth Humphries for her careful copy-editing and Kate Hopgood for her efficiency in handling the final stages of production.

Helen King
Reading, January 1998

NOTE ON TEXTS

In the interests of readers whose background is not in classics, I have chosen to give most Hippocratic references in the Loeb Classical Library editions, which offer Greek or Latin text with an English translation on the facing page. This is not possible, however, for some works, including the *Diseases of Women* treatises, so for these I have cited the edition with French translation published by Emile Littré (1839–61) *Oeuvres complètes d'Hippocrate*, 10 vols, Paris: Baillière (reprinted Amsterdam: Hakkert, 1961–2). The most recent and best edition of selections from *Diseases of Women* is that of Hermann Grensemann (1975b) *Knidische Medizin I*, Berlin and New York: de Gruyter, which uses a better range of manuscripts than that available to Littré and includes a German translation. Ann Ellis Hanson is currently preparing editions of the Hippocratic gynaecological texts for the Loeb and CMG series. For other classical authors, most passages can be found in the Loeb translations; other translations may have slightly different line numbers, but the reader should nevertheless be able to find what is needed. Non-specialists will find invaluable the third edition of the *Oxford Classical Dictionary* (ed. Simon Hornblower and Antony Spawforth, Oxford: Oxford University Press, 1996).

ABBREVIATIONS

7MC	[Hippocrates], *On the Seventh Months' Child*
Aen.	Virgil, *Aeneid*
Aesch.	Aeschylus
Aff.	[Hippocrates], *Affections*
Alc.	Euripides, *Alcestis*
Ant.	Sophocles, *Antigone*
Ant. Lib.	Antoninus Liberalis
Anth. Pal.	*Palatine Anthology*
Aph.	[Hippocrates], *Aphorisms*
Ar.	Aristotle
Aristoph.	Aristophanes
Art.	Callimachos, *Hymn to Artemis*
Ath. Pol.	[Aristotle], *Constitution of Athens*
AWP	[Hippocrates], *Airs, Waters, Places*
BL	British Library
BMJ	*British Medical Journal*
Call.	Callimachos
CIL	Corpus Inscriptionum Latinarum
CMG	Corpus Medicorum Graecorum
CML	Corpus Medicorum Latinorum
CP	[Hippocrates], *Coan Prognoses*
Cyn.	Oppian, *Cynegetica*
De uteri diss.	Galen, *On the Dissection of the Womb*
De prov. cons.	Cicero, *De provinciis consularibus*
Dec.	[Hippocrates], *On Decorum*
Diod. Sic.	Diodorus Siculus
Dis.	[Hippocrates], *On Diseases*
DK	H. Diels and W. Kranz (1967) *Die Fragmente der Vorsokratiker*, Zurich
DW	[Hippocrates], *Diseases of Women*
EG	G. Kaibel (1878) *Epigrammata Graeca*, Berlin
Elec.	Euripides, *Electra*

Ep.	[Hippocrates], *Epidemics*
Eur.	Euripides
Eust.	Eustathius
Fract.	[Hippocrates], *On Fractures*
GA	Aristotle, *Generation of Animals*
Gen.	[Hippocrates], *On Generation*
Geog.	Strabo, *Geography*
GLP	Martin West (1993) *Greek Lyric Poetry*, Oxford: Clarendon Press
Gyn.	Soranos, *Gynaecology*
HA	Aristotle, *History of Animals*
Hal.	Oppian, *Halieutica*
Hes.	Hesiod
Hippol.	Euripides, *Hippolytos*
IG	*Inscriptiones Graecae* (1873–)
Il.	Homer, *Iliad*
Isoc.	Isocrates
IT	Euripides, *Iphigeneia in Tauris*
Joly	Robert Joly (1970) *Hippocrate XI*, Paris: Eds Belles Lettres (Budé edition of NC)
K	Carl Gottlob Kühn (1821–33) *Claudii Galeni opera omnia*, 20 vols, Leipzig
L	Emile Littré (1839–61) *Oeuvres complètes d'Hippocrate*, 10 vols, Paris: Baillière
Lact.	Lactantius
Loc. Aff.	Galen, *On the Affected Parts*
LSJ	H.G. Liddell, R. Scott and H.S. Jones (1968) *A Greek-English Lexicon*, 9th edition with supplement, Oxford: Oxford University Press
Lys.	Aristophanes, *Lysistrata*
Med.	Celsus, *De Medicina*
Mem.	*Memorabilia*
Met.	Ovid, *Metamorphoses*
Mor.	Plutarch, *Moralia*
MW	Reinhold Merkelbach and Martin West (1967) *Fragmenta Hesiodea*, Oxford: Clarendon Press
NA	Aelian, *The Nature of Animals*
NC	[Hippocrates], *Nature of the Child*
NE	Aristotle, *Nicomachean Ethics*
NH	Pliny, *Natural History*
NM	[Hippocrates], *On the Nature of Man*
NW	[Hippocrates], *On the Nature of Woman*
Od.	Homer, *Odyssey*
Oik.	*Oikonomikos*
Oneir.	Artemidoros, *Oneirocriticon* (*Dream Book*)

Onom.	Pollux, *Onomastikon*
OSL	Obstetrical Society of London
P	Papyrus
PA	Aristotle, *On the Parts of Animals*
Pack[2]	R.A. Pack (1965) *The Greek and Latin Literary Texts from Greco-Roman Egypt*, 2nd edition, Ann Arbor: University of Michigan Press
Paus.	Pausanias
PCG	Rudolp Kassel and Colin Austin, *Poetae Comici Graeci*; vol. 1 (1983); vol. 2 (1991), Berlin and New York: de Gruyter
PGM	*Papyri Graecae Magicae*, 2nd edition, Karl Preisendanz and Albert Henrichs (1974), Stuttgart: Teubner
PL	J.-P. Migne (1841–64) *Patrologia Cursus, series Latina*, Paris
Plut.	Plutarch
PM	[Hippocrates], *Places in Man*
Pol.	Aristotle, *Politics*
PPF	H. Diels (ed.) (1901) *Poetarum philosophorum fragmenta*, Berlin: Weidmann
Prog.	[Hippocrates], *Prognostics*
ps-Ar.	pseudo-Aristotle
PSI	*Papyri Grece e Latini, Pubblicazioni della Società italiana per la ricerca dei papiri greci e latini in Egitto* (1912–)
RCS	Royal College of Surgeons
Reg. Ac.	[Hippocrates], *Regimen in Acute Diseases*
Sac. Dis.	[Hippocrates], *On the Sacred Disease*
SEG	Supplementum Epigraphicum Graecum
SF	[Hippocrates], *Superfoetation*
SLG	D. L. Page (1974) *Supplementum Lyricis Graecis*, Oxford: Clarendon Press
Soph.	Sophocles
Stat.	Statius
Suet.	Suetonius
Suppl.	*Suppliant Women*
T	O. Temkin (1956; repr. 1991) *Soranus' Gynecology*, Baltimore: Johns Hopkins University Press
Tac.	Tacitus
test.	testimonia in Emma J. and Ludwig Edelstein (1945) *Asclepius: a collection and interpretation of the testimonies* (2 vols), Baltimore: Johns Hopkins University Press
Th.	Hesiod, *Theogony*
Theb.	Statius, *Thebaid*
Thesm.	Aristophanes, *Women at the Thesmophoria*
Thuc.	Thucydides
TOSL	*Transactions of the Obstetrical Society of London*

Ulc.	[Hippocrates], *On Ulcers*
Virg.	[Hippocrates], *On the Diseases of Virgins*
[Xen.]	pseudo-Xenophon
Z	S. Zervos (1901) *Aetii sermo sextidecimus et ultimus*, Leipzig: Mangkos

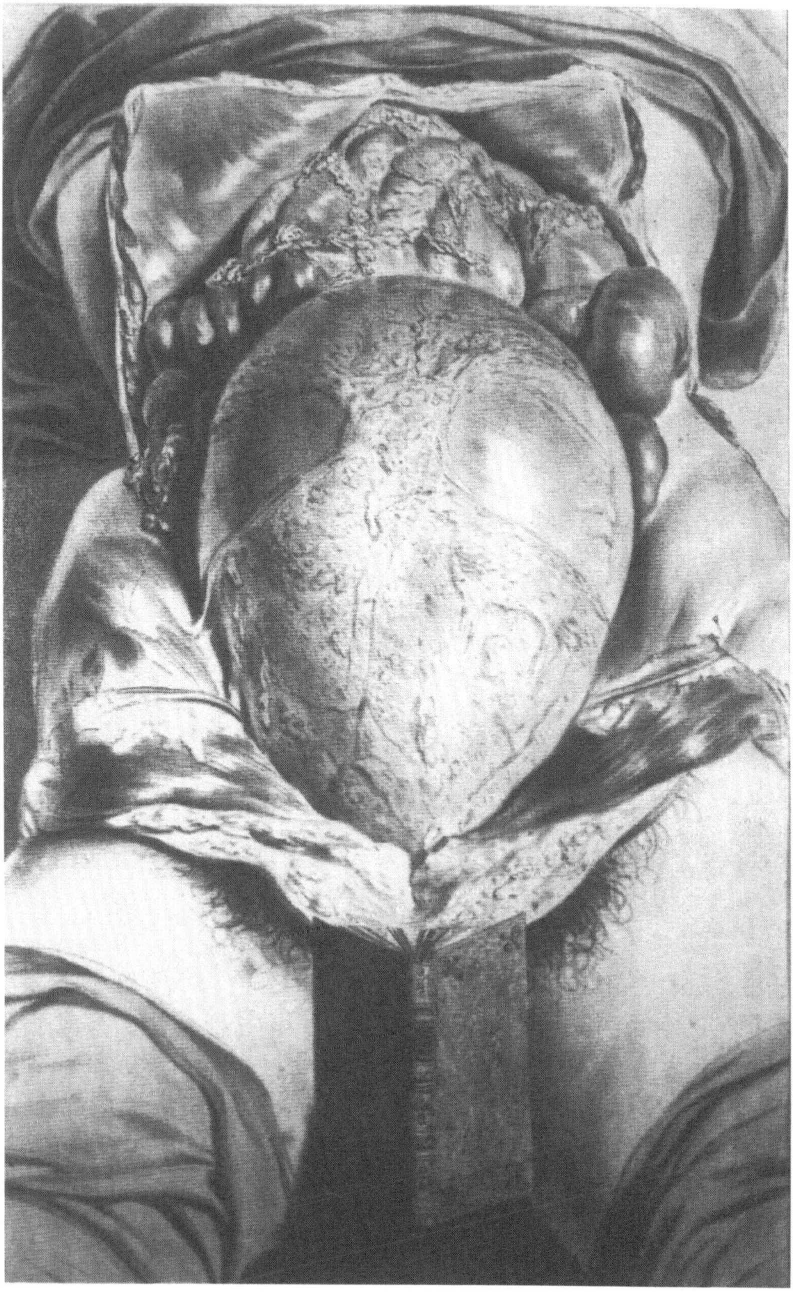

Jan van Rymsdyck
Tab. XXVI (front view of the womb)
Drawing from William Hunter's *Anatomy of the human gravid uterus*
Reproduced with permission of Glasgow University Library.

INTRODUCTION

'We, being men, have our patients, who are women, at our mercy'
(Seymour Haden, *British Medical Journal* 1867: 396)[1]

From the nineteenth century until the present day, gynaecology has been the branch of medicine which most strikingly manifests the inequality intrinsic to traditional patient/doctor relationships in Western culture. As many studies have shown, the sick role is feminised, while the doctor embodies what are considered to be the masculine virtues (e.g. Nathanson 1975; Weisensee 1986): in gynaecology, all the patients are women, and the majority of those deciding what counts as disease and how to treat it are men. We may think of gynaecology and obstetrics as separate areas, but they are commonly practised by the same individuals who define gynaecology as the medical speciality devoted to women's reproductive potential, with obstetrics focused on the realisation of that potential. For example, C. Scott Russell, Professor of Obstetrics and Gynaecology at Sheffield University, defined gynaecology as 'the part of doctoring that is centred on the woman's reproductive organs and functions' (1968: 1).[2]

This book concerns the nature, and subsequent historical interpretations, of gynaecology in the earliest period for which we have detailed written accounts: classical Greece of the fifth and fourth centuries BC, the period to which many of the texts now known as the Hippocratic corpus can be dated. Simon Byl (1989: 55) has estimated that approximately a quarter of the corpus concerns the diseases of women. By investigating Hippocratic gynaecology, this book will explore how claims about precisely which organs and functions are to be implicated in the reproductive process, and decisions on the situations needing medical intervention, should be understood as historical constructs. In studying this material, my purpose throughout remains twofold. First, I want to set the ideas about the female body which are found in ancient Greek gynaecology in the social and cultural context in which they were produced. This will involve seeing Hippocratic medicine as part of a wider discussion about the nature of humanity, and as an enterprise best understood by reading the texts in relation to ideas found in myth and religion about the place of woman in the world. Second, I want to examine the ways in which later writers have appealed to this ancient medical material in support of their own theories, in social contexts which may appear very different from the world of the classical Greek healer. For those arguing for the antiquity of their profession, trying to give the respectability of history to a new development or a new disease, or projecting into the past a model which would empower women in the present, Hippocratic gynaecology has had a lasting fascination.

In the period when Francis Seymour Haden served as a vice-president of the Obstetrical Society of London and expressed his view of the gender inequality fundamental to gynaecology, it was just beginning to be established as a medical speciality in the modern sense of the term.[3] The OSL itself was only founded in 1859, breaking away from the Royal Medical and Chirurgical Society (Moscucci 1990: 66); its interests covered matters related to childbirth but also the treatment of conditions of the uterus and vagina. It immediately enrolled 350 Fellows (*Transactions of the Obstetrical Society of London* 2, 1860: 1); by 1864 there were 535 (*TOSL* 6, 1864: 14). Why was there such enthusiasm for the Society? Its members voiced concerns about the training in obstetrics received by men in medical schools, and the need 'to raise the character of English midwifery in the estimation of our foreign brethren', as its first president, Edward Rigby, put it when addressing the Society (*TOSL* 2, 1860: 2), but there was also an interest for its individual members in upward mobility within the medical profession. Henry Oldham's presidential address in 1864 noted that, within a medical career, 'It is at a later period, when a man feels that it is often the stepping stone to practice, and the centre of his success, that obstetrics claim his earnest attention' (*TOSL* 6, 1864: 14; Loudon 1986: 94–9). It was also recognised that, by covering all diseases of the female generative organs (*TOSL* 7, 1865: 42), performing surgical procedures as well as recommending drugs, the nineteenth-century practitioner of obstetrics and gynaecology was crossing the boundaries between surgeon and physician established in the seventeenth century and maintained by the existence of separate Royal Colleges. In the words of the next president of the OSL, Robert Barnes, the 'obstetric physician seemed a sort of hybrid, sprung from the impure union of the pure physician and the pure surgeon'.[4]

For this hybrid, there was enormous concern to ensure that the potentially difficult situation of a male practitioner performing an intimate examination of a female patient was hedged around by agreed procedures. It was this situation, and known cases of its flagrant abuse (Porter 1987), that made it so important to establish 'Those rules of etiquette which should govern an honourable and scientific profession' (*Lancet* 1850: 706). After the introduction in 1821 of examination by means of the speculum, issues of propriety tended to focus on this (Dally 1991: 126–9); it was thought that the use of similar instruments in earlier historical periods had been restricted to dilating the mouth of the womb in labour (*Lancet* 1850: 701; West 1864: 17). Derided by its English critics as a 'French' invention, the speculum was considered to carry the potential risk not only of physical injury (Pattison 1866: 26) but also of 'dulling the edge of virgin modesty, and the degradation of pure minds, of the daughters of England'; 'the female who has been subjected to such treatment is not the same person in delicacy and purity that she was before' (M. Hall 1850: 660–1). Its negative connotations increased after its use in forcible examination of prostitutes under the 1864 and 1866 Contagious Disease Acts (Moscucci 1990: 112–17). Textbooks recommended that it should be avoided for unmarried women, except in very urgent cases (West 1864: 20; Churchill 1864: 18), but also questioned whether it really added anything to the practitioner's knowledge (West 1864: 22). Whatever their attitude to instruments – and the Fellows of the OSL took a particularly keen interest in developing their own variations on what were seen as the essential items of obstetric equipment[5] – gynaecologists often found themselves with knowledge of a patient, particularly relating to unwanted pregnancies or venereal disease, which was sensitive in the extreme. As doctors, they felt bound by the Hippocratic Oath, a code from another time and another culture,[6] which held that the doctor should preserve the secrecy of all that he learns in the course of treating patients. Yet as fellow men, their sympathies could lie with the fathers and husbands of the women they treated, a problem explored in the 1890s when the Kitson v. Playfair trial questioned whether a doctor could reveal a woman's adultery to her husband (A. McLaren 1993).

The social and economic context of Victorian gynaecology may seem very different from that of the Hippocratic corpus; issues of specialisation and the formation of professional groups were far from the world of the itinerant, unlicensed Hippocratic healer. But, as this example can illustrate, there were points of contact. The late third-century BC Hippocratic treatise *The Doctor* 1 (Loeb VIII, 302)[7] notes that 'Patients in fact put themselves into the hands of their physician, and at every moment he meets women, maidens, and possessions very precious indeed.' Similar problems of ethics and 'purity' were thus raised by the central scene of a male doctor examining a female body, while the concern with how best the interior of the body was to be viewed was one voiced in the Hippocratic corpus (see below, Chapter 2). Hippocratic texts were translated and read by doctors, while Victorian medicine retained its claim to Hippocratic origins through the concern with the Hippocratic Oath, which meant that a Victorian gynaecologist could see his role through a classical lens.

In this book I will be using limited cross-cultural comparisons in order to draw out features of the ancient Greek material, comparing it either with other historical data such as this, or with anthropological accounts both of contemporary non-Western societies and of our own society. Historians of ancient medicine will only ever have some pieces of the jigsaw: such comparative reports can at least give some idea of what the picture on the box could look like (Cohen 1991: 10). But Jack Winkler was right to warn that 'There is no magic phrase, such as "Anthropology!", that will guarantee success to our hermeneutic project' (1990: 98).[8] Arguing from Mediterranean anthropology, in which a network of competition and suspicion is commonly found, Winkler suggested that the élite literary texts of the ancient world should be seen as lying guides, manipulating us as readers much as an anthropological observer is manipulated by his or her informants. Anthropologists are well aware of the risk of 'the well-informed informant' who tells you exactly what you want to hear. Sjaak van der Geest (1991) worked with a man selling out-of-date Western drugs in a market in Cameroon, and noted how her questions led him to concoct answers, since saying 'I don't know' would not only make him lose face but, more practically, would mean that he risked losing her presence beside him taking notes, where she was perceived as his 'Western secretary' and thus provided a further boost to his prestige. When studying ancient medicine, we are always asking questions which our sources cannot readily answer, while assuming that medical texts are transparent accounts of reality,[9] and using ancient texts to promote the claims of particular types of modern medicine. All of these themes – their dangers, and the difficulty of transcending them – will recur throughout this book.

In addition to providing us with a healthy scepticism about our sources, comparative material enhances our sense of the possible. Modern Western biomedicine has been defined as an internalising, allopathic system in which disease is seen as a series of abstract, unchanging and universally valid entities and which is associated with literate, state societies and with professionally trained personnel given state funding (Fabrega and Silver 1973: 218–19; A. Young 1980: 108; Pearcy 1992: 595). 'Western biomedicine' may appear to be a far more homogeneous system than Hippocratic medicine, but anthropologists studying it have demonstrated that it too works with a large number of different explanatory models, including 'biochemical, immunological, viral, genetic, environmental, psychodynamic, family interactionist and so on' (Helman 1985: 294; cf. Good and Good 1981). If the only types of medicine with which we are familiar are biomedicine, and the humoral systems of ancient medicine which tend to treat a patient rather than a disease, we may have a misleading sense of what is normal, and therefore does not need explanation, and what is unusual and therefore needs to be explained.

One example of how awareness of other cultures can expand our sense of what is 'normal' is an activity which played a central role in ancient Greek definitions of woman: menstruation. We believe that it is normal for a woman of childbearing age to menstruate every month; so did the Hippocratics. But it would be insufficiently rigorous to leave the matter there, assuming that this is so obvious that it need not be questioned. The evidence from rural communities of the past, and from contemporary simple societies, suggests that – cross-culturally – menstruation is more likely to have been scanty and infrequent (e.g. D. McLaren 1975; Crawford 1978; Winslow 1980). Societies exist in which menstruation is considered dangerously abnormal and in need of medical treatment if it occurs more than once every two months (G. Lewis 1980: 123). We also believe that menstruation is 'a biological given', natural, spontaneous, and part of being a woman (Skultans 1970: 639); however, even for twentieth-century American society, Joan Jacobs Brumberg's study of the relationships between biological change and emergent consumerism in connection with menarche demonstrates a shift away from seeing the first menstruation in terms of 'becoming a woman' to what she calls 'the hygienic imperative', as immigrant groups learned the '"American way" to menstruate' (1993: 104). In other societies, menstruation may be seen not as a natural fact but as part of the present cultural order (G. Lewis 1980: 112). Many societies across the world with a strong opposition between the sexes have myths which tell how women invented the sacred objects now used in male ritual; men's appropriation of these objects by violence or stealth inaugurated the present sexual division of labour. The Barasana of Northwest Amazonia say that menstruation was forced upon women because they stole ritual objects from the men; in former times, it was men who menstruated (C. Hugh-Jones 1979: 137; S. Hugh-Jones 1979: 198; cf. G. Lewis 1980: 124). Menstruation can support opposition between racial or religious groups: Peter Biller has drawn attention to the medieval idea that, since the crucifixion, all Jews menstruate (1992: 199). As for spontaneity, some Melanesian societies in which men practise penis-bleeding use the same word for this as for female menstruation; with no linguistic indication that artificial and natural are to be separated, men are represented as doing the same thing as women (G. Lewis 1980: 112). Other societies in the same area categorically deny that female and male menstruation are in any way equivalent (G. Lewis 1980: 2), while a further variation is found in groups where women not only menstruate but also make themselves bleed by inserting wads of leaves into the vagina after menstruation and childbirth (Berndt 1962: 106). We do not see menstruation as under our conscious control, but it may be believed that women can stop it by using spells (Strathern 1972: 171). The Samo of the Upper Volta consider menarche so important that they will, if necessary, induce it after death; if a woman's blood is not released, not only will she have to be buried in the children's cemetery, but she may become a sort of vampire (Héritier 1978: 393). The range of the possible here brings home to us that menstruation may be seen in terms totally opposed to our own: as irregular, unnatural, controllable or even as an originally male activity.

Examples such as this demonstrate that the body is 'simultaneously a physical and symbolic artefact . . . both naturally and culturally produced' (Scheper-Hughes and Lock 1987: 7). We experience our bodies by living them, but the meanings we give to that experience are cultural, so that our experiences are also being shaped by the language and concepts medicine gives us to express our sensations (Wendell 1996: 136–7). We cannot therefore assume that there is some common 'reality' lying beneath the surface of medical texts such as the Hippocratic corpus: the human body, historically constant, naturally given.[10]

A related issue is that of rationality. The term can be used in studies of other medical systems in two ways. It may denote a type of medicine which searches for the cause in order to decide on treatment (Debru 1996: 241), or it may carry value-judgements about whether or not an argument makes sense in modern scientific terms. The two meanings can be combined, as in James Longrigg's book on the relationships between ancient philosophy and medicine, significantly entitled *Greek Rational Medicine*. Longrigg states as his opening gambit, 'One of the most impressive contributions of the ancient Greeks to Western culture was their invention of rational medicine' (1993: 1).[11] This is a revealing statement. Rational medicine is 'impressive'; this contrasts with Longrigg's later evaluation of coprotherapy, the use of excrement in drug recipes, as 'this nauseating practice' (1993: 9).[12] The importance of what the Greeks contributed to 'Western culture' is given priority; the Greeks are of interest principally as our ancestors. In a highly circular argument, we look at what impresses us, and what impresses us is what we define ourselves as being. Finally, the Greeks 'invented' a unitary thing called 'rational medicine', which appears to be independent of culture; not even 'a' rational medicine, but one monolithic, universally valid category. Longrigg grants that 'it should not be assumed that irrational elements were completely eradicated from Greek medical thinking . . . Then, as indeed is still the case at the present day, superstitious beliefs and irrational practices were rife in medicine' (1993: 3) but, by using words as value-laden as 'eradicated' and 'rife', he presents the irrational as a malign influence on the purity of rational medicine. For Longrigg, irrationality is a powerful but invisible force: beliefs and practices associated with it 'were frequently unconsciously adopted even by doctors, who were otherwise fiercely opposed to superstition and irrational practices' (1993: 4). 'Even by doctors' is a revealing phrase; although not himself a member of the medical profession, Longrigg, in company with the retired doctors who have traditionally written medical history, sees that profession as a group of brave and godlike men fighting the dragons of superstition while bearing aloft the banner of pure reason.

The assumptions by which we devalue other systems of knowledge are revealed not only by the use of 'rife' and 'eradicated', but also by our choices among words such as 'know', 'believe' and 'symbolic' (Browner *et al.* 1988: 682). For example, when Dan Sperber worked with the Dorze people of Ethiopia, he noted

> when a Dorze friend says to me that pregnancy lasts nine months, I think, 'So, they know that.' When he adds, 'but in some clans it

> lasts eight or ten months', I think, 'That's symbolic.' Why? Because it is false.
>
> (1975: 3)

We know: they believe. Our knowledge is real: their belief is symbolic. One way of studying the Hippocratic texts is therefore to assess their anatomy, physiology and therapy as either 'right' or 'wrong' in relation to the body we believe we now know; to compare representation and reality, and to judge the first accordingly. Comparative data contribute to reducing this ethnocentrism, but ideally we should use the same terminology for both our medical beliefs, and theirs: the Greeks believed in the wandering womb, while we believe in hormones.

New approaches to medical history explore discourse about the body as a means of reflecting, confirming or challenging dominant social values; they accept that even if 'Biomedicine may be scientific ideally; that does not mean to say that it is complete and perfect now' (G. Lewis 1993: 191). For example, the way in which differences between male and female bodies are expressed derives from particular social structures and the places of the sexes within these, but can also reinforce such structures by locating their origin in unquestionable, 'natural' facts.

The very existence of gynaecology as a speciality may be significant in a given culture. By concentrating on certain functions of the female, defining the limits of normality and deeming women in general as needing specialised care, it can reinforce the idea that women are a separate group rather than part of 'humanity'. Moscucci has shown how, in the late eighteenth and nineteenth centuries, the modern medical speciality of gynaecology developed in parallel with anthropology: the scientific study of humankind. Gynaecology appealed to 'nature' to reinforce its claims that 'the female body is finalised for reproduction' (1990: 2).

What are 'women' in ancient gynaecology? What is the body, and what is a female body? For us, sexual difference is intrinsic to humanity, so that there can be no such thing as 'the human body'; the physical body is always male or female. We assume that its maleness or femaleness depends on its genitalia, and thus on its reproductive capacity (Laqueur 1990: 31). In ancient Greek thought, however, Thomas Laqueur has argued that there was no such thing as the female body. Instead, there was one body, which if it was cold, weak and passive was female and if it was hot, strong and active was male; this is a 'one-sex body' in which 'at least two genders correspond to but one sex, where the boundaries between male and female are of degree and not of kind' (Laqueur 1990: 25). From this single body, he argues, it was almost a natural progression for the great second-century AD physician Galen to insist that the female genitalia are the male genitalia, but inside instead of outside. Some editions of the popular manual on the body, *Aristotle's Masterpiece*, which probably dates from the seventeenth century, include a poem which states,

For those that have the strictest searchers been,
Find women are but men turn'd outside in:
And then if they but cast their eyes about,
May find they're women with their inside out
(1791: 15, cited by Blackman 1977: 69–70)[13]

Here the subject, the 'searcher', is clearly male. It is men who survey 'women's secrets' only to discover the disturbing truth that, from one point of view, even men are women.

The material on which Laqueur based his discussion came mostly from Galen, although there is support for this 'one-sex body' in Hippocratic embryology. In his discussion of how the body first becomes male or female, the author of the Hippocratic treatise *On Generation/Nature of the Child* argued that both parents contribute seed, this being in each case a mixture of both 'male' and 'female' kinds (*Gen.* 6, L 7.478).[14] In the Hippocratic corpus as a whole, the sex of the foetus appears to be determined by three variables.[15] One is the influence of right and left, the left testicle producing girls and the right testicle boys (*Ep.* 6.4.21, Loeb VII, 252; *SF* 31, L 8.500); this can be linked to the statement of the pre-Socratic philosopher Parmenides that the left side of the womb produces girls and the right side boys (DK 28 B17), as well as to more general statements in the Hippocratic corpus of the superiority of right over left (e.g. *Ep.* 2.6.15, Loeb VII, 84). Dean-Jones (1994: 167) points out that the belief that physical sex depends on the side of the womb into which the seed falls treats the seed as 'sex-neutral until it was differentiated by its environment at conception'. Left/right beliefs of this kind survived into the nineteenth century in popular literature on the body, such as *Aristotle's Masterpiece* (Blackman 1977: 65); however, Föllinger (1996: 33–4) argues that they are not found in those Hippocratic texts which are 'gynaecological' in the narrowest sense of the term. Another possibility is the time of the cycle at which intercourse takes place, with a girl more likely to be conceived if menstruation is in progress. *Superfoetation* 31 (L 8.500) suggests combining this principle with a left/right one, tying up the right testicle if one wants a girl, the left if a boy is to be produced. A third possibility, used in *On Generation/Nature of the Child*, is the strength of the seed. When the seed from the male mixes with that from the female, a contest takes place in which sex and physical characteristics are determined by whether the mother's seed or the father's is victorious (*Gen.* 6, L 7.478; Laqueur 1990: 39; Föllinger 1996: 42). For example, the presence on a given occasion of a particularly strong seed coming from the father's nose will mean that the child too has this type of nose (*Gen.* 8, L 7.480–2). In sex determination, however, for most of the menstrual cycle 'strong' seed makes a boy, while 'weak' seed makes a girl; 'the male creature being stronger than the female must of course originate from a stronger sperm' (*Gen.* 6, L 7.478; trans. Lonie 1981: 3). Here, the speculations of a medical writer on the way in which sex was determined *in utero* reinforce social and cultural assumptions about the relative roles of the sexes, using the idiom of strength and weakness. Historically, these speculations have been treated very seriously as the basis for medical intervention, but it is possible that they were produced in a far less systematic way than this would suggest, with a Hippocratic writer pushing along one line of thought just to see where it would lead, without necessarily accepting these conclusions on another occasion and in a different context (cf. van der Geest 1991: 70).

The suggestion in *On Generation/Nature of the Child* that sex depends on the seed dominant at the time of conception certainly implies that there is a 'sliding scale' (Gleason 1990: 390–1) operating here rather than a simple opposition between two fundamentally opposed sexes. The possibility is left open that some individuals will be more or less masculine or feminine than others, with – for example – a feminine male emerging from a contest in which the 'male' seed only just succeeded in defeating its rival. The Hippocratic treatise *Regimen* goes further still, arguing that male seed is not necessarily stronger; even male seed can have a bad day. This treatise suggests that there are three kinds of men, and three kinds of women. If both parents secrete female seed, for example, the child will be a beautiful and highly feminine (*thêlukôtata*) girl; if the woman produces female seed and the man male seed, and the female seed is stronger, the child will be a girl who is bolder, but still behaves within the bounds of modesty. If the man produces female seed and the woman male seed, and the female seed dominates, then the child will be female, but 'masculine' (1.29, Loeb IV, 268–70; Föllinger 1996: 44).

In Greco-Roman antiquity, both sexes are equally fragile; all bodies consist of 'hard parts' and 'soft parts' (*Gen.* 3, L 7.474), but more importantly of various liquids which change in their relative proportions according to one's age, diet and lifestyle (Annoni and Barras 1993: 189). Ageing is experienced by all as a process of cooling and drying (*Regimen* 1.33, Loeb IV, 278–80). Foucault's work on the ancient world (1985; 1986), criticised for its failure to discuss the female body (Richlin 1991; B. Thornton 1991), is valuable precisely because it shows that it was not only women who maintained at best a precarious balance between fluid and its evacuation, between health and disease. Foucault demonstrates how élite males needed to adjust their diet and exercise according to the characteristics of the season, the place and the climate. Greco-Roman medicine even accepts the possibility of an adult body shifting to a different set of secondary sexual characteristics. A 'cold' woman can be heated so that she acquires a bodily exterior usually regarded as 'male'. The body of Phaethousa of Abdera became masculine after her husband left, as she ceased to menstruate and her bodily surface changed to reflect the internal processes:

> In Abdera, Phaethousa the wife of Pytheas, who kept at home [or, who was mistress of the house], having borne children in the

> preceding time, when her husband was exiled [or, when her husband fled] stopped menstruating for a long time. Afterwards pains and reddening in the joints. When that happened her body was masculinised and grew hairy all over, she grew a beard, her voice became harsh, and though we did everything we could to bring forth menses they did not come, but she died after surviving a short time. The same thing happened to Nanno, Gorgippos' wife, in Thasos. All the physicians I met thought that there was one hope of feminising her, if normal menstruation occurred. But in her case too it was not possible, though we did everything, but she died quickly.
>
> (*Ep.* 6.8.32, trans. Smith, in Loeb VII, pp. 289–91 [bracketed alternatives are alternative translations of the Greek text])

By forcing this Hippocratic text into the categories of biomedicine, we could perhaps 'diagnose' it as 'post-pubertal virilism caused by the adrenogenital syndrome'. But I would argue that this would lose its richness and complexity as a cultural product (cf. Laqueur 1990: 7); the slipper does not fit, and the solution is not to cut off part of the foot. The role of menstruation in defining the Hippocratic female body will be discussed later in this book.

The second-century AD medical writer Soranos of Ephesus (*Gyn.* 3.7; 133)[16] further suggests that women can stop menstruating if they take too much exercise, since this will use up any surplus blood; however, they remain 'women', and can resume their reproductive functions by changing their lifestyle once more (*Gyn.* 3.9; T 134–5). Myth challenges even more radically the fixed nature of the two sexes with stories, such as those of Caenis/Caeneus (*Aen.* 6.448) and Tiresias (Hes., fr.275 M-W; Brisson 1976; Loraux 1995), telling of individuals who experienced to the full both being a man and being a woman.

Another model which existed in classical antiquity suggested that men and women do not contribute to generation in an equal way. This model rejected 'female seed' entirely, instead reserving seed as a male prerogative; the female contributed merely 'matter', and a place in which the seed could grow. This is the model most famously articulated by Aristotle, who denied that women had the capacity to produce any sort of seed (*GA* 727b7–12; cf. pseudo-Lucian, *Erôtes* 19). For Aristotle, instead of male and female bodies there was 'the' body, a male body, of which a female body was an inferior form, too cold to heat up blood into semen and thus unable to reach perfection (*PA* 650a8 ff.; *GA* 775a14–20). The adult Greek free-born male represents the normal human form, with woman being 'a deformed man' (*GA* 728a17 ff.; 737a). In Aristotle, heat is always the positively valued pole, so that women must then be classified as the colder sex, since the female body is consistently inferior to that of the male. Women age more quickly than men because of their coldness; as inferior creatures, they reach their end sooner (*GA* 775a14 ff.). In this model both women and men are ranked on the same scale, with men at its pinnacle so that masculinity is 'an achieved state' (Gleason 1990: 391). But the model leaves open the possibility that, with a little extra heat, women can become men: with a little less, men risk feminisation.

So far, I have identified two models of sexual difference in ancient Greek medical thought. In one, sexuality exists as a continuum from female to male, with both sexes contributing an active seed to the process of reproduction. This model admits the possibility of a number of gradations of masculinity and femininity. In the second model, women lag so far behind men in body heat that their role in reproduction is entirely passive; they cannot produce seed. Both models, in Laqueur's sense, argue for one body, ranked as more or less male.

But Laqueur does not represent a further strand found in ancient Greek medical thought. This is the image of the female body underlying the Hippocratic *Diseases of Women* treatises, where it is assumed that women are not just cold men, but are creatures entirely different from men in the texture of their flesh and in the associated physiological functions (King 1985: 126; Dean-Jones 1994: 85). Both Schiebinger and Laqueur have argued that it was not until the late eighteenth century that the sexuality of the body was thought to extend to all its parts, including the mind (Schiebinger 1989: 189). Only then did the uterus cease to be an internal analogue of the penis, becoming an organ with no male counterpart. Sexuality came to be seen 'as penetrating every muscle, vein, and organ attached to and molded by the skeleton' (Schiebinger 1989: 191; cf. Laqueur 1990: 4–5). In the reading of Hippocratic gynaecology given in this book, I will be arguing that this model too existed in classical Greece, and forms 'Hippocrates' Woman'.

Although Stephen Clark has published *Aristotle's Man* (1975), it may seem perverse to call this book 'Hippocrates' Woman', when it appears unlikely that any treatise in the corpus as it now stands was written by the historical Hippocrates.[17] Indeed, diversity is the key to the corpus; there is an open acceptance by its writers of the point that they all disagree on what, precisely, goes on inside the body, so that the writer of *Generation* 2 ends a section with 'Such is my explanation of the facts' (L 4.474; trans. Lonie 1981: 2). In some Hippocratic texts, however, the model of the female body extended sexual difference into every particle of flesh. This is the aspect of 'Hippocrates' Woman' which the following chapters will explore: among the conflicting range of images of the female body given in the corpus existed one tradition of that body which saw it as radically unlike the male body, behaving in different ways and requiring different therapies. This female body was not at a different place in the continuum of humanity, but was something requiring its own special medicine: gynaecology.

In the later history of gynaecology, Hippocrates' woman was a resource drawn on by writers arguing for radical female difference. The question of how far gynaecology should be treated as a distinct medical sub-field could reflect just how 'different' women were regarded as being. In the second half of the sixteenth century, after the publication in 1525 of Marco Fabio Calvi's Latin translation of the complete Hippocratic corpus made the *Diseases of Women* texts available in full for the first time since antiquity, two short passages from the corpus were singled out for quotation on title pages, or discussion in prefaces, by medical writers who praised Hippocrates as the best guide to the particularly difficult field of women's medical treatment. The first was from *Diseases of Women* 1.62, a warning against treating sick women as if they were men, because 'the treatment (*iêsis*) of the diseases of women differs greatly from that of men' (L 8.126). This statement supporting gynaecology as a separate area of medicine, which Paola Manuli (1983: 154) described as the founding act of ancient Greek gynaecology, appears on the title page of Maurice de la Corde's commentary on the text *Diseases of Young Girls*, published in 1574. The second was *Places in Man* 47, 'the womb is the origin of all diseases of women' (Loeb VIII, 94), cited for example in Caspar Wolf's *Harmonia Gynaeciorum* of 1564. For sixteenth-century medical writers, these two passages suggested that women needed a separate branch of medicine. However, the second quotation is less radical than the first, since it concentrates the difference into one organ, even though ancient Greek views of that organ and its influence varied from our own. *Diseases of Women* 1.62 goes further, claiming that the diseases of women are difficult to understand, because they are experienced only by women; these women do not understand what is wrong with them, if they lack experience of 'the diseases coming from menstruation', but 'time and necessity' teach them the cause of their diseases. Women who fail to understand the origin of their illness call in a healer too late, while those who do understand are reluctant to talk to a healer. The healer must always bear in mind that the cause of women's diseases is different, and therefore the treatment must also be different (L 8.126).

The claim that gynaecology was necessary could have economic as well as theoretical implications (Moscucci 1990: 42). It was in the later sixteenth century, when there first seemed to be the possibility of performing a Caesarean section in which both mother and child survived, that women's reproductive bodies had started to enter the surgeon's sphere of interest (Blumenfeld-Kosinski 1990: 104). In the nineteenth century, as we have already seen, the treatment of women was a contested field between surgeons, physicians, and the new hybrid of the gynaecologist, but in classical Greece the contests were even more intense due to the absence of both institutionalised medical training, and professional bodies guarding standards. Although one healer would be most unlikely to earn a living by treating only women patients, in general medicine there was still some mileage to be gained by claiming that the female body needed to be read according to different criteria known only to particular healers.

The subtitle of this book, 'Reading the female body', not only serves as a reminder that the book concentrates on written texts rather than visual imagery. It is also an echo of a model of medical understanding based on seeing the body as something to be 'read' – a model which is entirely Hippocratic, taken up in the Renaissance by Vesalius' dissections which deferred to what he called 'the true book of ours, the human body'[18] – and an acknowledgement that the texts have their own history of being interpreted by readers from different backgrounds and with different agendas. Chapter 2 will discuss further how, in Hippocratic medicine, to read the body is to bring together a range of sensory evidence, and will give examples of how treacherous the act of reading can be to those who put their trust in instruments or who do not fully understand the language spoken by the body. Some texts in the Hippocratic corpus propose that the female body is actually more legible than the male body, because it has an extra exit and an extra function into which the healer should enquire: menstruation. In a striking image created by Jan van Rymsdyk for William Hunter's *Anatomy of the Gravid Uterus* (1774) (see frontispiece), the womb itself appears to be shown in the act of reading, as the female pudenda are conveniently hidden from the male gaze by a small, leather-bound volume propped up to cover the vagina.[19]

Hippocratic gynaecology, as a later construct, also has a history constructed by its readers. Most significant of these was Galen, who claimed as 'Hippocratic' those features of his own medical theory and practice for which he wished to gain powerful support (W.D. Smith 1979). Papyri show that Hippocratic recipes continued to be used for many centuries after they were first written down, with some changes in ingredients according to what was available (Hanson 1996b and forthcoming). In the Middle Ages, some sections of the Hippocratic gynaecological treatises were copied and recopied (see further Chapter 11 pp. 236–8). In the sixteenth century, after the whole corpus was translated into Latin by Calvi, the gynaecological treatises were reprinted immediately in a small-format, cheaper edition.[20] The authority of Hippocrates, as in sentences commencing 'Hippocrates himself did this', grew during the sixteenth century and remained largely unchallenged into the later nineteenth century, partly because the variety of the materials in the Hippocratic corpus is such that anyone looking for support for any new theory can find something in the texts to fit it, and can then use the buzz-word 'Hippocrates' to give it the authority of antiquity. The very diversity of the treatises linked together as the Hippocratic corpus gives the myth of Hippocrates its power.

My personal favourite among dozens of examples of the use of the name of Hippocrates to give authority to one's medical practice is the surgeon Isaac Baker Brown (1812–73). He became a Fellow of the College of Surgeons by examination in 1848, after which he worked as the Surgeon-Accoucheur, and subsequently as a lecturer in midwifery and the diseases of women, at the new St Mary's Hospital, Paddington (Plarr 1930: 152–3; Dally 1991: 162–84). He gained an international reputation as a surgical innovator, developing new methods of performing vaginal repairs and treating ovarian cysts, and experimenting with ovariotomy.[21] In 1858 he set up his own clinic, the London Surgical Home for the Reception of Gentlewomen and Females of Respectability suffering from Curable Surgical Diseases. Its mission was to alleviate 'the many sufferings to which the gentler part of humanity are the victims';[22] these included a range of disorders of the uterus, vagina and breasts, but also conditions of the bladder and rectum, hysteria, and even 'Disease of the knee-joint'.[23] Over the ten years in which the Home was open, Brown treated more than 1,200 patients, and carried out the operation of clitoridectomy on women to cure conditions as varied as urinary incontinence, uterine haemorrhage, hysteria, idiocy and mania.[24] The last three suggested that it was possible to cure insanity with surgical intervention, and were interpreted as a challenge to the established boundaries between medical specialities (*Lancet* 1866: 697). In 1865 Brown's standing in the profession was such that he was elected president of the Medical Society of London (*Medical Directory*, 1866; Scull and Favreau 1986: 248); supporters praised his skill, boldness and kindness.[25] But the following year he was expelled from the Obstetrical Society of London, leaving his career in ruins.

In the 1860s Hippocratic gynaecology was still very much a part of medical theory and practice, among orthodox and alternative practitioners alike. Emile Littré's edition and translation of the complete corpus was published between 1839 and 1861; Littré was a doctor who translated the Hippocratic texts into French, rather than the Latin which was still chosen by many translators of the period, with the explicit intention of improving current medical practice (Jouanna 1983: 293–5).[26] With Francis Adams, who aimed to make those Hippocratic texts he selected as being 'the genuine works of Hippocrates' intelligible to 'any well-educated member of the [medical] profession at the present day' (1849: v), Littré was among the last practising physicians to demonstrate that 'Until the nineteenth century, medicine nourished itself on Hippocrates – or at least on that which it believed it could find in Hippocrates' (Duminil 1979: 154).

How was this Hippocratism expressed in gynaecological knowledge? One area in which there was a clear Hippocratic debt concerned the theories and practices surrounding menstruation. The Hippocratic treatise *Aphorisms*, to be discussed in Chapter 3, states that suppressed menstrual blood can come out as a nosebleed, or in vomit, making the eruption of blood from the mouth or nose a good sign in women whose menstrual bleeding is not considered sufficiently heavy or frequent; another text, *On the Use of Liquids* 6 (L 6.130, Loeb VIII, 332), states that the menses can run back under the skin, and should be treated by cold topical applications. By the eighteenth century, bleeding from various orifices was widely accepted as 'diverted menstruation'. In a long section on unusual routes taken by the menses, Martin Schurig (1729: 83–118) included menstruation through the ears, skin, gums, fingers, saliva glands and tear ducts; as recently as 1953, some of these routes were listed in the *Nursing Mirror*, although the author commented on menstruation through tears and sweat, 'this is doubted' (Bender 1953: 159–60). In the same year that Brown published his book promoting clitoridectomy, the homeopath John Pattison wrote that, in women aged between 15 and 25, bleeding from the lungs could be due to menstrual suppression (1866: 13). Orthodox medicine concurred; Fleetwood Churchill's textbook *On the Diseases of Women*, first published in 1850, allows for 'vicarious menstruation' from the nose, eyes, ears, gums, lungs, stomach, arms, bladder, nipples, the ends of fingers and toes, the joints, and so on (1864: 204–5). Churchill gives the case of Mary Murphy, aged 21, who missed a period, then suffered losses of between 15 and 20 ounces of blood from her ears, and then moved on to a mixture of vomiting blood and bleeding from the ears; the sign that this blood was menstrual was that it did not coagulate (1864: 205–6; cf. Gubb 1879: 13).[27] Not all writers of the eighteenth and nineteenth centuries accepted vicarious menstruation; Thomas Denman (1788: 154–5; 1832: 102) believed that bleeding classified as such was more commonly due to disease, being independent of menstruation.

But not all aspects of Victorian gynaecology were so obviously rooted in Hippocratic medicine. Like many other medical writers of his day, Brown believed that female masturbation put excessive strain on the nervous system, specifically causing 'peripheral irritation of the pudic nerve' (Tanner 1867: 362; Brown 1866a: 7), affecting the clitoris and eventually the brain (Brown 1866a: 11); some thought that the use of treadle sewing machines caused excessive 'venereal excitement' to women factory workers (Duffy 1963).[28] Removal of the clitoris, Brown argued, was an operation of great antiquity which in no way unsexed a woman (1866a: 9–10); by subsequently becoming pregnant, several of his patients provided 'indisputable evidence that the clitoris is not an essential part of the generative system' (Brown 1866a: 23, 27, 28; 1866b: 305).[29] It is, however, interesting that one of the case histories Brown gives in *On the Curability of Certain Forms of Insanity, Epilepsy, Catalepsy and Hysteria in Females* involves a patient who did indeed consider herself 'unsexed' by his surgery, and told him that this was how she felt (1866a: 79).

Brown's book was favourably reviewed by the *Church Times* (April 1866), with the clergy being encouraged to recommend the procedure to their parishioners (Scull and Favreau 1986: 253). The Archbishop of York was a patron of the Home, and the Archbishop of Canterbury a vice-president.[30] A skit on Brown published in the year of his expulsion suggests that Brown was only taking to its logical limits a form of 'psychological surgery first indicated by Christ', that, 'If thy right hand offend thee, cut it off' (Scoffern 1867: 5, 3). One situation in which clitoridectomy was seen as a success was where women who had been seeking a divorce under the 1857 Divorce Act – an action so outrageous that it was a clear sign of mental illness – returned home to their husbands after the operation (Brown 1866a: 84; Scull and Favreau 1986: 250; Dally 1991: 167). Brown included the case of a woman who 'became in every respect a good wife' after clitoridectomy (1866a: 30).

The London medical establishment did not turn against Brown because of the nature of this surgical procedure, something which – his attackers claimed – he often described possessively as 'my operation' (*Lancet* 1866: 697).[31] Instead, for the writer of the 1866 *Lancet* editorial, Brown's operation was wrong because it was based on the empirical method rather than the 'rational method of studying medicine' which was historically established and proven (1866: 698). Doubts were expressed as to whether the procedure actually worked beyond the immediate post-operative period in which the genital area was so uncomfortable that masturbation was too painful.[32] Furthermore, significant ethical problems were identified in Brown's practice, such as his alleged failure to obtain consent from fathers and husbands of his patients (*British Medical Journal* 1867: 407; Dally 1991: 179–80); in ancient Greek terms, the men who were the patients' *kyrioi* or legal guardians. Francis Seymour Haden, who proposed the motion for Brown's expulsion from the Obstetrical Society of London, suggested that the medical establishment as a whole was the proper *kyrios* for Victorian womanhood: as obstetricians, he stated,

> we have constituted ourselves, as it were, a body who practise among women . . . we have constituted ourselves, as it were, the guardians of their interests, and in many cases, in spite of ourselves, we become the custodians of their honour [*hear, hear*]. We are the stronger, and they the weaker. They are obliged to believe all that we tell them. They are not in a position to dispute anything we say to them, and we, therefore, may be said to have them at our mercy. We, being men, have our patients, who are women, at our mercy.
>
> (*BMJ* 1867: 396)[33]

Brown's use of self-publicity and advertisements for the Home were also questioned, since advertising was seen as the mark of a quack; another definition of quackery, given by Seymour Haden, was 'The diagnosis of a disease which has no existence' (*BMJ* 1867: 397).

Not only the issue of whether Brown was a quack (Nichol 1969: 65) but also the related question of his 'reputation as a gentleman' was crucial to the episode (Scull and Favreau 1986: 256). In Victorian England, medicine in general had a very low status among the professions, regardless of the additional problems raised by the new gynaecologists' merger of the spheres of the surgeon and the physician. There has been much debate over whether this was due more to the social level of those entering the profession, or to its already inferior status deterring high status applicants. Jeanne Peterson (1978: 285) has argued that the sons of gentlemen were reluctant to enter medicine because the need for technical knowledge and practical skills – used, for example, in measuring out quantities of drugs – was not thought consistent with the image of a gentleman, an image comprising 'birth, classical education, manners and morals' with freedom from the need to earn a living (Peterson 1984: 470). Brown was the son of a gentleman (Plarr 1930: 152), and became a member of the small group of London practitioners who formed the medical élite; however, there are some indications that he was not one of the inner circle. For example, where Seymour Haden was a Fellow of the Royal College of Surgeons by election, Brown had gained his fellowship by examination; by making this explicit when giving his qualifications in his published works, Brown was dissociating himself from the suspicions surrounding the 'honorary' awards first made under the terms of the new RCS charter of 1843 (Loudon 1986: 283 n.58).

On 3 April 1867, over 200 members attended an emergency meeting of the Obstetrical Society of London which ended in Brown's expulsion.[34] There was standing room only at this noisy and acrimonious event, at which Brown appealed to medical history in his defence. In the preface to his book he had denied any originality for his surgical methods, and at the meeting he claimed that clitoridectomy

> is an operation, as Dr Aveling has shown, that has been performed from the time of Hippocrates again and again. Dr Barnes himself presided over a meeting of the Society at which instruments were shown – I think of Dyonius – invented on purpose for clitoridectomy.
> (*Lancet*, 6 April 1867: 434)

The *BMJ* version of this part of Brown's defence substitutes Dr Haden for Dr Aveling, which is an error; it was indeed the Sheffield gynaecological surgeon and medical historian James Hobson Aveling who outlined his version of the history of clitoridectomy to a meeting of the Society in 1866 (*TOSL* 8, 1867).[35] However, the *BMJ* does correctly give 'Dionis' as the originator of the instruments described. Pierre Dionis' *A Course of Chirurgical Operations* (1710: 149, fig. XVIII) gives an illustration of the full set of instruments required for operations on the womb; for amputation of an enlarged clitoris, one uses 'curve-knife H' (1710: 153–4). The *BMJ* also states that Brown's claims about the display of the instruments were met with 'cries of Oh! Oh!'[36] Hippocrates was also brought in by those on the other side of the debate. The *Lancet* editorial of 22 December 1866 stressed the importance of Hippocratic ethics, arguing that Brown's ethical behaviour constituted a departure from the principles which 'have governed medical men in the practice of their profession since the days of HIPPOCRATES' (1866, 2: 698). Brown, however, simply concentrated throughout on another aspect of Hippocratic ethics: the injunction in the Oath to preserve patient confidentiality. He insisted in specific cases that 'she extracted from me a solemn promise not to communicate the cause of her illness to her husband nor to anyone else. I sacredly maintained the secrecy so enforced' (*Lancet* 1866: 710) and 'The clitoris was cut away by her express sanction, she binding me to secrecy both from her husband and her medical attendant' (*Lancet* 1867: 427).

Brown did not go so far as to cite a specific Hippocratic reference for his assertions about the history of clitoridectomy, but other writers of the period did. At the regular meeting of the Obstetrical Society of London held on 5 December 1866, Thomas Hawkes Tanner (another vice-president of the OSL) read a paper criticising Brown's operation, likening it to the practices of 'savages' carried out in connection with 'gloomy rites . . . shrouded in almost impenetrable mysticism' in areas of the world known for 'licentious and depraved conduct' (Tanner 1867: 366–8). It was in the subsequent discussion of this paper that Aveling gave a full bibliography of clitoridectomy, including the Hippocratic treatise *Nature of Woman*, adding that 'From the time of Galen up to the last century, this method of treatment was constantly recommended' (Tanner 1867: 375–6). The Galenic passage he cites is *On the Affected Parts* 6.5, which does not describe clitoridectomy, but instead describes a woman suffering from symptoms caused by retained female seed, able to expel it only when a midwife advised that 'the traditional remedies' should be rubbed on to her 'female parts' (*hoi gynaikeioi topoi*); due to their warming effects, and to the pressure on her genitals, she felt 'pain (*ponos*)[37] and pleasure (*hêdonê*) just as in sexual intercourse'. Neither does *Nature of Woman* mention the operation; the passage usually taken by writers in the Renaissance as a description of clitoridectomy, Chapter 65 (L 7.400), instead recommends excision of a wart (*kiôn*) growing on the vulva, a condition also mentioned in *Diseases of Women* 2.212 (L 8.406).

The presentation of Tanner's paper provoked other responses; Charles F. Routh concentrated on his personal experiences of its value in practice. Routh, another fellow of the Obstetrical Society of London and physician in the diseases of women at the North London Consumptive Hospital, who was listed by Brown as one of his supporters (1866a: 13), cited the case 'of an idiot girl, who, after the operation, gradually improved so as to be able to read the Bible and converse, and who, he understood, was now in service' (Tanner 1867: 376). However, Routh argued that the operation should only be used 'after consultation with a brother practitioner' (Tanner 1867: 377), thus shifting the debate away from medical history and into medical ethics.

In the presentation of self within the London medical establishment, Brown was acutely aware of the role of appearance and style, issues thought to be particularly important in dealing with women patients (Peterson 1978: 129). 'He dressed always in black with a white tie . . . and on every day of the year had a flower in his buttonhole' (Plarr 1930: 153). Image in Hippocratic medicine was no less important, something which will be explored in Chapter 2. In his contribution to the discussion of Tanner's paper in 1866 Brown had thanked one of the previous speakers 'for the tone in which he had spoken' and added 'Magna est veritas et prevalebit' (Tanner 1867: 380). Gentlemen quote Latin tags; however, this one, 'Great is the truth and it will prevail', from the apocryphal book of 1 Esdras 4.41, may simply have been lifted from one of the dictionaries of quotations widely available in this period; it is included, for example, in Macdonnel (1809) and Riley (1856: 212). Although Latin was compulsory for medical students, many acquired it from a crammer (Peterson 1984: 469). The *Lancet* editorial of 22 December 1866 accused Brown of using 'barbarous jargon' in describing his surgical practice (1866: 697), objecting to his creation of new terms such as 'dilection' which sounded classical, but were not.

There is a self-consciously and almost awkwardly 'polite' tone to Brown's own words on occasion; for example, when he defended himself against the accusation of performing the operation without the consent of husbands and fathers, he said 'he had endured the ignominy of being held up to reprobation, because he was stated to have performed this operation on a lady without the consent of her husband, and without her knowledge; the fact being that the lady begged him to observe secrecy from her husband, and had afterwards, in polite phraseology, "sold" him, telling her husband that the operation had been done unknown to herself' (Tanner 1867: 382). Brown also asked for 'common fair play as an Englishman' (*BMJ* 1867: 401),[38] saying 'as an Englishman I stand upon the rights of an Englishman' (*BMJ* 1867: 403). He also tried to manipulate the ideal of 'manly' behaviour, asking that the Obstetrical Society should 'investigate . . . like men' the scientific, physiological facts of clitoridectomy, and begging that 'it is not manly to interrupt me' (*BMJ* 1867: 402).[39] While members of the Society stated and restated their status as 'gentlemen constituting a public body . . . men of honour and gentlemen' (Tanner, in *BMJ* 1867: 409), Brown accused the Society of thoroughly ungentlemanly behaviour, claiming that 'whippers-in' had been used to spur members into attending the meeting (*BMJ* 1867: 403).

Isaac Baker Brown died in February 1873; the Home had been closed since his expulsion from the Obstetrical Society. His story shows how Hippocratic gynaecology could be invoked not just to support the idea that women have a physical existence totally different from that of the male, requiring different medical interventions to cure its imbalances, but also to legitimise types of ethical behaviour and specific surgical procedures. It shows very strikingly that the myth of Hippocrates was alive and well and being used only a century ago to support what we now consider unnecessary operations on women. In the rest of this book I will explore how Hippocratic gynaecology grew out of its historically specific culture of production into a concept influencing the lives of real women over many centuries and across very different cultures. The first five chapters set Hippocratic gynaecology within the culture in which it was created, focusing on its relationship to the images of women presented in ancient myth and religion. After summarising some of the main claims of Hippocratic gynaecology in Chapter 1, Chapters 2 and 3 consider further the issues of 'reading' both the body and the Hippocratic texts which describe it. Chapters 4 and 5 turn to the context of myth and religion to see how they can help us to understand the cultural and social issues underlying Hippocratic gynaecology. The remainder of the book deals with the ways in which different interest groups have used Hippocratic gynaecology and other medical texts dealing with women to promote different versions of the classical Greek past. Chapters 6 and 7 examine the assumptions we currently bring to understanding the efficacy of ancient drug therapy, concentrating in turn on pain and contraception; they also explore further the nature of Hippocratic gynaecology by asking how the patient would have responded to the theories and therapies it offered. Chapters 8 and 9 look at the gender of those assisting in women's diseases, and examine how readers of the Hippocratic corpus have dealt with the apparent absence of nurses and midwives from its personnel. Chapters 10 and 11 investigate how the Hippocratic texts have been employed to construct two powerful disease categories: chlorosis and hysteria.[40]

1

CONSTRUCTING THE BODY

The inside story

This chapter is intended to provide an overview of the content of Hippocratic gynaecology: it summarises the assumptions about the female body with which it operates, the terminology it uses for some parts of that body, and the therapeutic procedures which it uses to restore the body to the functions it considers normal. In the process of constructing this summary, it also provides some idea of the range of types of text making up 'Hippocratic gynaecology'; subsequent chapters will consider in more detail the issues of the relationship between text and reality which the Hippocratics raise, and will apply the material outlined here to particular themes which arise not only in understanding Hippocratic gynaecology in terms of the ancient Greek world, but also in appreciating how these texts have been used in later medical debates.

Creating an overview of 'Hippocratic gynaecology' is an artifice which always risks falsifying its object; however, even in antiquity an attempt was made to define the main characteristics of a Hippocratic approach to the body.[1] Of the texts which have come down to us under the name of 'Hippocrates', possibly none was written by the historical 'Father of Medicine'. Instead, what has become the 'Hippocratic corpus' is a disparate collection in terms of geographical origin, date of composition and, most significantly for this chapter, theoretical position. The material given here must therefore have a certain provisionality, simply because there are so many variations within the texts of the Hippocratic corpus. However, with Ann Ellis Hanson (1996b: 307), I would argue that there are sufficient points of agreement – particularly within the *Diseases of Women* treatises – to make such an overview worth attempting.

It is also debatable how far any of the material presented here would have been exclusive to the Hippocratics. There are many areas of similarity between the Hippocratic medical texts and pre-Socratic philosophy (Longrigg 1993), and between the ideas put forward in the medical texts and those expressed in Attic comedy (Alfageme 1995), but in this book my focus is on the wider social and cultural context within which Hippocratic medicine was created, and in particular on the practical side of medicine. Medicine is not just about ideas; it is about making people feel better. These two aspects may be closely related, but to focus on the philosophical side may be to miss the point of the wider enterprise: 'The primary aim of medicine is to cure sick people' (Chaniotis 1995: 335). The social context within which a Hippocratic healer worked has been discussed in detail by Geoffrey Lloyd (1979, 1983), and characterised as highly competitive; different types of healer fought for patients, and the Hippocratic healer had little innate advantage over his rivals. Langholf (1990: 126–7) has argued that where Hippocratic theories such as *pepsis* – which covers the 'ripening' of a substance causing disease as well as the 'digestion' of food – seem rather vague to us, this may be because they were deliberately kept fairly vague in order to attract a wider clientele. The Hippocratic healer was 'materially dependent on a public with the broadest possible spectrum of religious and philosophical beliefs, and the less clearly he expressed himself about such matters, the better for him' (Langholf 1990: 239).

Effective healing can be the result of effective drugs – a topic to which I will return in Chapters 6 and 7 – but work on the anthropology and sociology of medicine shows that it also depends on some degree of communication between healer and patient. If the theories propounded by the healer make no sense at all to the patient, his explanations will be unlikely to reassure her, and his recommendations are less likely to be followed. Aline Rousselle's approach to Hippocratic gynaecology (1980; 1988) suggests that this material on the function and healing of the body is primarily women's lore, taken over by male medical practitioners. For Paola Manuli (1980; 1983), on the contrary, Hippocratic gynaecology consisted of men's fantasies about the female body. As Seymour Haden put it (above, p. 16), women 'are obliged to believe all that we tell them. They are not in a position to dispute anything we say to them.' But the medical encounter, then as well as now, is about patient and practitioner meeting to produce healing; it is in these terms that Lesley Dean-Jones (1994: 27) argues that the Hippocratic treatment of women 'must have been acceptable to them and have squared with their view of their own physiology'. If women patients found Hippocratic explanations preposterous, then how could these have been used to produce convincing explanations of why they suffered, let alone to provide the rationale behind therapies to restore their health?

One possible objection here is that the 'patient meets practitioner' model is anachronistic when considering ancient Greece. When a woman was sick, the person paying the practitioner would have been her male *kyrios*. Useful here is Joan Cadden's point, made in relation to the medieval West, that treatment needed to take place within 'the expectations and practices of the patient's family' (1993: 5). In ancient Greece, explanations for the woman's illness would thus have needed to convince the *kyrios*, rather than the patient, and may have been most successfully phrased in a way which reinforced his views of female nature. However, we may still ask whether, if these explanations made no sense at all to the patient, she would get better. This may be one of those questions which our sources cannot answer but, by bringing to it a range of comparative data, I will be returning to it throughout this book.

In this chapter I have chosen to start by setting the medical material within the context of the canonical myth of Pandora, the first woman, whose arrival in the world of men ushered in the age of iron, when 'diseases come upon men continually by day and by night' (Hes., *Erga* 102). In doing this, I am arguing from the outset that Hippocratic medicine needs to be seen within the widest possible context of ancient Greek culture, with aspects of its model of the body being shared with society more generally. In terms of the world in which the Hippocratic texts were produced and in which the Hippocratic physicians tried to win control of medical cases, the debate over whether gynaecology is necessary – whether the treatment of women should proceed along different lines from the treatment of men – may be seen as the logical consequence of Hesiod's programmatic account of the descendants of Pandora, the first woman, as a separate 'race' (*genos gynaikôn*, *Th.* 585–90; Loraux 1978). It is in this context too that the continuation of the debate on the proper treatment of the diseases of women in later classical texts should be seen.

Like a virgin

Thinking about Hippocratic gynaecology in terms of Pandora helps to avoid any assumption that our 'gynaecology' should be seen as a straightforward equivalent of what the Hippocratics meant by *gynaikeia*. *Gynaikeia* is a word which can mean women's sexual organs, menstruation, women's diseases, or therapies for these diseases, and it is the Greek name for the two long texts in the Hippocratic corpus devoted exclusively to the diseases of women (*Diseases of Women* 1 and 2). A major concern of Hippocratic gynaecology is the transformation of immature girls into reproductive women; in Greek terms, making a *parthenos*, a girl who combines the features of being 'childless, unmarried, yet of the age for marriage' linked on the epitaph of Philostrata (EG 463),[2] into a *gynê*. To be classified as a mature woman, a *gynê*, it was necessary to have given birth: the birth of the first baby ends the process of becoming a woman which started with the first menstrual period demonstrating the readiness of the body, in terms both of the availability of blood from which a foetus can be formed, and the possibility of male semen gaining entry to the womb. The classical Greeks tried to compress this process into the shortest possible amount of time, expecting menarche at age 13 and recommending that girls be married at 14 (King 1985: 180–6; Hanson 1992b: 49).

When Pandora was given to men by the gods, it was not as a *gynê*, but in the form of (*ikelon*, Hes. *Th.* 572; *Erga* 71) a *parthenos* or unmarried virgin (Loraux 1993: 81–2). To have become a *gynê* in the full sense of the term, she needed to have given birth, and 'from her comes all the race of womankind'.

Yet, as Froma Zeitlin (1996) has noted, sexual intercourse is absent from the Pandora myth. Although Pandora is dressed as a bride to be presented as a gift to Prometheus' foolish brother, Epimetheus, and is the origin of the race of women, there is silence about just what must occur between marriage and birth; instead, 'All is inference. Nothing is stated directly – neither sex nor procreation' (1996: 58). Zeitlin sees this as part of a deliberate suppression of women's sexual and reproductive roles on the part of Hesiod, who argues that only men have any work to do, while women, the source of men's hard work, remain inside the house taking in all that men can produce.

Hesiod tells the myth twice, both in his account of the origins of the gods, *Theogony*, and in his *Works and Days*. Nicole Loraux (1993: 80–1) suggests that, dressed, veiled, and wreathed by the Olympic deities, the Pandora of Hesiod's *Theogony* '*is* her adornments – she has no body'; the emphasis is placed on her elaborate and beautiful exterior which is like that of the immortal goddesses (cf. *Erga* 62–3). However, a reference which has not been noted in the context of Pandora's inside/outside mismatch occurs in the *Works and Days*: 'and he called this *gynê* (woman) Pandora' (*onomêne de tênde gynaika Pandôrên, Erga* 80–1). Taken with the repeated insistence on her virgin form, so that her introduction into the *Theogony* is formulated in terms of merging the two categories (*plastên gynaika parthenon*, 513–14),[3] this would suggest that from the outset Pandora is seen as a *gynê*, a fully reproductive woman, but masquerading as an innocent virgin. In *Works and Days*, as well as being 'like' a beautiful virgin (*parthenikês kalon eidos epêraton, Erga* 63), Pandora is described through two images which suggest the reality that is 'inside' (*en d'ara*, *Erga* 77) and which share a strong reproductive message: she is constructed by the gods with 'the mind of a bitch' (*kyneos noos*, *Erga* 67) and ravenous 'insides' (*gastêr*).

Homer's Agamemnon says that nothing is more like a bitch than a woman (*Od.* 11.427; Vernant 1979: 105). The domestic dog is comparable to woman in Greek thought, being a predatory beast taken into man's service, hovering between wild and tame (Redfield 1975: 193–203): as we will see in Chapter 4, the unmarried girl in particular was seen as naturally wild, 'untamed' (*admês*) and 'unyoked' (*azyga*), to be domesticated into the service of culture. In Aristotle, the dog is explicitly seen as an animal sharing some qualities of humanity. For example, in bitches, swelling of the breasts shows they are ready for intercourse 'just as in people' (*HA* 574b14–16). However, the later, pseudo-Aristotelian, *Problems* emphasise what is supposed to differentiate people from dogs: the bitch is often bad-tempered after childbirth, but women are not (894b13–15); the dog is prolific, but people are not (892a38–b1). This last point introduces a feature of the dog which human beings may want to emulate. The bitch was thought to give birth more easily than other animals (Plut. *Mor.* 277a–b) and to have many wombs, hence the appearance of offspring in litters (Aelian *NA* 12.16). Even in a human context, while *kuôn* means 'dog', *kuein* means 'to be pregnant'. But dogs also represented 'dissolute impudence' (Lilja 1976: 22): *kuôn* is used in comedy for the sexual organs (Henderson 1975: 127, 133). Dogs were thought to have exceptional sexual appetites (Redfield 1975: 194), remaining together in coitus for a particularly long time (Ar. *HA* 540a24), and having intercourse at every stage of their lives (Ar. *HA* 574b27), although elsewhere Aristotle says that bitches stop being sexually active at 12 or, at the latest, 18–20 (*HA* 546a28–34).

Which of these aspects is Pandora's bitch-mind supposed to evoke? Insatiable sexual desire, or desirable fecundity: or, perhaps, the fear that one cannot achieve the second without experiencing the demands of the first? The dog features as an ingredient in recipes given in Hippocratic gynaecology, but puppies, rather than mature dogs, were used to cure failure to conceive. The fat of puppies could be cooked and eaten (*DW* 2.217, L 8.420), or a whole puppy disembowelled, stuffed with aromatic substances, and then used as the basis of a fumigation (*DW* 2.230, L 8.440; see Chapter 11, pp. 218–19), a procedure in which vapours were passed into the uterus through the cervix in order to open it, return it to its correct position if it had moved elsewhere in the body, or expel substances such as retained menstrual blood which were causing disease. When the respective qualities of the flesh of dogs and puppies are described in the treatise *Regimen* 2, 'dog's flesh dries, heats and strengthens but does not evacuate . . . the flesh of puppies moistens and evacuates' (2.46, Loeb IV, 318). Intercourse moistens the womb, discouraging it from moving elsewhere to seek moisture, and agitates the body, easing the passage of blood within it. Similarly, puppies moisten the female body, encouraging reproduction. But mature dogs 'dry' the body; dog's flesh also appears, roasted, in a list of drying foods in *Regimen* 3.79 (Loeb IV, 406). Pandora is like a bitch, drying in the same way that Hesiod sees the female body more generally taking man's moisture and leaving him desiccated: Pandora is given to man *anti pyros*, 'in place of fire' (*Th.* 570; *Erga* 57), in the sense both of being 'equivalent to fire' – hot and burning – and of being 'opposed to fire', as an evil to a good (Vernant 1974; 1979; cf. Eur. fr.429 Nauck^2), while 'the greedy wife will roast her man alive, without the aid of fire' (*Erga* 704–5; *Anth. Pal.* 9.165).

Pandora's bitch-mind, then, evokes a fertility which entails exhausting lust for her man. What of her *gastêr*? *Gastêr* is an ambiguous word which can indicate 'belly' in the dietary system, or 'womb' in the reproductive system; to receive, to have, or to hold in the *gastêr* means 'to be pregnant' in both medical and non-medical texts.[4] The concept of two separate systems is, in any case, ours rather than the Greeks', so that one should perhaps think of the *gastêr* as a single organ. In one of the many polemics against this organ in the *Odyssey*, Odysseus exclaims that there is nothing more like a bitch (*kunteron*) than a *gastêr* (7.216). The context makes it clear that they share shameless and inappropriate appetites; Silvia Campese has pointed out that a woman both *has* a *gastêr* through which society is reproduced, and *is* a *gastêr* which must be controlled by a man, as a master must control a slave (1983: 16). This also applies to Pandora, but in a more concrete sense. She has not only a voracious *gastêr*, but also a *pithos*, a jar of the type usually used to store food (*Erga* 94). She herself is also a jar, in that she is fashioned from earth and water, 'molded like a vase by Hephaistos, and [.] described as a container into which the gods put something' (Pucci 1977: 88). As I will discuss further below, in Hippocratic gynaecology, the womb is seen as a jar. The specific identification of the womb with Pandora's jar is not new (*contra* Zeitlin 1996: 65; cf. King 1985: 161–3; Sissa 1990: 154–5) but has been widely represented in Western art. Dora and Erwin Panofsky use the Pandora of Abraham van Diepenbeeck, who holds her goblet/jar exactly over her pubic triangle (Panofsky and Panofsky 1956: 75); de Marolles noted that this was because it is the part 'from which flowed all the sorrows and concerns of men' (Panofsky and Panofsky 1956: 76 n.21), while Klee's extraordinary 1920 drawing shows Pandora's jar as a goblet with handles resembling the Fallopian tubes, an obvious vulva emitting black smoke, and a base ridged like the muscular lining of the vagina (Panofsky and Panofsky 1956: 112). When closed, the Hippocratic womb-jar may be securely holding a foetus in the process of formation, but its closure outside pregnancy is negative, causing disease in the woman by blocking normal menstrual flow, while preventing the entry of male seed and thus impeding normal human reproduction. The closure of Pandora's jar initially maintained a golden age: its subsequent opening brought a range of evils, *kaka*, including disease, to both men and women (*Erga* 101), evils of which Pandora herself is one, since she was planned by Zeus explicitly as a *kakon* (*Erga* 57; *Th.* 570 and 600). When the jar is closed again, all that is left inside is *elpis*, 'hope'; not a positive hope for good, but a neutral hope, with the sense of waiting for an uncertain future (Vernant 1979: 125–32; Pucci 1977: 105). The womb, too, contains this *elpis*, since in pregnancy it is impossible to know whether it contains a child or a shapeless mass of flesh.[5] Zeitlin suggests that, in opening her jar herself, Pandora is performing an act 'equivalent to breaching her virginity', while closing it can represent the beginning of pregnancy (1996: 66). This suppression of the male role in reproduction, making Pandora alone responsible for defloration and conception, gives woman 'an intrinsic power over man' (Zeitlin 1996: 71).

Like Pandora, the *gastêr* brings 'many *kaka* to mankind' (*Od.* 17.284 = 474) and can be called evil-doer, *kakoergos* (*Od.* 18.53–4). As a manufactured *kakon* and as bringer of *kaka*, as well as in her inauguration of sexual reproduction, Pandora is not only a bitch but also a *gastêr*.

Where Pandora differs from the *gastêr* is in her deceitful combination of outside and inside. In the absence of human dissection, the Hippocratics argued from the outside to the inside; they assumed equivalence between the seen and the unseen. A further feature of Pandora relevant to our understanding of Hippocratic gynaecology is, however, her consistent failure to match. As Vernant's masterly study (1974) of the two versions of the Prometheus myth in Hesiod has shown, the myth proceeds according to a pattern of giving and withholding, appearance and reality. In the trick he played on Zeus at Mekone, Prometheus presented to the god two packages; one looked good but contained the inedible parts of the ox; the other, the ox *gastêr*, looked unappetising but in fact contained the best parts. When Zeus uses Pandora as a trick to play on mortal men, he mirrors Prometheus' technique. She is not just a *kakon*, but a *kalon kakon* (*Th.* 585), a 'beautiful evil'. Unlike the ox *gastêr* package, she is externally desirable, but she contains the mind of a bitch and a ravenous *gastêr* which will compel men to work in the fields to satisfy its demands.

The complete woman

In the myth of Pandora, then, woman is 'different'; a late creation, a construct, an artifice and an illusion, containing a bitch-mind and a womb-jar. What of Hippocratic gynaecology? In Hippocratic medicine the terms of female difference are developed in a more complex way than in Aristotle's characterisation of woman as 'a deformed male' or 'a mutilated male' (*GA* 728a17 ff. and 737a; Horowitz 1976; Dean-Jones 1989; 1994). The main statements of difference occur in the two parts of *Diseases of Women*, but the Hippocratic corpus also includes a third text dealing specifically with the problem of infertility (*Diseases of Women* 3 = *On Sterile Women*), as well as a further redaction of some of the material given in *Diseases of Women* 1 and 2 (*Nature of Woman*), a merger of parts of *On Sterile Women* with apparently later material on difficult births (*Superfoetation*), texts on conception and foetal growth (*On Generation/Nature of the Child)*, discussion of the risks encountered in premature birth (*Eight Months' Child*), a description of the removal from the womb of a dead foetus (*Excision of the Foetus*), and a short text on diseases of young unmarried girls at puberty (*On the Diseases of Virgins*) (Diepgen 1937). The gynaecological treatises, unlike other parts of the corpus which deal with a predominantly dietetic approach to disease, have a polemical tone (Edelstein 1931: 96 n.16), and most suggest that women are sufficiently different from men to merit a separate medical approach; however, texts such as *Eight Months' Child* 9 argue that the same principles of prognosis and healing which are applied to diseases, healthy conditions and death in all humans – such as the principle of 'critical days' according to which certain days in a condition are particularly significant – can equally well be applied to conception, miscarriage and childbirth in women (L 7.446–52; Joly 170).

Medically, in what does women's difference consist? The Hippocratic texts never restricted women's difference to the function of childbearing and the organs associated with it. There are many statements in the Hippocratic corpus of areas of bodily experience in which men and women differ; for example, in how they shiver (*Ep.* 6.3.11, Loeb VII, 238). Paola Manuli suggested that the major anatomical feature distinguishing women from men is the existence of a *hodos*, a route extending from the orifices of the head to the vagina; woman has 'an uninterrupted vagina from nostrils to womb' (1980: 399; 1983: 157; cf. Hanson 1981; 1989). At each end of the tube is a mouth (*stoma*; Sissa 1990: 53) which can be used as a sign of the condition of the tube, and as a site for the administration of therapy. There is no explicit anatomical description of this tube, but its existence is implied in many ways, through vocabulary, and through context. Where the mouth of the womb closes and tilts, the nostrils too become 'dry and blocked, not upright' (*DW* 2.133, L 8.282). When a menstrual period is about to start, pain is felt in the throat (*CP* 537, L 5.706). Treatment aimed at the womb is to be applied 'from the top' and 'from the bottom' (*anô/katô*) of the tube (*DW* 2.137, L 8.310).[6] An abnormal flow is treated from above and from below, but first of all from above – the opposite direction (*DW* 1.66, L 8.136) – while *Nutriment* 45 (Loeb I, 358) states that 'the way up and the way down are one'. The analogies between top and bottom, which continued in medical literature up to the nineteenth century (Laqueur 1990: 36) and are still present in modern Latinate medical terminology in the usage of 'labia' (lips) and 'cervix' (neck), become explicit in the third-century BC work of pseudo-Aristotle, who says that the womb 'breathes in' the male semen in much the same way as the mouth and nostrils inhale substances, and that the route from the vulva to the inside of the womb is like the *poros* from nostrils to larynx (*On sterility* 634b35; 636b17–18; 637a21–35).[7] In a further variation, Greek and Roman writers believed that it was possible to tell when a girl had lost her virginity because her voice became deeper (Hanson and Armstrong 1986). It is interesting that the writer of a pamphlet ridiculing Isaac Baker Brown's practice of clitoridectomy pretended throughout that his operation consisted in the division of muscles in the hand to cure kleptomania, and – using another example of the analogy between the top and the bottom 'mouth' of the female body – in the tongue, to stop women spreading scandal. The operation does not 'injure the female utterance', he claims, but makes the voice even more charming, removing from it any metallic quality so that it is capable only of 'temperate conversation and agreeable singing' (Scoffern 1867: 12–13).

Even the *hodos* was not however the most powerful tool in a Hippocratic physician's conceptual vocabulary. More fundamental still in defining the anatomy of female difference was the texture of the flesh, used to explain why women are 'wetter' than men (*AWP* 10, Loeb I, 98–100; *NC* 15, L 7.494), their inclination towards water meaning that they flourish from foods, drinks and activities that are cold, wet and soft (*Regimen* 1.27, Loeb IV, 264). Their wetness gives them an affinity with the natural world, accounting for both their emotional reactions and their hungry sexuality (Carson 1990: 137–43). According to *Glands* 16 (Loeb VIII, 124), the physiological basis for their wetness is that their bodies retain moisture due to being loose-textured (*araios*), spongy (*chaunos*) and like wool (*eirion*). The opening chapter of *Diseases of Women* accepts these beliefs; the bodies of mature women are soft to the touch (*hapalos*), loose-textured, wet and spongy, while male flesh is drier and firmer. In a woman who has not yet given birth, there will be greater discomfort if her menstrual blood is obstructed, because her body is more resistant, firmer and more 'thickly-packed' (*ischyros*, *stereos*, *pyknos*). The main analogy used to describe the gender difference aligns mature female flesh with wool, and male flesh with a closely woven garment (*DW* 1.1, L 8.10–14: cf. *Glands* 1, Loeb VIII, 108 and 16, Loeb VIII, 124); this also suggests that women are 'raw material', while men are the finished product of a manufacturing process. The analogy is associated with a Hippocratic 'thought experiment' by which the writers advise anyone doubting the truth of their statement to take a fleece and a woven garment of equal weight, stretch them over water for two days and two nights, and note that the wool will weigh more at the end of this time because it has absorbed more fluid (Heidel 1941: 91; Hanson 1975; 1981: Dean-Jones 1994: 55–9). The absorbent qualities of fleece were used both in purificatory ritual (Parker 1983: 230) and in Hippocratic therapy; in *Superfoetation* 34 (L 8.506), warm lambskins are placed on the abdomen of a young girl who has failed to menstruate and oscillates between hunger, thirst, fever and vomiting blood, the intention perhaps being to draw out the suppressed blood.

Because of the anatomical difference constituted by the looser texture of their flesh, women experience a major physiological difference.[8] Due to absorbing more fluid from their diet than men do, women need to menstruate in order to evacuate the surplus accumulated. This, in the words of the Hippocratic *Nature of the Child* (15, L 7.494, trans. Lonie 1981: 8; Föllinger 1996: 37), is 'simply a fact of her original constitution' and it is why, as Clologe correctly noted almost a century ago, 'Les anciens s'étaient beaucoup occupés de la menstruation' (1905: 63). Menstruation, as Soranos later put it, is 'the first function' of the womb (*Gyn.* 3.6; T 132). The Hippocratics, as well as naming the menses *gynaikeia*, 'women's things' (*DW* 1.20, L 8.58; *CP* 511, L 5.702; *Ep.* 1.19, Loeb I, 174) and *ta hôraia*, 'the ripe things' (*SF* 34, L 8.504–6), call it by names which evoke its ideally 'monthly' appearance: *katamênia*, *epimênia* and *emmênia* (*Aph.* 5.39, Loeb IV, 168; *DW* 1.58, L 8.116; *NW* 8, L 7.322 and 16, L 7.334). They also refer to it as *hê physis*, 'nature' (*Ep.* 7.123, Loeb VII, 414), and *ta kata physin*, 'the natural things' (*Ep.* 6.8.32, Loeb VII, 288–90; *DW* 3.230, L 8.444).

If menstruation does not occur, then the surplus blood will continue to build up in the body, putting pressure on different organs, until disease or even death results: 'if the menses do not flow, the bodies of women become sick' (*Gen.* 4, L 7.476) so that regular heavy menstrual loss is a necessity (*AWP* 21, Loeb I, 124). Menstrual bleeding should occur every month, be sufficient in quantity, flow freely and in equal amounts, and occur on the same days of the month, according to *Prorrhetic* 2.24 (Loeb VIII, 270). These Hippocratic ideas were to have a long history: as the homeopath John Pattison wrote in 1866, 'No female between the ages of sixteen and forty years of age can be said to enjoy good health unless this discharge takes place with regularity, is sufficient in quantity, and lasts a proper length of time; which is from three to six days' (1866: 1–2). Orthodox medical textbooks of the same period also insisted on regularity, but varied in their estimates of loss from 4 to 6 ounces, to 4 to 10 ounces, taking place over two to four or two to ten days (lower estimates, Gubb 1879: 13; higher estimates, McMurtrie 1871: 215–16).[9]

In the *Diseases of Women* treatises, menstrual loss is expected to be both regular and heavy. The correct quantity of blood loss per month, 'if she is healthy', is two Attic cotyls – probably about a pint – in two or three days (*DW* 1.6, L 8. 30). In fact, the capacity of the womb is only 2–3 fluid ounces, and a menstrual loss of a pint of blood would represent pathologically high blood loss by today's standards.[10] However, comparisons are made difficult because it is not clear what we are comparing; about half a pint of fluid – of which about half is blood – is now considered the maximum of the normal range, and as the Greeks could not distinguish between the components of menstrual fluid I assume that their figure was for total loss rather than blood loss. The figure of two Attic cotyls is a persistent one in ancient gynaecology: Soranos was still using it in the second century AD, although as a maximum rather than the norm (*Gyn.* 1.20; T 17). Lesley Dean-Jones (1994: 89–91) has correctly noted that two cotyls is taken elsewhere as the maximum amount of fluid one should pour in when washing out the womb (*DW* 1.78, L 8.190), based presumably on perception of the size which the womb could reach during pregnancy. The assumption behind this figure for the amount to be lost at every menstrual period is thus that the container which is the womb fills completely each month and must empty itself completely. In pregnancy, blood flows into the womb gradually over the month, drawn in by the embryo on a daily basis (*DW* 1.34, L 8.78), but outside pregnancy the movement into the womb occurs only once, immediately before flowing out of the body (*NC* 15, L 7.492–4; Dean-Jones 1994: 62).

Where Pattison considered a period should last between three and six days, the writer of *Diseases of Women* 1.6 expected the massive blood loss on which he insisted to be compressed into two to three days; anything more or less constituted disease (*epinosos*, *DW* 1.6, L 8.30) and would lead to sterility. Some Hippocratic texts accept variation in the amount lost; for example, *Nature of the Child* 30 (L 7.534) states that some women lose much less than others, but then adds that these will have difficulty in providing sufficient nourishment to allow a foetus to reach full term. Heavy loss is therefore assumed to be healthier than light loss. Other passages of *Diseases of Women* take into account the individual *physis* of each patient, based on visible signs: the fair and the young are wetter and more liable to flux, while darker, older women have firmer flesh and bleed less (e.g. *DW* 2.145, L 8.320; *NW* 1, L 7.312). Outside the *Diseases of Women* texts, it seems to be possible for some women to survive even a prolonged failure to menstruate. Phaethousa survives, but only by becoming masculine (*Ep.* 6.8.32, Loeb VII, 288–90). In *Epidemics* 5.11 (Loeb VII, 160–2) the wife of Gorgias stops menstruating for four years, 'except for a very small amount'; she experiences heaviness and throbbing in her womb. She nevertheless becomes pregnant, after which she bleeds heavily and, eventually, 'she became healthy'. A servant who had not menstruated for seven years had a poor colour and a hard area on the right of her abdomen with some pain, but became 'healthy'; then her period started, the tension in the abdomen eased, and her skin colour improved (*Ep.* 4.38, Loeb VII, 132). In both cases, however, complete health only follows menstruation. In passages like this, where the possibility of survival exists for those who do not menstruate heavily, the 'sliding scale' model of the one-sex body seems to be edging its way back, but the model of total difference between the sexes is not to be overcome; as another passage puts it, 'Generally, most treatment is the same for all women' (*DW* 1.11, L 8.44). Furthermore, as words such as *katamênia* imply, women are generally expected to shed some blood every month without fail, except in pregnancy or when very young or old; prolonged absence of bleeding is sufficiently exceptional that it is noted, and is seen as the cause of symptoms elsewhere in the body.

Obstacles to pregnancy included a womb which was excessively dense, hot, cold, dry or wet (*Aph.* 5.62, Loeb IV, 174), since in these situations the seed could not survive. Obesity was a further barrier, since it was thought to cause narrowing of the mouth of the womb which prevented the male seed from gaining entry (*Aph.* 5.46, Loeb IV, 170). According to Aristotle, obese women did not menstruate, because all their excess blood was used up by the body (*GA* 746b27–9). In the Hippocratic texts, the potential fertility of a woman could be detected by using scented substances and discovering whether the odour could travel freely through her body, thus showing that the *hodos* is free from obstructions (*Aph.* 5.59, Loeb IV, 174); 'Obstruction of passages is a very frequent explanation in Greek medicine' in general (Lonie 1981: 113; cf. *Dis.* 4.39, L 7.558). Garlic or another strongly scented substance was placed at the bottom end of the *hodos*; if the smell reached the top end, the woman could conceive (*DW* 2.146, L 8.322; *NW* 96, L 7.412–14 etc.).

The Hippocratic healer could detect pregnancy and the sex of the unborn child by looking at the woman's complexion – if poor, the child must be female (*Aph.* 5.42, Loeb IV, 168 and *DW* 3.216, L 8.416) – and her appetite. According to the Hippocratic *Aphorisms*, pregnancy could be ascertained by investigating whether the womb was open or closed, since it was believed to close upon conception (*Aph.* 5.51, Loeb IV, 170), or by administering hydromel, a mixture of honey and water; if colic followed, then the woman was definitely carrying a child (*Aph.* 5.41, Loeb IV, 168). Further tests for pregnancy are listed in *On Sterile Women* (*DW* 3.214, L 8.414–16). However, pregnancy without any signs (*en gastri asêmôs*) is mentioned in one of the *Epidemics* case histories, where it is associated with a difficult delivery and menstrual insufficiency (*Ep.* 4.24, Loeb VII, 116),[11] while another *Epidemics* passage states 'If she was pregnant, I don't know' (4.26, Loeb VII, 122).

But if a woman had not menstruated when she was expected to do so, and pregnancy tests and Hippocratic observation proved negative, what then? Dean-Jones (1994: 95) refuses to believe that 'an extended menstrual cycle by itself would call down upon a woman who was sexually active the battery of Hippocratic measures for dealing with suppressed menses' – including beetle pessaries and fumigations – but the logic of the wet and spongy flesh steadily accumulating blood would have made this eventuality very likely. In our terms, menstruation at the level expected in the Hippocratics would indicate that a woman was suffering from a disease, and that she would be in danger of becoming anaemic at the very least: in Hippocratic terms, most Western women today are very sick indeed.

The only let-out clause was the belief that women themselves 'know' when they have conceived, because they can feel the womb close, or because they note that the man's seed has remained inside them (*NC* 13, L 7.488–90). Aristotle adds that women have a particular feeling in the flanks and groin which tells them they are pregnant (*HA* 582b10–12; 583a35–b3; cf. 584a2–12). It is only 'inexperienced' women (*hai gynaikes hai apeiroi*) – a category to be discussed further in the next chapter – who think that the absence of menstruation, in conjunction with a swelling of the belly, is alone sufficient to indicate pregnancy (*NC* 30, L 7.534). This reinforces the suggestion that, for the Hippocratics, pregnancy was not the first answer to the question posed by a late period.

Even when blood flows out monthly, symptoms may occur in some women. If menstruation is to be painless, the body must be completely female, in that it must be 'broken down' and its internal channels opened to provide a properly spongy texture throughout; this breakdown can occur only through childbirth, after which, 'in consequence of violence, pain, and heat' (*hypo biês te kai ponou kai thermês*), a bloody discharge secreted from all over the body and head opens up a *hodos* for the lochial flow (*NC* 30, L 7.538). By breaking down the flesh, giving birth creates within the body open spaces in which the blood can rest before travelling to the womb and leaving the body each month (*DW* 1.1, L 8.10–14).

While Aristotle later claimed that women were too cold to concoct blood into semen (*PA* 650a8 ff.; *GA* 775a14–20), there is evidence from the Hippocratic corpus suggesting that, because menstrual blood is 'hot', it is equally possible to argue that women in general may be the hotter sex. *Diseases of Women* 1.1 (L 8.12–14) states that 'the woman has hotter blood'.[12] According to Aristotle (*PA* 648a28–30; *GA* 765b19), the fifth-century philosopher Parmenides 'and others' argued that women must be hotter, because they possess more blood, the hot and wet humour. When Plutarch later constructed a debate over whether men or women are 'hotter', it was a doctor who proposed the position which Aristotle had attributed to Parmenides

(*Mor.* 650a–1e). But not all Hippocratic writers used the existence of menstruation as evidence that women are hot; although *Regimen* 1.34 (Loeb IV, 280) agrees that menstrual blood is hot it argues that, since women purge the hot every month, they must end up being 'cold' (Föllinger 1996: 31–2).

The version of gendered body temperatures which influenced the West through the medieval and early modern period was not that of the Hippocratic *Diseases of Women*, but that of Galen. Galen accepted the Aristotelian configuration in which women are 'cold' while men are 'hot', and also focused on 'female seed' rather than menstrual blood as the fluid which is the most dangerous if it is retained in the body.[13] For the Hippocratic *Diseases of Women* texts, however, excess blood is always at the root of the problem; it accumulates both because of women's sedentary lifestyle and because of their wet and spongy nature. Galen argues that a change in a woman's lifestyle combined with the influence of climate could, in theory, actually reverse male/female norms; in *On the Causes of the Pulse* 3.2 (K 9.109–10) he claims that, if a cold wet man lived in the damp climate of Pontus, and a hot dry woman in the heat of Egypt, and the man was idle while the woman worked in the open air, her pulse would be greater than his.

Tube, flesh – what about the organ which we now see as emblematic of femininity, the womb? I have deliberately left the womb to the end of this chapter, although it has of course entered the discussion as jar, as container and as a means for the evacuation of blood. Despite *Places in Man* 47 asserting that 'the womb is the origin of all diseases of women', in the *Diseases of Women* texts the womb was seen as secondary to female difference; it was made necessary by the nature of the flesh, which needed somewhere to send and store the blood it could not use.

Cross-culturally, the womb is a rich source of imagery. Janice Boddy's study showed that, in the Sudan, it can be represented as a house with a door (1982); Greek comedy too used doors and gates in sexual imagery (Henderson 1975: 137). The womb can also be a container (Murphy and Murphy 1974: 102) or a garden to be cultivated (Richards 1956: 205–6 and n.180). In classical Greek imagery, whether women were seen as 'hot' or 'cold', the womb was seen as 'hot', its role being to cook the seed. In a powerful analogy, retained even by Aristotle, for whom women were 'cold', the womb was likened to an oven (*kaminos*; *GA* 764a12–20). In the Hippocratic *Generation/Nature of the Child* the womb is seen successively as an oven in which the seed is 'baked' – reminiscent of Herodotus' phrase for the necrophilia practised by the tyrant Periander of Corinth, who 'put his loaves in a cold oven' (5.92) – and a field in which seed is sown (4, L 7.474–6; 12, L 7.486; 30, L 7.536); 'the condition of the plant depends on the condition of the earth in which it grows' (*NC* 22, L 7.514; Lonie 1981: 13). In the *Dream-Book* of Artemidoros, a hearth (*hestia*) and a baking-oven (*klibanos*) can represent woman, because they receive things that produce life. Dreaming of seeing fire in a hearth means that your wife will become pregnant (*Oneir.* 2.10).

In the Hippocratic texts, organs are often of less importance than fluids. *On Ancient Medicine* 22 (Loeb I, 56–60) looks at bodily 'structures' (*schêmata*) as different shapes and textures first, and as named organs only secondarily. The type of structure best for pulling in fluid from the rest of the body is one which is broad, hollow and tapering, such as 'the bladder, the head, and the womb in women' (Annoni and Barras 1993: 190). Where the womb is given any separate identity, the most common words for it are *mêtrê* and *hysterê*, both of which are normally used in the plural; the belief that the womb has many chambers was derived from observation of animal wombs (Fasbender 1897: 73, 141; Manuli 1983: 188), although Aristotle argues that the human womb is always two-chambered because the male is the model for humanity and a man has two testicles (*GA* 716b33). Galen too insisted that, although the womb is one organ, it contains two chambers sharing a single neck, and he suggested that this makes it valid to use either singular or plural forms for it (*On Anatomical Procedures* 12.2, Duckworth *et al.* 1962: 113–14). The fullest ancient discussion of the etymology of the terms most commonly used is given by Soranos, who links *mêtrê* to the womb as 'mother of all the embryos borne of it' or 'because it makes mothers of those who possess it' (*Gyn.* 1.6; T 8). The womb continued to be called 'the Mother' in English Renaissance medicine. *Hysterê*, for Soranos, is linked to *hysteron*, to indicate that the womb 'yields up all its products afterwards' and 'lies after all the entrails' (*Gyn.* 1.6; T 8). Modern etymologists suggest that it is connected with a Sanskrit word and means 'upper/back part' (LSJ), or with *hyderos*, meaning 'dropsy' or 'swollen belly' (Chantraine 1968). The verbs *hystereô* and *hysterizô* mean 'to come late' and 'to come after'. Athenaeus, an excellent source for word usage, gives a pun which suggests that this temporal sense could be linked to 'womb'; Leontion was upset because her lover was paying attention to a woman called Glykera who had arrived later than she, and when asked what was the matter replied *hê hystera mê lypai*, 'my womb hurts' or 'she who arrived after me hurts me' (585d). But there is another sense in which *hystera* for womb invokes lateness; the presentation of Pandora as a late arrival on the human scene. Woman is generically *hystera*, and this name for womb should remind the listener of Pandora and thus of the origin of female difference.

A further term for womb is 'jar', *angos*. *Epidemics* 6.5.11 (Loeb VII, 258) says that paleness in the nipples and areola indicate disease in the *angos*, and Galen's commentary on this passage identifies this organ as the womb. In terms of Hippocratic anatomy, this makes sense because the womb and breasts are very closely connected; breasts are part of the essential sponginess of the female body (*NC* 15, L 7.494). Breast milk is menstrual blood diverted and refined (*Glands* 16, Loeb VIII, 124). Very excessive or inadequate menstrual flow were both seen as unhealthy (*Aph.* 5.57, Loeb IV, 172); one way of stopping abnormally heavy menstruation was to apply the largest size of cupping-glass to the breasts (*Aph.* 5.50, Loeb IV, 170), so that the blood would come out from them rather than from the womb. Aristotle, for whom women were 'cold' and men 'hot', developed this argument further, claiming that menses, milk and semen were the three successive stages of development of a single substance, with only the male of the species being sufficiently 'hot' to achieve the final stage of transformation into semen (e.g. *PA* 650a8 ff.; *GA* 774a1).

Generation 9 (L 7.482) draws an analogy between womb and jar; as a plant grows to fill its container, so if the womb is small like a cup (*arystêr*; Lonie 1981: 143) then the child will be small and weak, but if the womb is larger the child can grow properly, like a cucumber growing in an *angos*. Soranos uses *angeion* for one of the membranes which 'encases the embryo like a vessel' (*Gyn*. 1.57; T 58), while pseudo-Aristotle uses it to mean either the womb or a foetal membrane (635b14). The theme throughout is the role of the womb as container. A section of *Diseases of Women* says that a difficult delivery is like shaking a fruit stone out of a *lekythos*, a jar with a narrow mouth (1.33, L 8.78).

Thus, like any jar, the womb has a mouth, *to stoma tês mêtrês* (*DW* 1.85, L 8.210) or, since the womb can be plural, *to stoma tôn mêtreôn* (*DW* 1.2, L 8.14). Occasionally there are references to plural 'mouths of the womb(s)' (e.g. *DW* 2.146, L 8.322; 2.162, L 8.338), perhaps suggesting that the neck of the womb-jar has both a mouth into the body of the jar and another out into the vagina.[14] More commonly, the mouth of the womb must be aligned with a second mouth at the bottom of the tube, or blood will not be able to pour out. This is called the 'mouth of the vagina' (*to stoma tou aidoiou*, *DW* 1.40, L 8.96; *Ep*. 2.4.5, Loeb VII, 72)[15] or the 'mouth of exit' (*to stoma tês exodou*, *Virg*., L 8.466). The condition of the inner, uterine mouth can be determined by the female patient, who can tell by touching it whether it is hard or soft, open or closed, upright or tilted (e.g. *DW* 2.119, L 8.260; 2.133, L 8.280–8; 2.134, L 8.304).

From the passages cited, it is clear that the *Diseases of Women* treatises and the other gynaecological and embryological texts of the corpus are not the only places in which material on women's diseases can be found. Case histories of female patients exist throughout the seven books of *Epidemics*, while a number of Hippocratic treatises on disease in general include a section devoted specifically to women's diseases; for example, *Aphorisms* 5, *Coan Prognoses* 503–44 (L 5.700–8) and the last part of *Places in Man* (47, Loeb VIII, 94–100). The presence of such material in a 'general' treatise is suggestive; the addition of a section on 'women' to a text recalls Pandora's arrival as an afterthought tacked on to male humanity. *Places in Man* 47 keeps a certain distance from the proposal that women's diseases are 'separate' by opening with the words, 'Diseases of women, as they are called'.[16]

As we have seen (p. 12), whereas the focus in *Diseases of Women* rests on suppressed menstruation as the primary cause of a variety of symptoms experienced by women, *Places in Man* 47 regards the womb as the main cause of women's diseases. Movement of the womb in a forward direction is seen as the most serious problem, not only producing pain but also obstructing the menstrual flow; upward movement of the womb may lead to pain in parts of the body as far away as the head. *Diseases of Women* also includes descriptions of womb movement. Ann Hanson (1991: 82) has proposed that, because the male is the norm for the human race,[17] the womb is an organ with no natural home; it therefore tends to wander around the body in search of moisture. It is not enough to label the wandering womb 'this curious notion' or call it a 'bizarre phenomenon' (Blundell 1995: 100–1); to the Hippocratics, it was a central tenet of medical theory and practice.

For Hippocratic anatomy of the female body, this raises an important question, one to which I will return when considering hysteria in Chapter 11. How far is the womb thought to be able to move? In Plato's *Timaeus* (91c4) it can move 'through the whole body', but there is some debate over whether the Hippocratic womb was considered capable of passing through the diaphragm. I have been criticised by M.J. Adair (1996: 159) for suggesting that the womb moves to the head, on the grounds that the Greek *trapôsin hai hysterai* (*DW* 2.123, L 8.266)[18] means that the womb 'turns', rather than 'moves'. However, the chapter in question opens, 'When the womb turns to the head and suffocation stops there, the head is heavy.' The ensuing description of the symptoms and recommendations for therapy suggest that the head is indeed the focus of the problem. The patient says that the passages in the nose and under the eyes hurt; the treatment is to wash her with hot water and, if this does not work, to pour cooled infusions of myrtle or laurel over the head, anoint the head with rose oil, and fumigate with sweet smells below, foul smells under the nose. Thus, no matter how far the womb itself can travel, its effects are very wide-ranging; and, in the corpus as a whole, it 'rushes' and 'moves swiftly' through the body, and 'falls upon' other organs (Dean-Jones 1994: 70).

Therapy for the diseases of women was based on the belief that, although nothing could change the essential wetness and sponginess, it was nevertheless possible to make adjustments to a woman's way of life which would improve her health. The interventions carried out included alterations to the amount of blood being produced, which could be achieved by instigating dietary changes (King 1995c). As the preparation of food was an important part of a woman's role in the household, the Hippocratic recipes and dietary advice could be seen as usurping her role, perhaps because her illness means that she cannot fulfil it successfully.[19] Other interventions included the expulsion of suppressed blood, and measures to move the womb away from inappropriate locations, such as the liver, to which it was liable to travel in search of additional moisture (see further Chapter 11, p. 217). Also practised as therapies were washing, oiling, and wrapping bandages around the body to keep the womb in place (e.g. *DW* 2.127, L 8.272 and 2.129, L 8.278). Usually a combination of measures would be taken to achieve the goal. A drying diet and frequent exercise were prescribed for a woman whose menses were phlegmatic, but her treatment involved vapour baths – aromatic substances thrown on hot ashes under a cloth – as well as emetics and purgative pessaries (*DW* 1.11, L 8.44–6). A wide range of pharmacological substances was employed, including materials also used in purificatory ritual – such as sulphur, asphalt, squill and laurel – as well as animal excrement (von Staden 1991). The range of substances listed to treat most conditions may have been in order to cater for a range of abilities to pay among potential patients, or to allow for seasonal variation in the availability of materials (Nutton 1985a). Scented substances, such as myrrh, were thought to have warming qualities to draw out suppressed blood, and were administered as fomentations, fumigations, vapour baths and pessaries (surveyed by Byl 1989). The womb could be lured downwards by the use of the *hodos*, with sweet scents being applied to the vagina, accompanied by foul smells inhaled at the nostrils (e.g. *DW* 2.123, L 8.266; 2.154, L 8.330); prolapse of the womb was treated by applying the scents from the opposite direction (e.g. *DW* 2.125, L 8.268). Vomiting could also be used to jolt the womb upwards, with foul odours being applied to the vulva at the same time (*DW* 2.142, L 8.314; Joly 1966: 44–5). A method of expelling the retained afterbirth is to make the woman sneeze, but to block her nostrils and mouth at the moment of sneezing (*Ep.* 2.5.25, Loeb VII, 80).

How did the Hippocratic writers claim to know about women's bodies? Because they did not dissect the human body, the female anatomy on which these therapies were based came from deducing the inside from outside manifestations, connecting bodily events by means of analogy and assumption. Even if the Hippocratics had dissected a woman, however, they could always have accounted for the womb being found in the same place post-mortem by arguing that it tends to drift down at death. Technology can work with, rather than against, prevailing cultural beliefs. 'Accidental' anatomy was practised in classical Greece; for example, prolapse of the womb made the normally invisible dramatically visible. As Annoni and Barras (1993: 194–5) have pointed out, 'imaginary' dissection of human bodies was carried out in the mind of the Hippocratic writer of *On Joints*, who imagines what would be seen if one were to strip off the flesh from the arm to see the humerus (1, Loeb III, 200–2), and even speculates about the possibility of opening the body and inserting one's hand to reduce a dislocation from inside (46, Loeb III, 292). Analogies with animal anatomy were also made, since butchery, sacrifice and medicine were closely related; Galen makes it clear that the knowledge of the 'slaughterers of oxen' of his own day included the insertion of the knife between the skull and the first vertebra, which immediately paralyses the animal.[20] The order in which Aristotle takes the parts of the body in *On the Parts of Animals* also reflects sacrificial practice; but, as Vegetti (1979: 32; cf. Durand 1979a: 149) has shown, medical knowledge in the fourth century BC attempted to deny its sacrificial origins. Aristotle gives two identical descriptions of abnormal gall bladders (*HA* 496b24ff. and *PA* 676b35ff.) but, whereas the former states that this knowledge comes from sacrificial victims (*en tois hieriois*), the latter passage omits this information.[21]

It was not until third-century BC Alexandria that systematic anatomy was carried out on human bodies.[22] This was associated in particular with Herophilos, in whose work women first came to be seen more as reversed males than as a separate 'race'. Where men's reproductive organs are outside, women were seen as having analogous organs inside their bodies. Herophilos discovered the ovaries (von Staden 1989, fr.61), although he did not understand their function; he was aware of the Fallopian tubes, but he did not know their purpose, believing that they went to the bladder. It appears to have been Galen who discovered that they terminated in the womb (*De uteri diss*. 9; CMG V.2,1 p. 48).

Some of the assumptions made about the interior of the female body in Hippocratic medicine were challenged by Alexandrian anatomy, but there was no straightforward 'medical progress' as a result. When Herophilos described the uterine ligaments which technically made extensive womb movement an impossibility (von Staden 1989, fr.114), the Hippocratic 'wandering womb' theory was merely rephrased, being seen in terms of 'sympathy' between the upper and lower parts of the body permitting the latter to cause symptoms in the former (see further Chapter 11, pp. 231, 235). In terms of therapy, there was also little change as a result of Alexandrian anatomical developments, although the rationale behind scent therapy for womb movement was reinterpreted by writers such as the first-century AD Celsus, who accepted that the womb was attached to the ilia (*Med*. 5.1.12), and argued that the purpose of scent therapy was to rouse the unconscious patient (4.27.1) rather than to entice the womb into a different location.

In later classical medicine the debate over whether women were sufficiently different from men to merit their own branch of medicine continued. In the second century AD, when Soranos asked whether women have conditions peculiar to their sex (*Gyn*. 3.1; T 128), he summarised the position taken on this question up to this time: writers such as the early fourth-century BC Diocles of Carystos (fr.169 Wellmann) and the Empiricist sect believed that there were conditions specific to women, while the third century BC Erasistratos and Herophilos, together with writers of the Methodist sect, a group whose approach to medical knowledge was particularly strong in first-century AD Rome, denied that this was the case. Instead, Methodists thought that the same principles governed all diseases. They put their trust in a strict division of causes of symptoms into three conditions of the body: *status laxus*, in which the body or affected part is lax and wet, leading for example to a flux; *status strictus*, a constricted and dry state such as amenorrhoea; and *status mixtus*, a combination. Treatment characteristically began with fasting, then built up the patient through diet and exercise, before aggressive interventions causing the patient to vomit, shake or sneeze.[23] Soranos himself claimed that men and women were made of the same materials behaving according to the same rules; although the womb is unique to women and has its own functions, while some conditions, such as pregnancy and lactation, are specific to women, their diseases are not generically different (*Gyn.* 3.5; T 132).

There is no place in Soranos' gynaecology for the Hippocratic theory that menstruation is essential to female health; on the contrary, Soranos argues that menstruation is actually bad for women's health, except insofar as it is necessary for conception, while intercourse is harmful, and perpetual virginity represents the best option for both men and women (*Gyn.* 1.27–32; T 23–30). Pregnancy, far from relieving certain gynaecological disorders, is bad for women, causing exhaustion and premature old age. It is ironic that the author of the fullest *Gynaecology* surviving from antiquity – a hazard of preservation which will be discussed further in Chapter 9 – should also have been one of the writers who minimised the need for gynaecology at all. Although coming from a very different theoretical position Aretaeus, another medical writer of the second century AD, took up a similar stance to that of Soranos on the need for gynaecology (2.11; CMG 2.34); however, he argued that the mobility of the womb leads to special problems which women do not share with men, these being hysterical suffocation, prolapse and the female flux.

So the issues addressed by Hippocratic gynaecology did not go away. The nature and extent of female difference, and hence the necessity of gynaecology itself, continued to be debated. For the Greeks of the classical period it is Pandora, the separate creation who is the origin of the 'race of women', who makes gynaecology necessary. She is a womb-jar, insatiable in her appetites, lustful and deceitful, but fertile. Hippocratic gynaecology states female difference in terms of structure and function. Structurally, women have an entirely different texture of flesh from men, being wet, soft and spongy. This means that they accumulate blood, and need to menstruate with relentless regularity to avoid the diseases caused by menstrual retention. They also have powerful connections between breasts and womb, and between the top and bottom of their bodies. Yet Pandora, while supporting the need for gynaecology, also undermines the whole Hippocratic enterprise by her combination of the features of the immature girl, or *parthenos*, with those of the mature woman, the *gynê* who is the object of Hippocratic *gynaikeia*, and by her persistent refusal to match the inside to the outside. In the next chapter I will discuss the issues raised by 'reading the body' in Hippocratic medicine, looking at the role of the healer confronted with a female patient in terms of the issues of appearance and reality raised by Pandora. Chapter 3 turns from the mythical girl-woman, Pandora, to an apparently more realistic female patient, the 'daughter of Leonidas', who not only demonstrates further the hazards of menstruation but also introduces the issue of how our understanding of Hippocratic gynaecology has been affected by the ways in which historical readers have chosen to approach particular types of Hippocratic text.

2

DECEITFUL BODIES, SPEAKING BODIES

How was a Hippocratic healer supposed to understand the body of a woman patient? How did reading her body differ from the process of interpretation involved in understanding the signs presented by a male body? The Hippocratic healer, the *iatros*, relies on reading the external signs in order to know the inside, which remains unseen; on the rare occasions when instruments are used to see inside the body, these are treated with considerable caution. Pandora, presented to male humanity as a beautiful, marriageable *parthenos*, threatens the work of the healer because her outside is deceptive, concealing the fact that her body contains a voracious womb-jar and the mind of a bitch. But when Hippocratic writers discussed how to read the female body, they proposed that certain types of woman were easier to read than others.

The fullest Hippocratic description of reading the body occurs in the treatise *Regimen*, where – in keeping with the competitive nature of many of these medical texts – the author claims that he alone has discovered how to tell when a patient is about to fall ill (*Regimen* 1.2, Loeb IV, 230). He argues from basics, stating that all things in the universe are composed of water, which nourishes, and fire, which moves (1.3, IV, 230–2). He then discusses the place of medicine as one of a list of *technai*, arguing for example that, like divination, it knows the unseen by means of the seen (1.11, IV, 248) and, like shoe-making, it cuts and stitches to create wholeness (1.15, IV, 252). What constitutes a *technê*? Ferrari and Vegetti (1983: 202) have characterised it as a 'practical activity that required intellectual competence as well as manual dexterity, was based on scientific knowledge, produced results that it was possible to verify, and was governed by well-defined rules that could be transmitted by teaching' but, as the inclusion of divination in this list suggests, a *technê* was equivalent neither to a 'science' nor a 'craft' today. Von Staden (1996: 412, 416) defines a *technê* in terms of its creation of a sense of belonging to a collectivity extending over the generations. The writer of *Regimen* further compares the *technê* of medicine with writing, which is described as 'putting together' (*synthesis*) the symbols of the human voice, having power to recall the past and to show what is to be done (1.23, IV, 258). The author then links the seven Greek vowels to the seven senses of hearing, sight, smell, taste, speech, touch and breath; together, these bring knowledge to the trained healer (1.23, IV, 258–60).[1]

In the ancient world, reading the body was never considered to be a straightforward activity. As Maud Gleason has shown for the second century AD, masculinity and femininity 'constituted a system of signs' (1990: 402) which could be taught to anatomical males and females. From birth, a baby was to be swaddled in such a way that its future shape would be that considered most becoming to its sex (Soranos, *Gyn.* 2.15; T 85), and then massaged into shape by its child-nurse (*Gyn.* 2.32; T 105). Moralists and physiognomists advised on how to discipline the body, holding it posturally and using it in speech and gesture in order to present it in the best possible light. Gleason has linked this to the pressures of a face-to-face society in which image is all. However, conscious self-presentation carried to this level carries with it the risk of deceit, and physiognomic literature of the second century AD revealed anxiety about those who tried to cover up unacceptable character traits with adroit use of gesture and posture.

The danger of deceit was also something with which Hippocratic healers were closely concerned; not only because the body could deceive its reader, but also because healers needed to pay close attention to the way they presented themselves to potential patients. Arriving in a new location with no licence, and no recognised training, these healers needed to display an image which would convince patients of their worth. In the competitive context of early medicine, in which not only different protagonists within one medical discourse, but also adherents of different medical discourses, could be in dispute (von Staden 1992e: 585), rhetoric was important; healers needed to present their arguments verbally, sometimes to defeat a rival in public debate (Lloyd 1979: 96–8), but more commonly to persuade the client or potential client of the value of specific therapies. But self-presentation went beyond rhetoric into every aspect of the healer's own appearance.

There was no single word for 'quack' in the Hippocratic vocabulary, but the specific issues of what we could call quackery in their culture were bound up with their concern for self-presentation and their awareness of the role of deceit within this. The definition of 'quack' for any historical period is of course fraught with difficulty. As Porter (1989) has shown for the period 1660–1850, for the medical practitioner a quack is always someone else. Our dominant image today is of someone who lacks any qualifications, knows very little, tricks patients and lies about his or her results. When Isaac Baker Brown was accused of being a quack, it was his use of self-publicity through advertisements which was most commonly criticised although, as we saw in the Introduction, quackery could also be defined as 'The diagnosis of a disease which has no existence' (Seymour Haden, *BMJ* 1867: 397). For the ancient world, there was no qualification system; what was 'known' was disputed within the *technê*; and, on one occasion at least, frank admission that trickery of patients occurs is found in the Hippocratic corpus (below, pp. 46–7). As for self-publicity, it is an inevitable part of trying to gain clients, but some who considered themselves as working within the *technê* regarded others as going beyond reasonable limits in their presentation of self.

What were the specific constituents of quackery for a Hippocratic writer? Several passages in the corpus attack either fellow *iatroi*, or those professing different modes of healing, for language or behaviour seen as deceiving the patients. What is specifically condemned in such passages is failure to match appearance, whether verbal or visual, with reality, a situation reminiscent of Pandora.

The late fourth-century BC text *The Doctor* and the early third-century BC, or later, *On Decorum* provide the most guidance on the presentation of the Greek medical self, instructing the healer in how to dress and act so that he will attract custom. These are lasting concerns; because he only wanted to cite the section relevant to 'what was anciently considered good manners and good behaviour for doctors' (Loeb II, 305) Jones translated only the first chapter of *The Doctor*, but in the recently published Loeb VIII it appears in full. These texts warn that quackery is implied by wearing extravagant clothing and hats, while using elaborate perfume and quoting from the poets when at the patient's bedside (*Dec.* 2, Loeb II, 280; Lloyd 1979: 89–90).[2] Another writer makes the theatrical analogy even more explicit, comparing those who have only 'the appearance, dress and mask' of doctors with non-speaking parts in tragedy, played by people unable to act but nevertheless costumed and masked in character (*Law* 1, Loeb II, 262). These texts recommend as the costume appropriate to a true doctor a naturally healthy appearance, with simple, undecorated clothes and pleasant but unobtrusive perfumes (*Dec.* 3, Loeb II, 280; *The Doctor* 1, Loeb II, 310 = Loeb VIII, 300).

The central irony of texts such as these is that, in the very process of condemning deception, they are simultaneously teaching it. In her study of an interesting parallel from early modern France, Alison Lingo (1986: 586) noted that the regular physicians interpreted only the dress of their competitors, the empirics, as being 'costume', despite the fact that physicians too advertised their identity through a formal dress code. As for the Hippocratics, the extravagant clothes and flowery language of the bad *iatros* are considered wrong because they deceive the crowd (*Dec.* 2), while the simple dress and direct language of the good *iatros* are to be emulated. Yet the texts show awareness that the latter may be as much a costume as the former, particularly if the reality beneath is an incompetent practitioner.

The Doctor 4 (Loeb VIII, 304) moves from the appearance of the *iatros* to his therapeutic activities: it singles out for attention the use by the bad *iatros* of bandages that are 'elegant and theatrical' (*epidesias kai theêtrikas*), labelling these as thoroughly tasteless (*phortikos*) and pretentious (*alazonikos*). This recalls the *alazones* or 'deceivers' condemned in *On the Sacred Disease*, classed with magicians, purifiers[3] and begging-priests who, because they have no idea how to help a sick person, provide purification, chanting, food taboos and divine intervention; the Hippocratic writer says that they 'claim superior knowledge' and construct a name for the disease, calling it 'sacred', then 'add a plausible story and establish a method of treatment that secures their own position' (*Sac. Dis.* 2, Loeb II, 140). In terms of healing, as I will be suggesting in Chapter 6, this use of narrative may well have been effective; here, however, what is significant is the Hippocratic healer's attempt to distance himself from this type of medicine, in favour of what he presents as real knowledge of the individual patient in relation to her environment. In ancient medical texts, we briefly meet others whose claims to heal are not made within the bounds of the *technê*, including priests, midwives, and root-cutters (Lloyd 1979: 15–29; 1983: 208–9); drugs were also sold in the market, where anyone could buy them (ps-Ar. *Oik.* 1346b22; Aristoph. *Clouds* 766–8). The root-cutters, like the *iatroi*, are supposed to have written books; fragments survive of the *Roots* written by a first-century BC root-cutter called Crateuas. But not all of these alternatives to the Hippocratic healer are guilty of deceit. What specifically constitutes deceitfulness in the *alazones* and their kin is their failure to admit their ignorance; here they are comparable with the *manteis* whose advice to female patients in *On the Diseases of Virgins* is condemned as 'thoroughly deceitful' (*exapataô*; see Chapter 4, pp. 78–9).

Precisely why are theatrical bandages so bad? Because they are not only excessive, but often do harm to the patient. The patient is said to be interested not in fine appearances (*kallôpismon*) but in benefit (*sympheron*). In the discussion of treatment for a broken nose in *On Joints* 35 (Loeb III, 264–6) the writer claims that this is the injury for which those who 'take delight in pretty bandages' can do the most damage, displaying their manual skills (*eucheiriê*) in producing something intricate. The patient is as thrilled as the doctor with the effect, at least for the first day or so, after which the bandage becomes uncomfortable. Such bandages are thus more than merely silly; they are potentially harmful (Edelstein 1931: 94), putting more pressure on the nose than may be helpful, and possibly exacerbating the effects of the fracture (cf. *Joints* 44, Loeb III, 288). It is shameful for any *technê*, especially medicine, to make a show of so much trouble, display and talk, and then to do no good. Similar language occurs in another chapter of *The Doctor* (2, Loeb VIII, 302), where the author recommends that bronze should not be used except for surgical instruments – where it is particularly appropriate due to its strength and resistance to rust (Longfield-Jones 1986: 84) – because 'it seems to me tasteless ornamentation (*kallôpismos phortikos*) to have all one's equipment in bronze'. Galen's attack on his fellow practitioners in Rome in the second century AD deliberately echoes but also goes beyond these Hippocratic pronouncements, when in *On Prognosis* 1 (CMG V 8, 1 p. 68.13) he condemns their use of silver medical instruments.

The Hippocratic texts show considerable ambivalence not only about the role of dress, as a sort of theatrical costume which can conceal a good or a bad healer, and about the props of the medical actor, but also about the intelligence of the patient. Is the patient to be seen as discerning, able to identify the best healer, or as gullible and easily impressed by a good performance? A well-known passage from a treatise probably dating to the fourth century BC, *Joints* 42 (Loeb III, 282), describes the effect on the crowds of watching a performance of the spectacular therapy of public succussion in which the patient is tied to a ladder and violently shaken, for a case of humpback caused by an accident.[4] The writer says there is nothing wrong with the technique itself – it is an established method which is sometimes very useful – but it is often carried out for the wrong motives, by practitioners who care little for results but only want to make the crowd gape and stare (Edelstein 1931: 94). The writer claims that he is too embarrassed even to try the procedure because of its association with deceivers (*alazones*).

Deceit may then stem from one's personal appearance, medical equipment or therapeutic practices: it is condemned because it does not have the patient's interests at heart, but instead is more concerned with looking good and impressing the crowds. The true *iatros* should be a gentleman (*kalos kai agathos*, *Dec.* 1) who is above such flashy vulgarity. However, it is also acknowledged that part of the problem may lie with the patients who positively encourage such spectacular displays.

Deceit is not only unworthy of a gentleman, it is also feminine. In a passage of the *Iliad*, Hera 'being a woman deceived Zeus with her treachery (*dolophrosynê*)'. Knowing that Alkmene was about to give birth to his son Herakles, Zeus declared that a man related to him to be born on that very day would be the ruler of his people. After making him swear this, Hera went to Argos where she knew the wife of Sthenelos was also pregnant with a son, and brought him to birth although he was only a seven-months' child. At the same time she delayed Alkmene's labour (*Il.* 19.97–119). The child born also happened to be related to Zeus, so this type of deceit used as its starting point verbal ambiguity of which the speaker was unaware. The deceit which concerns the Hippocratics tends to be centred on the visual: what you see is not necessarily what you get, so seeing should not be believing.

In the circle of the good *iatroi*, whose discreet demeanour and healthy appearance appeal to discerning patients (*The Doctor* 1), their medical activity is aimed at discovering and exposing deceit. This is deceit of a different kind: the deceit implicit in the human body, which can confuse both doctors and patients. In reading and writing, the same symbol keeps the same meaning whenever it is encountered; but, in reading the body, the signs do not always mean what one expects (*PM* 41, Loeb VIII, 80). Phantom pregnancies deceive women for many months (*Prorrhetic* 2.26, Loeb VIII, 274), while the swelling of dropsy deceives patients so that they disobey the doctors' instructions, and may die (*Prorrhetic* 2.6, Loeb VIII, 238).[5] Here it is personal experience of the body which deceives: the symptoms do not match the reality. Deceit on the part of the patient may be deliberate; *On Decorum* advises the healer, 'Keep a watch on the faults of the patient, which often make them lie about the taking of things prescribed. For through not taking disagreeable drinks, purgative or other, they sometimes die. What they have done never results in a confession, but the blame is thrown upon the physician' (*Dec.* 14, Loeb II, 296). Alternatively, failure to follow the instructions given by the *iatros* may be intrinsic to the state of ill health:

> It is much more likely that the sick cannot follow out the orders than that the physicians give wrong instructions. The physician sets about his task with healthy mind and healthy body . . . The patient knows neither what he is suffering from, nor the cause thereof . . . Which is the more likely: that men in this condition obey, instead of varying, the physician's orders, or that the physician, in the condition that my account has explained above, gives improper orders? Surely it is much more likely that the physician gives proper orders, which the patient not unnaturally is unable to follow; and not following them he meets with death, the cause of which illogical reasoners attribute to the innocent, allowing the guilty to go free.
>
> (*The Art* 7, Loeb II, 200–2)

Edelstein summarised this side of Hippocratic medicine by writing, 'The patient is believed to be credulous, devoid of real judgement, and a liar' (1931: 99).

Some texts associate these faults more strongly with female patients. As we saw in Chapter 1, pregnancy was supposed to be something which women 'knew' from their own sensations on conception, and which Hippocratic healers could usually detect by bodily signs or by tests. In a case history in the *Epidemics*, a report from a female patient that she had lost a male foetus towards the twentieth day of pregnancy is modified by the *iatros* adding the phrase, 'If this was true, I do not know' (*Ep.* 4.6, Loeb VII, 94). This suggests that women's bodies may deceive them, and therefore that the healer's assessment does not match their experience. A group of descriptions of women which is found further on in the fourth book of *Epidemics* casts more doubt on women's knowledge of their own pregnancy and of its progress: Antigenes' wife 'did not know whether she was pregnant' (*Ep.* 4.21, Loeb VII, 112); the woman from Tenedos aborted, 'so she said', a male foetus of 30 days' gestation (*Ep.* 4.20g, Loeb VII, 112); while the wife of Apemantus' brother aborted a female foetus of 60 days, 'she said' (*Ep.* 4.22, Loeb VII, 114).[6] Elsewhere in the *Epidemics* we are told that another woman patient 'would not take orders' (*Ep.* 3.2.14, Loeb I, 280; cf. Lloyd 1983: 68 and n.38).

For the *iatros*, who is one stage further away from the reality of the disease, the main problem lies with the uncertainties of the different forms of sensory perception which provide him with access to knowledge. Faced with possible deceit or simple confusion on the part of the patient, the senses are the doctor's main means of reading the body; Langholf (1990: 51–2, 134) cites in particular two passages from the *Epidemics* which detail the ways in which the body gives access to the body, whether one's own or that of another. In *Epidemics* 4.43 (Loeb VII, 136–8) we read that 'we [observe] with the eyes, the ears, the nose, the hand . . . [on the one hand, there is] the patient; [on the other hand, there is] the practitioner,[7] who, in each case, touches or smells or tastes and is informed about the rest . . . these are the means by which we observe'. *Epidemics* 6.8.17 (Loeb VII, 284) states that 'It is necessary to use the body for observation: sight, hearing, nose, touch, tongue, intelligence.'[8]

But touch may not be an accurate guide: although examining a patient by touching the abdomen and veins makes one less liable to be deceived than if one does not touch at all, if the patient does not follow a constant regimen then any form of examination by looking, touching, smelling or listening may produce an inaccurate impression (*Prorrhetic* 2.3, Loeb VIII, 226). Ignorant practitioners are deceived by touching the ridges of the spine, which they wrongly assume to be the vertebrae themselves; the postures of patients with spinal problems can further deceive the unwary *iatros* (*Joints* 46, Loeb III, 292).

Even more deceptive than touch is the sense of sight. On several occasions Hippocratic writers warn 'do not be deceived' when discussing how to read visual body signs (e.g. *Prog.* 12, Loeb II, 28; *Dis.* 3.16, Loeb VI, 54). The appearance of a recent wound may deceive you into thinking that the bone is not coming up, yet it does (*Fract.* 28, Loeb III, 160). Wasting of the flesh at the joint can deceive *iatroi* into thinking that the shoulder has dislocated forwards (*Joints* 1, Loeb III, 200) and a tumour in the ear may deceive a healer into expecting it to contain excess humoral fluids, so that he cuts into it in order to release them (*Joints* 40, Loeb III, 276; cf. *On Setting Joints* 5, L 4.346).

Although the Hippocratics usually interpreted the inside of the body in terms of the signs displayed on its surface (DuBois 1991: 87–90), they also developed instruments to enhance the sense of sight by enabling them to see inside the orifices of the body. However – as in the nineteenth-century attacks on the vaginal speculum mentioned in the Introduction – instruments were thought to be even more deceptive to the careless user than unassisted sight. The *katopteris* used to examine the rectum is described in these terms in *Haemorrhoids* 5 (Loeb VIII, 386; cf. *Fistulas* 3, Loeb VIII, 392), but its inherent potential for deception can be overcome by the skilled user, who is aware that it should be kept closed; opening it up risks flattening the very lump one is supposed to be examining.

Perhaps the most surprising use of deceit in the Hippocratic corpus is the one passage in which it appears to be recommended to the good *iatros*. In *Epidemics* 6.5.7 (Loeb VII, 256) the writer describes blatant deceit, ending the passage with the frank admission, *apatê*, 'deceit'. Pain in the ear, he says, can be treated by a doctor who, having previously concealed in the palm of his hand a piece of wool soaked in warm oil, puts his hand over the ear so that, to the patient, something appears to have come out. After producing this 'foreign body' the doctor is advised to throw it in the fire, perhaps so that nobody has a chance to examine it too closely. Rather than accepting that this therapy is openly being described as deceit, ancient commentators preferred to believe that there were some words missing after *apatê*. Dioscorides preferred to omit as spurious everything after the description of the doctor holding his hand over the affected ear, making the text into a straightforward account of warm oil as a cure for ear pain. However, in their edition of this book of the *Epidemics*, Manetti and Roselli (1982: 111–13) argue on structural grounds that all but the final word of the paragraph is authentic, so that, even if the statement 'Deceit' is a later gloss, the description of the *iatros* as active deceiver remains.

There is thus a very fine line for the doctor to tread between deceit and honesty, between unduly elaborate self-promotion and necessary attention to the need to attract custom. Neither bandages nor succussion is inherently bad; their value depends on the motive for their use. Nor is there anything wrong with medical instruments, but they should be for use rather than display, and they must always be used with caution. The utmost care must be taken in understanding the deceptive signs the body offers to its reader.

Where the patient is a woman, the difficulties a male *iatros* encounters may be outweighed by a positive advantage offered by the female body to its Hippocratic reader. This is not a verbal advantage although, like men, women can tell the doctor how their bodies feel, as when the wife of Polemarchos says that she feels 'gathering around the heart' (*Ep.* 5.63, Loeb VII, 196). Culturally, however, it may have been expected that the healer would have to rely more on reading the deceptive body in the case of a female patient, because women were expected to provide less information verbally. Women are often represented as silent patients, reluctant to tell male *iatroi* about what they feel. I have discussed elsewhere (King 1995a) how Galen's second-century AD description of the woman patient infatuated with the dancer Pylades represents her as almost entirely silent, turning over in bed and covering her head rather than speaking to the doctor. Yet her pulse tells him the source of her symptoms is love; her body speaks to the trained reader, even when her mouth remains firmly shut. *Diseases of Women* 1.62 (L 8.126) claims that women are prevented both from knowing what is wrong with them, and from speaking to a *iatros* if they do know, by their youth, inexperience and embarrassment. This comment is usually set beside the passage in Euripides' *Hippolytos* (293–6) where Phaedra's nurse tells her, 'Here are women to help you calm your disease' and adds, 'But if it's something one can tell men, say so, so that it can be revealed to doctors.' This speech tends to be taken at face value; women prefer to keep some things to themselves, but others can be revealed to men, and hence to doctors (cf. Jouanna 1992: 173–5).

Is this the picture we find in the Hippocratic corpus? Geoffrey Lloyd (1983: 70–9) sees 'a certain ambivalence in the relationship between the male doctor and the female patient' here. Sometimes the doctor carries out internal examinations; sometimes the patient examines herself and reports her findings; and on other occasions 'another woman' (*heterê gynê*, e.g. *DW* 1.21, L 8.60; *Ep.* 5.25, Loeb VII, 176) examines the patient. The distancing of the doctor from the body of the patient in the last two options recalls, for us, Victorian accounts of the examination of the patient under a sheet so that a male doctor should not see her external genitalia; but this may be a misleading comparison in its implications about the relationship.

The ideal pattern of interaction between doctor and female patient is represented by the model patient Phrontis, who is described as having examined her vagina, recognised (*egnô*) the problem and reported it (*ephrase*) to the Hippocratic physician (*DW* 1.40, L 8.96–8).[9] Rousselle uses Phrontis as her sole evidence to support the claim that 'In general, women examined themselves while they were in good health' (1988: 25), but I contest whether one swallow makes a summer, even though the bird count could be raised to four if Rousselle had included the passages *Diseases of Women* 1.59 (L 8.118) and 2.155 (L 8.330) where women are described as having detected a problem by examining the mouth of the womb and finding it narrow and moist, and 3.213 (L 8.410) where self-examination shows that the mouth of the womb is closed or tilted. Not all the women of the Hippocratic corpus are, however, prototypes of the *Our Bodies, Ourselves* model of the woman who is trained to know her own healthy body and can therefore detect its changes.[10] Inexperienced women, *hai apeiroi*, think they must be pregnant because their menses stop and their bellies swell, but in fact all they have is wind (*DW* 2.133, L 8.280–2). Phrontis' problem is the absence of the lochia, so she clearly counts as an 'experienced' woman, a complete woman; one who has been through childbirth and has thus become a more trustworthy witness to her own body's potentially deceptive messages (Hanson 1990: 309–10). Danielle Gourevitch (1984: 163–4) has drawn attention to the persistence of these categories outside medical texts, by looking at the example of Calpurnia, the third wife of Pliny the Younger. In a letter written to her grandfather, Pliny says that she had not realised that she was pregnant, due to her lack of experience; as a result, she failed to do what she should have done while pregnant, and paid the price of her inexperience by miscarrying (*Letters* 8.10). In the next letter, to Calpurnia's aunt, Pliny says that the miscarriage was not Calpurnia's fault; it happened because of her age (8.11) The woman who lacks the experience usually brought by age is doubted; it is this type of woman who does not know whether or not she is pregnant.

Where the patient is 'experienced' according to this definition of what counts as experience, her word should be taken seriously, and she should be allowed to examine herself under the healer's supervision; but where she is young, ashamed or inexperienced, the healer has to decide whether to examine her himself or to use an intermediary. This Hippocratic approach to the female patient, by which she is graded on the scale of experience, contrasts with the blanket approach to 'women' taken in a popular work on the role of the gynaecologist published in 1968, where it is suggested that the patient's own history should not be taken until after the gynaecologist has performed a physical examination, since there is a risk that the 'woman draws attention to and underlines some trifling fault' which will mislead the doctor so that he misses something more serious (Russell 1968: 15; cf. Laws 1990: 142). As for treatment, the experienced Hippocratic woman can participate as an active partner in this; in a description of the insertion of a tube into the womb, down which milk will be poured, the writer advises that this can be left to the patient because 'she herself will know where it is to be' (*DW* 3.222, L 8.430). This patient is married, has previously been able to conceive, and reports that her womb is receiving the male seed so that her present failure to conceive cannot be due to an unduly open, or entirely closed, uterine mouth. She is therefore, by Hippocratic standards, an experienced and co-operative woman, and can be trusted. Even here, however, the patient's word is not always infallible. In *Diseases of Women* 2.157 (L 8.332), the woman examines herself,[11] touching the mouth of her womb to check if it is soft; if so, the treatment can proceed. A similar situation occurs, with the woman reporting whether the mouth of her womb is 'straighter' before the next stage of treatment can take place, at 2.146 (L 8.322). But in 2.157 (L 8.334) the writer goes on, 'But if it seems to *you* (*ên soi dokeêi*) that she needs more purging . . . '; that is, the opinion expressed by the female patient only counts up to a point, beyond which the healer uses his own judgement.

But there is another context in which the female body is positively loud in its messages to the Hippocratic physician. This is the experience of epidemic disease, in which women are easier to read than men because they have an extra mouth (*stoma*), the vaginal orifice.

Historically, one of the most influential Hippocratic treatises is *Prognostics*. Dominated by the terminology of intellectual activity – observe, examine, evaluate, think, predict (Lichtenthaeler 1963: 49) – it was a highly influential text in medieval and Renaissance medicine, appearing with *Aphorisms* and *Regimen in Acute Diseases* on the medical curricula of Paris and Oxford in the fifteenth century, and as one of the six core medical texts in a group of medical writings widely used as a textbook for teaching medicine, the *Articella* (Kristeller 1976: 59, 65).[12] Despite its very general title, it is restricted to the acute malarial-type fevers,[13] diseases of short duration and predictable course in which a cyclical pattern of symptoms is experienced due to the build-up of micro-organisms in the blood (Demand 1994: 82). Depending on the precise parasite carried by the mosquito, the attacks may come every third (tertian fever) or every fourth day (quartan fever).

As part of its claim that the doctor can know in advance which patients will live and which will die, *Prognostics* lists the signs of impending death. The author makes a clear bid for control of some women's diseases, stating 'The crises which women undergo after childbirth follow the same plan too' (20, Loeb II, 44), suggesting that what we would probably want to diagnose as puerperal fever is seen in terms of the malarial fevers. But would he interpret all female conditions in terms of this model?

Prognostics opens with the statement, 'It seems to me that the best doctor is one with foreknowledge (*pronoia*)' (1, Loeb II, 6). At the bedside of the sick, the physician – like Homer's Calchas (*Il.* 1.70) and Hesiod's Muses (*Th.* 38)[14] – will know in advance (*progignôskô*) and speak in advance (*prolegô*) the present, the past and the future. In a section of *Epidemics* (1.11, Loeb I, 164) a similar passage occurs, in which the doctor must 'speak (*legô*) the past, know (*gignôskô*) the present and predict (*prolegô*) the future'. This order – past, present, future – may seem the more obvious; in choosing instead present, past, future the author of *Prognostics* may be deliberately situating the medical art beside those of prophets and Muses (Pigeaud 1990: 30–1). The doctor gains the confidence of patients and their families by his knowledge of the past and present, telling them points about the origin of their sickness which they had omitted when describing it to him. If his predictions for the future are wrong, of course – as *Prorrhetic* 2.2 (Loeb VIII, 222) reminds us – he will be hated, and even thought to be mad. But by controlling time, he controls the case, and increases his chances of success in treating it, because he can see in advance what is to come. He also produces let-out clauses; some patients will die before he can treat them, due to the power of the disease (*Prog.* 1, Loeb II, 6), while others die because of environmental factors (25, Loeb II, 54).

The interest in what came to be known as the *indicia mortis*, the physical signs predicting death, is part of a reluctance to take on hopeless cases, since these can do nothing for one's reputation. The author combines an individualist approach – the best way anyone can look is like him- or herself – with a more generalist, 'prognosis by numbers' approach in which a pointed nose, sunken eyes, cold ears, dry forehead and a complexion which is yellow, black, livid or leaden should always be taken as signs of the approach of death (*Prog.* 2, Loeb II, 8).[15] Sleeping on the stomach signifies delirium or abdominal problems – unless one always sleeps in that position when in health. Grinding the teeth is bad – unless one has done this since childhood (3, Loeb II, 12). The body may produce further hints; diarrhoea and hunger are good signs (2, Loeb II, 8), perhaps because they indicate that basic appetites remain. Examination of the eyes is valuable: do they avoid the light? Are they full of tears? Out of focus? One smaller than the other? Are the whites red? These are all bad signs (2, Loeb II, 10).

From the eyes, the doctor goes on to examine movement of the hands, breathing irregularities, sweating, the condition of the hypochondria (the area just above the navel), swellings, sleeping habits, stools, urine, vomit, expectoration, headaches, ears and throat. It is from the combination of signs that a decision must be made (25, Loeb II, 54).

But do men and women exhibit the same signs? Do their bodies speak the same language, let alone say the same things? In the application of the prognostic principles in another group of Hippocratic texts, *Epidemics*, women appear not as Aristotle's incomplete men, but as men with a bonus: that bonus is the womb and its lower exit from the *hodos* which, by providing an extra route through which blood can leave the body, not only enables women's bodies to communicate more effectively than men's bodies, but even gives them the edge in surviving acute fevers.

This is best illustrated by looking at a section of the *Epidemics*, the description of a particular seasonal pattern of diseases in the population of Thasos given in a passage known as the 'third constitution' (1.13–17, Loeb I, 164–72). In the early spring *kausoi* – or acute fevers – struck, and these continued into summer. Those who suffered from such fevers in spring or early summer tended to survive: but those affected after the arrival of the autumn rains were struck by a more dangerous form that killed a greater number of sufferers. Those who had a heavy nosebleed were always saved from death by it (Loeb I, 166). *Prognostics* 7 (Loeb II, 16) stated that nosebleeds were beneficial in acute fevers, and suggested that these were more likely in the under-35 age group; *Epidemics* agrees that nosebleeds were more common in young people or adults with this fever, and that those in this age group who did not have a nosebleed were more likely to die (Loeb I, 168). If the fever turned to dysentery, patients were again more likely to survive.[16]

The writer of *Epidemics* 1 then turns to the effects of this particular fever on women (Loeb I, 170). Many were ill, but fewer women than men. In women, the outcome was less likely to be death; the typical female fatality was a woman suffering a difficult labour and becoming ill after giving birth. All pregnant women who contracted this disease miscarried. In most women, their period (for which the term *ta gynaikeia* is used here) started during the fever, and many *parthenoi* experienced their first menstrual period. Some women had both a nosebleed and a period at the same time, among them the daughter of Daitharses, a *parthenos*, who experienced both menarche and a nosebleed (Loeb I, 170); the writer adds that, to his knowledge, no woman who had both forms of blood loss died. In other words, women who could menstruate, did – some for the first time – and thus escaped death.

To understand what is happening here in Hippocratic terms we need to remember that menstrual blood was thought to be the excess from the diet. Outside the acute fevers, nosebleeds in women were seen simply as menstruation by a longer and less orthodox route. *Epidemics* 1.18–22 (Loeb I, 172–80) describes further changes in this *kausos* during the winter, when the writer says that the signs clearly indicated a fatal conclusion. These signs include cold extremities, sweating restricted to the area around the head and neck, insomnia and dark urine. These are all identical with the most fatal signs of all listed in *Prognostics*. *Prognostics* 6 (Loeb II, 14) says that sweating fits are excellent when they occur on the critical days and when the whole body is involved but, as the worst kinds of sweating, it singles out those that are cold and occur only around the head and neck; if accompanied by a high fever, such sweating means death. *Prognostics* 10 (Loeb II, 22) singles out insomnia as a bad sign, because it either indicates severe pain, or causes delirium: 'The worst thing is not to sleep either during the day or during the night.' *Prognostics* 12 (Loeb II, 24–6) states that 'urine is best when the sediment is white, smooth and even'; periods of clear urine are a sign that the disease will last longer and recovery is less likely, while black urine is always a bad sign in adults. The most hopeful signs of this particular fever in *Epidemics* are again those described in *Prognostics*: a nosebleed, plentiful urine with a lot of sediment, a bilious flux, and dysentery (Loeb I, 174). Of these encouraging signs, nosebleeds feature as beneficial for swelling in the hypochondria in *Prognostics* 7 (Loeb II, 16), but this is not a feature of this particular *Epidemics* disease picture; they also help in headaches (*Prog*. 21, Loeb II, 44). However, in his description of the condition prior to its transformation in winter, the *Epidemics* writer notes that the humour of blood was the dominant one in the disease (1.15, Loeb I, 168), and this dominance continues even when other manifestations of the condition change; hence the writer's concern that any nosebleed which occurs should be a properly heavy one.

In mature women and young girls, in addition to these four good signs, the writer lists as a hopeful sign a heavy period. Once again, women are at an advantage. The writer states that he knows of *no* women who died after showing any of the five signs, except one: the daughter of Philon, who had a heavy nosebleed but dined at an inappropriate time on the seventh day and died (Loeb I, 174).[17] Women are therefore thought to be just as likely as men to suffer from acute epidemic diseases but, because a cure is thought to follow from purging, and they have one extra route from which excess fluid can escape, they are also believed to be more likely to recover (see also Dean-Jones 1994: 136–46).

From this it also follows that diagnosis is easier with women. We know from *Prognostics* that Hippocratic doctors decide on the likely outcome of a disease by looking at movements of the hands, breathing irregularities, sweating, swellings, sleeping habits, stools, urine, vomit, expectoration, headaches, ears and throat. If we return to the *Epidemics*, the case histories there repeat these signs, but add to them, where women are concerned, the hopeful, encouraging sign of a heavy period. By providing an extra sign to examine, women's bodies are easier to understand.

We have seen that *Prognostics* explicitly identifies the signs of death in the acute fevers with those of fever in women after childbirth. Again, this can be illustrated from the *Epidemics*. The progress of fever from its onset on the second day after childbirth in the wife of Dromeades (*Ep*. 1 case 11, Loeb I, 204–6) fits precisely with the picture of a hopeless acute fever case in *Prognostics*. The key features indicating that the outcome will be death are insomnia, hallucinations, cold extremities and irregular breathing. These also feature in other fatal fevers in women which arise after miscarriage; for example, the woman of Pantimides' household who died on the seventh day of a fever after miscarrying (*Ep.* 3.1 case 10, Loeb I, 234), and the wife of Hicetas who also died on the seventh day of a fever after miscarrying in the fifth month (*Ep.* 3.1 case 11, Loeb I, 234–6).[18] Another case of this group is a woman aged about 17 who gave birth to her firstborn, a boy, after a difficult labour (case 12, Loeb I, 236–8). She suffered from a fever which included insomnia, cold sweating around the head, cold extremities and hallucinations. Despite a nosebleed on the fourteenth day, she died later that day.

By applying the theoretical criteria of *Prognostics* to the women patients of the *Epidemics* it is thus possible to see that the signs of death remain constant across the gender barrier; the possible outcome of women's fevers is judged by the same criteria as those applied to men. However, women's bodies speak more loudly than men's, for there is an extra 'favourable' sign which they can give, one which is not mentioned in *Prognostics*: a heavy period. Just as suppressed menses can come out via the nose, so blood which in men could only come out of the nose can, in women, take an alternative or simultaneous route through the vagina. Because they have this extra route available, women are thought more likely than men to survive an acute fever.

Where fevers arising shortly after childbirth are concerned, a menstrual period cannot occur because, the Hippocratics believe, the excess blood is diverted to the breasts where it is converted into milk. Thus, although – in the words of *Prognostics* – fevers after childbirth 'follow the same plan' as the acute fevers in general, a heavy period is impossible – and these fevers are more likely to be fatal than other fevers affecting women.

The Hippocratic body is thus difficult to read, offering many pitfalls to the untrained reader who is unaware of the risks of deceit. The body of Hippocrates' woman, however, while sharing these risks, also offers to the trained reader the sign of menstruation, a sign which permits knowledge and which also eases recovery. When Hippocratic gynaecology confronts its patients, it assumes that, within the general category of the female body, not all bodies follow the same rules; the healer must first decide who is fully a *gynê* and who is not before interpreting the signs the body offers to its reader. An important theme in the Hippocratic texts is the relationship between identity and imitation, truth and deceit, echoing Hesiod's representation of Pandora with which this study opened. Meanwhile, the body of the doctor himself is available as a guide to the patient who needs to distinguish quack from effective healer.

3

THE DAUGHTER OF LEONIDAS

Reading case histories

In the previous chapter, Hippocratic views on how the female body should be read were used to demonstrate the importance of menstruation as a sign communicating with the *iatros* and as a process which can lead to recovery. But it also emerged that the healer needs to decide whether or not a woman is sufficiently 'experienced' to be trusted as an authority on her own body. We will now turn to a named patient in the Hippocratic *Epidemics*, the daughter of Leonidas, who suffers from menstrual diversion. Her history once more emphasises the competitive nature of the medical *technê* in ancient Greece, as the writer apparently criticises a fellow *iatros* for his failure to understand the subtleties of the female body. But the story of her illness also introduces the theme of how later categories imposed on the Hippocratic corpus have influenced the understanding of Hippocratic gynaecology.

The texts which make up the Hippocratic corpus have a wide range of formats (see Chapter 1, p. 27). Some, such as *Aphorisms* and *Coan Prognoses*, take the form of lists of short, pithy statements about different symptoms which are signs of disease, without providing any general theoretical framework within which these should be set. Other types of text give the broad picture of how an organ works but do not suggest how it is to be transformed into a healthy condition. Thus, for example, the third-century BC text *On the Heart* describes the anatomy and physiology of that organ, but neither discusses heart diseases nor gives remedies for them. Some texts describe the course of disease but do not give lists of therapeutic interventions: *Airs, Waters, Places* describes the diseases affecting people in areas influenced by different environmental features, but not their treatment. The *Diseases of Women* treatises look at conditions specific to women and incidentally hint at the anatomical beliefs about women's difference from men which underlie their claims about appropriate treatment; here, long sections of the text are lists of different ways of treating particular conditions, which will be discussed further in Chapter 7.

However, for many readers of the Hippocratic corpus in the centuries since its formation – probably in the third or second century BC (W.D. Smith 1979: 199–204) – the texts which resonate most strongly with their own ideas about what medicine is (Brody 1987: 1–2) are the case histories which form the bulk of the material in the seven books known as the *Epidemics*, a title that may best be translated as 'Encounters' (Langholf 1990: 78 n.33). For Charles Singer, for example, the cases in *Epidemics* 1 and 3 constituted 'The chief glory of the Hippocratic collection from the clinical point of view' (1923: 219). These case histories do not strike the modern reader as polished literary products; instead, they give the impression of notes jotted at the patient's bedside.[1] Their sense of careful observation of the course of the disease, their image of a doctor fighting bravely and often in vain against diseases which will prove fatal, and the opportunities for diagnosis which the lists of symptoms provide, all exert a strong attraction, in particular for the medically trained reader. As Jackie Pigeaud has demonstrated, the form of the case histories makes them particularly amenable to retrospective diagnosis; because these Hippocratic texts rest at the level of description of named individuals, relating a succession of events, rather than going on to a definitive, generalising diagnosis and a statement of cause and effect, successive generations of medical historians have been left free to give their own diagnoses based on changing modern medical theories (Pigeaud 1988: 320, 328). The poignancy of the frequent ending of case histories in variations on 'Seventh day: died' sends a sympathetic but relieved shiver up the spine of the reader whose only experience with medicine is as a patient; sympathetic to the suffering of this distant fellow human being, but relieved to live at a time when medicine appears to be able to offer more answers to more questions.

As modern readers of the Hippocratic corpus, we may think we know what case histories are: objective texts based on careful, direct observation. Of course, even in Western biomedicine, they are not; in their studies of the Harvard Medical School from an anthropological point of view, Byron and Mary-Jo DelVecchio Good have shown how trainee doctors are taught how to 'do a write-up', in the process of writing transforming an individual into a 'case' (Good and Good 1993; B.J. Good 1994: 76–83). Nor does there appear to have been any direct equivalent in Greek for our positivist ideal of 'observation' providing the data from which theories will subsequently be derived (Lloyd 1979: 129 f.); in the Hippocratic corpus, 'looking at' something occurs only according to particular rules and standards (Langholf 1990: 193–4).

Case histories are written for a specific audience, and have to create a pattern out of the confusion which is reality. One way in which they do this, common in the *Epidemics*, is to impose a numbered pattern of days on to the succession of events. For example, in a case mentioned in the previous chapter,

> A woman from the household of Pantimides, after a miscarriage, was seized with fever on the first day. Tongue dry, thirst, nausea, sleeplessness. Bowels upset, thin, copious and raw stools. Second day: rigour, acute fever, copious stools, no sleep. Third day: pains worse.

> Fourth day: delirium. Seventh day: died. Throughout, bowels loose, copious, thin, raw stools. Urine scanty and thin.
>
> (*Ep.* 3.1 case 10, Loeb I, 234–5)

These numbered patterns have been linked to the Hippocratic theory of 'critical days', which anticipates the 'crisis' on particular days in the progress of the condition. Although it may be connected to beliefs about the magical power of certain numbers, the origin of the idea may lie in observation of disorders such as malaria, which follow a cyclical pattern (Demand 1994: 82).

But is this all there is to the numbering of days in these texts? Anthropological studies of patients in chronic pain have shown how they give an 'origin myth' of their pain (M.D. Good *et al.* 1992: 16) and have also examined the sense in which pain is 'performance': to name a pain is to tame it. In Chapter 6 I will be examining the significance of pain vocabulary in the Hippocratic corpus; pain affects the view of the self, experienced in the world of everyday life as the originator of our actions – as in 'I do this' – and of the body as the subject of these actions, through which we act upon the world (B.J. Good 1992: 38–9). In pain, the body is experienced as being separate from the self, the pain as within me rather than part of me; so that, more generally, 'illness forces an awareness of the body as separate from self' (Garro 1992: 132; cf. Gadow 1980: 174, 179; Brody 1987: 29). In particular, pain has been shown to dissolve the sense of time which is now so central to our construction of the world of everyday life that our first question on waking or on recovering from fainting is often 'What time is it?' (Berger and Luckman 1966: 42). In the *Epidemics*, the Hippocratic writers' structuring of the case histories in terms of the successive days of the illness has usually gone unmentioned, perhaps because it seems to us such an obvious thing to do; but it could be linked to the statement in *Prognostics* 1 (Loeb II, 6), discussed in the previous chapter, that the doctor should 'know in advance and speak in advance the present, the past and the future'. In this case, it could be interpreted as a deliberate attempt to regain control of time on behalf of the patient.

The case history of Phaethousa of Abdera (*Ep.* 6.8.32, Loeb VII, 288–90; given in full in Introduction, pp. 9–10) does not use this structuring method, perhaps because the development of symptoms was thought to have occurred over a long period of time, or because the doctor did not observe the stages for himself. Nevertheless, the selection of significant points within this text needs further consideration.

Lee Pearcy has stressed 'the choices made by the Hippocratic author in telling his stories' (1992: 605), while for modern biomedicine Byron Good has shown how case histories select what he calls 'the important stuff' (1994: 79). What is regarded as important is never self-evident, but is a matter of culture. The absence of Phaethousa's husband is seen as sufficiently important by the Hippocratic writer that he juxtaposes it with the crucial absence of menses ('when her husband was exiled she stopped menstruating for a long time'), and he repeats this absence of menses three times. No husband, no menses: this reflects the use in the ancient Greek language of the same word, *gynê*, for 'mature woman' and 'wife' and, as we saw in Chapter 1, makes one name for the menses *gynaikeia*, 'women's things', the things appropriate to a woman/wife. Menstruation and marriage are so closely bound up here that to lose one's husband raises not just the risk of losing one's status as wife, but also the possible dissolution of one's physical womanhood. In the order of symptoms, what is selected begins with the protracted absence of the menses, and ends with the outward manifestations of maleness, the body hair, facial hair and vocal deepening which represent the internal change forcing its way to the outside.[2]

In the *Epidemics*, case histories such as this one occur alongside 'aphoristic' remarks, such as 'In moist women the menses last long' (*Ep.* 6.1.6, Loeb VII, 221), recommended therapies, such as 'Suppuration under the fingernail: black oak gall in honey' (*Ep.* 2.6.27, Loeb VII, 89), and descriptions of 'constitutions' (*katastaseis*). A constitution summarises the general condition of a population at the time of the year when the Hippocratic healer visited the area, and these summaries appear to have been written as 'carefully crafted literary pieces', possibly intended for publication (Demand 1994: 38).

The *Epidemics* are, in general, self-consciously literate texts. In *Epidemics* 3.16 (Loeb I, 256) we read, 'The power, too, to study correctly what has been written I consider to be an important part of the art of medicine'; earlier in this book, the writer refers to 'the cases written above' (*tois progegrammenoisin*, 3.9, Loeb I, 248). Prose-writing was at a very early stage in fifth-century Greece (Lonie 1983; Lloyd 1983: 115–19), and many of the surviving texts illustrate Jack Goody's arguments for the effects of literacy on societies new to it (Goody 1968; 1986). For example, Goody describes the role of the list in stimulating critical reflection. Once symptoms have been listed, the writer can then consider how they should be arranged and under what headings. The Hippocratic text *Coan Prognoses* lists symptoms according to the age group of the sufferers, while in *Diseases of Women* remedies for what is perceived as the same condition are grouped together, but not in such a systematic way; instead the author lists 'another remedy', 'another' and so on. By Goody's standards these texts are thus at an intermediate stage between listing and analysing their material. Iain Lonie (1983) applied Goody's work on early literacy to the *Epidemics*, locating them as early examples of the shift from an exclusively oral to a partially literate culture, and there has since been widespread agreement that their persuasive appearance of being the crude data from which a doctor will later generalise may be misleading. Following Paul Potter (1989), Nancy Demand has shown that there is an 'editorial process at work in shaping the raw materials of bedside observations into case histories'; she gives the example of two case histories in which the author has apparently chosen to bring out the similarities he perceived by repeating similar phrases and by reporting the symptoms in the same order (1994: 45–6). I would however argue that our reading of the *Epidemics* still tends to assume, with Demand, that the case histories we now have did at least originate in 'the raw materials of bedside observations'. Reading the *Epidemics* thus takes place under certain assumptions about basic similarities between then and now, held in conjunction with a reassuring sense of medical progress.[3]

In this chapter I want to use a specific example from the *Epidemics*, a case of a young girl who died after a nosebleed, in order to illustrate not only the way we read case histories but also, within the traditions of reading the *Epidemics*, how artificial divisions set up within the Hippocratic corpus by subsequent readers have influenced our understanding of Hippocratic medical theories and practice. The case of the fatal nosebleed of the daughter of Leonidas may challenge whether there are any such 'raw materials'; the process of observation can only take place in a cultural context.

After setting the case of the daughter of Leonidas within the context provided by an apparently conflicting text on women's nosebleeds, I will consider some traditional ways of 'reading' the Hippocratic corpus in general before returning to nosebleeds to show why they are so important in Hippocratic gynaecology. In the process, I will propose a further interpretation which reverses many established assumptions about reading ancient medicine – and which, inevitably, has implications for reading other ancient sources.

The daughter of Leonidas as a pink raven

Aphorisms 5.33 (Loeb IV, 166) reads: 'In a woman whose menstrual periods (*katamênia*) have stopped, blood flowing out of the nostrils is a good thing.' This information is repeated by Aristotle (*HA* 587b35–588a2; cf. Byl 1980: 60).

The *Aphorisms* is one of the most copied, most edited and historically most popular texts in the Hippocratic corpus (cf. L 4.445–57; Müller-Rohlfen 1980; Beccaria 1961; Kibre 1976). As a set of practical tips (Kibre 1945: 380), it was thought to have universal applicability. It circulated both in the West and in the Arab world, and was one of the first Hippocratic texts to be printed.[4] Probably in AD 175 (D.W. Peterson 1977), Galen wrote a commentary on *Aphorisms*; in the eleventh century this was restored to the West when Constantine the African translated it from Arabic into Latin and, in terms of its printed editions in the Renaissance, it became the third most popular Galenic treatise after *Ars medica* and *De differentiis febrium* (Durling 1961: 243). It also held a central position in Western medical education, being one of the oldest texts included in the *Articella*.[5]

As a result of this popularity, there are some textual variants, but for this aphorism there is only one. A number of later manuscripts omit 'In a woman', *gynaiki*; however, in the rest of this section almost all aphorisms start with *gynaiki*, and the aphorism clearly refers to women because *katamênia* can only mean 'monthly periods'.

In its format, 5.33 is highly representative of Hippocratic aphorisms; a short general principle, with nothing to explain why this should be a good thing, and no specific empirical examples to support it. One of the traditions associated with *Aphorisms* claims that 'Hippocrates composed it in his old age as a summary of his vast experience' (W.H.S. Jones 1931: xxxiv), making it a distillation of the wisdom of a lifetime's experience, and thus one of the most 'genuine' works (Adams 1849: 50–4; Chance 1930; *contra*, W.D. Smith 1979: 238). Whatever the relationship of this tradition to its 'real' authorship, the tradition provides an accurate description of its effect on us as readers, for whom it suggests distillation from years of clinical encounters; a large number of particular observed cases, from which this general law of nature has been derived by the principle of induction (Chalmers 1982: 1–37). Such a methodology is sometimes explicit in the Hippocratic corpus; for example, *Precepts* 1 (Loeb I, 312) describes how reason builds up many examples of sense-perception, from which theories can be deduced, and *Epidemics* 6.3.12 (Loeb VII, 239–40) suggests that the 'method' (*hodos*) consists of gathering together and studying a large number of accounts and noting similarities and dissimilarities.

Here, however, the perceived format (general principle, scientific law) is, for us, seriously at odds with the content. In our understanding of nature, there is no way that suppressed menstrual blood can come out of the nose. Laqueur therefore interpreted this aphorism to mean only that 'nosebleeding was a prognostic sign that blocked courses, amenorrhea, would soon resolve' (1990: 36). We could also link the aphorism to Western biomedicine's category of 'vicarious menstruation', a rare condition in which the mucous membranes of the nose bleed at menstruation in response to stimulation by oestrogen.[6] But, as was noted in the Introduction, in medical texts from the seventeenth to the nineteenth century, lists of alternative routes by which menstrual blood can leave the body are both commonplace and exhaustive; in her study of the medical practice of the eighteenth-century German physician Johannes Pelagrius Storch, Barbara Duden (1991) suggested that the body was seen as open and changeable, with bodily fluids emerging through orifices almost interchangeably. Taken in a wider historical perspective, then, the aphorism has most commonly been understood not to mean that a nosebleed is a prognostic sign, but that actual menstrual blood can travel up the body and leave through the nose. These examples from medical theory and practice suggest that, rather than using our current standards and judging the derived law as 'wrong', we should be asking what it can tell us about the image of the body in Hippocratic medicine and the effect of this image on the observation of cases.

But another Hippocratic text, *Epidemics* 7.123 (Loeb VII, 414), appears to contradict the *Aphorisms* principle that a menstrual nosebleed is a 'good thing': 'In the daughter of Leonidas the *physis*, having made a start, turned aside; after it had turned aside, she bled at the nose. When she had bled at the nose, a change occurred. The doctor did not understand, and the young girl (*pais*) died.'

As Lee Pearcy (1992: 615) has shown, 'In ancient accounts of disease the tale of an illness must often be the tale of a patient.' Here, the patient is not named except in terms of her father. This avoidance of personal names is characteristic for the women in the Hippocratic corpus, who are usually identified as 'daughter of' or 'wife of', in keeping with classical Greek practice in which women are not named unless they are dead, or are of ill-repute (Schaps 1977). In the passage of *Epidemics* given in the Introduction, one could argue that Phaethousa and Nanno are named not just because they died, but because their bodies became masculine, and thus moved beyond the conventions on 'the naming of women'. The use of names in the *Epidemics* in general can be seen, on a positivist reading, as evidence of the reality of the people behind the text as 'historically verifiable patients' (Horstmanshoff 1990: 179–80); Deichgräber (1982) dated a section of the *Epidemics*, in which cases seen on Thasos are described, by comparison with epigraphical evidence from there. Although she is not named, 'the daughter of Leonidas' is nevertheless brought before us as a specific, identified individual; in contrast to the *Aphorisms* example, our inclination as readers is therefore to perceive this as a particular observed case. However, Langholf has recently demonstrated that the authors of *Epidemics* 'saw their disease cases (individual and collective) always through a filter of preconceived ideas' (1990: 208). The 'case' is most commonly given in order to confirm these ideas, or to extend their applicability (1990: 190); sometimes, as Daniela Manetti (1990: 149) has shown, its purpose is 'to communicate a disappointed expectation to a public who shares the same theory as the author'. What ideas lie behind the daughter of Leonidas?

Hê physis, 'nature', here means the menstrual period. As I noted in Chapter 1, this is one of a number of different terms for menstruation used in the Hippocratic corpus, each of which reveals something of ancient Greek ideas about menstruation; the contexts for which the less common of these terms are selected may be particularly instructive. Most texts use a variation on 'monthlies'; *gynaikeia*, 'women's things', can mean any menstrual period, but it may be significant that this is the term chosen to be modified by *prôton*, 'first', when discussing menarche in three passages of the *Epidemics*.[7] As Chapter 4 argues, the 'first' menstrual period is an important step on the road to womanhood. *Ta hôraia* is used only once, but also occurs in a context which implies menarche, suggesting that it was chosen because the first menstrual period is a sign of 'ripeness'; in *On the Diseases of Virgins* (L 8.466), it is when the girl is 'ripe for marriage', *hôrê gamou*, that absence of menstruation comes to be seen as a serious symptom. *Ta kata physin* is not specifically menarcheal; the implications of *hê physis* here must, for the moment, remain open.

We are told that the menstrual period of the daughter of Leonidas started, but then turned aside, and came out through her nose. There was a change (*diallagê*); in his translation of the *Epidemics*, Wesley Smith translates *diallagê* as 'she was relieved', taking the word in the sense of 'reconciliation', but elsewhere in the Hippocratic corpus the verb *diallassein* is used in the sense 'to change' or 'to differ'. The doctor did not understand; the term used here is *syneiden*, implying shared knowledge. Since these texts prefer the first person, 'the doctor' is probably not the writer himself, but another practitioner; this would make the text parallel to another case history in which 'the *iatroi*' failed to understand the curative powers of a nosebleed in a male patient (*Ep*. 2.1.7, Loeb VII, 26). In the latter case, other practitioners failed to understand that nosebleeds can heal; in the former, however, the other doctor did not understand the change, and the patient subsequently died.[8] The writer shares a smile of complicity with his audience – which may consist of fellow specialists, students, the public or even himself[9] – in their superior knowledge which means that they understand what 'the doctor' did not; namely the reasons why the patient's condition changed and she died.[10]

So, why should she have died, when her death appears directly to contradict the *Aphorisms'* statement that a nosebleed is good when the menses are suppressed? On a common-sense reading of the corpus, the aphorism appears to be a general principle, with the *Epidemics* story as a particular observed case. The central problem of the inductive method, moving from the latter to the former, is that the next particular case may be the one which disproves the rule: I have seen 302 black ravens, and therefore propose the rule 'All ravens are black'; but what if the 303rd is pink? How many ravens are necessary to formulate the principle? Three hundred and three? 30? Are 30 more persuasive than 29? Where do we draw the line (Chalmers 1982: 13–17)? And is the daughter of Leonidas the pink raven?

As Clifford Geertz has reminded us, however, 'Common sense is not what the mind cleared of cant spontaneously apprehends; it is what the mind filled with presuppositions . . . concludes' (1983: 84). There are several types of presupposition present in the explanations traditionally used when two Hippocratic texts apparently contradict each other in this way, and these must now be discussed in terms of approaches to the Hippocratic corpus as a whole.

Permitted questions in the Hippocratic research programme

What sort of texts are these apparently contradictory sections of *Aphorisms* and *Epidemics*? How have they been seen by readers of the Hippocratic corpus? A useful model to apply to traditional Hippocratic studies is that of Lakatos (1978), which regards any scientific discipline as possessing a set of questions, methods and assumptions followed by all those who work in that discipline

(1978: esp. 16–17, 48–52; Chalmers 1982: 80–7). This set is called a 'research programme', and it has a 'hard core', an area the assumptions of which are accepted by all scholars working in the field and which are unfalsifiable. This is surrounded by a 'protective belt' of hypotheses to digest anomalies which would otherwise threaten the hard core. A research programme also has a set of questions which can be asked ('positive heuristic') and a set which cannot be asked ('negative heuristic'). The positive heuristic of the Hippocratic research programme included such questions as 'Who was Hippocrates?', 'Which are the "genuine works" written by the great man himself?',[11] 'Who wrote the other works?' While acknowledging the variations within the corpus, the hard core assumed that at least some – maybe a dozen – of the works it contained really were by Hippocrates, and its image of Hippocrates was largely based on a set of letters composed from the first century BC onwards, which were supposed to be between Hippocrates and such notable figures as Artaxerxes and Democritos. In these letters, Hippocrates and his sons travel around classical Greece and intervene at significant points of its history, for example curing a 'plague from the land of the barbarians' affecting the Greeks (*Epistula* 25; W.D. Smith 1990: 106).

The traditional research programme traced the origin of the Hippocratic medical texts to the institutions within which it assumed early Greek medicine functioned. It saw the temples of Asklepios as proto-hospitals or health resorts (C. Singer 1923: 224; Kelly 1939; Kee 1982); their 'case notes' were assumed to be texts such as the *Coan Prognoses* (L 5.588–732) and *Prorrhetic* 1 (Loeb VIII, 172–210), which were thought to have been written up from inscriptions bearing details of case histories and treatment. Pliny (*NH* 29.2.4) refers to case notes kept at the shrines of Asklepios, which he says Hippocrates copied out; similar stories exist in Strabo (*Geog*. 8.6.15; 14.2.19). Although Clologe (1905) demonstrated that the format of the extant inscriptions at the sanctuary of Asklepios at Epidauros bears no relation to the lists of symptoms found in the Hippocratic texts supposedly based on them, and Withington published a thorough refutation of the case note theory in 1921, its underlying assumptions remain: in particular, that many of the texts which have survived stand in a close relation to 'the real', that is, to real doctors, patients and diseases. I will return to the relationship between Hippocratic and temple medicine, and women's treatment in the temples of Asklepios, in Chapter 5.

The research programme used a combination of classical texts and its own assumptions about rationality to help it decide on the 'genuine works' of Hippocrates. Plato's dialogues show that Hippocrates existed as a healer, writer and instructor famous in his own time (*Phaedrus* 270b–d; *Protagoras* 311b–c), but it is difficult to use Plato's references to the 'Hippocratic method' to show beyond any doubt that particular treatises of the corpus were 'by Hippocrates' (W.D. Smith 1979; cf. Joly 1983; Mansfeld 1983: 49–76). The research programme also favoured what were seen as the most rational parts of Hippocratic medicine, such as the denial of divine causation for what was traditionally called the 'sacred disease', at the expense of other sections where remedies are, in our terms, apparently magical; the rats' droppings and stag's penis school of medicine (Lloyd 1983: 132). Historically, Hippocrates was supposed to have been responsible for the treatises seen as the most 'rational', with others having been added in to the corpus by mistake. The recent rediscovery of what was once seen as the 'irrational' strand in the corpus has led to some valuable new work; for example, Heinrich von Staden's demonstration that therapy based on excrement is only used for female patients in Hippocratic medicine, and the subsequent debate on the cultural meaning of this gender division (von Staden 1992a; Hanson forthcoming).

In its 'protective belt', the traditional programme of Hippocratic research contained various strategies to deal with the complexity of the Hippocratic corpus as it now stands. Hippocrates developed sons, a wicked son-in-law who betrayed him, and eventually a full genealogy of seventeen generations traced back to Asklepios, based on the twelfth-century Byzantine commentator Tzetzes (Edelstein and Edelstein 1945; T 213). The identity of his mother remained open, although the name of Phaenarete, supposedly the mother of Socrates and a midwife, also attached itself to Hippocrates as his mother or grandmother (Hanson 1996a: 159–62). Why were all these additional characters necessary? Because they allowed differences in style between treatises to be easily accommodated: two works could be 'by Hippocrates' even if they are not in the same style, because one may come directly from the hand of Hippocrates, the other via subsequent editing by his 'son' Thessalos (Pigeaud 1988: 306–7). Both of his sons were supposed to have called their sons 'Hippocrates', a common naming convention, but conveniently making four members of the family bear the same name: the father of medicine, his grandfather and his two grandsons. Like the 'edited case notes' idea, this is very useful for the protective belt. A further strategy accounting for the inclusion of works which later readers considered 'irrational', or 'unscientific', in a corpus bearing the name of the great founder of scientific medicine, was to blame the textual history; in a reaction appealing to every academic who has ever blamed the library staff for failing to locate the right book, the tradition decided that an incompetent librarian in third-century Alexandria had classified the works of all four men called Hippocrates under the same name.

In the words of Wesley Smith, this whole enterprise should be seen as 'an etiological myth, an analytical scheme dressed up as a narrative of events' (1979: 30). He traces this myth back to the 'letters' and to two writers of the first and second centuries AD: Dioscorides, whose *Materia Medica* dates to around AD 65 and covers over 1,000 substances, and Galen. There is little that one would wish to add to his excellent study of the 'Hippocratic myth'; only perhaps that the progress of the Hippocratic research programme from antiquity shows us that the ancient world was as obsessed as we are with finding an author or authors, with reference to whom differences within the text could be 'explained'.[12]

In Lakatos' research programme model, the function of the protective belt of hypotheses is to absorb anything which emerges as a threat to the integrity of the hard core. The classic example of such a development, used by Smith, was the publication in the 1890s of new evidence; the first- or second-century AD Anonymus Londinensis papyrus, which includes what are usually assumed to be excerpts from Aristotle's pupil, Menon.[13] The research programme had already decided from one of Galen's commentaries (K 15.25–6) that Menon's lost work would provide accurate and valuable information on early medical history: yet, of the known works of the Hippocratic corpus, the piece from which Menon gave extracts and which he attributed to Hippocrates seemed most closely to resemble a text called *Breaths* (Loeb II, 226–52), not previously considered as a 'genuine work' (W.H.S. Jones 1947: 19). In this potentially threatening situation, historians adjusted the protective belt of the programme; for example, one suggestion was that *Breaths* was by one of the other three members of the genealogy with the same name (Smith 1979: 36–8). Menon was right to say that it was by Hippocrates, but it was not by the great Hippocrates. Strategies such as this maintained the research programme intact.

The power which the programme exerts even now can be most effectively demonstrated by the otherwise surprising fact that Wesley Smith, who in so many ways has broken through its influence by exposing much of the hard core as myth, also felt obliged to conform to its assumptions by identifying a 'genuine work'. Using as a basis pre-Alexandrian evidence – for example, Plato's description of the method of 'Hippocrates the Asclepiad' in *Phaedrus* (269e ff.), used by Littré (L 1.294–320) to argue that *On Ancient Medicine* is a 'genuine work' (Edelstein 1939) – he claimed that Hippocrates wrote *Regimen* and that Menon's references are to this rather than to *Breaths* (1979: 44–59). Mansfeld subsequently used precisely the same evidence, but this time to 'demonstrate' that it is *Airs, Waters, Places* which is by the real Hippocrates (1980; cf. Kucharski 1939; Jouanna 1977), while Langholf, after noting with amazement that even Wesley Smith feels the need to play the 'genuine works' game (1990: 3 n.7), immediately refers the reader to his own piece arguing that it is *Breaths* which is authentically 'Hippocratic' (Langholf 1986). Even where the traditional research programme is being eroded, there apparently remains an entrenched need to find a 'genuine work'.

For those historians who have abandoned the attempt to match up texts to Hippocrates, other nameless 'authors' can be still made to emerge from the corpus. For example, treatises can be linked on the basis of perceived similarities of doctrine, language or style, or on the evidence of self-citation of the form, 'As I say in my treatise on x.' A persuasive example is Iain Lonie's excellent edition of *On Generation*, *Nature of the Child* and *Diseases 4* (1981: 43 ff.). Alternatively, groups which are established in the manuscript tradition may be challenged; thus Grensemann has tried to distinguish two or more authors, separated by at least fifty years, within *Diseases of Women* 1 and 2 (1975a: 164; 1982). The grounds on which he does this are open to criticism; where Grensemann argues that his 'author A', who seems to favour *epimênia* for the menses, predates 'author C' who prefers *katamênia*, Joly used the same evidence in 1977 to reach the opposite conclusion on relative dating (1977: 137–8). If we assume that the difference in terminology is due to a different author and date rather than to personal preference or total interchangeability of terms, the problem remains that there is hardly any external evidence on which dating can be based, since there is almost no discussion of menstruation in fifth-century literature outside Hippocratic gynaecology. The possibility of deliberate archaising – of chronologically later writers consciously imitating the style of earlier writers – also exists, making dating even more complicated.

The question raised by all such attempts to produce authors for anonymous texts is why so much effort is invested in them. The answer is simply that this is how the Hippocratic texts have traditionally been read, in order to explain apparent differences in therapy or theory by different dates – as change over time – or by different authors – as variation within one period (Hanson 1996b: 295). Authors are useful explanatory devices, one of the interpretative models traditionally favoured by historians being to identify the ancient writer's personal slant, his political stance, his biases and so on, and then to strip these off in a triumphant dance of the seven veils to reveal the naked truth gleaming underneath (Gellner 1964: 30). This way of working is so entrenched that, before structuralist and post-structuralist approaches to the text reached classical studies, an authorless text such as the Hippocratic corpus was seen as a positive embarrassment; generations of medical historians have therefore endeavoured to produce some authors for it, and to assign contradictions between texts to different authors, or groups of authors.

A related way of reading the Hippocratic corpus is to assign texts to 'schools' of medicine alleged to have existed at Cos and Cnidos in the classical period; the incompetent librarian at Alexandria not only confused the four writers called Hippocrates, but even catalogued some medical works from a rival school under Hippocrates' name. Further questions from the traditional research programme's positive heuristic are therefore 'What were the doctrines characteristic of the ancient medical schools of Cos and Cnidos?' and 'Which treatises in the corpus belong to each school?' (Joly 1966: 31) The school of Cos is the rational, scientific one supposedly linked with Hippocrates, and has been seen as responsible for all the best treatises of the corpus – however each age wishes to define 'best' – while the 'more primitive' (Kudlien 1968: 321 and n.67) or 'pre-rational' (Kudlien 1968: 325) level of medicine is represented by the Cnidian school (Sarrazin 1921: 9). Cnidos trusted patients' subjective statements, while Cos relied on objective investigation: Cnidos related symptoms to parts of the body, while Cos set them in the context of the whole body (Baas 1889: 92–3; C. Singer 1923: 206–7).

Of the texts being considered here, *Aphorisms* is traditionally seen as coming from the hand of Hippocrates himself: a 'genuine work'. *Epidemics* 1 and 3 are also usually taken to be 'Coan' and 'genuine works', on the basis of their emphasis on observing the course of a disease. *Epidemics* 7, with its description of the daughter of Leonidas, is thought to be somewhat inferior; Galen regarded books 5 and 7 as 'bastards' (Pigeaud 1988: 307). Now, however, *Epidemics* 7 is gradually moving into favour; Grmek and Robert (1977: 290) have pleaded for it to be assessed more positively, on the grounds of the 'admirable' quality of its observations.

But it is when it looks at the *Diseases of Women* treatises that the negative heuristic of the research programme shows its full force. It has classified them not only as being by someone other than the great Hippocrates, but also as belonging to the inferior and irrational 'school of Cnidos'. Historically, as a result of this classification, they have been judged as being of only marginal interest, seen as evidence of the primitive form from which Coan medicine developed, but with little value as objects of study in their own right. It is worth noting that this blanket rejection of Hippocratic 'authorship' for *Diseases of Women* was not repeated in antiquity; in the 'letters' attributed to Hippocrates he is imagined to have written 'As I said in my treatise on *Diseases of Women*, give purges when the womb needs to be purged' (*Epistula* 21, W.D. Smith 1990: 100), while in the second century AD Galen regarded them as genuinely Hippocratic (W.D. Smith 1979: 142). Yet, as Ann Hanson has demonstrated, by the seventh century AD medical students were advised to leave *Diseases of Women* to the end of their reading of the corpus, because of the texts' supposed focus on 'faeces, urine and the like' (Stephanus Philosophus, *In Hippocratis prognosticum*, preface and on 1.1, CMG XI.1.2, 32.25–7, 34.8–9; Hanson 1991: 75). A further problem relevant to the two passages being considered here is that, within the traditional research programme, it has been considered somewhat heretical to read a 'Cnidian' text such as *Diseases of Women* beside the 'Coan' *Aphorisms* or 'inferior' *Epidemics* 7.

An alternative model of the Hippocratic corpus, which cuts across such divisions, has gained much support over the last twenty years (W.D. Smith 1979; Lloyd 1975, 1983; Thivel 1981). This suggests that there is no heuristic value whatsoever in separating treatises as genuine and secondary works, 'Coan' and 'Cnidian', and that we should instead emphasise the common assumptions of the writers in the corpus (e.g. Jouanna 1961: 463; Joly 1966: 64–9; 1983; Langholf 1990: 5) and their stock of shared knowledge and beliefs. For example, the anatomy and physiology of the female body outlined in Chapter 1 derives from the whole of the Hippocratic corpus; it is common to so-called 'Cnidian' and 'Coan' works. The final nail in the coffin of the 'pre-rational' Cnidian school was hammered in by Lonie, who demonstrated conclusively that it is entirely a construct of the dominant research programme; it 'comes into existence to fill an historical vacuum, the absence of any direct information on the character and development of Greek medicine before Hippocrates' (1978: 50). As Hanson (1991: 76) wrote, the attempt to assign Hippocratic treatises to Cos or Cnidos 'now appears to have been a futile exercise in scholarly ingenuity and an invalid model for the fifth century BC'. Differences within the corpus should be traced not to different men called Hippocrates, nor to competition between 'schools', but to rivalry at the individual level, where practitioners tried to innovate within the limits set, in order to gain patients (Lloyd 1979). In the absence of any form of professional licensing, employment depended upon one's ability to persuade; rhetoric became highly important (Jouanna 1984), as did the presentation of self in a way which would convince patients and their relatives of one's abilities, through dress, manner, language and so on.

Indeed, it is only by reading across the traditional boundaries between groups of texts that the scope of Hippocratic medicine can be appreciated. The *Epidemics* are presented as the work of a doctor who sees every type of case, male and female; case histories chart the progress of the symptoms to the critical point of the disease, but information on treatment is less common. *Diseases of Women* gives long lists of remedies for the symptoms described, but rarely ties descriptions of disorders to identified individuals. The brief comments on women's diseases in *Aphorisms* 5 similarly need to be set within the context provided by the fuller accounts of *Diseases of Women*.

The range of explanations offered by the traditional research programme for the difference between the two texts on nosebleeds in women may now be summarised: they could derive from different authors, different schools, or different dates. Since we assume that we are right to think that menstrual blood cannot be diverted to come out of the nose, the first of these options would challenge the hard core, since the aphorism – from a 'genuine work of Hippocrates' – appears to be 'wrong', and the passage of *Epidemics* 7 'right'. The second option also upsets the hard core, since the 'Coan' *Aphorisms* seems to stand corrected. As for the third option, we would need to classify the *Epidemics* passage as 'late' because it suggests that the aphorism is 'wrong', so that the case history becomes a step forward, as the earlier hypothesis is falsified. 'The doctor didn't understand' would thus mean 'The doctor was baffled that his theory, namely that the nosebleed of the daughter of Leonidas would help her, did not seem to be borne out in practice.' On this reading, the daughter of Leonidas is the pink raven, the observed case which falsifies the (erroneous) general rule.

The daughter of Leonidas as a black raven

I would propose, in direct opposition to this, that any reference to a medically correct 'reality' here is entirely misplaced: the daughter of Leonidas is not a case of observation falsifying a general law, but is another black raven.

Only the traditional research programme prevents us from taking the two texts under consideration here at precisely the same level. As I indicated at the beginning of this chapter, case histories, with their real place names, identified individual patients including 'names and addresses' (Pigeaud 1988: 327) and descriptions of the course of diseases, intuitively feel closer to reality than more theoretical texts. However, Lloyd points out that these 'star examples of detailed observations in early Greek science' nevertheless rely on prior theory and on motivations very different from those behind modern case histories (1979: 154–5; Pearcy 1992). While doctors in our society write up case notes because of particular historical developments in medical institutions, and because of their own positions and responsibilities within such institutions (Lonie 1983), such a social context is absent for the authors of the *Epidemics*. Unlike the case histories with which we are familiar, those of the Hippocratic corpus appear to be private notes of points which interest the doctor, and to which he may later return. They provide directions for further enquiry, and they begin the process of putting a structure on that which is observed. They therefore seem to provide evidence, not so much of what 'really happened', but rather of 'the observer's private and unexpressed sense of what is interesting, relevant, of what may turn out to be useful' (Lonie 1983: 155).

In Foucault's terms, all sources are equally 'representations'; action, text, speech: observed, read, heard (1970). Each is a veil between the observer and 'reality'; there is no such thing as direct, common-sense access to 'reality'. Furthermore, the search for an ultimate, 'correct', true meaning is futile: there is no single 'meaning of', but rather, as the anthropologist Gilbert Lewis has shown in a study of the 'meaning' of a particular ritual practice, there are many 'meanings for' (1980). First-hand reports such as case histories cannot report reality accurately; they do not present reality, but they 'represent' – re-present – reality.

Now if both Hippocratic texts are taken as representations in this sense, as equally far from – or near to – reality, they are best referred not to our ideas of the reality of the body, but to their own cultural context. Beneath the apparent difference between their evaluations of nosebleeds lies a shared belief that a menstrual period may be diverted and come out through the nose. Rather than eliding this with Western biomedicine's category of vicarious menstruation (above, p. 59), we need to set this belief within the intellectual framework common to the *Aphorisms*, *Epidemics* and *Diseases of Women*: the internal anatomy of Hippocratic woman. Only then will we be able to discover why, in the terms of Hippocratic medicine, a nosebleed was thought to cause a fatal change in the daughter of Leonidas.

In Chapter 1, the medical uses of the *hodos* were outlined; it is this route from nose and mouth down to vagina which makes it possible for menstrual blood to find an exit from the top of the body. The nostrils are important in Hippocratic medicine in general as indicators of health; for example, cold *pneuma* coming from the nostrils when the skin is producing warm vapour is a sign of death (*Ep.* 6.4.22, Loeb VII, 252). They also have affinities with the reproductive organs: naturally damp nostrils and watery, plentiful sperm show a healthy constitution (*Ep.* 6.6.8, Loeb VII, 264) and sexual intercourse dries up the nasal discharge of Timochares (*Ep.* 5.72, Loeb VII, 200). These last examples demonstrate that an affinity between the nostrils and the organs of reproduction also exists in the male, but the affinity seems to be more pronounced in the female; the nostrils respond like the mouth of the womb (*DW* 2.133, L 8.282).

Women absorb more fluid from their food because of the spongy texture of their flesh; if this surplus does not appear in menstruation, this may be because the mouth of the womb has closed, blocking its way outside, or because the womb-jar has tilted, pouring the blood in the wrong direction. Where the mouth of the jar is not aligned with the bottom of the *hodos*, the blood may accumulate or may force a new way out. In *Diseases* 4.41 (L 7.562) it is said that, just as there are four humours and four bodily sources of the humours, so there are four routes out of the body which the humours can take: mouth, nostrils, anus and urethra. *Epidemics* 2.1.7 (Loeb VII, 24) gives several more routes, and particularly recommends, if possible, a loss from an opening below and a long way from the site of the disease. One area in which the *Diseases of Women* does differ significantly from many other treatises of the corpus is that the theory of the four humours plays a very small part in its vision of the body (Thivel 1981: 98–9; 1983: 230). This is because the nature of woman is dominated by one organ, the womb, and hence by only one humour, the hot and the wet: blood. There are many routes which suppressed menstrual blood may take; it may come out through the groin, the side or the rectum (*DW* 1.2, L 8.20–2; *CP* 511, L 5.702).

Because of the general affinity between the top and the bottom of the *hodos*, suppressed menstrual blood may cause headaches (*Ep.* 5.12, Loeb VII, 162), and the easiest route for blood to take in a woman is that which leads to the mouth and nostrils. The aphorism under consideration here, encouraging menstrual nosebleeds, is preceded by one saying that vomiting blood ceases when the menses flow (5.32, Loeb IV, 166).[14] These aphorisms imply that blood can only move in one direction at a time; however, in the *Epidemics* it is possible to find several cases in which blood changes direction abruptly, and others in which it uses both routes simultaneously. The fever affecting both sexes at Thasos (*Ep.* 1.13–17, Loeb I, 164–72) was discussed in Chapter 2, where I noted that women were less likely than men to die from it, unless they suffered after a difficult labour, when their menstrual blood would be diverted to their breasts and unable to come out (*Ep.* 1.16, Loeb I, 170). In male sufferers, a heavy nosebleed always led to recovery: in women, the fever often brought on the menstrual period, and *parthenoi* suffering from it had their first menses. What is most significant here is that, for some, nosebleed and menses flowed at the same time, while the daughter of Daitharses, a *parthenos*, had her very first period as well as a nosebleed.

The combination of first menses and a nosebleed is also favourable in the cases of the *parthenos* of Larissa (*Ep*. 3 case 12, Loeb I, 276) and the *parthenos* of Abdera (*Ep*. 3 case 7, Loeb I, 268), who have similar symptoms of fever, thirst and insomnia. The girl from Abdera experienced menarche at the beginning of the illness, and a heavy nosebleed on the seventeenth day: the Larissan girl had the nosebleed first, and menarche shortly afterwards.

Where these cases differ from both *Aphorisms* 5.32–3 and the daughter of Leonidas is that they describe fevers in which natural blood loss is considered to be beneficial to both sexes (cf. *Ep*. 4.17, Loeb VII, 104), rather than menstruation suppressed for reasons of individual physiology. An intermediate case is the daughter of Philon (*Ep*. 1.19, Loeb I, 174), who suffers from another fever in which nosebleeds are thought to be beneficial for both sexes. There are four favourable signs in the course of this disease, one of which is the nosebleed; in *gynaikes* and *parthenoi*, the writer adds, there is a fifth sign, a heavy period. However, although the daughter of Philon had a copious nosebleed, she died on the seventh day. The writer is clearly aware that this requires explanation, and he therefore adds that 'she dined at an inappropriate time' (*akairoterôs*).

The daughter of Leonidas is not described as having a fever, or being ill in any way; her surprisingly fatal nosebleed should therefore be seen as a diversion of her normal menses. The daughter of Philon is ill before her salutary nosebleed occurs, but dies because she then eats at the wrong time (Langholf 1990: 213). It is possible to reconstruct the reasoning by which both deaths could be explained without falsifying *Aphorisms* 5.32–3, by investigating two variables in the 'jar and tube' anatomy and physiology of woman: the age and the reproductive status of the patient.

The age of the patient, of either sex, is taken into consideration by several Hippocratic writers. *Aphorisms* 3.24–31 (Loeb IV, 130–4) and *Coan Prognoses* 502 (L 5.700) list the diseases most likely to affect particular age groups; texts which apply such a division to women include *Diseases of Women* 2.111 (L 8.238–40) and *Nature of Woman* 1 (L 7.312). Only one section of the *Diseases of Women*, that which concerns fluxes, consistently gives comments on the age of the patient (*DW* 2.115–21, L 8.248–64, except 2.117). A younger woman is given a different regimen (*diaita*, *DW* 2.115, 118; cf. 2.177, L 8.360): a white flux is difficult to cure in older women (2.116, 118, 119), and other fluxes too are more likely to strike and to kill if the patient is older (2.120, 121). Elsewhere in the *Diseases of Women* similar distinctions are drawn. Movements of the womb cause more difficulties in older than in younger women, especially if the woman is near the menopause (2.137, L 8.310). Some conditions are worse in pregnant women (2.174–1742, L 8.354–6), others more common in the childless

(2.145, L 8.320). The variables of age and reproductive status would often, but not always, coincide, young women being more likely to have no children.

To discover why fluxes and womb movement are more of a problem in older women, two parallel texts on sudden movement of the womb to the liver in a healthy woman are instructive (*DW* 2.127, L 8.272–4 = *NW* 3, L 7.314–16). Those affected are mostly older *parthenoi* and young widows, but it can affect any childless or sterile women who are *ek tôn tokôn*, which Manuli translated as 'outside the logic of generation' (1983: 156). This is the case because such women do not experience the bloodshed of the lochia, the discharge after childbirth, thought to be composed of stored menstrual blood (see below, Chapter 4, pp. 85–6); the womb 'does not swell up or become soft or emit [blood]'. The treatment for the widow includes sweet wine poured in the mouth, foul odours applied to the nostrils with sweet smells administered to the womb, followed by a purgative and cooked asses' milk, an aromatic fumigation of the womb, beetle pessaries (another purgative) and an aromatic injection into the womb. These procedures have in common the drawing down of the womb from the liver; it is significant that they assume the connection between nostrils and vulva. It is best of all, the writer continues, if the widow conceives. As for *parthenoi*, they should take a husband. So far, this is fairly standard Hippocratic advice. The remainder of the section is, however, of a different type, consisting of advice on what one should *avoid* doing if the patient is a *parthenos*. In such a patient, nothing should be applied to the nostrils (*DW* 2.127; *NW* 3 reads 'to the womb' here), no purgative should be administered, although strong-smelling substances in sweet wine may be drunk, and she should neither put any perfumed oil on her head, nor inhale any.

Variation in disease frequency and treatment in different categories of woman may be explained by the physiological differences believed to exist between them. Women's loose-textured flesh, complete with channels, develops gradually over time. In *Diseases* 4.39 (L 7.558) the network of passages (*phlebes*) throughout the body is described. During the whole of the person's life they are normally open, allowing the humoral fluids to pass, but at death they close, and in illness they may become narrow. In *Breaths* 8 (Loeb II, 240), a feverish headache is caused by hot blood being forced through narrow channels. *Diseases of Women* and some other texts modify this theory to take account of change over time. In children of either sex, 'the channels are narrow' (*NC* 20, L 7.508); normal growth includes the widening of these channels so that fluids can move around more easily:

> But as both boys and girls grow, the vessels which extend in the boy's case to the penis and in the girl's to the womb, open out and become wider in the process of growth; a way is opened up through the narrow passages, and the humour, finding sufficient space,

> can become agitated. That is why when they reach puberty, sperm can flow in the boy and menses in the girl.
>
> (*Gen.* 2, L 7.472, trans. Lonie 1981: 2; cf. Diogenes DK 64 B 6)

Boys show that they are mature once and for all by producing semen, but the channels in girls continue to widen after puberty. Puberty (*hêbê*) is in general a time of sudden changes (*Ep.* 6.1.4, Loeb VII, 218)[15] but in girls a more gradual series of events is necessary to complete the process of becoming a woman. Normal growth opens the channels to make 'a way through and a way outside' (*Gen.* 2, L 7.472–4), but all three transitional bleedings – menarche, defloration and childbirth – cause further changes in the body. For example, a childless woman of any age has denser, more tightly packed flesh than a woman who has given birth, with less space into which suppressed menstrual blood can travel and consequently more pain if her blood does not leave her body. In a childless woman the *stoma* of the womb will be narrower (*DW* 1.1, L 8.12; 1.2, L 8.14), although it may be closed by disease in any woman. As I showed in Chapter 1, childbirth eases menstruation not only because the passage of the child opens the 'way out' (*exodos*, *NC* 30, L 7.538), but also because it breaks down the flesh, opening up spaces in the body (*DW* 1.1, L 8.10) and widening the channels carrying blood to the womb (*NC* 30, L 7.538).

A woman who has given birth has loose-textured flesh, open channels and a complete tube from nostrils to vulva, which can be used in therapy. A young unmarried girl has not given birth and possibly has not even completed the growth process of puberty, so her channels are narrow and her tube may not be complete: this is why attempts to apply anything to her head or nostrils would have no effect on the womb. These distinctions between women made by age and reproductive status would also suggest that the reason why fluxes affect older women more is that their bodies are more open. Women near the menopause are more subject to movements of the womb not only because their bodies are drying out as they age, so that the womb is more likely to travel in search of moisture (cf. *DW* 2.137, L 8.308–10), but also because there is more open space in their bodies into which the womb can move.

In terms of Hippocratic theory, *parthenoi* are thus physically incomplete women; some are still growing towards menarche, while others have bled but their channels are narrow and, in any case, their flesh has not yet been broken down (*katarrêgnymi*, *DW* 1.1, L 8.10) by childbirth. Chapter 4 will show how menarche is a time of particular danger for *parthenoi*; if menstrual blood, unable to come out of the bottom of the tube, travels upwards, it can become lodged in the region of the heart and diaphragm where the channels are 'at an angle' (L 8.466–8), causing illness. A nosebleed is therefore only unequivocally 'a good thing when the menses are suppressed' in a mature *gynê* (*Aph.* 5.33, Loeb IV, 166). In *Diseases of Women* 1.41 (L 8.100) it is explicitly lochial blood which comes out of the nose, showing that the patient has obviously given birth and can therefore be considered a complete woman; the complete woman (*gynê*) can be treated by purges and by fumigations at the nose, and can lose blood from the nostrils, because her internal anatomy permits it. In a *parthenos*, a nosebleed is particularly significant – and thus worth noting in a case history – because it should show that the dangerous areas of the body have been successfully traversed, and hence that a certain point of internal physical maturity has been reached.

How does the daughter of Philon (*Ep.* 1.19, Loeb I, 174) fit into this model? It is not stated that she is a *parthenos*, and her nosebleed is not seen as menstrual. However, the attribution of her death to 'dining at an inappropriate time' recalls a phrase of *On the Diseases of Virgins* where blood is said to accumulate at menarche because of 'food and the growth of the body' (L 8.466). Since the origin of blood is food, more food means more blood (e.g. Homer, *Il.* 5.341–2; Aristotle, *PA* 650a34–5; Duminil 1983: 235 ff.). Having successfully purged the excess, by eating too soon the daughter of Philon foolishly created more blood before her body was ready for it: the output of blood was correct, but the input was excessive.

What of the anatomical status of the daughter of Leonidas, whose nosebleed is due not to a fever but to the diversion of normal menstrual blood? After her menstrual blood had 'made a start' – something which could only be known after she had bled from the vagina – it turned aside, and she bled at the nose. This should have been a good sign, showing that she was internally mature, with open channels, but – after she had bled at the nose – a change occurred. It is not possible to know whether *hê physis* does or does not suggest menarche in her case, while being 'daughter of' rather than 'wife of' is not necessarily any guarantee of being a *parthenos*.[16] The case histories of *Epidemics* 7, like those of the other *Epidemics* collections, often end with the bald statement of the death of the patient, sometimes also giving the number of days since the illness began.[17] In no other case in this volume, however, is the age, sex or any other status of the patient given at the point at which death is stated as the outcome; yet, for the daughter of Leonidas, we read *hê pais apethanen*, 'the (female) child died'.

If Hippocratic gynaecology is to be appreciated as literature, then the chosen ending must affect our perception of the whole. What is selected as the 'end' explicitly links her death to the status of *pais*,[18] just as that of the daughter of Philon is linked to 'dining at an inappropriate time'. There is no reason to repeat her identity as 'daughter of', which is why I would suggest taking *pais* here as 'child'. How old is she supposed to be? The category of *parthenos* can extend at least to 20, the age of the 'pretty daughter of Nerios' in *Epidemics* 5.50 (Loeb VII, 190). *Weeks* 5 (L 8.636) uses *paidion* from age 0–7, *pais* from 7–14; the next section of *Epidemics* 7 concerns a *pais ephebos*, a 'boy in military training' (7.124, Loeb VII, 414), which would suggest the upper limit of the *Weeks* category. These references cannot be pushed too far. In terms of her internal anatomy, being a *pais* would simply suggest that the daughter of Leonidas is, as yet, an incomplete woman; in her compact body there are insufficient spaces where excess blood can rest. However, she is old enough that menarche appears to be an imminent possibility. She dies because, although her body is almost ready to menstruate properly – the *physis* 'made a start' – it cannot survive such a large amount of blood forcing its way up to the nose through channels which are too narrow to cope. The young daughter (*paidiskê*) of Olympiodoros survived a loss of blood from the right nostril (*Ep.* 4.33, Loeb VII, 130); but this blood was not seen as a diverted menstrual period, perhaps because she was too young for this even to be considered as a possibility. In *Epidemics* 5.28 (Loeb VII, 178), a *paidiskê* is described as being aged around 12. 'The doctor didn't understand': he failed to realise that the nosebleed principle only safely applies to mature women, to *gynaikes*. This would also explain why suppressed menstrual blood is more likely to come out through the rectum in a *parthenos* than in a *gynê* (*DW* 1.2, L 8.22);[19] unable to move up the tube so freely, in a *parthenos* the blood may 'make a passage' through the next nearest orifice.

The 'Coan' and 'Cnidian', 'genuine' and 'spurious' works of the Hippocratic corpus together demonstrate further the details of the jar and tube anatomy of woman, such as the affinity between nostrils and vagina, and show some of the concerns raised by the process by which a girl grows to become a woman. If we commit the heresy of reading the texts as if the traditional research programme had never separated them, the death of the daughter of Leonidas becomes another black raven for the theory of menstrual nosebleeds. This interpretation does not treat the case history as the rationally observed particular case which causes the general rule to be questioned; instead, like the work of Langholf (1990: 179–90), it emphasises the point that the particular case can only be observed within the conceptual framework provided by the general rule, so that 'Nothing is ever dismantled in the *Epidemics*, the steadfastness of the foundation walls is never doubted' (1990: 212). I would suggest that the author of *Epidemics* 7.123 is fully aware of the rule that menstrual nosebleeds are salutary and that he defends this foundation wall by noting that this patient was a *pais*. Any description involves selection (Pigeaud 1988: 311); as historians, our role is to take into account both the points which the text brings to our notice, and the points which are so obvious that they are not stated. The medical case history shows that it is precisely those sources which appear to report reality directly which need to be read with the closest attention.

4

BLOOD AND THE GODDESSES

Historians of the mid-nineteenth century have argued that it was only then that the adolescent girl was 'discovered' and seen as a problem; ideally pure and innocent, but also liable to sexual experimentation and possible pregnancy (e.g. Nathanson 1991: 6, 79). Joan Brumberg (1993: 102 n.6) furthermore suggests that, 'In the nineteenth century, menarche was the critical site for establishing female difference.' She notes that the age at menarche had fallen from an average of 15 in 1877 to 13.9 in 1901, while the age at marriage had risen, and suggests that these statistics were at the root of an increased concern about the proper way to manage the potentially dangerous gap between what was perceived as the onset of sexuality, and its proper fulfilment (1993: 106–9). This contrasts sharply with the ancient Greek world and with the Middle Ages, when Schultz (1991: 528, 530) has argued that 'the age of marriage for girls will often coincide with the age of menarche', so that 'there simply is no stretch of time between puberty and adulthood'.

But the case of the daughter of Leonidas shows that, for the Hippocratic gynaecological texts, concerned as they are with the mature female body and its flows, puberty could pose particular difficulties. We have seen how Pandora was sent by the gods as a mature woman disguised as a *parthenos*, a young girl of the age for marriage. One consequence of this is that, by merging two normally separate stages of the female life-cycle, Pandora by-passes puberty: but her daughters, the 'race of women', cannot. A short Hippocratic text, the *Peri Partheniôn*, 'Concerning *parthenoi*', known historically as *On the Diseases of Virgins* or – more accurately, but less familiarly, as *On the Diseases of Young Girls* – gives a physiological explanation of why puberty is a time of considerable mental and physical danger for the girl passing through it. In this chapter, following on from the case of the daughter of Leonidas, I will discuss the place of female puberty in Hippocratic medicine, moving from the uses made of *On the Diseases of Virgins* in the traditional Hippocratic research programme to the interpretation of the text which follows from setting it in the context of the ways in which medicine and religion handle the transition from *parthenos* to *gynê*. I will then look at a related aspect of Hippocratic body symbolism which aligns mature women with sacrificial victims, presenting their bleeding as an essential part of the life of the city.

The date of *On the Diseases of Virgins* (L 8.466–71)[1] is not known; Christine Bonnet-Cadilhac (1993) argues for the late fourth century on the grounds of alleged Aristotelian influence, but Flemming and Hanson (forthcoming) see no such influence and suggest a date in the late fifth or early fourth century. The text's location of the seat of intelligence at the heart and *phrenes* would also support an early date (Langholf 1990: 41, 45 n.40). Bonnet-Cadilhac also rejects any suggestion that our text is to be identified as the work on virgins' diseases mentioned twice in *Diseases of Women* (1.2, L 8. 22; 1.41, L 8. 98), in passages which discuss diverted menstrual blood coming out orally or in the stools. *On the Diseases of Virgins* mentions neither route, raising the possibility that what survives as our text was originally the introduction to a lost treatise which went on to describe alternative routes for the menses. Still other possibilities exist: our *On the Diseases of Virgins* may have opened a lost work dealing exclusively with virgins, one which concentrated on types of seizure (Flemming and Hanson forthcoming), or one on diseases in general (Jouanna 1992: 548).

In Hippocratic gynaecology, to be a woman is to menstruate. This poses the problem of women who do not menstruate: they may be ill, in which case drugs or mechanical procedures can be used to induce menstruation; they may be pregnant, in which case there is no danger to their health because the excess blood is contributing to the foetus; or they may be past the menopause, that natural process of 'drying out' which transforms even a wet and spongy female body into something that does not need to bleed.

Puberty lies in a different category. A girl who has never previously bled begins to bleed: why? What invisible changes occur inside her body before blood appears to view? Or, far worse in terms of a model of woman which sees the norm as regular heavy loss, a girl who is apparently mature in other ways does not begin to bleed: why not, and when and how should a doctor intervene?

The images familiar from myth and ritual represent female maturation as a process of taming and ripening. All women start their lives as outsiders to male society; through maturation they are taken 'inside' in order to reproduce it. Children, for the Greeks, are by nature wild (Plato, *Timaeus* 44a–c; *Laws* 2, 653d–e, 666a–e) and the *parthenos* is untamed (*admês*) to the extent that she needs to be 'tamed' (*tithaseuein*) before a man can even carry on a conversation with her ([Xen]. *Oik*. 7.10). In some versions of the myths associated with the rituals at Brauron by which Athenian girls entered maturity after 'acting the bear' for Artemis, a tamed bear living in the sanctuary went wild, and scratched or tore out the eyes of a *parthenos*.[2] While it becomes wild, the girl who dances as a bear in ritual will become tame. A girl's upbringing is often represented as the 'breaking in' of a filly (Soph. *Ant*. 477–8; Aristoph. *Lys*.

1308; Eur. *Hippol.* 546–7; Vernant 1979–80: 456; Loraux 1987: 36), with marriage – submission to the 'yoke of Aphrodite' – as the end of this process (Calame 1977: 411–20, 330–3). The co-operation of the filly/girl is not necessary to her taming; of Poseidon and the daughter of Nereus we read that 'he broke her in, although she was not willing' (Oppian *Hal.* 1.390).

In contrast to the violence and the cultural character of taming, ripening may strike us as a softer and more 'natural' image. Unmarried girls – like those in *On the Diseases of Virgins* – are 'ripe for marriage' (L 8.466), 'tender ripe fruit', while innocent girls carried off in battle are 'plucked unripe', and unmarried but deflowered girls are 'rotted fruit', 'corrupted' or 'gone off' (Aesch. *Suppl.* 996–1005; *Seven Against Thebes* 333). As Anne Carson has pointed out, because Greek men were not expected to marry until the age of 30 (e.g. Hes. *Erga* 699–701), a man's 'ripeness' was an extended period of full enjoyment of sexual activity: for a woman, ideally married as young as 14, 'ripeness' would be only a fleeting instant between reaching physical maturity, and first sexual experience (e.g. Aristoph. *Lys.* 596; Carson 1990: 145–7).

However, it should be remembered that the ancient Greeks classified ripening and taming differently from ourselves. They considered some foods to be partly 'tamed' by nature, needing only a little human intervention to cook them and make them fully edible (Vernant 1979). This is a good model to apply to medical constructions of female puberty, where ripeness seems to consist of a process involving signs such as breast buds, body hair and menarche but, in addition to these changes, needs a little extra male intervention to complete it. The natural changes outlined in the Hippocratic *On Generation* 2 (L 7.472–4) were discussed in the previous chapter; the process of growth gradually opens up the flesh so that it acquires the spongy texture characteristic of the female. But full 'sponginess' does not occur until childbirth 'breaks down' the flesh,[3] so there is a sense in which medical maturity depends on becoming a mother. Where the girl appears to be otherwise 'ripe', but the first menstruation does not occur, then – according to *On the Diseases of Virgins* – the solution also lies with male intervention, whether the male is husband or Hippocratic healer.

The text opens with a statement of the origins and eternal nature of the medical *technê* and a reference to the seizures characteristic of the 'sacred disease'.[4] Such symptoms, the writer explains, may result in suicide by hanging/strangulation.[5] This is more common in women than in men, because female nature is weaker, but most common of all at the descent of the menses among *parthenoi* who, despite being 'ripe for marriage' (*hôrê gamou*), remain unmarried.

Demand (1994: 98–9) has argued that the initial statement that men too can suffer from these symptoms, taken with the similar terminology of Aristophanes when, in *Wasps* (1037–43), he described fevers which choked and suffocated men, means that 'the explanation cannot be framed exclusively in terms of references to female anatomy' (Demand 1994: 214 n.62). I would argue against this that *On the Diseases of Virgins* states that it is more women than men (*pleones de gynaikes ê andres*), and 'particularly' (*mallon*) young girls at menarche who suffer in this way; what is there about their anatomy which makes them particularly susceptible?

The problems start *hama tê kathodôi tôn epimêniôn*, at the same time as the 'going down of her menses', in a girl who is otherwise ripe for marriage. Is first menstruation, or any menstruation, implied here? In *Diseases of Women* 1.41 the expression used for menarche is the unambiguous *ta epiphainomena prôta*, 'the first showings',[6] and the fact that the reference to the 'going down' is followed by the remark 'suffering disorders to which she was previously (*proteron*) not exposed' supports reading *On the Diseases of Virgins* too as a text on menarche.[7]

Girls at puberty produce more blood than their body can use, due to what the writer of *On the Diseases of Virgins* describes as 'food and the growth of the body' (Dean-Jones 1994: 48–50). This blood flows down, moving as if it were going to pass out of the body; here, menarche is thought of as an internal process occurring before the outward manifestation of blood. But, in the girls described here, the blood is unable to leave, due to the closure of the 'mouth of exit' (*to stoma tês exodou*). Instead, it moves up again, towards the area of the heart and diaphragm, where it produces numbness; this, the writer explains, is like the feeling in the feet after sitting still for a long time. But, where the heart and diaphragm are involved, there is great danger, since the channels in this area are 'at an angle', so the blood cannot easily return to its proper place, while the area itself is a vital one in terms of its influence on insanity. Due to the pressure of blood here, the *parthenos* exhibits a number of symptoms: she is delirious, she fears the dark, and she has visions which seem to compel her to jump, to throw herself down wells and to strangle herself. In the absence of visions she shows an erotic fascination with death; literally, 'she welcomes death as a lover' (*erai tou thanatou*).[8] The text ends,

> When her senses are returning, the *gynaikes* dedicate many other objects to Artemis and also the most splendid women's clothing. They are ordered to do this by diviners (*manteis*)[9] who thoroughly deceive them. But relief from this complaint comes when nothing impedes the flow of blood. I order (*keleuô*) *parthenoi* to marry as quickly as possible if they suffer this. For if they become pregnant, they become healthy. If not, then at puberty or a little later she will be caught by this or by some other disease. Among married *gynaikes*, the sterile suffer most from these conditions.

The interpretation of this text is made more difficult by the apparently indiscriminate shifts between singular and plural. If we take all the singular forms as referring to a *parthenos*, and all plurals as referring to mature *gynaikes*, then the passage can be understood. The one section which remains problematic is the first; the senses return to a single individual, a *parthenos*, but this is followed by a dedication to Artemis performed by plural *gynaikes*. These women could be the close female kin of the affected girl offering their garments in thanksgiving for her recovery;[10] or, following Fasbender (1897: 229), they could include the recovered *parthenos* who, by recovering, has at last established herself as a *gynê*. 'The flow of blood' can then be understood as the mechanism by which her senses have returned. By ordering sufferers to marry, and adding 'if they become pregnant . . . ', however, the author suggests that the successful transition from *parthenos* to *gynê* depends on compressing menarche, marriage and childbirth into as short a space as possible. The maligned diviners, however, seem to see things rather differently, believing that Artemis can intervene to help the disturbed *parthenos*.

On the Diseases of Virgins shares a number of themes with other Hippocratic gynaecological texts. *Superfoetation* 34 (L 8.504–6) discusses delayed menarche causing mental disturbance, but attributes the symptoms to womb movement (Demand 1994: 98); *On Sterile Women* (3.213, L 8.408 and 228, L 8.436) mentions closure of the 'orifice of exit' preventing normal menstruation and parallels the use of 'I order', *keleuô*, by the doctor; *Diseases of Women* mentions terror (2.182, L 8.364) and feelings of suffocation accompanied by the desire for death (*thanein eratai*, 2.177, L 8.360), and advises *parthenoi* to marry (2.127, L 8.274). The attack on the diviners for 'deceit' reflects the wider Hippocratic interest in deceit and truth in medicine (see above, Chapter 2 p. 43).

In assessing the text, many scholars have been tempted into retrospective diagnosis. G. Stanley Hall used *On the Diseases of Virgins* in his 1904 study of adolescence, but changed the plural subjects into the singular in order to make it into a case history: 'Hippocrates describes a girl who at the dawn of pubescence saw a vision, leaped and tried to throw herself into a well and then to hang herself, deeming death more desirable than life' (1904: 265). The text has often been read by assimilating it into the category of hysteria, to be discussed at length in the final chapter of this book. Laín Entralgo described these *parthenoi* as 'certain ill – perhaps hysterical, to judge by what is said of them – women' (1970: 158) and commented more generally on the gynaecological texts, 'In all these clinical and therapeutic descriptions the predominantly psychic state of the symptomatic picture is quite obvious' (1970: 168). A psychiatrist, Jean-Philippe Catonné (1994: 386), makes the Hippocratic text 'the very first description in medical history of what nineteenth-century authors called hysterical insanity'. In recent work on the text by women there has been more sympathy shown towards the patients; the text has been seen as 'medical terrorism' (Manuli 1980: 404) and as an 'instrument of socialization' (Pinault 1992: 129), designed to scare women into acting as society requires, by marrying and giving birth at the ages seen as socially appropriate. Geneviève Hoffmann sees this text as a representation both of menarche (1992: 303) and of hysteria (1992: 305–7), emphasising that the behaviour of the disordered *parthenos* is the reverse of that of a well-brought-up young girl, moving as she does between silence and logorrhoea, prostration and agitation, apathy and heightened sensibility, and seeking death when she should be entering marriage (1992: 306).

When she comes to the two methods of suicide, hanging and drowning in wells, Hoffmann suggests that drowning is chosen as a means of expressing the 'wetness' of the female body (1992: 307). Valeria Andò (1990) prefers to link both to myths of ritual 'death' as part of initiation practices. However, the forms of suicide chosen have in common not only relative ease for a young girl, but also lack of blood loss. It is this factor, and its relationship to the unique glimpse offered by this treatise of an alternative cure given by religious healers through a cult of Artemis, that I will next explore.

The strangled goddess

The symptom of feeling strangled and the girls' desire to hang or strangle themselves both use the verb *(ap)ankhô*. This may seem to link the text to the sensation of *pnix*, traditionally translated as suffocation, found in many sections of *Diseases of Women* and often – but not always – connected to menstrual retention. Later lexicographers and medical writers tend to view the verbs *ankhô* and *pnigô* as equivalent; for example the tenth-century encyclopaedia known as the Suda gives, under *apankhonisai*, '*pnixai*', while Galen gives *pnigomenos* as the meaning of *ankhomenos* (K19.69). In classical Greece, however, there may have been some difference in emphasis between these verbs. *Ankhô*-related words imply pressure on the neck blocking breath, and may best be translated in terms of 'strangulation' or 'hanging'. *Pnix*-related words suggest heat – *pnigos* and *pnigmos* mean stifling heat, and a *pnigeus* is an oven – so that 'stifling' may be a better translation than 'suffocation'. Where strangulation implies pressure on the neck, stifling suggests something over the mouth and nose preventing respiration, or a hot atmosphere in which breathing is difficult. Overlap between the two sensations is possible, since strangulation may also cause a feeling of heat. In Aristophanes' play *Frogs*, the god Dionysos asks the hero Herakles for a way to Hades which is neither too hot nor too cold. Herakles suggests 'by rope and stool' – that is, to hang oneself. 'No,' replies Dionysos, 'that's stifling' (*paue, pnigeran legeis*; 122). Herakles goes on to suggest hemlock, which is rejected as 'too cold'. Within a hot/cold opposition, hanging oneself is seen as a 'hot' way to go. But I would argue that Dionysos chooses a *pnix*-related word because these carry a more obvious suggestion of heat. Using *ankhô* words exclusively, as in *On the Diseases of Virgins*, rather than mixing them with *pnix* words, shifts the emphasis more to the surface of the neck. By evoking the anatomical affinity between the top and the bottom of the female body, which lay behind the belief that a girl's virginity – or loss of it – could be detected from the pitch of her voice,[11] the physical emphasis of *ankhô*-words hints at the need for the lower mouth to be opened by sex and marriage.

For Renaissance readers, the girls of the Hippocratic text recall another classical source by hanging themselves. This is Plutarch's *Moralia* ('On the virtues of women') 249b–d, which describes a condition said to have affected the *parthenoi* of Miletos. Here, in an act of mass suicide brought on by the sensation of a 'desire for death' (*epithymia thanatou*), girls hanged themselves; and, again, the verb is *(ap)ankhô* and the text covers both 'divine' and 'medical' explanations of the incident.

Giovanni Battista Donati's commentary on the text *On the Diseases of Virgins*, published in 1582, appears to have been the first to link the Hippocratic material to this section of Plutarch. Commenting on the line 'She welcomes death as a lover' Donati writes, 'The new kind of madness now comes to my mind, that of the Milesian virgins of whom Plutarch of course [writes]. Those girls choked themselves *en masse*. Some people thought that inclement air contributed to that disease; those who were considered wiser men attributed it to the gods. But our most ancient and prudent author [i.e. Hippocrates] expressed the opinion that all the blame for those diseases should be traced to the holding back and suppression of menstrual blood' (1582: 38–9).[12]

This story was told twice by Plutarch, not only in the *Moralia* but also in a lost work, *On the soul*, where it featured in a section on disorders of the mind which is preserved in Aulus Gellius' *Attic Nights* (15.10). Plutarch does not mention the Hippocratic *On the Diseases of Virgins*, although in both versions the girls of Miletos are struck with 'a desire for death', wording which certainly recalls 'She welcomes death as a lover', and a mass suicide by hanging ensues. Neither parental argument nor friendly comfort has any effect, until at last a decree is passed that all victims should be carried to their graves naked. In the *Moralia* they are carried 'through the marketplace' while in *Attic Nights* they are taken with the rope they have used. In both cases the shameful exposure after death apparently acts as a deterrent.[13] Another ancient author, Polyaenus, gives a short summary of this story but, whereas Plutarch attributes the instigation of the decree to 'a man of good sense', Polyaenus credits 'a Milesian woman' (*Stratagems* 8.63).

Donati's link between the Milesian mass suicide and the Hippocratic virgins is repeated by Stephanus' commentary (1635: 32); confusingly, Stephanus claims that the Milesian girls in Plutarch 'threw themselves into Wells', perhaps a simple error, or perhaps an indication of the extent to which hanging and drowning have come to be seen as equivalent and interchangeable modes of death because of their relationship in *On the Diseases of Virgins*. The stories are also discussed in non-medical literature of the late sixteenth and early seventeenth centuries. In the *Treatise of Specters* of Le Loyer, *On the Diseases of Virgins* is again seen as providing a medical explanation for the behaviour of the Milesian girls (1605: 110^{r-v} [first published 1586]); the merging of Plutarch's Milesian suicides with the Hippocratic text always results in Hippocrates' 'ancient and prudent' explanation of the condition being given precedence.

More generally, it has been suggested that the *parthenoi* of myth have what almost amounts to an 'elective affinity' with hanging and strangulation (Brelich 1969: 443–4 n.2).[14] This even applies to the goddess Artemis, granted eternal *partheneia* by her father Zeus (Callimachos, *Art.* 5 ff.), who includes among her epithets *Apankhomenê*, the Strangled Lady. Blundell (1995: 25) notes that, of the six female Olympians, three are virgins: Hestia, Artemis and Athena. Hera is a semi-virgin, in that she renews her virginity annually, while Aphrodite is the goddess of sexuality but remains unmarried, leaving Demeter as the 'only true mother goddess'. Blundell argues that such a high percentage of goddesses are unmarried virgins because this gives them independence; if they were wives, they would be subordinate to their husbands (1995: 44). However, the divine *parthenoi* do not act as role models for normal women, who are expected to undergo the transition from *parthenos* to *gynê* when they are ripe to do so.

Of the divine *parthenoi*, Artemis alone is linked to strangulation, through the epithet of *Apankhomenê* which she holds at Kaphyae in Arkadia. The earliest discussion of *On the Diseases of Virgins* that I have been able to find making the connection with this epithet is by a Dutch medical practitioner, Evert D. Baumann (1939), who argued that the medical description provides an insight into a folk disorder specific to classical Greece; what we would now call a 'culture-bound syndrome'.[15] Pausanias (8.23.6–7) explains the origins of the title. Once some children tied a rope around the cult image of Artemis in the course of one of their games; playfully, they said that Artemis was being strangled. For this apparent sacrilege, the adults stoned them to death. The *gynaikes* of Kaphyae were then struck with a disease, as a result of which their babies were stillborn. The Pythia, the priestess of Apollo, was consulted; she ordered that the children should be buried and should receive annual sacrifices, because they had been put to death wrongly. From then on, Artemis was called *Apankhomenê*.

The explanation reflects the role of the goddess in children's lives. Artemis, whose own virginity 'expressed an attitude to the wilderness, that it was not to be tamed' (Sale 1965: 26 n.33), tames the wild child; she released the daughters of Proitos from their wildness (*ap'agrion*, Call. *Art.* 233 ff.) and Proitos then dedicated a temple to Artemis Hêmerê, 'She who tames' (Vernant 1980–1: 393). As Kourotrophos she protects their upbringing and leads them to adulthood, receiving dedications of childhood toys (van Straten 1981: 90 n.126). The story follows a pattern, common in myths of Artemis, by which an error is made, the guilty are struck by disease, and equilibrium is restored after the Pythia gives advice (Calame 1977: 281). But what is most significant about the incident described is that it is correct to call Artemis

'Strangled'. The children were right to give her this title: their innocent game revealed the truth.

Assuming that the origins of legends such as this lie in ritual, scholars have suggested that *Apankhomenê* arises from the practice of hanging images of vegetation deities on trees (e.g. Farnell 1896: 428; Nilsson 1967: 487). This misses the pertinence of the epithet to Artemis. It should be noted that the punishment for the adults in this text is not merely a disease, but more specifically an interruption in the process by which the city is reproduced through its *gynaikes*. Artemis, who herself never gives birth, has the power to give or withhold a successful labour (e.g. Call. *Art.* 122 ff.; Cahen 1930: 123); here she chooses to prevent birth, because the people of Kaphyae will not acknowledge her as 'Strangled'.

Why should Artemis be 'Strangled'? Strangulation and hanging, for the Greeks, meant shedding no blood (Loraux 1984: 213; 1995: 111). In the field of sacrifice, for example, Herodotus (4.60) says that the Scythians strangled their beasts; 'normal' Greek sacrifice of animals shed blood, thus ensuring communication between men and gods (Hartog 1980: 191–4). As a form of death for humans, strangulation or hanging evoked horror, as in the reactions to Phaedra's suicide (Eur. *Hippol.* 778, 802; Hartog 1980: 195 n.4), but as methods of suicide they are also related to shedding no blood. A bloodless suicide is, for example, a particularly appropriate way of avoiding the bloodshed of unwanted defloration. The chorus in Aeschylus' *Suppliant Women* threaten to hang themselves rather than sleep with men they hate (465, 788), and young girls such as Aspalis (Ant. Lib. 13) and the Caryatides (Lact. ad Stat. *Theb.* 4. 225) move beyond threats to action when they fear rape (Calame 1977: 270). Other girls in Greek myth hang themselves *after* being raped (e.g. *Contest of Homer and Hesiod* 323). Like hanging, jumping down wells is presented as a culturally appropriate response to unwanted sex; in a passage praising pagan women renowned for their chastity, Jerome mentions the daughters of Phidon, who 'threw themselves down a well, to preserve their virginity by death' (*Against Jovinian* 1.41, Migne, *PL* 23.285). In his famous condemnation of Piso's term of office as a provincial governor in the late Roman republic, Cicero alleged that Piso's lust was such that, at his approach, well-born virgins would leap into wells, preferring a voluntary death to inevitable dishonour (*De prov. cons.* 3.6). Whether or not this really happened is irrelevant here; what is important is that suicide, whether threatened or performed, is thought to be a plausible response to the threat of rape and, furthermore, that hanging or drowning are the preferred means to this end. The action of Phaedra is not merely a negative gesture performed from fear that Hippolytos will tell Theseus the truth (as in Diod. Sic. 4.62); it is a positive action, for by choosing hanging as her mode of death she inserts herself into an established tradition and thus strengthens her false claim that Hippolytos has raped her.[16]

Strangulation and hanging can thus be culturally opposed to unwanted sex;

the avoidance of the latter may be appropriately achieved through the former, although it may be carried out after the event, as if to restore the non-bleeding, closed body of the virgin. Where the *parthenoi* of the Hippocratic text are wrong, however, is that their actions are inappropriate; what faces them is not violent defloration before they are 'ripe', but menarche and marriage at the proper times.

Herodotus (4.180) tells of a Libyan festival of another eternal *parthenos*, Athena, in which the most beautiful human *parthenos* is dressed in a Corinthian helmet and full Greek panoply, then driven along the shores of a lake in a chariot. After this, the other *parthenoi* are divided into two groups and proceed to fight with sticks and stones. Those who die of their wounds are called '*pseudoparthenoi*'; that is, 'they distinguish the true from the false by metaphor: the true virgin is inviolate or unwounded, hence the survivors are true virgins' (Benardete 1969: 125). The true *parthenos* does not bleed, let alone die from her wounds;[17] the eternal *parthenos* Artemis does not shed her own blood in the hunt, in sex or in childbirth. Artemis *Apankhomenê* can therefore be seen as expressing her *partheneia*, and the strangulation symptoms and chosen mode of death of the Hippocratic *parthenoi* identify with her as 'Strangled'.

Artemis does not bleed, but she sheds the blood of others, both as huntress and as director of the process by which a *parthenos* becomes a *gynê*. The 'true' *parthenoi* in Herodotus' story similarly shed the blood of others.[18] Those in *On the Diseases of Virgins* are, however, 'ripe for marriage', ready to bleed and thus to enter into the series of bleedings in menstruation, defloration and childbirth that will transform them into *gynaikes*. The *gynê* is constructed as the opposite pole to the *parthenos*: she should bleed, as part of her role in reproducing society – and the Hippocratic writers supply theories to support this idea – but she should not shed blood. Only a man may shed blood in war and sacrifice (Detienne 1979: 187–9), while, as we shall see later in this chapter, the *gynê* is explicitly compared to the sacrificed beast which bleeds.

Pausanias' story reflects Artemis as both the goddess who sheds none of her own blood, and the goddess who makes others bleed. The Kaphyan *gynaikes* only accept the second aspect; by denying that Artemis is strangled they claim her as a *gynê* like themselves. The children, appropriately, recognise the first aspect. In *On the Diseases of Virgins* the *parthenoi* cling to the first when it is time for them to accept the second, and in dedicating garments to Artemis they finally acknowledge her role in initiating the transition which takes them further towards becoming full *gynaikes*.

Parallel to the opposition between bleeding and strangulation in stories of *parthenoi* and Artemis is that between releasing and binding. Artemis is Lysizônos, releaser of the girdle: she is also Lygodesma, bound with the *lygos* or *agnos castus*.

Artemis releaser

The use of the *zônê* or girdle in female clothing reflects the stages of a Greek woman's life. A young girl is 'ungirdled' (Call. fr.620A) and the first girdle, put on at puberty, is later dedicated to Artemis as part of the marriage process; a special girdle, tied with a ritual knot, is worn on the wedding night and untied by the spouse; a married woman unties her girdle in labour (Schmitt 1977). Loosening hair and garments can be a necessary precaution in dangerous situations and when performing magic (Heckenbach 1911: 78 ff.) but the association between Artemis and the *zônê*, worn throughout the *parthenos* to *gynê* transition, deserves to be seen not as one of many examples of the release of all knots at times of transition, but as a far more specific reference to the powers of Artemis.

As protector of childbirth, Eileithyia, Artemis is invoked by women calling on her, often as Lysizônos, in labour (e.g. Theocritus 17.60–1; Eur. *Hippol.* 166–9); after the birth, breast bands and girdle may be dedicated to her (*Anth. Pal.* 6.200, 202, 272).

Birth is not, however, the only time when Artemis releases. The phrase *luein tên zônên*, to release the girdle, is used not only in labour (Sor. *Gyn.* 2.6; T 74) but also for defloration (*Anth. Pal.* 7.164, 324; Eur. *Alc.* 177; EG 319.3, 684.3) and the epithet Lysizônos evokes the presence of Artemis on both occasions. She releases the blood from those who are 'strangled' in *On the Diseases of Virgins*, and she performs a similar action at the transitions of defloration and parturition, where she 'releases' the *parthenos* to cross the threshold of bleeding into a fuller expression of the status of *gynê*.

The girdle is released at these times of bloodshed: it can also be tied as a noose when *parthenoi* commit suicide. Kylon's daughter Myro, 'loosing her girdle and making a noose of it', should be seen in this context; she is a '*parthenos* ripe for marriage' but instead of her spouse releasing her girdle in defloration she must release it herself so that it may be tied as the instrument of her death (Plut. *Mor.* 253c–e). Marriage and death – more specifically, sexual bloodshed and hanging – are inverted, and from this the story derives its pathos.

There remains one other transition that needs to be considered here. The birth of the first child is particularly important in making a woman into a true *gynê* (Schmitt 1977: 1064; cf. Lysias 1.6) and this is completed by the first lochia, the discharge from the womb after childbirth. Among the epithets referring to her role in childbirth, Artemis is called Lochia (Eur. *Suppl.* 958; *IT* 1097; SEG III 400.9). When a woman dies in or just after childbirth she remains 'not fully a *gynê*' (EG 505.4), suggesting that the lochia are an essential part of the process. Medical texts regard the absence of this discharge as a threat to future fertility or to life itself (*DW* 1.29, L 8.72; 1.40, L 8.96–8; 1.41, L 8. 98–100), and state that the most difficult lochial bleeding is that after the first birth (*DW* 1.72, L 8.152; *NC* 18, L 7.502). The symptoms of lochial displacement are explicitly compared to those caused by displacement of menstrual blood in *parthenoi* (*DW* 1.41, L 8. 98), while both menstrual and lochial blood are 'like the flow of blood from a sacrificed beast', an image to be discussed further shortly.

Artemis thus supervises transitions, assisting other women to cross the very boundaries she will never experience. As *Apankhomenê* she expresses the ideal of the *parthenos* who does not bleed; but as Lysizônos she 'releases the girdle' in both defloration and labour, while as Lochia and Eileithyia she assists in childbirth.

Chaste herb, virgin goddess

A further epithet of Artemis combines the 'strangled' *parthenos* who sheds none of her own blood with the goddess who makes other women cross boundaries of bleeding. This is Lygodesma, meaning bound with the plant called *lygos* or *agnos castus*, used in wickerwork and perfumery (Pliny *NH* 24.38.59), medicine and ritual.[19] Pausanias (3.16.7 ff.), who gives the epithet as an alternative title of Artemis Orthia, explains it by a story that the cult image was found in a thicket of this plant which made it stand upright (*orthos*).

The most important work to date on this epithet is that of Meuli (1975),[20] which places it in the context of other 'bound gods' and of myths such as those of Daidalos, who made images so lifelike that they had to be tied down to prevent them from running away (Plato, *Meno* 97d; *Euthyphro* 11c–d). Frontisi-Ducroux (1975: 100–6) notes that 'bound' images of the gods were all *xoana*, small, light and easily movable figures, and she suggests that to bind the statue was to ensure the continuing presence of the god in the sanctuary (cf. Vernant 1982–3: 443–5). The method used here involves linking deities by a shared feature; however, following Vernant's method of reading the Greek pantheon by concentrating on a single deity's 'mode of operation' as the key unifying apparently diverse facets, I prefer to focus instead on the links between different attributes of Artemis, in order to demonstrate how the epithets intersect in such a way that it can 'make sense' that Lygodesma, *Apankhomenê* and Lysizônos 'are' one goddess. This method contrasts with, for example, the approach of Burkert (1977: 192), who states that 'The great goddess of Ephesos, the cruel Laphria and the goddess for whom girls dance at Brauron are obviously different but are nevertheless called "Artemis"'; instead, following Detienne and Vernant (1974), it asks how the Greeks could see what to us are 'obviously different' aspects as one goddess with a consistent mode of operation.

No detailed study of the connections between Artemis and the *lygos* or *agnos castus* exists, although Nilsson (1967: 487) links it to *Apankhomenê*. Detienne has investigated the uses of the plant at a festival of Demeter, the Thesmophoria, where its apparently opposed associations with fertility and with chastity seem to be related to the image of the ideal *gynê*, fruitful but faithful (Detienne 1972: 153–4; 1976: 79–80; 1977: 130 n.197; 1979: 213–14), while von Staden (1992b) has covered the broad picture of the uses of this plant in Greek culture.

Calame (1977: 285–9) isolated three possible connections between the *agnos* and Artemis. First, Artemis is associated with the plant world; not just with wild trees, as Farnell (1896: 429) supposed, but also with cultivated trees. Near the sanctuary of Artemis Kalliste in Arkadia were many trees, *akarpa* and *hêmera* (Pausanias 8.35.8): in human terms, both *parthenoi* who bear no fruit,[21] and tamed *gynaikes*, are under the protection of Artemis. Secondly, both plant and goddess are associated with wet and marshy areas (Farnell 1896: 427–8; Motte 1973: 93 ff.; Calame 1977: 262). This in turn links both to women, regarded in Hippocratic terms as 'wetter' than men.

Finally, and most importantly here, Calame considers the medical qualities of the *agnos*, which reduces sexual desire, but encourages menstruation and lactation. In the Hippocratic texts – which Calame does not use – these opposite qualities appear even more clearly. Outside the gynaecological texts, it is used to reduce inflammation (*Ulc.* 11, Loeb VIII, 352; *Aff.* 38, Loeb V, 60), because it is seen as being colder than the wound or sore being treated. The wide range of ingredients in Hippocratic gynaecology also includes the *agnos*, used as an astringent in a severe flux (*DW* 2.192, L 8.374; *NW* 32, L 7.356), to encourage conception (1.75, L 8.162), to bring on birth in an unusually long labour (1.77, L 8.172) and to expel the afterbirth (1.46, L 8.106; 1.78, L 8.184). The last two uses, where the *agnos* expels, are supported by other texts which say that it drives away snakes and acts as an abortifacient (Eust. in *Od.* 1639.1–5; Moïssidés 1922: 135), while the first two suggest that it can also encourage retention. The expulsive and retentive faculties cannot simply be reduced to the part of the plant used; the leaves both stop a flow of blood and expel the afterbirth. Instead, I would suggest that the dual function of the *agnos* mirrors that of the womb, which both retains (male seed, a foetus, and sometimes blood which should be expelled) and expels (a child, menstrual blood, and the lochia).

Calame (1977: 289) suggests that when young boys were beaten until they bled at the altar of Artemis Orthia the intention was to stimulate the forces of growth; he then argues that girls may have similarly been consecrated to Artemis at menarche, so that, for them, Lygodesma implied the stimulation of the menses. Such a conjecture, while consonant with the suggestions I have already made, concentrates on only one side of the *agnos*, thus detracting from the dual mode of operation of both plant and goddess. The *agnos* as repressive astringent corresponds to the strangled *parthenos* Artemis and to the *parthenos* whose *stoma* is closed so that her menses cannot flow out: the *agnos* that promotes menstruation to the Artemis of *On the Diseases of Virgins* and to Artemis who releases. The epithet Lygodesma makes explicit the parallel between the *agnos* in the plant code[22] and Artemis in the schema of deities concerned with women; Artemis is bound with this plant because she is eternally a *parthenos* but encourages sexual bloodshed at the appropriate time in other women.

The analogy can be taken further. The strength and flexibility of the *agnos*/*lygos* make it ideal for use in bonds, thongs and ropes, but these uses also recall the role of the girdle in a woman's life. Artemis is both bound with the *lygos* and releaser of the girdle, spanning the two temporal aspects of 'woman': strangled, non-bleeding *parthenos* and released, bleeding *gynê*.[23] Yet although she is concerned with the transitions between them, she herself stays firmly on one side. She who sheds the blood of others is 'strangled': she who releases others is 'bound'.

This suggests that the problem of *On the Diseases of Virgins* is a category problem. Because the Greeks separate out the category 'woman' into an undisciplined threat to social order versus a tamed, reproductive *gynê*, puberty becomes problematic. It makes it obvious that the two are really one and the same: the reproductive *gynê* used to be a wild *parthenos*, and this raises the fear that she may become one again. The *parthenos* is supposedly ignorant of 'the works of golden Aphrodite' (Hes. *Erga* 521), yet she whispers about love (Hes. *Th.* 205) and is highly attractive to men (Aesch. *Suppl.* 1003–5; Ar. *HA* 581b11–21; Loraux 1978: 50; Calame 1977: 189, 256). It is, logically, impossible to make the *parthenos* wholly asexual, because every *parthenos* – other than the divine *parthenoi* – is a potential *gynê*. Every *gynê* was also once a *parthenos*, and may return to the infertility of that category if struck by disease. The two terms thus drift back towards their original fusion in the ambiguous term 'woman'. The girls in the text identify with the wrong image of Artemis, who spans both categories while remaining firmly in one rather than the other. The doctor, trying to claim superiority, also separates out his own cure as entirely different from that recommended by the 'deceitful' diviners. Yet both groups of healers want to initiate the sequence of bleedings which will bring the *parthenos* to maturity: if she follows the advice of the doctor, she will still dedicate objects to Artemis on marriage, at defloration and at childbirth.

The menstrual sacrifice

In this discussion of menarche, I have noted that the comparison is drawn between menstruation and sacrificial bloodshed. What does such an analogy imply? Robert Parker (1983: 100) pointed out that many societies see menstruation as pollution; he cites material from New Guinea, as well as from Mediterranean anthropology, linking women's status to menstruation making them inferior or dangerous. But, he notes, although the Greeks had similar ideas about women, they did not fear menstrual blood. Only late sacred laws of non-Greek cults include purity from contact with menstrual blood as a condition for entering the sanctuary (1983: 101–2). Parker speculates that menstruation could be seen as so very 'secret and shaming' that it was not even mentionable in a sacred law. Yet medical writers link menstrual blood to sacrificial blood, which is 'public' blood displayed as part of the essential maintenance of normal human relations between the human and the divine.

Analogy is a well-documented aspect of ancient medicine (Lonie 1981: 77–86; Lloyd 1966). In his study of Celsus' construction of a female body in the Latin language, von Staden showed the continued importance of blood in medical writers' descriptions of women's healthy and sick bodies; women are expected to bleed more than men undergoing the same surgical procedure ('there is no need to be frightened if more blood flows from a woman', Celsus, *Med.* 7.26, 4) and when suppressed menstrual blood erupts through an abscess, 'the bloodier the better' (2.8, 7; von Staden 1991a: 274). But in the analogies by which he describes female anatomy, Celsus – in contrast to the Hippocratics – consistently uses associations which suggest 'impurity and . . . the aesthetically disagreeable' (von Staden 1991a: 279). For example, he draws analogies between the vagina and the male anus (*Med.* 6.18, 9A; cf. 7.26, 4); between a woman's breasts or nipples, and nasal polyps (6.8, 2A); and between the labia, and the edges of a wound or ulcer (von Staden 1991a: 279).

This approach to Celsus suggests the importance of the analogies chosen by medical writers. Should we see the Hippocratic physiological analogy between menstrual and sacrificial blood as no more than an example of the excellent powers of observation and description exhibited by the ideal – or idealised – Hippocratic doctor, appropriate because it encapsulates certain key empirical features of menstrual and other bleeding? I will instead argue that the sacrificial analogy provides further evidence of the extent to which ancient gynaecology in general carries cultural values.[24]

In what contexts does the sacrificial analogy appear? The general description of normal menstruation in *Diseases of Women* 1.6 (L 8.30) states that, in a healthy woman, 'the blood flows like that of a sacrificed victim' (*chôreei de haima hoion apo hiereiou*)[25] and it clots quickly. This is the opposite view to that taken in Victorian gynaecology where, as mentioned in the Introduction, the distinguishing feature of menstrual blood was that it did *not* coagulate.[26] Lonie (1981: 196) comments on such analogies: 'Sacrificial animals are of course in prime condition, and their blood is of a good colour and coagulates rapidly.' The type of bleeding which is meant here is further explained by the text *On the Nature of Man* 6 (Loeb IV, 18). This refers to those who think blood is the spirit (*psychê*) of mankind; in support of this, they point to the amount of blood lost by those who have had their throats cut (*aposphazomenoi*), in whom 'the blood first runs hottest and most red, then flows with more phlegm and bile'. The context here is explicitly human; the meaning is therefore not 'those who have been sacrificed' but simply those killed by having their throats cut. However, as this is also the normal way of collecting blood in sacrifice, it is valid to use the passage to illustrate the type of bleeding expected in sacrificial victims. Aristotle may also be thinking of the sacrificial context when he says that the blood of a bull clots the most quickly (*PA* 651a4–5). To bleed like a sacrificed victim is thus to lose hot, red and quickly-clotting blood. The idea that menstrual blood is humorally 'hot' and 'wet' is shared by the philosopher Empedokles (DK 31 A 81.4), the Hippocratic corpus (*DW* 1.1, L 8.12; 3.217, L 8.418) and Aristotle (*PA* 648a31). Aristotle also uses an expression which distances female bleeding from the sacrificial process, but continues to link it with animal slaughter: a young girl's menstrual blood is *hoion neosphakteon*, 'like that of a freshly-slaughtered beast' (*HA* 581b1–2; cf. Detienne 1979: 213; Sissa 1983: 85). Byl (1980: 53) takes this passage as evidence of Aristotle's close knowledge of the gynaecological sections of the Hippocratic corpus, but it could instead be read as implying that this was a common analogy in the Greek world. It is also used in medicine after the classical period, but there it has lost its exclusive link with normal female blood loss: Aretaeus 2.11 (CMG 2.34) says death following haemorrhage in women is 'like in a slaughtered beast', *hokoion ti en zôôi sphagê*.

Diseases of Women 1.6 is not however the only Hippocratic text which uses such an analogy. In *Diseases of Women* 1.72 (L 8.152), and the related *On the Nature of the Child* 18 (L 7.502), identical and all but identical wording is applied to the normal lochia. Lloyd-Jones (1983: 99) notes that 'the ancients did not always clearly distinguish blood from amniotic fluid' (cf. Strathern 1972: 166–7). This application of a distinction made in our medical knowledge to the ancient world is somewhat misleading; indeed, far from even trying to draw a 'clear' distinction, the Hippocratics developed theories to explain why the two fluids are identical. By using the same analogy for menses and lochia, they supported their belief that the discharge after childbirth is in fact composed of menstrual blood. Aristotle says that the foetus absorbs most of the excess blood which a woman produces as part of her 'wet' physiology (*GA* 775b11–14); the Hippocratic writers believed that, in the later stages of pregnancy, the foetus consumes all the excess blood which would normally be evacuated in regular menstruation. In the first weeks of pregnancy, when the foetus is very small, there is rather more blood than it can use; that which is surplus to its needs is stored, coming out as the lochia after the womb has been opened by childbirth (Lonie 1981: 170, 192). If a pregnant woman menstruates, this is a sign that her foetus will not be healthy (*Aph*. 5.60, Loeb IV, 174). This theory can also be used to account for *Diseases of Women* 2.113 (L 8. 242), in which a pathological red flux is described as *hoion haima neosphageos*, 'like the blood of a freshly-slaughtered beast'. This flux occurs when the foetus has decayed and has not come out; that is, when a discharge formed of the normal stored menstrual blood of the first weeks of pregnancy flows out but, because the foetus has not been born, it is not appropriate to describe this blood as lochia, 'of childbirth'. As there is no birth, the analogy is not with a specifically sacrificial animal, *hiereion*, but simply with a slaughtered beast.

Other Hippocratic descriptions of women's body fluids may seem comparable to the sacrificial analogy. For example, a dangerous discharge is 'like the juice of roasted meat' (*DW* 2.115, L 8. 248); abnormal lochia are 'like water in which bloody meat has been washed' and do not clot (*DW* 1.30, L 8.74) and, supporting the theory that lochial blood is only unused menstrual blood, abnormal menses can be described in almost identical terms (*DW* 1.61, L 8.124). These descriptions of lochia, menses and pathological discharges could be read as support for the proposal that the sacrificial analogy requires no further explanation; sacrifice, like the preparation and cooking of meat, is merely an aspect of ancient life in which blood is naturally encountered.

However, although there are good empirical reasons why sacrifice and cooking should be sources of descriptive analogies for types of blood flow, two important points should be noted. First, at a conceptual level, in classical Greece there are culturally specific connections between sacrifice, cooking and medicine, noted by Vegetti (1979) and Berthiaume (1982), which reinforce such analogies. Sacrifice and cooking are closely related because the *mageiros* acts not only as sacrificer but also as butcher and cook (Detienne 1979: 207; Annoni and Barras 1993: 192–3); the sacrificial victim becomes the butcher's meat (Casabona 1966: 32–3; Vernant 1979: 114) and the same vocabulary applies both to killing in sacrifice and to killing for consumption. However, as Osborne (1993: 394–5 n.11) has demonstrated, it is misleading for Detienne to argue from this connection between sacrifice and cooking that the *only* animals available for consumption were sacrificial victims; in addition to animals killed at altars in the course of religious activities, some animals were killed by butchers in their shops, this act being accompanied by only 'minimal ritual'. Another pair, medicine and cooking, are related not only through some doctors' concerns with diet in general, but also through texts in which the doctor takes on the role of the cook, advising on the method of preparation of the foods which he recommends (e.g. *DW* 2.115, L 8. 250; Vegetti 1979: 24–5). Of most interest for the present argument are medicine and sacrifice; medical knowledge of anatomy depends directly on sacrificial procedure (above, pp. 37–8). The shift from the Hippocratic 'the blood flows like that of a sacrificed victim' to Aristotle's 'like that of a freshly-slaughtered beast' may reflect a deliberate distancing from the act of sacrifice as medicine seeks to separate itself from its sacrificial roots.

Second, and more importantly here, although sacrificial blood may appear to be an obvious empirical source of analogies with any bleeding from the human body, it is significant that, like the medical use of excrement as therapy (von Staden 1992a), comparisons of this kind are restricted to the gynaecological treatises (Duminil 1983: 207–8). In addition, in the Hippocratic texts only two, closely related, kinds of bleeding are analogous to sacrifice: menstrual/lochial bleeding. These are one and the same substance, the production and loss of which derives from woman's distinctive loose-textured and absorbent flesh.

Some general remarks on the significance of such blood are in order here. Blood is important to the Greeks' definition of humanity in a number of ways. First, from Homer onwards, the presence of blood in the body acts to separate human from divine; the gods, because they do not eat the products of the agricultural cycle, *sitos*, are bloodless and immortal, but people consume *sitos*, have blood in their bodies, and are mortal (*Il.* 5.339–42). Blood is thus distinctive to mortals, and bound up with the conditions of life of the present day (King 1986a). Second, as we have seen, within the category of 'mortal men' the production and loss of excess blood can distinguish men from women. Women's bodies are wet and spongy, and need to evacuate excess fluid at regular intervals; amenorrhoea is almost always seen as pathological, and the writers aim to achieve regular and heavy menstrual loss in their patients. The Hippocratic texts lead towards a definition of the *gynê*, the mature childbearing married woman, as she who bleeds. A third use of blood in creating categories involves emphasis on the differences between the flesh of the immature girl who does not yet bleed – the *parthenos* – and the *gynê* who does (*DW* 1.1, L 8.10–14; *SF* 34, L 8.504–6; *Glands* 16, Loeb VIII, 124).

I would therefore suggest that the meaning of the analogy between menstrual/lochial and sacrificial blood should be pursued further, into ideas about gender and society which can be found outside medical sources; in particular, it lies in the overlapping contexts provided by more general work on the role of sacrifice in ancient Greek models of the world, myths about the origin and nature of woman, and a fragment of a pre-Socratic philosopher. This unlikely collection of sources allows us to reconstruct an important aspect of Greek ways of thinking about women.

There has been much interest in recent decades in the role of animal sacrifice in ancient Greek thought and practice (Detienne and Vernant 1979; Loraux 1981a; Étienne and Le Dinahet 1991). The selection of animal sacrifice as a practice requiring interpretation and understanding relates to its 'otherness' in a post-Christian society in which it is perceived as a messy, noisy intrusion into the 'glory that was Greece'. The accounts of its origin given in myth, and enacted in ritual, place it as a central institution of society, part of the divinely ordained present order along with the connected institutions of agricultural labour, marriage and sexual reproduction. The first animal sacrifice, that of the ox by Prometheus at Mekone (Hesiod, *Th.* 535ff.), is linked in a sequence of transgression and punishment to the creation of the first woman, Pandora (Vernant 1974: 177–94; Loraux 1978). Sacrifice serves to re-establish communication with the gods, and to set humanity apart from the beasts (since a beast is taken as victim); but it also acts as a bitter reminder of a lost age when men and gods dined together (since now gods receive certain parts of the sacrifice, and men others) (Hesiod, *Th.* 535–41 and fr.1 MW; Detienne 1972: ch.2; 1977: ch.3; Vernant 1974; 1979: 43–4). Sacrifice makes other ideological statements; for example, about the separation of male and female spheres of action. Detienne (1979: 186–8) argued that women were excluded at a number of levels, since the act of sacrifice could only be performed by a man, and women normally participated only in the 'outer circle' of the distribution of meat, and then only by virtue of their status as wives or daughters of male citizens. Responding to these claims, Osborne (1993) challenged Detienne's implicit assumption of different 'levels' of participation in sacrifice, with killing and consuming the beast being singled out as the two most important parts; he points out that not only could women pay for the victim and pray over it, but also the verb *thuein*, 'to sacrifice', could be used for the whole of the ceremony (1993: 400–1). Osborne also showed that the picture of women's 'normal' exclusion is not supported by epigraphic evidence; sacred laws point to inclusion as the norm in many cults, since 'cases of specific exclusion of women are much more numerous than specific inclusions' (1993: 397). Why should it be necessary to specify exclusion, unless inclusion was normally expected?

Greek women were thus involved in many of the stages which constitute an act of animal sacrifice, including the parts occurring after their ritual cry, the *ololygê*; here, however, my interest lies in their exclusion from one action, that of shedding blood. To pick up the reciprocal relationship between men's role in war and women's role in childbirth investigated by Nicole Loraux (1981b) and found as an expression of gender difference in many simple societies (cf. Rosaldo and Atkinson 1975: 43, 69), men shed the blood of others: women naturally bleed from their own bodies. Osborne argues that the application here of any such 'women bleed: men shed blood' division should logically mean that ancient Greek women would be excluded from all 'the bloody bits of sacrifice . . . at least from menarche to menopause' (1993: 397), but it is neither historically correct nor logically necessary to go this far. I would argue that their exclusion from this act, within the context of their general inclusion in sacrifice, forms part of a wider system of classification of male and female, in which women do not perform culturally significant acts which involve shedding the blood of others (war, sacrifice, butchery), and that it can be extended to the way in which female anatomy and physiology are said to work.

In his discussion of the reluctance to perform human dissection in ancient Greek science, von Staden (1992d) argued that cultural attitudes to the skin played an important role alongside beliefs concerning the pollution incurred by contact with a corpse. Central here are the 'cultural reverberations' (1992d: 225) raised by the act of cutting. The Greeks asserted the inviolability of the skin, whether animal or human; hence the preservation and, often, the subsequent public display of the skin of a sacrificed beast. The unity of the skin may represent the cohesion of the community which performs the act of sacrifice (1992d: 228). The earliest uses of *temnein*, 'to cut', occur in the context of sacrifice performed to accompany a sacred oath; the person making the oath cuts hairs from the victim's head, and shares these among those present. The oath is finally sealed by the cutting of the victim's throat. Von Staden notes that the oath (*horkos*), linked since antiquity with the sense of 'enclosure' or 'boundary' (*herkos*), involves violation of another boundary; to make an oath, to create a boundary, one violates the skin boundary of the sacrificed beast (1992d: 230). 'Cutting' is thus seen as acceptable only to create new boundaries or to resolve a crisis, whether this is one threatening the state or an individual body. In the first case, the violence of war may ensue: in the second, surgical cutting for therapeutic purposes (1992d: 230 and n.44). On this reading, in which cutting the skin is seen as violent and invasive, dissection became unthinkable because it lacked the legitimation of crisis.

Menstrual/lochial bleeding is anomalous because it occurs without the need to cut: no boundaries are violated. In this, it forms a strong contrast with the act of sacrifice. The menstrual/sacrificial analogy draws not on the significance of cutting but on other aspects of sacrificial practice, related to the role of women as victims and to the use of a bowl to collect blood.

Gynaecological imagery of woman as sacrificial victim recalls Hesiod's descriptions of the first woman, Pandora. Hesiod describes Pandora's preparation for mankind in terms of a *parthenos* being made ready for marriage (*Erga* 63, 71; *Th.* 572; Vernant 1974: 184–5; Pucci 1977: 97). In myth and tragedy it is most commonly a *parthenos* of the age for marriage, rather than a mature, married and childbearing *gynê*, who becomes the sacrifice. Many elements of the Greek wedding evoke the preparation of a beast for sacrifice; for example cutting hair, washing, giving a sign of consent and wearing a garland (Segal 1975; Foley 1982), elements which are found in other rites of passage, including the funeral (Redfield 1982; Jenkins 1983). In *Iliad* 10.293, and in *Odyssey* 3.382–4 and 430–63, the heifer chosen for sacrifice is untamed, *admês*, and unyoked by any man – language used typically of the Greek *parthenos* (Kahn 1973: 111–12; Burkert 1966: 106; Loraux 1981a: 619) – with horns overlaid with gold. Pandora, created like a *parthenos*, is made to appear even more attractive, with gold necklaces placed on her by Peitho and the Charites (*Erga* 73–4) or crowned with gold by Hephaistos (*Th.* 578). It is implied that the bride is being prepared to be a 'sacrificial victim'; that is, to shed her blood. Blood and sacrifice thus separate humans from gods, and men from women. Not only does the first woman appear in the world as a direct result of the circumstances of the first sacrifice; she herself recalls the sacrificed ox.

This cultural imagery of the female body may provide a background for fragment 70 of the work of the philosopher Empedokles, given by Rufus and Pollux. Rufus writes, 'The foetus is enclosed in a thin, soft covering: Empedokles calls this "amnion"' (229 p. 166.11 Daremberg = DK 31 B 70; cf. Pollux *Onom.* 2.223 = PPF fr.70); he uses this fragment to explain a title given to Eileithyia, the goddess of childbirth. She is known as 'Amnias', he says, not because of 'the harbour in Crete' (Amnisos), but because of

Empedokles' name for the foetal sac.[27] Two other possible reasons why Empedokles may have used *amnion* for this covering were mentioned by Charles Singer in an article explaining the origin of selected anatomical terms to a medical audience. He wrote,

> Galen and his older contemporary, Rufus of Ephesus (*fl. c.* AD 150), have the form *amnios*. This I believe to be more correct, though the dictionary maker, Julius Pollux . . . prefers *amnion*. *Amnion* would mean a little lamb (diminutive of *amnos*), or else a vessel to hold the blood of a sacrificial victim. *Both are irrelevant to the nature and function of the amnion*.
>
> (Singer 1959: 3; my italics)

Is Singer's rejection of these meanings entirely warranted? The gynaecological use of sacrificial imagery would, I suggest, support either or both of them. The fragment of Empedokles is the earliest known reference to either *amnios* or *amnion* in a medical context; however, in Homer *amnion* occurs with an apparently different meaning, to which Singer refers. In both Homeric and classical blood sacrifice, an essential part of the equipment is the receptacle into which the blood of the animal is directed (Durand 1979a: 137–9; 1979b: 176–9). The beast is knocked senseless; as it falls women, who may be present but may not kill the beast, raise the ritual cry (Aesch. *Seven against Thebes* 230–2; Detienne 1979: 207; Berthiaume 1982: 30–1). While others hold its head above the ground, an officiating priest then cuts the victim's throat and collects the blood. Finally, the animal is butchered according to strict rules, and the blood is poured over the altar; it is not clear which of these last two acts is chronologically prior (Burkert 1966: 108). Rudhardt (1958: 292; cf. 254–5 and 259–62) emphasises that the collection of the blood is in no way an incidental by-product of the sacrificial process, but is an essential part: 'The blood must flow: the spurt is directed: it is carefully collected.'

The bowl used in classical blood sacrifice is called the *sphageion* (Aristoph. *Thesm*. 754–55; Eur. *IT* 335; Eur. *Elec*. 800), but the Homeric word is *amnion* (*Od*. 3.444). In his commentary on this passage of the *Odyssey*, the twelfth-century scholar Eustathius discusses the etymology of *amnion*, saying, 'The Cretans call the *angeion* in which the blood of sacrificed victims is collected an *amnion*' (1476.35ff.). He then tries to link *haima*, 'blood', and *amnion*; an etymology also favoured by the twelfth-century lexicon, the *Etymologicum Magnum*. Folk etymologies are a valuable source for discovering what connections writers in the ancient world found both possible and plausible; the desire to link *haima* and *amnion* underlines the point that the function of the sacrificial bowl was to collect the blood. Furthermore, it seems that *amnion* 'bowl' was just as subject to folk etymologies as was *amnion* 'membrane', while the Cretan connection with a cult at Amnisos could be extended to the more obviously sacrificial meaning of *amnion*.

Another response to *amnion* is to link it to *amnos*, 'lamb'. In his remarks on fragment 70, Diels considers that Empedokles was referring to sheepskin, *amneion*, rather than to *amnion*, 'little lamb' (cf. Zafiropulo 1953: 268–9); this is supported by Rufus' own description of the membrane as finely textured and soft. Pollux specifies that Empedokles used this term for the inner membrane – the outer being the *chorion* – because of its delicacy and softness. These descriptions recall Hippocratic gynaecological theories of female flesh in general as soft and spongy, with a capacity to absorb fluid which makes it directly analogous to wool or sheepskin. Chantraine finds no real etymological connection between the *amnos* group and *amnion* as sacrificial bowl; the true root of *amnion* as sacrificial bowl is, according to both Chantraine and Frisk, *amaô* or *amaomai*, meaning 'to collect'.

'Bowl' and 'lamb' may not be linguistically related, but this does not prevent popular etymology from connecting them with the *amnion*. The sacrificial bowl 'collects' blood; so does the foetal membrane, since during pregnancy blood is attracted to the womb to nourish the foetus. *On the Nature of the Child* 16 (L 7.496) describes how the membranes (here called *hymenes*) around the foetus collect blood as the foetus draws it (*helkei*) from all over the body (*NC* 15, L 7.494); in his commentary on these passages, Lonie (1981: 176) recalls the Empedoklean use of *amnion* and suggests that the function of the membranes may be regarded as analogous to that of the bowl into which the blood of a sacrificed beast is directed. When Hunain ibn Ishaq edited a Syriac translation of Galen's work *On Anatomical Procedures* in the mid-ninth century, comparing it with three Greek manuscripts which have subsequently been lost, he may have added to Galen's description of the *amnion* as 'the covering which envelops and contains the embryo' a note referring to 'a sacrificial animal offering its blood into the bowl, or "*amnion*"'; alternatively, he may have found this reference to the sacrificial bowl in one of the lost Greek manuscripts of book 12.[28]

There is thus a possible functional analogy between *amnion* as sacrificial bowl and *amnion* as foetal membrane, based on the collection of blood. Not only is menstrual/lochial blood like that of a sacrificed beast; inside the woman is an anatomical 'sacrificial bowl' which receives this blood.

It would therefore appear that Singer is too hasty in rejecting the 'bowl' and 'lamb' connections of Empedokles' fragment 70. There may be no real etymological link between *amnion*, 'sacrificial bowl', and *amnos*, 'lamb', but that need not mean that Empedokles' term for the inner foetal membrane should be restricted in meaning to only one of these words. I would suggest that he calls the membrane *amnion* primarily because it is a bowl to collect and pour out menstrual blood and that the name is particularly appropriate in view of the Hippocratic writers' readiness to see menstrual/lochial blood as analogous to that of the sacrificed beast. At the same time, however, he may be alluding to *amneion*, 'sheepskin', and thus to ideas of the female body being more absorbent than the male body. His name for the membrane could thus cover both of the ways in which the membranes of the womb work: they *absorb* blood (as sheepskin absorbs fluids) and *pour out* blood (as sacrificial blood is poured out on the altar).

It is common to emphasise the debt owed to Empedokles by Hippocratic writers (e.g. Jouanna 1961; Longrigg 1993: 90–2), while Geoffrey Lloyd has shown that

> The search for likenesses between different objects, phenomena or processes is a recurrent feature of Empedocles' physical and biological inquiries. Occasionally he constructed elaborate analogies in his attempts to throw light on obscure natural phenomena . . . many of his metaphors too seem to have a similar underlying purpose.
>
> (1966: 366)

Even so, is the double analogy which I am proposing too 'elaborate' for Empedokles? A glance at another medical fragment, DK 31 B68, suggests that this it is not. Discussing blood in the pregnant female body, Empedokles says, 'On the tenth day of the eighth month it became *puon leukon*.' The passage of Aristotle within which this fragment is preserved (*GA* 777a7 ff.) sets it in the context of ancient debates about the relations between blood, milk and semen (Longrigg 1985; 1993: 74). Aristotle's theory of concoction suggests that each fluid is a more thoroughly 'cooked' version of the last; the female body is too cold to cook menstrual blood into semen (*PA* 650a8 ff.; *GA* 774a1). Aristotle criticises Empedokles for suggesting that milk is formed at a particular point in pregnancy, not by internal 'cooking', but by *de*composition of blood. In so doing Empedokles calls milk white 'pus' (*púon*), but also glances at *puós*, the word for the first milk after birth, colostrum (Lloyd 1987: 184).

Lloyd (1983: 149–67) has investigated the relationship between popular and scientific vocabulary in the origin and development of Greek anatomical terminology, showing that newly discovered parts were frequently named by analogy with other objects; Vivian Nutton (1985c: 31–2), writing on Herophilos of Alexandria, has demonstrated how this particular anatomist 'drew his coinages for his new discoveries from everyday life'. I would suggest that *amnion* provides an excellent early example of the popular associations underlying a technical usage. When it is set beside the wider medical analogy between menstrual/lochial and sacrificial blood, it can be seen to represent far more than the practical debt owed by medical knowledge to sacrificial procedure. It is only menstrual/lochial blood which is analogous to the blood of a sacrificed beast, because only woman, by her origin and nature, is comparable to the first sacrificial victim. She bleeds, and her blood is evidence of the fundamentally different quality of her flesh, reminding us that she is unlike man in her creation and her structure. Both Empedokles' use of *amnion* and the sacrificial analogy rely on such images, making reference both to the function of the membranes of the womb in collecting the 'sacrificial' blood, and to the absorbent flesh which is the origin of that blood. In the present age, in which man must work in the fields, sacrifice to the gods and reproduce sexually, 'the blood must flow' in sacrifice (Rudhardt 1958: 292) as, for women, in all cases other than immaturity, pregnancy and old age, 'if the menses do not flow the bodies of women become sick' (*Gen.* 4, L 7.476; cf. *DW* 1.1, L 8.14, and Ar. *GA* 775b8–9). Dorothy McLaren (1975) has argued that women's diaries in the early modern period demonstrate that a menstrual period could be welcomed as a blessing, showing a woman that she still remained fertile. For an ancient Greek woman, 'health' is to bleed like a sacrificial victim; but this analogy proposed that menstruation was not only a sign of health, but also something as fundamental as animal sacrifice to the maintenance of the present order.

5

ASKLEPIOS AND WOMEN'S HEALING

In the previous chapter, some of the connections between Hippocratic medicine and religion were explored. I argued that the apparent rivalry between the Hippocratics and Artemis over the treatment of girls who failed to menstruate when expected can mislead us into seeing religion and medicine as opposed, when in fact they agreed on the place of women's bleeding in the proper ordering of the world. Like sacrificial ritual, Hippocratic gynaecology is about ensuring blood is shed at the proper times and in the proper ways. Menarche, the point at which women's bloodshed begins, is problematic. Although it provides visible evidence of the internal changes comprising puberty, it does not in itself constitute maturity, but is only the beginning of a series of bleedings that define womanhood. By admitting that a non-bleeding, 'strangled' and 'bound' *parthenos* will become a woman, menarche calls up its shadow: the anxiety that an apparently mature woman may cease to bleed, losing her reproductive capacity. The discussion of *On the Diseases of Virgins* suggested further ways in which medicine shared its models with other aspects of Greek culture; these include the symbolism of plants, important to ancient pharmacology, which will be discussed in more detail in the next two chapters.

But the criticism of the cult of Artemis in *On the Diseases of Virgins* reminds us above all that, in the fifth and fourth centuries BC, Hippocratic medicine coexisted with religious claims to heal. In this chapter I will compare the models by which the traditional Hippocratic research programme has approached religious healing with alternative models drawn from contemporary societies in which religious and secular healing coexist. The Greek myth of Prometheus and Pandora accounts for the presence of diseases in the world in terms of the revenge taken by Zeus on Prometheus after the latter attempted to trick him into taking the inferior portion of a sacrificed ox, a story discussed in Chapter 1, p. 27. Taking the proffered portion, Zeus planned his revenge. After Prometheus had stolen fire from the gods to give to the mortal men whose helper he traditionally was, Zeus caused the creation of the first woman, Pandora. Moulded by all the gods into the deceptive form of a marriageable virgin containing 'the mind of a bitch' and an insatiable *gastêr*, she was sent to earth, where she opened the jar containing all the evils the world now knows (Hes. *Erga* 102): pain, grief, old age and disease. Disease therefore goes back to Pandora; to Prometheus, whose trickery caused the anger of Zeus; and to Epimetheus, the foolish man who accepted her as a gift.

In the ancient world, religious healing could be the 'temple medicine' which was predominantly, although not exclusively, associated with the god Asklepios; in the fourth century BC, when many of the Hippocratic medical treatises were composed, around 200 temples of Asklepios were founded in Greece. But many other gods and local heroes had healing, or the promotion of health,[1] among their functions; as we have seen, Artemis was associated with women's diseases, difficult childbirth, and the transition to womanhood, while dedications of models of the breasts and uterus at shrines of Asklepios indicate an interest which extended to women's reproductive functions.[2] The normal mode of healing in these cults was through offerings made at a local shrine; in the case of Artemis, women offered articles of clothing. At Brauron and in Athens, women dedicated these to Artemis Brauronia (Linders 1972).

The use of cross-cultural comparisons to suggest possible ways in which religion and medicine could have interacted in the ancient world does not mean that we must necessarily see ancient patients as being like modern patients in their assessment of the options available to them. For example, the Porters have argued that patients in the long eighteenth century were highly demanding, choosing the practitioners they wanted, discussing their treatment, and carrying out self-treatment. The dominant ethos, based on the Protestant work ethic and Locke's individualism, was 'busy, energetic, and practical' (Porter 1989: 31; Porter and Porter 1989: 8). This model of the individual patient choosing within the medical marketplace is open to criticism as the product of the Thatcherite England of the late 1980s when the Porters were writing. It cannot be applied to the ancient world, far from the individualism of Thatcherite economics, but it does have the value of shifting our focus away from the Hippocratic healers whose written theories and remedies survive, making us more aware of the alternatives – some of them 'religious' – available to patients (Nutton 1995a: 13). Anthropological work on less-developed societies today points out that most episodes of sickness are caused by infectious or parasitic diseases, poor nutrition or injury, and that most such episodes are self-limiting. In this sense, the intervention chosen – whether it be medical or religious – makes little, if any, difference to the outcome but, from the patient's point of view, it may feel helpful to 'play all reasonable options against unwanted physical, social, and economic outcomes' (A. Young 1980: 105).

Even at the limited level of comparison with which I am operating here, one valuable point of difference emerges immediately. The 'medical' model in modern anthropological studies is almost always taken to be Western bio-medicine, representing the imported medicine of the former colonial powers. Medicine which comes from 'outside' can be thought to have power simply because of its novelty (Lingo 1986: 584; G. Lewis 1993: 192; van der Geest *et al.* 1996: 169), so that – particularly in the gynaecological texts – the Hippocratics often specify substances from distant countries such as Ethiopia (Byl 1995: 230–1). In the classical world it was not the 'medical' model of the Hippocratics, but the 'religious' model of Asklepios which was exported to many other parts of Greece and, in 291 BC, to Rome. Associated by Homer with the northern Greek area of Thessaly, Asklepios does not appear to have been the object of worship at Epidauros until the early fifth century BC, when he replaced an earlier healing deity (Homer, *Il.* 2.729–32; see Garland 1992: 116–18). The geographer Strabo, however, claimed that Asklepios' 'oldest and most famous sanctuary' was at Trikka in Thessaly (*Geog.* 9.5.17). It remains far from clear whether Epidauros or Trikka was the first sanctuary, but when other cities decided to import the cult it was to Epidauros that they sent for sacred objects. Athens established a sanctuary of the god in 420 BC, perhaps as a result of the plague's effects on Attica, or because of the enthusiasm of an Epidaurian who happened to be resident in Athens (Garland 1992: 116–35; Parker 1996: 175–85; Aleshire 1989). Comparing the models of healing available, the structural position of Hippocrates in relation to Asklepios was therefore not like that of Western biomedicine in relation to traditional healing systems in non-Western societies; Hippocratic medicine did not come from 'outside' and it did not carry the values of the colonial powers as Western biomedicine now does.

In 1983 the ancient historian Robert Parker wrote that 'A scholarly account of Greek healing gods in general seems not to exist' (1983: 248 n.70). With the exception of Graf (1992) that remains the case. Among the many healing gods of the ancient world, Asklepios appears as an exception both because of his cult's promotion as an 'international' one (Burford 1969: 15) and because of the role of the 'divine dream' experienced by the patient at the sanctuary. If, in pre-modern times, 'the meaning of dreams were shaped by their dreamers' (Fissell 1992: 91), what does this imply for Asklepian temple dreams? The dream interpretations given in the second century AD by Artemidoros show clearly that, by then, ancient dreams were understood in terms of a culturally specific set of ideas regarding gender and power; Jack Winkler's analysis of the role of sexual intercourse in Artemidoros' *Dream Book* notes that what is important is not the act being performed, but domination and submission based on who penetrates whom. Dreaming of sex with a sheep is not 'bad', because it has no social meaning: 'If a man gains advantage over a sheep, so what?' (Winkler 1990: 39). Because the mother symbolises the earth, a dream of sleeping with one's mother is good for holders of political office, because it means keeping control of one's native land; but if mother is 'on top', it can become a 'bad' dream for a sick man to experience, not because of something intrinsic to that sexual position, but because to have earth on top of you means to be dead and buried (Artemidoros, *Oneir.* 1.79; Winkler 1990: 213–14). While some dreams (*enhypnia*) only showed the condition of the dreamer in the present, others (*oneiroi*) were the key, not to the unconscious, but to the future (Artemidoros, *Oneir.* 1.1; S.R.F. Price 1990: 366, 371; Langholf 1990: 246). Hippocratic healing also took account of dreams as potentially important signs indicating the present state of the body (e.g. *Ep.* 1.10, Loeb I, 180; von Staden 1989: 306–7; Oberhelman 1993); a dream of polluted rivers indicates bowel disturbance, and high rivers indicate an excess of blood in the body (*Regimen* 4.89, Loeb IV, 438), while the patient with a swollen liver dreams of enemy warriors and believes he is fighting them (*Regimen* 4.93, Loeb IV, 446 = *Critical Days* 3 and *Internal Affections* 48).

But Hippocratic healers believed that dreams are not always as significant as the patient fears (*Ep.* 4.57, Loeb VII, 150), and healing in Hippocratic medicine took place in the physical world of bodily fluids and material substances, in contrast to Asklepian medicine, where the patient's dreams also included the god's healing acts, achieved by surgery, drugs or touch. From the *iamata*, the inscriptions recording cures performed at the temple of Asklepios at Epidauros, we read that the god appeared in dreams to stretch out the hands of the paralysed, pour drugs into the eye to restore sight to the blind, restore the voice, tie on a headband which removed a birthmark, extract a spearhead from the jaw, operate on an abdominal abscess, and apply drugs to the head to cure baldness.[3] Many questions about the *iamata* remain unanswered. Were they written by the priests, or at least under their supervision (Edelstein and Edelstein 1945: 146–7)? Kee (1982: 122) regarded them as a form of 'preconditioning', encouraging the pilgrims to feel courage and hope, while Dillon (1994; 1997: 79) stressed their 'didactic nature', arguing that they should be understood as demonstrations to sceptics and doubters of the power of the god, and warnings to suppliants to pay what they have vowed – or expect divine punishment. Later literary accounts of Asklepios' healing methods suggest that the god sometimes gave unexpected advice, such as exercise when the patient had expected to be told to rest; this sounds like a deliberate challenge to the faith of the believer.[4]

As we saw in Chapter 3 (p. 62), earlier scholars, operating with a model of science as progress out of superstition, thought that the origin of Hippocratic medicine lay in the temples of Asklepios (e.g. Festugière 1948: vii), and saw the *iamata* as early case notes. They then envisaged a later conflict between 'the scientists of the Hippocratic period' and 'the general population . . . still close to their gods' (Veith 1965: 15–16).[5] In *Greek Rational Medicine*, Longrigg defined 'rational medicine' as 'free from magical and religious elements and based upon natural causes' (1993: 1). This definition should be challenged as misleadingly dependent on our own cultural concepts. We may not see the gods' anger as part of the 'natural world', but one could argue that the Greeks did. As post-Enlightenment beings, we separate medicine from both magic and religion, and call this liberation, or progress: the Greeks' categories were not equivalent to ours.[6]

Indeed, rather than Hippocratic medicine breaking 'free' from temple medicine, there is evidence that the dream repertoire of temple medicine copied Hippocratic and subsequent secular medicine; for example, in the late fourth century BC surgery was in vogue, and the Asklepios seen in dreams duly practised surgery (Edelstein and Edelstein 1945: 166). But, being a god, he kept ahead of the real world, performing operations superior to any on offer there. When compound drugs were fashionable, Asklepios used them too, but his were invariably more effective (Edelstein and Edelstein 1945: 167). One could argue that the successes of Hippocratic medicine actually led to an increase in the Asklepios cult, with patient expectations rising and cures for a wider range of symptoms being sought (Parker 1983: 250; Demand 1994: 92), or that Asklepios' appropriation of the symbols and prestige of Hippocratic medicine was a smart career move: as Parker puts it, 'The truest explanation for the rise of Asklepios may be that he was, as it were, in partnership with Hippocrates' (1996: 184).

Temple medicine did not present itself in opposition to Hippocratic medicine. 'There is neither competition nor enmity between the god [Asklepios] and the physician' (Temkin 1953: 216), and Asklepios was the 'friendly ally' of the doctor (Edelstein and Edelstein 1945: 139). Nor is there evidence that Greek physicians objected, in principle, to temple medicine. No Hippocratic writer criticises Asklepios – indeed, the Hippocratic oath invokes Asklepios, among other gods – and doctors were present at his temples, serving as priests themselves (von Staden 1989: 8; Nutton 1985c: 46), making individual dedications (Aleshire 1989: 65–6) or collective sacrifices to the god (Nutton 1995a: 4). There is even an example of a woman from a family of *iatroi* dedicating to Artemis at Brauron (Linders 1972 on IG^2 1517.214; Demand 1994: 90, 95). Our current construction of 'priesthood' and 'medicine' regards both as 'professions', a concept utterly alien to the ancient Mediterranean, where in some states any number of priesthoods could be held by a man who was also serving on the ruling body of his state, leading its armies, and treating the medical disorders of his family or soldiers. Those whose primary identity appears to have been 'physician', at least insofar as they practised for a fee, could be exempted from civic or military service, but there was nothing to keep them from holding priesthoods. On the few occasions when a Hippocratic text tells us what religious healers do in a particular situation, what is criticised is not the invocation of the gods as such, but the search for any cause outside the human body. In the two texts in which such criticisms are levelled at religious forms of healing, *On the Sacred Disease* and *On the Diseases of Virgins*, the cause of the distressing symptoms is seen by the Hippocratic healer as the accumulation of a bodily fluid in a vital area of the body. The cause is mechanical, so the therapy must also be mechanical, removing the blockage so that the fluid can move. In many texts the Hippocratic authors recommend the use of opposites – the dry must be made moist, the hard must be softened – which may be a deliberate distancing from the like-cures-like approach of magical therapy (Hanson, forthcoming).

Studies of the interaction between Hippocratic and temple medicine reveal how difficult it is to bracket out contemporary ideas about rationality and irrationality, order and chaos, sense and nonsense. The traditional images used in medical history to think about the relationship between Asklepios and Hippocratic medicine present them as analogous either to Lourdes and the general practitioner, or to a health spa and Harley Street. The first model concentrates on the religious element of temple medicine, taking up a narrowly post-Enlightenment view to assume the 'obvious' superiority of science over religion,[7] or distinguishing between acceptable and unacceptable manifestations of religion, as Charles Singer did when, in 1923, he stated that ancient physicians, although worshipping Asklepios, were as devoid of 'the baser theurgic elements of temple medicine . . . as a modern Catholic physician might be expected to be free from the absurdities of Lourdes' (1923: 207–8). The second, while concentrating on temple medicine as a harmless, but socially enjoyable, experience (C. Singer 1923: 224), also accepts at face value the Hippocratic healer's assertion of his personal superiority over anything else available; whereas current work, in contrast, suggests that 'The boundary between the self-acknowledged doctor and the educated layman was very narrow' (Nutton 1985c: 38). Seeing the Asklepieia, the sanctuaries of Asklepios, as health spas accords with Vitruvius' statement of the principles on which healing sanctuaries should be sited in a healthy location (*De architectura* 1.2.7), and also with the known sites of Asklepieia outside towns, although it is likely that the latter was due to a desire to separate ritual space from normal life (Graf 1992: 166–7, 198). The Roman sanctuary, on the Tiber island, may seem to us to occupy an unhealthy location, but makes sense as a way of achieving ritual separation (Edelstein and Edelstein 1945: 158). However, the health spa model removes the religious aspect entirely; here, one could argue that the position of the Greeks as our cultural ancestors encourages us to play down their religious life. A further variation removing the religious dimension was proposed by Howard Kee (1982: 136), who suggested a shift from the 'out-patient clinic' of Hellenistic Epidauros to the 'all-purpose sanatorium' of Pergamum in the second century AD.

The Edelsteins provided what remains a valuable historiographical account of modern explanations for the cures recorded for Asklepian medicine. These include seeing them as miracles (but, since they were performed by a pagan god, they must be deeds of the devil), 'natural remedies', a form of spiritual healing, or 'trickery'. A further possibility is that people were more willing to follow the treatment given because it carried the authority of the god; Galen mentions those who will obey the god, but not a doctor who gave identical advice (Edelstein and Edelstein 1945: 168–71; test. 401). After the tablets from the sanctuary of Asklepios at Epidauros were first published in 1883, the cures were seen as 'fraud': this was followed by a counter-reaction interpreting them as real cures, performed by the then fashionable methods of dream interpretation or hypnosis. As the Edelsteins put it:

> The miracle, a dish so distasteful to the modern palate, had been cooked until it became acceptable and digestible; the irrational had been worked on until it finally evaporated into nothingness; the amoral had been sifted until it had cleared off a useful and orderly substance.
>
> (Edelstein and Edelstein 1945: 144)

The historiography of responses to temple medicine thus illustrates clearly how our images of the Greeks and our relative valuations of Hippocrates and Asklepios change with our own medical preferences.

Perspectives provided by materials from the social sciences may help us to look at the relationship between Hippocratic and temple medicine not by de-sacralising temple medicine and converting it into something else,[8] nor by romanticising the priests of Asklepios as 'holistic' traditional healers, nor indeed by condemning them as quacks (Finkler 1994: 179).

All formulations to date of the relationship between Hippocratic medicine and the cult of Asklepios assume that, in some way, they were perceived by patients as 'alternatives', in which the patient had to follow one or the other independently, shifting between sectors only after one failed. In addition, recent work on women and ancient medicine assumes not only that 'women continued to have recourse to traditional medicine over Hippocratic physicians more often than men did' (Dean-Jones 1994: 35) but specifically that 'A woman facing childbirth probably looked first to the gods for assistance' (Demand 1994: 87). This assumption can be based on another, namely that Hippocratic medicine would have failed Greek women; for example, Sue Blundell argues that ancient methods of curing sterility were ineffective, so that 'Not surprisingly, some women resorted to more mystical methods in their efforts to conceive' (1995: 105). Certainly, ancient women were among those making pilgrimages to religious and healing sites, often travelling long distances by land or sea (Dillon 1997: 183 ff.), and a fifth-century AD account survives of a girl who could not be cured by the physicians and was therefore prayed for at an Asklepieion (test. 582).

But is there any evidence to suggest that women were more likely than men to look to non-Hippocratic methods of healing, or to support the assertion that Hippocratic medicine would necessarily have been assessed and then dismissed by women in the way that recent feminist work assumes? Literary and epigraphic evidence from the ancient world suggests entirely one-way traffic; it only tells us of people shifting from physicians to god but, since physicians did not encourage their patients to put up inscriptions, it would be unwise to assume that the reverse never occurred. Where patients moved, as in an inscription stating that a patient had consulted thirty-six doctors before the god, the failure of the medical sector is however stated 'in sadness rather than in anger' (Roesch 1984: 290, discussed by Nutton 1995a: 14; cf. Nutton 1985c: 47).

But how far apart were Hippocrates and Asklepios? Not only were doctors present at Asklepieia; Von Staden's recent study of the Hippocratic Oath (1996) has pointed out that the structure of this document has significant affinities with the inscription that appeared over the entrance to the healing temple of Asklepios at Epidauros. This inscription read:

> Pure (*hagnos*) must be the person who goes inside the fragrant temple,
> and purity (*hagneia*) is to think holy (*hosia*) thoughts.[9]

The Oath too links purity and holiness, in the phrase 'I shall guard my *bios* and my *technê* in a pure and holy way.' Von Staden argues that *bios* (life/livelihood) is here closer to 'manner of living', encompassing both the private and the professional life of the practitioner. 'Pure' (*hagnos*) is a religious term, meaning 'undefiled', and thus able to approach the gods. Defilement in Greek religious thought comes from contact with the physical events of birth, death and sex (Dillon 1997: 187–8). A doctor could not keep away from all these, but he could make sure that he observed the correct exclusion period afterwards to restore purity, and purified himself by washing or by fire. 'Holy' (*hosios*) means 'in a way that does not offend the gods'. The doctor is therefore stating that he will stay free from pollution and will act in a way sanctioned by the gods. Both the Epidauros inscription and the Oath suggest that purity is an internal state, but both also take it as a moral, cognitive category.

Studies of contemporary groups who have access both to traditional healers and to Western-style clinics also suggest that ancient perception of the two sectors as clear 'alternatives' is most unlikely to have been universally the case. Indeed, practitioners themselves may combine sectors, so that a medical officer in a rural Indian health centre, qualified only in traditional Ayurvedic medicine, 'almost exclusively gave allopathic medicine to his patients' (Kamat 1995: 89). As for patients, they often begin in the 'popular' or lay sector, where they attach meaning to their illness; on the basis of that meaning, they may next choose to move either to the Western healer, or to the traditional healer (Brody 1994: 80; van der Geest 1991: 77). They then proceed by what Sjaak van der Geest (1991: 85) has called 'therapeutic shopping', in terms both of the therapies they seek and the explanations they give for their condition. Tola Olu Pearce's work on Yoruba communities in south-west Nigeria suggests that, both in times of crisis and in everyday preventative care, 'people consistently combine different traditions' while also believing that particular traditions work best for particular conditions; Western medicine may be used for surgery, accidents, aches and pains, while indigenous practitioners and prophets are consulted for what is perceived as mental illness (1993: 154). These patient expectations in turn influence the services offered by practitioners, and thus the further development of the various types of medical care on offer (1993: 155). In rural Mali, Sarah Castle concluded that women seeking a cure for a sick child do not perceive traditional and Western medicine as opposed: 'mothers tended to cross sectors substantially in their search for treatment' (1994: 328). In early modern England, too, 'People used many different kinds of practitioner without being troubled about the distinctions between them' (Wear 1992: 17). In their study of the eighteenth century, the Porters concluded that, 'Probably few sick people restricted themselves solely to regular, or to unorthodox medicine' (Porter and Porter 1989: 106–8). Mark Nichter's work on South India (1978) showed that patients could combine systems in a way which suggests that they believe Western medicine alleviates the symptoms, while traditional medicine removes the underlying cause of the sickness episode. As the next chapter will show, in the surviving account of one patient's experiences of Asklepios – the story of Aelius Aristides – we do not find a simple opposition between medicine and the temple; although he presents the relationship between doctors and god as a 'dramatic conflict' (Pearcy 1992: 609), Aristides nevertheless uses both, even employing doctors to carry out the god's instructions (Behr 1968: 169–70).

If Hippocrates and Asklepios were not perceived as incompatible alternatives, what differences can we identify between them which would tend to lead a patient – particularly a female patient – to choose one rather than the other? Since both are intended to heal, it would be misleading to follow Laplantine's general suggestion that medicine aims at determining cause and cure, while religion is concerned with meaning (Laplantine 1986: 350). The type of disease is a possible area of difference, as Asklepios seems to have cornered the market in three- and five-year pregnancies (test. 423.1; 423.2; Dillon 1997: 189–92).[10] He was able to cure sterility (test. 246), often by using his sacred snake as intermediary, but Strabo clearly stated that the god could cure 'diseases of every kind' (test. 735), and the snakes were also believed to cure non-reproductive problems in male patients (Dillon 1997: 191).

Access and cost are important variables in dealing with suffering (A. Young 1980: 113; Kamat 1995: 91). Access to a healing sanctuary depended to some extent on where one lived, but many gods were associated with healing, and pilgrimages were made to distant shrines (Dillon 1997). Access to a Hippocratic healer was unpredictable when physicians travelled from city to city. For the ancient world information on costs is rarely available, but doctors did charge fees. In a possible reference to physicians leaving Athens in a time of crisis, a character in Aristophanes' *Ploutus* asks: 'Is there a doctor in town at the moment? There's no fee now the profession has gone' or perhaps 'With no fees, there's no skill' (407–8). However, temple medicine also charged, and we do not have sufficient information to know how the two areas compared.

A further variable is the experience of the suffering patient within both types of healing. Kaja Finkler's work on the relationship between spiritualist healing and Western biomedicine in Mexico today emphasises the similarities between the systems, as perceived by the patients. In both systems, the patient presents with chronic bodily pain and is treated as passive by the healer: in both, the patient expects the healer to 'see inside' the body, either by using the technology of X-rays and blood tests, or with the aid of the spirits (1994: 181–2). Looking at the situation from outside, however, Finkler argues that significant differences do exist. Spiritualist healing can start from a group consultation, whereas the biomedical encounter is one-to-one. Where spiritualist healers blame impersonal spirits for the illness, biomedicine may implicate equally impersonal pathogens, but often suggests individual blame due to poor habits. Biomedical practitioners ask the patient questions which seem intrusive and which would be irrelevant to spiritualist consultations: Finkler argues that, 'Whereas patients were concerned with anguish and pain often associated with culpability and unresolved contradictions, [biomedical] physicians focused on the nature of the patient's excrement and frequency of sexual intercourse' (1994: 185). Where biomedical healers blame individual lifestyle, spiritualist healers remove blame from individuals and place it on the spirits. Finkler also argues that the interest of the biomedical practitioner in the individual, reflected in the one-to-one privacy of the contemporary medical encounter, is something which we value positively only because in our own society the individual is so highly valued at the expense of the family and the community (cf. A. Young 1980: 110–11).

How can this material apply to Asklepios and Hippocrates? Two aspects may be considered: the group dynamics of the medical encounter, and the way in which blame and suffering are handled. When we consider group dynamics, at first sight the Asklepian medical encounter may appear to be between the individual and the god in the dream; how the priests mediated between the two is not clear. The Hippocratic encounter may look like more of a group affair; the consultation takes place within the household, not at some distant and neutral location, while we read of other household members assisting the *iatros* to carry out healing procedures (see further Chapter 8 pp. 166–7).

A further anthropological study of a society in which temples play a role in healing may however make us question the assumption that temple medicine is, by its nature, individualistic. Vieda Skultans has worked on a Mahanubhav healing temple in rural Maharashtra, where the sick stay for some time in order to gain a diagnosis and effect a cure. The diagnoses most commonly given are of spirit possession, which comes out of the blue and is relatively simple to cure, and witchcraft, which comes from other family members. In neither case is suffering the patient's fault. She has also shown the importance of gender expectations in the treatment of men and women with mental disorder. The dominant ideology – incidentally, very similar to that of the ancient Greeks (Padel 1983; 1992) – claims that women have less will-power and self-control than men, so are more likely than men to suffer mental affliction (Skultans 1991: 349, 347), but Skultans argues that there are more women than men in the temple not because these women are ill, but because they are staying there as care-givers to male family members, while many women patients arrive unaccompanied (1991: 349). She writes of the 'religious pluralism within the temple' itself (1987: 671), as the women she interviewed offered images of themselves and of their roles differing from those provided by the male priests. Women may enter a trance to lift illness from male relatives; in the view of these women, sharing the affliction of a family member affirms 'the legitimacy of their connection with that family' (1991: 352).

Skultans found that six out of ten men at the temple, as against one out of twenty-one women, had had psychiatric treatment before entering the temple; another nine women had received medical treatment elsewhere. She therefore argues that 'the temple is likely to be a first resort for women, particularly if they are unaccompanied, and a last resort for men' (1991: 349). The cure records from Epidauros, which show more men (thirty-three cures found) than women (thirteen cures extant) amongst those seeking healing at the temple, suggest at first sight that the dynamics in the ancient world were very different in this respect, but could indicate merely that the priests responsible preferred – for some reason – to display male cures on the *iamata* (Dillon 1997: 191). However, Lesley Dean-Jones (1994: 136) has suggested that the case histories in the Hippocratic *Epidemics* show men outnumbering women in the ratio of two to one because women were seeking help from traditional healers rather than from Hippocratics. This is not, however, the only possible construction we can place on the data. If the *Epidemics* are the notes of individual *iatroi* on points of interest to which they could return later, we could speculate – following the suggestions made in Chapter 2 – that women's bodies were thought to be more straightforward than those of men in the signs offered to the healer, so that female patients were less likely to generate such notes. We could alternatively give a single explanation for the apparent absence of women from both the Epidauros *iamata* and the *Epidemics*. Perhaps most women consulted neither the temple nor the Hippocratic healer when ill; possibly they treated themselves. A further possibility is that neither the priests nor the writers of the *Epidemics* regarded women's illnesses as particularly interesting, a suggestion which would make the writers of the *Diseases of Women* treatises unusual in their insistence on the importance of understanding the female body and the role of menstruation in its health.

In Skultans' work, some women were found to be living at the Mahanubhav healing temple as 'spiritual hostages' for the continued health of their sons, who had previously been cured there; a similar phenomenon was found in the temples of Asklepios, since it was possible for women and for men to travel there in order to dream on behalf of a sick family member who remained at home.[11] In Athenian healing cults in general it was possible to pray for another family member or to make a vow on behalf of someone else, while votive reliefs at Asklepieia often show a family group making offerings (van Straten 1992: 255–6, 279). Greek temple medicine is also familiar with the idea that another family member can be the cause of an illness; one of the Epidauros *iamata* involves a man whose chest is opened by Asklepios so that the god can remove the leeches which had been put in his drink by his stepmother (test. 423.13). The temple is not then as 'individualistic' as one may think; furthermore, anyone who travels there – particularly if going to one of the most famous shrines from a considerable distance away[12] – would presumably have had to find family support in order to leave fields, business and family in good hands. So perhaps we should reverse the provisional opposition – that temple medicine focuses on the individual, while Hippocratic medicine operates within the family – and consider instead that in religion, someone can go and dream for you, and your family needs to support your quest for healing, but in Hippocratic medicine, you are on your own.

As for blame, in contrast to the views shown on inscriptions from Lydia and Phrygia in the second and third centuries AD, where disease was seen as a divine punishment to be transferred on to animals, birds and fish (Chaniotis 1995), from the surviving evidence it appears that neither the priests of Asklepios nor the god himself had any interest in morality or in culpability (Parker 1983: 249; Nutton 1985c: 47); the only time blame is mentioned is when a patient fails to give the dedication promised in the event of a cure and is then punished by the god. Otherwise, the god intervenes to heal without telling the patient why he or she is sick (Parker 1983: 249). While the god refrains from asking questions about one's medical history, Hippocratic prognosis, as we saw in Chapter 2, is based on observing the patient and asking questions in order to determine the present, the past, and the future of the condition (*Prog*. 1, Loeb II, 6). The patient is sick because of past life-style, or because of the interaction between individual humoral balance and a particular combination of the location of the city, the prevailing wind and the time of year. This can be illustrated from the case histories of the Hippocratic *Epidemics*, where it has been suggested that there is a 'residual moralising tone' (García-Ballester 1994: 1648); for example, 'She drank a purgative for the sake of conception, had pain in the *gastêr*, and twisting in the intestines, and swelled up' (*Ep*. 5.42, Loeb VIII, 184); 'The man from Baloea, who lived on the hill, had been careless in his way of life' (7.17, Loeb VIII, 322); 'The mother of Terpides, from Doriscos, miscarried twins after a fall in the fifth month . . . nine years later she had terrible pains in the *gastêr* for a long time' (7.97, Loeb VIII, 394); 'In Larissa, the servant of Dyseris, when she was young, whenever she had sexual intercourse suffered much pain . . . she never conceived . . . When she was sixty, she had pain from midday, like strong labour. Before midday she had eaten many leeks. When pain seized her, the strongest ever, she stood up and felt something rough at the mouth of her womb . . . another woman, inserting her hand, pressed out a stone like a spindle top, rough' (5.25, Loeb VIII, 176). The main focus in Hippocratic prognosis is on what the physician can observe in the present, and the writers sometimes doubt information given them by patients about past events (e.g. Ep. 4.6, Loeb VIII, 94; see above, Chapter 2 p. 45); but, as these cases illustrate, although recent history is the most commonly reported, distant history can also be relevant. It is therefore possible that Asklepios may be preferred over Hippocrates because of his lack of interest in potentially embarrassing questions about the past.

In terms of providing a cure, however, Hippocrates may be more effective than Asklepios. This is not a judgement on Hippocratic pharmacology; indeed, it is often assumed that temple treatment was more pleasant than some invasive Hippocratic therapies. Instead, it is a reflection on the importance of narrative in providing an explanation for symptoms that will lead to their alleviation. In all cultures, patients need treatment which is 'congruent with their explanatory model' (Garro 1992: 130–1). As Roy Porter has argued in connection with medicine in England in the late Stuart to Georgian periods, for medicine to work it needed to 'offer visions of health, sickness, and recovery, which made sense from the sick person's point of view'; it had to tell 'plausible stories' (1989: 132). Medical anthropologists, most notably Arthur Kleinman, suggest that the search for meaning in suffering – whether carried out through what we would categorise as 'medicine' or as 'religion' – should be seen in terms of narrative. Explaining illness leads to reflection on one's life, in a specific cultural context (Kleinman 1992: 181). Reflection leads on to narrative, as previously unconnected events are perceived to have been linked in ways unseen at the time. Following Elaine Scarry's highly influential study of pain (1985), the anthropologist Byron Good proposed that suffering 'unmakes' the world while, by creating a narrative representation of illness, medicine can reconstruct it (1994).

The creation of narrative can be carried out alone, but even then it may need to be given authority by a specialist, whether priest or healer, as in the case of Aelius Aristides to be discussed in the next chapter. Alternatively, the patient may expect the specialist to construct the narrative, within a cultural context in which the explanation makes sense to the patient; Linda Garro noted that, where a patient in chronic pain tried many doctors, the treatment which worked best was that given by the doctor who provided a key element of the patient's explanatory model, making sense of the past, and suggesting options for the future (1992: 130–1). The narrative itself may thus heal. However, just as there is a sort of 'placebo effect'[13] when patient and healer agree on the diagnosis, so there can be a 'nocebo effect'; a medical diagnosis can lead a patient to behave in a 'sicker' way than before (Helman 1985: 323).

The construction of a narrative linking past to present and providing expectations for the future is a central part of Hippocratic medicine. The theory of critical days, using models of regular crises taken from malarial-type fevers, gives even greater control of the future, predicting exactly when the patient will feel worse or better. But Asklepios too uses time management; votives, the objects promised to the god in the event of a cure, are 'a major human strategy for coping with the future', making time manageable by creating a public, and thus social, contract of the 'if . . . then' type (Burkert 1987: 13; Nutton 1985c: 47).

When creating a narrative, how do the Hippocratics apportion blame? Wujastyk (1998) considers the death of a child as the supreme event raising the question, 'Why does God permit this?'; in the Indian material he uses, the mother is blamed for laying herself open to demonic powers. Sarah Castle has worked on contemporary rural Mali, an area of high childhood mortality in which over 50 per cent of children die before reaching the age of five. Here, the death of a child may be attributed to *foondu* ('the owl') or to *heendu* ('the wind'). *Foondu* is caught if a child cries at the same moment as an owl shrieks, if dust falls from an owl on to a child, or if an owl flies over a pregnant woman. *Heendu* is caused by a sorcerer or a spirit drinking the patient's blood. The central points about both diagnoses are that they are rarely given to living children and that they are both seen as untreatable, although amulets and inhalation of smoke may be attempted (Castle 1994). To diagnose a living child as having *foondu* or *heendu* makes the diagnosis into a self-fulfilling prophecy. To diagnose a child post-mortem as having been a victim removes any suspicion that its death was the responsibility either of the mother, or of the healer. An important element of these diagnoses is that they are given only by traditional healers, clerics or senior women of the patrilineage, thus reinforcing the hierarchical transmission of knowledge (Castle 1994: 330–1). Here, explanations for disease are couched in such a way that they exonerate all parties, while reproducing socially significant structures.

We do not know how Greek religion accounted for the death of a child. Wujastyk's Indian material on Lady Opulence – represented with wings, talons and beak, and killing foetuses and young children – as 'Child-Snatcher' suggests to a classicist the Greek mythical figures of the harpies (literally, 'snatchers') who, on the Xanthos tomb, are represented carrying away small human figures. But, thanks to an important article by Ann Hanson (1987), we do know how Hippocratic medicine coped with the death of a newborn child. The Hippocratic solution to the problem refers not to gods or spirits, but to an unavoidable law of nature related to numbers. Based on beliefs about gestation, the Hippocratics insisted that the eight-months child never survives, while the seven-months child is at risk of death (*Fleshes* 19, Loeb VIII, 162). This meant that a child born dead could be hastily redefined as an eight-months child – 'They always die – there's nothing anyone can do' – while the statement 'This is a seven-months child' became a convenient shorthand to warn everyone involved that the child might not live long. It was in the interests of doctor, mother, family and midwives to go along with these statements and thus to avoid all blame or guilt.

The advantage of using suffering as a way into the relationship between Asklepios and Hippocrates is thus that it helps us to avoid issues of rationality in looking for answers as to why a patient may prefer religion or medicine. The different systems handle the issues of blame and suffering in different ways. Work on chronic pain suggests that – at least in the industrialised West – the construction of a narrative can be part of the healing process; Hippocratic medicine duly allows the creation of meaning from suffering by anchoring it to the patient's experience. In Hippocratic medicine you are on your own; you, as an individual, are the focus of enquiry. Not everyone, however, wants to feel the medical gaze; as Alcinda Honwana (1998) has reminded us in the context of post-civil-war Mozambique, not everyone wants to research their past. Both the focus on the present in prognosis and the power of numbers in Hippocratic medicine respond to this problem but, if you still fear the implications of the narrative which a Hippocratic would create for you, you may prefer what the temple offers. The patient who opts for the narrative-free neutrality of temple medicine may also have gained a much greater investment of symbolic capital from the family and friends whose support makes the journey to the temple possible, so that the network of expectations surrounding him or her makes a cure even more likely.

6

WHAT DOES MEDICINE MEAN?

The pain of being human

In this and the following chapter, I want to investigate further some aspects of the ways in which Hippocratic medicine intervenes in the female body, and in the process to challenge some of the assumptions made by the Hippocratic research programme about how we can best apply models based on Western biomedicine to ancient texts. In this chapter, I will concentrate on the meaning of pain, arguing that women's pain in childbirth was divided into that which was necessary to the process, and that which was excessive and needed to be treated. This will involve looking in more detail at how medicine, as a *technê*, fitted into wider ancient Greek views of what it is to be human. I will then use comparative materials taken from the sociology of medicine to suggest that ancient medicine may best be understood not by focusing on the chemical efficacy of its pharmacopoeia but by investigating its uses of narrative; here, I will be using an example of a patient who used both doctors and temple medicine in his search to find a meaning for his pain. Chapter 7 will develop this argument in a different direction by challenging the assumptions behind recent work on the early history of contraception.

Medicine is never neutral. In any society it carries cultural values, including beliefs about the human body and about the roles and relative importance of different age/gender groups. It constructs its object in a dialogue with culture; before treating sickness, it is necessary to decide who is sick and who is not, what behaviour is abnormal and what is normal (Kleinman 1992: 171). Resources for treatment are allocated in accordance with a particular definition of 'life'. Anthropological studies of societies in which the aged are left behind by some nomadic tribes to die are echoed by debates in contemporary 'high-tech' medicine about whether it is worth spending money to keep alive those whose 'quality of life' is defined as being too low even to count as 'life'.[1] Different cultures operate with different ideas about the origin of medicine, its place in relation to other social systems, and its development over time. We today see medicine as moving ever onwards to cure more people of more diseases; we act as though we believe that sufficient research money will find cures for everything. This view has received some setbacks – for example, from the emergence of AIDS as a new disease of disputed aetiology, apparently with the capacity to shift its form – but the very fact that research money has been put into finding a cure for AIDS demonstrates that we still believe in the ideal of the conquest of all disease.

What of the ancient Greeks? In broad terms, the Greeks operated with two different models of the past incorporating different valuations of disease and medicine. One representation of human history, of the development from past to present, held that mankind had fallen from a Golden Age in which men and gods shared a common way of life; this is the view put forward in Hesiod's poetry. According to this version, diseases entered the world at the opening of Pandora's jar (*Erga* 102), along with death, hard work, sacrifice and marriage (Vernant 1974; 1979). Here disease becomes an inevitable part of the present, with medicine fighting to keep it under control. The other strand stressed progress rather than a 'Fall'; it postulated that, by gradually acquiring the skills of the various *technai*, man was able to climb up from a past in which people were little different from beasts, towards the present level of civilisation (Cole 1967). In this version of the past, the *technai* thus define what it is to be a civilised human being; they stand between humanity and the world of the beasts, and they contain the promise of even greater progress towards sharing the life of the gods.

Some Hippocratic texts explicitly identify medicine as a *technê* and show concern to maintain its boundaries against deceit and ignorance. *Regimen*, discussed in Chapter 2, emphasises the language of discovery and research in the development of medical knowledge, and claims a place for medicine in a long list of all the *technai*. This includes the *technai* of diviners, iron workers, fullers, cobblers, carpenters, builders, musicians, cooks, curriers, gold workers, makers of statues, potters, writers and athletics trainers, all of whose skills are presented as in some way resembling the actions of the healer as he cajoles the patient's body into shape and creates harmony from its elements (1.12–24, Loeb IV, 251–63). But in fifth-century Greece the interest in the *technai* as the defining features of human civilisation extended far beyond such medical texts, forming part of a general interest in what it means to be human. For example, in Aeschylus' play *Prometheus* (478–83), the culture hero Prometheus describes medicine as the greatest of all the *technai*. In the distant past, if someone suffered from a disease, they could not be cured, but then Prometheus showed man 'how to drive away diseases'.

Medicine's place among the great *technai* was, however, open to question in the ancient world. Was medicine unique to human beings, or something shared with the animal kingdom? One line taken, most consistently argued by Plutarch in the *Moralia* (992a, 973e), was that the beasts are self-taught doctors, and that teaching oneself implies even greater *logos* than does the ability to learn from others. In the history of pharmacy in general, the question of how those plants which have medicinal uses were first isolated remains unanswered (Riddle 1987: 39–40). Plutarch argues that animals have taught mankind how to use drugs, diet and surgery – the three traditional branches of medicine – by taking herbs, purging themselves with salt water, fasting and surgery; elephants even remove arrows from each others' bodies (*Mor.* 974a–d; cf. Theophrastos 9.20.3). In myth, too, men can be presented as having learned medicine from observing animals; Polyeidos saw a snake placing a certain herb on the body of another to restore it to life, and then used the same herb to revive Glaukos (Hyginus, *Fabula* 136; Apollodorus 3.3.1; Ovid, *Met.* 7.232–3). Each species of animal is thought to have its own remedy (*Mor.* 974a–d; cf. Aelian *NA* 2.18; 5.46; 8.9); for example, Oppian (*Cyn.* 2.287) describes a *pharmakon autodidakton*, a 'self-taught drug', used by the stag. These arguments for the superiority of beasts over man should, however, be seen in context; Plutarch puts one defence of the beasts' medical skills into the mouth of Gryllos, one of Odysseus' sailors who was turned into a pig by Circe and wanted to stay that way. Animal medicine can thus be placed in a series of comic inversions of the normal belief in the superiority of man over beast; for example, the comic poet Philemon (fr.88 Kock; cf. frr.3 and 93) gave several comparisons between man and beast in which the latter came out on top, so that man became the most wretched of animals because, unlike the others who are cared for by the earth, man has to work hard all the time in order to obtain enough to eat.

But the impassioned defences of the place of medicine as a *technê* are also significant because of the limited type of medicine they include in this category. Alongside their claims for their own brand of medicine, the Hippocratic writers go out of their way to criticise certain other groups of people who provided healing in ancient Greece as 'deceivers'. In the competitive climate within which Hippocratic medicine existed, however, even others acknowledged as being *iatroi* could be criticised on the grounds that their interventions were showy appeals to the crowd rather than actions backed by knowledge. Confronted by other forms of healing, the Hippocratics do not close ranks in defence of their *technê*; they show a far stronger spirit of individualism than did medical men in later historical periods when medicine had become a 'profession' in the modern sense.

While believing that disease was an inevitable part of the present, then, the Greeks also saw it as something which could be controlled through medicine. The Hippocratics set the limits to that control in different places to us, sometimes arguing that only a particular type of medicine involving a balance between manual skill and critical intelligence could overcome disease; some *iatroi* who have the manual skills necessary to the *technê* lack the intelligence (*Joints* 33, Loeb III, 262). There is one occasion on which they may also suggest that the patient needed to be sufficiently 'human' to benefit from the medical *technê*; when a female slave in *Epidemics* 5.35 (Loeb VII, 182), who was purged and then produced a little bile 'up' and a lot 'down', subsequently died, the writer adds 'she was a barbarian'. If, following Lonie (1983), we understand these texts as *aides-mémoires* for the healer, this could be added simply to jog a writer's memory at a later date. But if the ending of the case should also affect how we should read it, I would argue that this suggests barbarians are somehow beyond the pale for Greek medicine, thus forming a direct contrast to the approach taken in *Airs, Waters, Places*, a text which explicitly applies the principles of Hippocratic medicine to other peoples, and to the claim that the same symptoms have the same meaning 'in Libya, in Delos and in Scythia' (*Prog.* 25, Loeb II, 54).

In ancient Greece, medical 'progress' could derive from observation of the beasts, which at the same time lifted man up from their level, or from the superior application of mental and manual skill. But, whatever techniques were applied, medicine remained unable to heal the rupture between gods and mortal men instigated by the opening of Pandora's jar. In contemporary Western biomedicine, it is chronic illness[2] and – above all – chronic pain, defined as pain lasting over six months for which there is no detectable organic cause (Morris 1991: 70), which most challenge our ideal of continuous medical progress by their resistance to current treatments. Recent anthropological work has pointed out that chronic pain is seen as anomalous in Western biomedicine because it is an inner experience which cannot be measured objectively, since there is no 'pain thermometer' (Jackson 1992: 139; M-J. DelVecchio Good *et al.* 1992: 5–6). The idealised objectivity of measurement in Western biomedicine has been questioned; for example, the work of Annemarie Mol and Marc Berg (1994) on anaemia shows not only that the symptoms listed vary considerably between textbooks, but also that haemoglobin levels used to diagnose the disease fluctuate according to posture, whether blood is taken from a vein or from the fingertip, the time of day, weather conditions, how much fluid has been drunk, and the method of measurement used. Nevertheless, the ideal of objectivity remains intrinsic to biomedicine. Chronic pain is also problematic for biomedicine because it cannot be visually represented by scans, X-rays or biochemical tests (Kleinman 1992: 200); even more significantly, it has been argued that biomedicine generally has 'little interest in treating suffering that it cannot eliminate' (Wendell 1996: 137).

In addition, chronic pain challenges the Cartesian mind/body divisions (Morris 1991: 76) which are part of our culture. The use of 'twilight sleep' at the beginning of this century demonstrated the phenomenon of patients who, under anaesthesia, cried out and writhed as if in unbearable pain, but remembered no pain on awakening (Morris 1991: 158–60). Was the body, or the mind, to be privileged here? David Morris writes of chronic pain as 'this contemporary epidemic' (1991: 60), 'the gray tide of affliction now sweeping across the land', and he links its spread to the advent of 'a world in which pain has become almost utterly without meaning' (1991: 56).

If pain had meaning in antiquity, what did it mean? Were chronic and acute pain understood in different ways, and how was chronic pain made explicable? Morris would respond that, where other treatment fails, the attribution of meaning to one's pain has a real power to reduce that pain. In the first part of this chapter I will concentrate on pain in the context of Hippocratic medicine, and particularly the gynaecological texts. I will look briefly at the kinds of substance used to relieve it, before examining more closely ancient Greek ideas of what pain is and thus how it should be handled. In the second part, I will set Aelius Aristides' *Sacred Tales* beside material on chronic pain and chronic illness from the social sciences, in order to show how a patient in the early Roman empire succeeded in giving his pain meaning. This strategy means that the first part will focus on doctors' narratives, the second on the account of one of the most vociferous patients in the ancient world. Such an account is not available from any female patient in this period, and it may be doubted whether any woman would interpret her pain in the precise terms used by Aristides.

Translating Hippocratic pain

Studying pain in the ancient world brings us directly up against the problem of translation. I do not mean simply the issue of pain terminology and its precise nuances in another culture; the issue is deeper than this, and concerns whether there exist human universals which somehow escape from the control of culture. The fact that the ancient world was acquainted with a number of anodynes known today can lull us into a false sense of security, making us assume that pain was both felt and relieved in the same ways as now. The Hippocratic text *Affections* mentions several times a work called *On Drugs* which apparently listed painkilling drugs as a distinct category:[3] 'To those suffering from these pains, one gives the *pharmaka* listed in *On Drugs* as those which stop pain' (15, Loeb V, 28; 27, Loeb V, 48, etc.). Three types of henbane (black, yellow and white; Greek *hyoskyamos*), which contains hyoscyamine alkaloids, were known and were used as anodynes in topical applications (e.g. Dioscorides 4.68). A number of other plants containing tropane alkaloids – hyoscyamine, atropine and scopolamine – are also listed in Dioscorides' *Materia Medica*, which dates to around AD 65 (Riddle 1985: 107–8). These include belladonna (*strychnos manikos*), black nightshade (*strychnos*) and mandrake (*mandragoras*). Opium is an important ingredient in many ancient remedies (Scarborough 1995); in particular, it has been suggested that it is the only active constituent of the cure-all called theriac.[4] A medicine with a vast number of ingredients which varied according to the physician making it up, and according to the availability of different substances (Nutton 1985a: 142), theriac was supposed to cure snakebite, headache, vertigo, deafness, apoplexy, epilepsy, asthma, colic, jaundice, the stone, fever, and many other conditions.

When giving the effects of drugs such as these, most ancient medical texts do not however give the quantities to be administered. This makes it difficult to assess what would have 'worked', even in a narrowly chemical sense of efficacy. The absence of quantities is not because the authors thought them unimportant since, as Riddle (1985: 67–9) points out for Dioscorides, doses were more likely to be specified when the substance in question was highly toxic. In general, however, medicine was supposed to be something learned from experience as well as from instruction, so that the practitioner would gradually learn how to weigh up all the variables both on the side of the patient and on the side of the drug.[5] A passage of the Hippocratic *Epidemics* (2.3.2, Loeb VII, 50) stating these variables was cited frequently in ancient drug manuals, acknowledging that, with so many factors to be considered, no handbook could possibly guarantee the best dosage:

> We know the characteristics of drugs, from what ones come what kinds of things. For they are not all equally good, but different characteristics are good in different circumstances. In different places medicinal drugs are gathered earlier or later; also the preparations differ, such as drying, crushing, boiling, and so on (I pass over most things); and how much for each person and in what diseases and when in the disease, in relation to age, appearance, regimen, what kind of season, what season and how it is developing, and the like.
>
> (trans. W.D. Smith)[6]

This means that, even where quantities are given, we cannot necessarily use this information to assess the efficacy of an ancient remedy, because we may not know whether the methods of harvesting and preparation of the materials for drugs were comparable with contemporary practices nor, indeed, whether the chemical makeup of the plants was the same as that which we find today (Shorter 1983: 187). Even attempts to match a modern plant to an ancient description or illustration are rarely straightforward; the different illustrations of the herbs *dracontea* and *vettonica* given in manuscripts of the Latin writers on herbs are so unlike each other that one despairs of ever finding a single modern equivalent.[7] Furthermore, a plant which we now believe has certain chemical properties was not necessarily used in a way which would exploit those properties (Riddle 1987: 37); the antibacterial qualities of garlic are irrelevant, if it is worn around the neck by a patient with a stomach disorder. Ancient ideas about human anatomy, often very different from our own, influenced the site of drug administration, as in the Hippocratic use of both ends of the *hodos* in gynaecology. We of course have a similar idea – substances taken orally affect uterine function – but support it with a rather different rationale.

But there is a further problem still in assessing ancient painkillers. Substances which we continue to use as painkillers were used within an explanatory framework entirely different from that of the tropane alkaloids today. In her *History of Pain*, Roselyne Rey claims that 'the Hippocratic doctors knew how to use narcotic plants' (1993: 32) but in a survey of the narcotics in Hippocratic texts Monique Moisan notes in passing that some of these 'uses' do not correspond to those we would recognise today; for example, twenty-one out of twenty-five Hippocratic uses of the opium poppy occur in the gynaecological texts, but the most common purpose of its administration is to recall a wandering womb (1990: 386). This suggests that the Greeks were indeed using narcotic plants, but not necessarily as narcotics.

In the Hippocratic *Places in Man* 45 (Loeb VIII, 90), a drug is defined as a substance that changes the state of the patient. In ancient medicine, the primary language of drugs is that of temperature. For example, looking at the plants we define as containing tropane alkaloids, John Riddle notes that in Dioscorides wild lettuce is 'a little cooling', while opium is 'cooling' (2.136 and 4.64; Riddle 1993: 106). How should we understand such language? Is it translatable? In our medical beliefs, opium makes a person hot to touch, so clearly hot and cold are not being used in our empirical sense here. Similarly, plants which are thought to bring on a delayed period, ease childbirth and cause abortion are described by the people of highland Oaxaca in Mexico as 'warming' the womb to make it open, 'irritating' it to make it expel its contents, and 'drying' it so that it cannot nourish a foetus. Browner *et al.* comment that 'Whether or not these plants actually warm (i.e., change the quality of) the blood or body is not currently amenable to empirical validation using standard bioscientific methods' (1988: 687). If 'warming' and 'cooling' do not mean what we would expect, then what do they mean? Riddle proposes that Dioscorides was aware that too much opium kills; in ancient thought, death is 'cold' (Lloyd 1966: 44–5, 62–3) so opium becomes 'cooling'.

This form of translation echoes the practical and development-oriented field of medical anthropology, which looks at humoral systems in developing countries in order to try to map on to them disease categories and therapeutic methods used by Western biomedicine. For example, it has been shown that aspirin is not used for fevers in a humoral system until it is presented to a society in humoral terms; since a fever is 'hot', aspirin has to be introduced as a 'cold' drug (Logan 1977). If efforts of this kind are not made, then the drug will not be taken properly.[8] The effect of translating across cultures may however lead to practices which Western medical practitioners regard as dangerous; where a traditional treatment for infected wounds is to sprinkle silt or termite dust on them, penicillin powder which looks very similar will be used even against the advice of the aid post orderly who knows that there is a risk of a hypersensitivity reaction (G. Lewis 1993: 207).

Byron Good has also argued that the use within a humoral system of terms like 'warm' can only be understood in relation to the rest of that system; 'warm' and 'cool' have no meaning 'external to culture' (1994: 101–2, 107). In particular, in Greco-Roman medicine warming relates to what Good singles out as the 'master metaphor' of cooking (1994: 103). Normal bodily processes involve a series of stages of cooking which gradually transform food into blood, tissue and humours, while abnormal symptoms appear when rotting occurs due to too much or too little heat being applied, leading to the generation of morbid humours. To say that a remedy is 'warming' can only be understood by reference to these beliefs, and there is thus no point in trying to relate it to variables we can measure, such as bodily temperature. Humoral medicine has a 'holistic' quality, in that it demands changes in the entire way of life; there is no private area here, since sexuality, diet and exercise are all thought to influence the internal 'cooking' of humours and are thus all implicated in the health of the person.

Even if we could translate from a humoral system to a biomedical one, however, to study pain in the ancient world by concentrating on the drugs known to be effective painkillers today is to give a misleading impression both of the ancient pharmacopoeia and of the rationale behind its use. As Morris points out, it is very much a contemporary attitude to put our faith in 'chemical assaults on pain' (1991: 61). In the Hippocratic materials, a treatment which is perhaps more typical of pain relief than the use of orally administered substances is the fomentation (Rey 1993: 31). *Regimen in Acute Diseases* describes pain in the ribs, and recommends the application of a skin, a bladder or a metal or clay container filled with hot water, with something soft placed between container and skin to prevent further discomfort. It also discusses dry fomentations, woollen envelopes filled with grain (21, Loeb II, 78–80).

A focus on the pharmacopoeia is even more seriously flawed by its failure to take into account culturally specific attitudes to pain. Within the Hippocratic corpus we can discover many, conflicting, approaches not only to pain relief but also to its causation. A long discussion of pain (*odynê*) in *Places in Man* 42 (Loeb VIII, 84) tells us that pain is produced by cold and hot, by excess and deficiency. It should at once be noted that the precise connotations of 'hot' and 'cold' differ from those in Dioscorides since, within the basic theme that life is 'hot', this writer suggests that some people are naturally much hotter than others. In persons of a cold constitution pain is produced by heat, and in those of a hot constitution by cold. In the dry it is produced by wetness, in the wet by dryness. This is because pains are produced every time there is a change and corruption of the natural constitution (*physis*). Pains are therefore cured by contraries, each disorder (*nosêma*) having a cure which is right for it. So hot constitutions, made sick by the cold, need a remedy which heats, and so on. This particular brand of ancient medicine, seeing everything in terms of the principle of opposites, would therefore not use any single substance as 'a painkiller', applicable to all situations; instead the type of painkiller given would depend on the healer's assessment of the constitution of the patient. To know your painkiller, you must know yourself.

Another Hippocratic text, *Epidemics* 6.6.3, gives a series of general principles for relieving pain anywhere in the body; you should purge the nearest cavity of blood, using cautery or incision, or apply hot or cold substances, or induce sneezing, or use vegetable juices where these have power, or use the ancient multipurpose remedy called *kykeôn*, a mixture of wine and barley-flour (Loeb VII, 262). For even worse pains, milk, garlic, boiled wine, vinegar and salt are recommended. I would emphasise that the vegetable juices (*phytôn chymoi*) are to be used 'where these have power' – again implying that certain types of ancient medicine would regard as alien the idea of a single drug having the same properties in all cases and situations. Another passage, *Aphorisms* 2.46, says that if someone has two pains (*ponoi*), in different places, the stronger will cancel out the weaker; the implications of this position for pain relief would suggest that you create a worse pain somewhere else to remove the one you started with, rather than considering a drug (Loeb IV, 118; Rey 1993: 31). There is thus no single medical attitude to pain or to the use of pain-relieving substances in Hippocratic medicine.

What cultural criteria were available to medical writers against which to judge pain and pain relief? It may be misleading to foreground the Hippocratics as if they were the only source of drug materials in ancient society; they clearly were not, since drugs were available to all members of ancient society, made up by *pharmakopôloi* (Scarborough 1991: 148–51) and sold by root-cutters, *rhizotomoi*, in the marketplace and at fairs (Nutton 1985a). Root-cutters sometimes collected their materials with the aid of rituals, prayers and chants; when, however, a drug was given by a doctor employed for the purpose, its efficacy would perhaps have been improved by the whole ritual of consultation and therapy, as well as by the doctor's explanation of why it would work.

The old idea that primitive peoples are less sensitive to pain has been criticised for relying on 'ethnic caricatures', where the current focus in anthropology is on real individuals and the complexity of their experiences (Good *et al.* 1992: 2), and in fact the picture is far more complicated; cultures seem to have certain situations in which the expression of pain is encouraged, and others in which stoicism is required (Zborowski 1952). Pain response may not be a fair reflection of the pain felt: as in the example of 'twilight sleep' already cited, what is observed by others may not relate to what the subject feels (Wolff and Langley 1968). Pain not only accompanies injury and disease, but is also part of normal physiological changes such as childbirth; it can be caused by the processes of diagnosis and healing themselves (Helman 1984: 95–105). The presence of pain in healing was acknowledged by ancient Greek writers; Plato implies that it is painful to take a drug and unpleasant to be treated by medicine, but adds that the pain must be endured if the patient is to recover (*Gorgias* 467c; 478b–c). Whatever their theories on its treatment, the ancient Greeks regarded pain as a central element in diagnosis, often giving its location as the first point in their lists of symptoms; thus for the Hippocratic writers as for Galen, writing over 500 years later, pain was seen as an important indicator of the precise location of a disease (Siegel 1970: 184–93). They believed that pain might be a natural part of some conditions,[9] and that sometimes the cessation of pain was far more dangerous than the pain itself: the Hippocratic *Coan Prognoses* states that 'Pains which go with no cause are fatal' (19.364, L 5.660).

In the Hippocratic texts I have already cited, two words for pain have so far been mentioned: *odynê* (as in our 'anodyne') and *ponos*. Others include *algêma*/*algos* (as in our 'analgesic') and *lypê*. The extent to which one word for pain is used rather than another is partly a matter of the date and authorship of the treatise; thus, for example, *Epidemics* 7 and *Coan Prognoses* seem to prefer words of the *algos* group. The work of Fabrega and Tyma (1976), however, suggests a further class of factor governing the selection of word: cultural considerations, which allow us to deduce something of a culture's attitude to pain from the words chosen to describe it. They argue that, since the English 'pain' derives from the Latin *poena*, 'punishment', the idea of disease being caused by divine vengeance still hovers behind the word's use; Scarry (1985: 16) argues more generally that the pain/*poena* connection has now come to suggest a search for a cause of pain external to the interior sensation. Where Fabrega and Tyma argue that the vocabulary of pain shapes the phenomenon of pain itself, Diller's study of Thai terms for pain (1980) warns that there will not be a perfect match between words and feelings; the lexicon of pain may not reproduce physiological or psychological distinctions. We may nevertheless be able to apply material such as this to the ancient Greek texts, even if our findings must remain provisional. In the medical texts, *ponos* seems to be used for long-lasting pain, or dull pain: *odynê* for sharp pain, pain which pierces the body. Rey (1993: 21) argues that *odynê* is 'a sharp, shooting pain' associated with cutting. In this, it corresponds to the Thai term Diller classifies as $PAIN_3$, a 'sudden piercing or stabbing pain, highly focused'.

To understand the full field of meanings for *ponos* in classical Greece we must however look outside the medical texts. Hippocratic medicine may be seen as the medicine appropriate to the Greek *polis*, a city-state within which there is an emphasis on particular parts of the body; the arms and hands which bear weapons and practise crafts, and the voice which is central to the oral culture of the *polis*, based as it is on the ideal of participation by all citizens.[10] Activities such as athletics and body-building, which in our society are performed for the sake of the individual, were performed for the state. In Aristotle's *Constitution of Athens* (*Ath. Pol.* 49.4), the exposure of the invalid male body to the Council is described; since being unable to work means being given a state allowance, it is logical that this scrutiny (*dokimazein*) of the body should be made. In Athens, there was also an annual parade of the deme's youths to check on their physical development, with it being left to the members of the deme to vote on whether or not these boys had reached the age of 18 (*Ath. Pol.* 42.2). Aristophanes (*Wasps* 578) also suggests that the Council inspected these adolescent male bodies, and that demes could appeal against a Council decision to a law court, at which the jurors would subject these bodies to further scrutiny. The male body was matured and maintained in a healthy condition not primarily for itself, but for military service: in his claims about the lives of Spartan women, who were seen as being unique among Greek women in training their bodies as men did, Plutarch suggests that for them too fitness was seen as something necessary in order to facilitate their own particular brand of service to the state, in this case bearing healthy children (*Life of Lycurgos* 14). Spartan *parthenoi* exercise to prepare for the *ôdines* of giving birth; *ôdines* has as its primary meaning 'labour pains', and is then used figuratively for other mental and physical suffering.

In ancient Greek culture further parallels were drawn between fighting and, if necessary, dying for his city, as the most highly valued male social activity, and childbirth, as the corresponding activity by which women prove themselves to be proper women (Loraux 1981b; cf. von Staden 1991b: 45). However, men's role in war was seen as active while women's role in childbirth was essentially passive,[11] since it was up to the baby to force its way out of the womb 'much as a chicken hatched from its egg' (Hanson 1992b: 54; *NC* 30, L 7.530–2). According to Plutarch (*Life of Lycurgus* 27.2–3), the Spartans were allowed to commemorate only two classes of death by inscriptions on the tomb: men dying in battle, and women dying in childbirth. In a famous passage from Greek tragedy, Medea draws an explicit comparison between the two spheres of activity when she says that she would rather stand in the line of battle three times than give birth once (Eur. *Medea* 248–51). This should probably not be taken as evidence that the Greeks expected normal childbirth to be even more painful than battle injuries; Medea is not a typical Greek woman, but a foreign sorceress who murders her own children, and these lines occur in a long speech on the miserable condition of women, written by a man. However, a fragment of Aeschylus' play *Europê* (fr. 99. 7–8 Nauck[2]) includes the lines 'Three times in childbirth, I have endured *gynaikeioi ponoi*', making it clear that the pains of labour are most definitely classified as *ponoi*. Both war and childbirth were viewed as forms of combat involving pain, but in childbirth the enemy was labour itself (Loraux 1981b). Where this is the case – where some degree of pain is seen as necessary to the process – the idea of using any form of painkiller would perhaps be out of place (Zborowski 1952: 18). The precise word used for pain in both war and childbirth is usually *ponos*, or the plural *ponoi*, but its use does not stop here. Loraux (1982) argues that, for the classical Greek city, *ponos* became a positive, glorious sensation linked to war and childbirth; outside this civic context, however, *ponos* kept its earlier associations of pain and fatigue.

One of the earliest uses of *ponos* is with the meaning agricultural labour, or hard work. In Hesiod it is presented as an unpleasant, but integral, part of human existence, associated with Pandora opening her jar to release the evils which make up the world as we know it; it is ordained by the gods and thus inescapable (*Erga* 92, 113). It hurts but, whether experienced as war for men or as childbirth for women, it remains part of a process necessary for the continuation of human life. *Ponoi* is also used in medical texts for strengthening exercises; that is, for the training necessary for those who want to face the situations in which pain will occur. However, *ponoi* in the sense of 'exertions' of any kind can also cause disease, if undertaken with insufficient care; in several passages of the Hippocratic *Diseases 1 ponoi* cause a vessel in the lung to burst (Loeb V, 100).[12] *Ponos* in its wider uses is thus primarily pain with a goal, a means to an end (Loraux 1982: 172); for example, in *Epidemics* 5.2 (Loeb VII, 152), the case of the madness of Timocrates of Elis, he took the necessary purgative drug to cure his excess of black bile, had 'much pain (*ponos*) in the purging', but was cured. This pain, part of the process which led to a cure, may be contrasted with the fatal case of Eupolemos of Oineiadae whose condition began with severe *odynai* in the hip and groin; he drank a purgative, and at first improved, 'but the pains (*odynai*) did not leave him' (*Ep.* 5.7, Loeb VII, 156). In the first case the pains are *ponoi*, and part of the healing process: in the second they are the *odynai* which remain untouched by the treatment. Something similar may be found in *Regimen in Acute Diseases*, which uses *odynê* for pain throughout its descriptions of fomentations for pain in the ribs, with one exception. This occurs when the writer warns, 'but if warm fomentations do not relieve the *ponos*, do not continue using them, because they dry out the lung' (*Reg. Ac.* 22, Loeb II, 80). I would emphasise that this is the only occasion in this passage when *ponos* is used; elsewhere the pains/pain are *algêdonai* or *odynê*. Is *ponos* therefore chosen here to convey the sense 'pain which cannot be relieved'?

When *Regimen* 3.75 (Loeb IV, 396–8) discusses cases in which a person has taken too much food in proportion to their exercise, one possibility raised is when, the morning after the over-indulgence, the sufferer brings up undigested food and passes a large amount of stools – although insufficient for the food previously eaten – but there is no *ponos*, used here in the sense of 'pains'. The cause of this condition is considered to be cold intestines, which fail to digest the food overnight. *Ponoi* 'exercises' and *ponos* 'pain' are both associated with warming, essential to digestion in a humoral system. The treatment for cold intestines which do not digest the food is warmth, both from warm foods and from *ponoi*, used this time in the sense of 'exercises'. Where too much exercise is taken in relation to the food intake, the regimen proposed is 'soft' and feminine (Loraux 1982: 175); warm baths, soft beds, sex and alcohol, and easing off the *ponoi* (*Regimen* 3.85, Loeb IV, 418).

I would therefore argue that Hesiod's foregrounding of *ponos* as an essential part of the world of the present, the Age of Iron, continues to influence the choice of pain terminology in the early medical writers. This would in turn suggest that, if a pain is defined as *ponos* at the onset, it may be considered culturally inappropriate to offer pain relief for it.

In the early gynaecological and other medical texts, pains during childbirth can be described either as *ponoi* or as *odynai*. What could these alternatives signify? The first choice regards the pain as a necessary part of the process and thus something to be endured, while the second sees it as excessive and thus demanding special attention. This can be supported from *Diseases* 1.8: a warning that, if a woman in labour has pain (*odynê*) in her womb, and the doctor 'gives her something' but she worsens or even dies, then he will be blamed (Loeb V, 116–18). This reference shows that drugs were sometimes given to women during labour; the use here of *odynê* rather than *ponos* may suggest that there is a line being drawn between pain which is necessary to a successful outcome and is therefore to be endured, and pain which is excessive and which therefore should be treated. The particular problem here could be that the doctor defines the woman's pain as being in excess of what is needed, but those members of the family and neighbourhood involved in the birth believe that the pain falls within the limits of 'normal and necessary'. The subsequent death of their kinswoman and friend would then make them blame the doctor for having interfered to minimise what they saw as the 'necessary' pain, thus jeopardising the outcome.

What of chronic illness and chronic pain in the Hippocratic medical texts? Chronic illness is recognised in Hippocratic medicine; there is the belief that it arises from minor conditions which are wrongly treated (e.g. *Aff.* 18, Loeb V, 30). Acute diseases are, however, said to cause the most deaths and to be the most painful or most wearisome (*epiponotatai*, *Aff.* 13, Loeb V, 22). Sciatica is considered long and painful (*epiponos*), but not fatal; arthritis – in sharp contrast to our own experience in a historical period when life expectancy is much higher than in classical Greece – is described as short, acute, not fatal and affecting the young; gout is the 'most chronic' (*polychronios*) and the most intractable condition (*Aff.* 29–30, Loeb V, 52). *Diseases* 1 gives a full classification of conditions according to whether they are invariably fatal, only fatal if there are complications, long-lasting, quick, and so on (1.3, Loeb V, 102–4). Taken with the example of labour pain, these observations and the difficulty of knowing whether the disease labels or even the experience are translatable suggest some of the limitations of any study of pain in the ancient world. Where much pain was seen as a normal part of human life, and was regarded as 'warming' in a system in which heat was considered essential to many bodily processes, patients may have been as reluctant to complain as healers were reluctant to administer painkilling treatments.

Aelius Aristides: a patient in pain

Publius Aelius Aristides, born in AD 117, was a public orator during the Second Sophistic, a period in which public displays of rhetoric were a major art form, and orators not only performed but also taught others and travelled as envoys. As the most famous patient from antiquity, Aelius Aristides certainly did complain. Modern commentators have very little sympathy with his ill-health. Charles Behr (1981: 425) describes him as 'a deeply neurotic, deeply superstitious, vainglorious man'. A prime example of his vanity is his dream which compares his achievements in oratory to those of Alexander in war (*Sacred Tales* 50.49; Rutherford 1995). E.R. Dodds' assessment of his condition for his entry in the 1970 edition of the *Oxford Classical Dictionary* ran as follows: 'At the age of 26, when on a visit to Rome, he was struck down by the first of a long series of maladies, apparently psychosomatic in origin, which put an end to his hopes of a great public career and drove him to spend much of his time as a patient at the Asclepieum of Pergamum', a temple founded in around 350 BC (Paus. 2.26.8–9). Neurotic? Having 'many psychosomatic symptoms' (Behr 1968: 162)? Hypochondriac (Beagon 1992: 214–15)? An 'introspective neurasthenic' (Holden 1907: 23)? Whatever we may think of his 'inordinate fixation on bodily pain and suffering', and however unsettling we find the details of his own bodily experiences (Perkins 1992: 246) and the lists of symptoms and treatments – 'enemas and phlebotomies, as many as no one has ever counted' (*Sacred Tales* 47.59) – so graphically described in the *Sacred Tales*, in his own terms Aelius Aristides 'suffered from chronically poor ill-health' and was 'in almost constant pain' (Perkins 1992: 259, 264). Life, for him, was a succession of 'tempests of my body' (*Sacred Tales* 47.1): health was a safe harbour only too briefly experienced in their midst (*Sacred Tales* 46.1).

Aelius Aristides is best known for his devotion to the healing god Asklepios; he spent AD 145–147 at the Pergamum Asklepieon in 'incubation', the procedure by which the sick person slept at the temple and dreamed there. Aristides' interpretations of his dreams are relentlessly physical; a dream indicates how the body is to be treated (Perkins 1992: 252). He then returned to his political career, but he continued to suffer and also to maintain a close relationship with Asklepios until his death in AD 171 (Perkins 1992: 247–8).

However, it is clear from his public speeches that he continued to use doctors; Behr suggests that, while doubting specific doctors and recommendations, he continued to believe in 'an ideal medicine, which remained unaffected by the bunglers who practised it' (1968: 169). Modern studies of patients in chronic pain suggest that this behaviour, mixing and matching treatment from a range of healing systems, characterises those still seeking for a pain story. One doctor – Behr suggests that it was Porphyrio – listened to Aristides' dreams and 'being a sensible man, he also yielded to the god' (*Sacred Tales* 47.57 trans. Behr 1981). After one dream sent by the god, in 146, Aristides summoned the doctor Theodotus and told him his dreams: 'He marveled at how divine they were, but was at a loss as to what he should do, because it was winter time and he feared the excessive weakness of my body' (*Sacred Tales* 48.34). They decided to call the temple warden Asclepiacus, in whose house Aristides was living at the time; Asclepiacus said that the other temple warden, Philadelphus, had had a significant dream very similar to that of Aristides. Aristides therefore drank wormwood, which had featured in both dreams, and it helped him. When he developed a swelling in the groin, Aristides started with doctors, who recommended surgery or cauterisation by drugs, or gave a prognosis of death (*Sacred Tales* 47.62). The god, in sharp and clearly preferable contrast, suggested that he should 'endure and foster the growth. And clearly there was no choice between listening to the doctors or to the god' (*Sacred Tales* 47.63). When the growth worsened, Aristides' 'friends' put in their contributions; some praised his endurance, others thought he put too much trust in dreams, and others said he was a coward to forbid surgery or drugs. The god explained the condition as being dropsy diverted downwards; this made the swelling a good swelling, as an appropriate diversion of matter from above, and it coincided with – and thus legitimised – Aristides' own feeling that his head and upper gut were healthy throughout the four months of this condition (*Sacred Tales* 47.61 and 64). The god's treatment was dramatic: Aristides had to run a race barefoot in winter, ride horses, and sail in stormy weather after eating honey and acorns, and then vomit (47.65). Finally 'a certain drug' which contained salt was successfully applied at the recommendation of Aristides' foster father Zosimus who was told it in a dream from Asklepios (47.66). This stopped the doctors' criticisms; instead they said 'that it was some other greater disease, which he secretly cured' (47.67). But the doctors did consider surgery necessary to deal with the loose skin left after the growth had disappeared; however, the god commanded Aristides to rub on an egg, which cured the problem to the extent that nobody could even tell which thigh had been affected (47.68). In a further bout of ill-health soon after the swelling in the groin, the god advised enemas; the doctor called to apply them was unwilling to do so, as Aristides seemed so weak, but Aristides persuaded him and immediately recovered (47.73).

Reading the *Sacred Tales* it becomes clear that, in this chronic illness extending over many years, Asklepios offers something which the doctors do not: an explanation of suffering acceptable to the patient. If acute symptoms are to be read as messages sent by illness, then chronic pain feels like an all but indecipherable message (Morris 1991: 74). In AD 144 'the doctors were wholly at a loss not only as to how to help, but even how to recognise what the whole thing was' (48.5), while the doctors and gymnastic trainers at Smyrna were also unable to help, not recognising 'the variety of my disease' (48.68).

This is not simply a question of giving a disease label to the condition; the god does not do this either. However, for Aristides, the worst aspect is his difficulty in breathing and the associated pain (48.6). A public orator needs, above all, to feel confident in his delivery. But the doctors do not seem to appreciate the patient's priorities. In the 144 episode, when his intestines swelled and his breathing was blocked, the doctors (48.63) purged him with elaterium, and he then had a bloody discharge, plus more fevers, 'and everything was despaired of, and there was not any hope even for my survival'. Doctors made an incision from chest to bladder and used cupping instruments; at which, he stopped breathing, and 'a pain, numbing and impossible to bear,[13] passed through me and everything was smeared with blood, and I was violently purged. And I felt as if my intestines were cold and hanging out, and the difficulty in my respiration was intensified' (48.63). The god's prescriptions may sound to us even less helpful, including washing at a frozen spring while only wearing a linen tunic (48.79), going without shoes in winter (48.80), ' countless thousands of medicines' (48.10) and very limited 'exclusion diets'. Aristides sometimes eats no greens except wild ones and lettuce, refuses all sweetmeats, and for a period of time is permitted only one food by the god; he chose chicken (49.34). For six years up to AD 170–1 he refused all fish, and for many years pork (49.35). When a physical explanation for the symptoms is given by the god, such as the description of dropsy moving downwards causing the swelling in the groin, it is one which could equally well have been provided by doctors.

What Asklepios offers and the doctors do not, however, is a focus on the symptom which most disturbs his patient, in what we could call a 'holistic' approach to the condition. As Lee Pearcy puts it, 'To heal Aristides' body and to inspire his literary efforts are for Asklepios the same activity' (1988: 391). The god understands his patient's anxieties about oratory, and appreciates that having had to abandon oratory has made Aristides feel despondent (50.14); he eases his difficulty in breathing, convincing him that once he starts to speak his problems will fade, so that although Aristides begins short of breath, he finds he is soon able to breathe well (50.22).[14] In her study of patients coping with chronic illness today, Kathy Charmaz (1991: 101) demonstrates how the self can be overwhelmed by the body, leading someone with chronic illness to ask the questions, 'Who *will* I be?' and 'How can I continue to be myself?' But the god tells Aristides his identity remains that of an orator (Kee 1982: 133); he teaches him which ancient writers to study (50.24), instructs him in techniques (50.26) and even gives him the words to write (42.11). Indeed, Pardalas the orator once says to him that he had become ill 'through some divine good fortune' in order to improve his oratory (50.27; cf. Rutherford 1995: 198). Sometimes Aristides copes with his anxiety about breathing by learning speeches word for word (50.29). At the god's command, he also starts to write lyric poetry (50.31) and to keep a chorus of boys who can sing his verses if he ever finds himself physically unable to speak (50.38); it is the doctor Theodotus, who was his doctor during his incubation in Pergamum, who tells them to sing at the critical moment.

In addition, Asklepios encourages narrative. In part, it seems to be the very frequency of the god's interventions which is so soothing; there are so many signs from him to Aristides, given in response to the dangers which beset him 'every night and every day' (48.25), a phrase reminiscent of Hesiod's view of the onset of the evils of the present age, when 'diseases come upon men continually by day and by night' (*Erga* 102). Asklepios 'gave me one day after another' (48.37); this can be read in conjunction with Charmaz' remarks on perceptions of the self and time by contemporary patients managing chronic illness (1991). The chronically ill live in a continuous present, one day at a time; they may be unable to think about the future, because they are not sure that they have one (1991: 88, 170). Or they may look back, 'searching the past to explain the present and predict the future', seeing fresh significance in past events as a result of their illness (1991: 200).

Arthur Kleinman has shown how the search for why they are ill makes people today become 'archivists researching a disorganised file of past experiences' (1988: 48). Aristides' excavation of the past is deliberate, and is performed at the instigation of the god. *The Sacred Tales* were composed during the winter of AD 170–1, and Aristides gives every occasion in his life when Asklepios has helped him, in particular claiming to use his recollections of a diary kept for a period of a month and a half in AD 166.[15] He says that 'each of our days, as well as our nights, has a story, if someone, who was present at them, wished either to record the events or to narrate the providence of the god' (47.2). But it is hard to tell the story when pain intervenes; Morris compares 'The normal failure of language under the assault of acute pain' with the experience of chronic pain, in which 'There is simply nothing that can be said' (Morris 1991: 72–3, following Scarry 1985: 13, 54). Only with the prompting of the god is Aristides able to become his own archivist (48.2):

> Come let us also recall earlier events, if we are able. In the beginning it did not occur to me to write about any of these, because I did not believe that I would survive. Next my body was also in such a state that it did not give me leisure for these things. Again as time passed, it seemed to be an impossibility to remember each thing and to tell it precisely. So I thought that it was better to keep completely silent than to spoil such great deeds.
>
> (48.1)

In the *Sacred Tales* Aristides breaks the silence by breaking the chronology of his diaries to create/discern a pattern which shows more clearly than did 'real life' the influence of Asklepios, the god who understands that oratory is central to his patient's life. Morris (1991: 274–5) describes a woman with chronic pain in her elbow who breaks down because she can no longer play the organ for her church choir, because it was this activity which gave her life shape and meaning. Facing the loss of his public career, Aristides nevertheless comes to believe that his suffering, that 'seemingly incoherent mass of symptoms' (Behr 1968: 162), has meaning. He tells the full extent of the suffering because it shows 'more clearly the power and the providence of the god, and . . . the honor which I had' (48.59).

Aelius Aristides and the story he creates demonstrate that Hippocratics did not have a monopoly on the healing power of narrative. But the narrative provided by Asklepios for this patient in the second century AD differs from Hippocratic narrative in the way it manages to avoid any suggestion that Aristides' way of life is to blame for his symptoms. Just as *ponos* could be seen as necessary pain, so the pain story of Aelius Aristides suggests that pain can be inescapable; but, in the latter case, it comes to be taken as evidence of the continual presence of a benign god. Rather than studying ancient accounts of pain and its treatment from the viewpoint of Western biomedicine, with its focus on drugs and the power of their constituents, I would argue that we will have a better understanding of ancient medicine if we take seriously the role of narrative in healing.

7

READING THE PAST THROUGH THE PRESENT

Drugs and contraception in Hippocratic medicine

In the previous chapter, I suggested how material from the sociology of medicine on chronic pain can illuminate the behaviour of Aelius Aristides. This raises important epistemological questions for studying the medical systems of any other civilisation. What role should our contemporary medical beliefs play in the enterprise? How far is it valid to use our categories, and how far is it possible to do anything else?

One area of Hippocratic gynaecology which has aroused considerable interest in recent years is its pharmacology. As Riddle (1987: 39) noted, in the Hippocratic corpus many references to drugs come from the two collections of *Diseases of Women*. Concentrated in the closing chapters, 74–109 (L 8.154–232), of the first book, these references often take the form of lists of different therapies for a condition; other than grouping recipes together, they are generally unsystematised, rarely rating cures within groups by their relative efficacy. Only occasionally is a recipe is marked approvingly, as 'does well' (*kalôs*, *DW* 1.78, L 8.184), or as 'the best' (*DW* 1.34, L 8.80), while the squirting cucumber is recommended as a uterine expulsive with the words, 'You will find nothing better' (*DW* 1.78, L 8.178). These recipes are currently seen as traditional or 'folk' material, taken over by *iatroi*; for example, Lesley Dean-Jones (1994: 30) states that 'The gynaecology incorporates more elements of folk practice, such as a wider materia medica . . . than other sections of the corpus.' Aline Rousselle (1980: 1091–2) was the first to argue that Hippocratic medicine was based on 'an empirical science' derived from women in which they 'made the most detailed observations of their own bodies' and collected facts 'patiently over the years' (Rousselle 1988: 24, 26);[1] this was subsequently hailed by Nancy Demand (1994: 63) as 'a claim of the greatest importance to the interpretation of women's role in the history of medicine', making the recipes 'women's lore' (1994: 65), a privileged source allowing us to reach ancient women and their own views of their bodies. But how special are the gynaecological treatises in their therapy? The number of references to drug ingredients is striking – 'In no other segment of the early Greek medical writings are the medicaments that cure, or at least alleviate, awarded such prominence' (Hanson 1992a: 235) – but, as Heinrich von Staden (1992a: 12) has shown, more specific claims for the unique *range* of the gynaecological materia medica are unfounded; almost all the ingredients mentioned in *Diseases of Women* also occur in recipes given in general works such as *On Diseases* 2 and 3, *Affections* and *Places in Man*.

In this chapter I want to discuss some of the problems raised by attempts to assess the gynaecological recipes. For a full assessment of ancient drug lore, we need to investigate not only its origins in male science or women's traditional lore, but also its efficacy. Hanson's phrase 'cure, or at least alleviate' raises the issue, while keeping the options open. Where the aim is contraception or abortion, alleviation may seem irrelevant; you either conceive, or you do not, and either abort, or do not (Riddle 1997: 67).

What counts as contraception?

Before the publication of John Riddle's *Contraception and Abortion from the Ancient World to the Renaissance* (1992) and *Eve's Herbs* (1997), studies which make extensive use both of comparative studies of folklore surrounding plants in contemporary third world societies and of laboratory work on the chemical efficacy of the plant materials used in such societies, it was assumed that ancient methods of contraception using herbal substances were almost entirely ineffective.[2] In his 1990 *History of Contraception*, for example, Angus McLaren argued that these recipes are 'clearly "female knowledge" of which male writers were simply the chroniclers' but rated this knowledge as largely worthless, 'working' only in what he saw as the very limited psychological sense of giving women the illusion of control over their own bodies (1990: 28). Sue Blundell generally regards the ancient gynaecological recipes as 'women's wisdom' but, on the efficacy of Soranos' contraceptives, which she characterises as 'homely', she nevertheless writes, 'None of these methods can have been very effective' (1995: 108). In particular, the widespread ancient practice of polypharmacy, by which several different agents were applied simultaneously, would have made it difficult to discover what worked, and what did not. These agents included spells; a contraceptive using a lodestone as an amulet is preserved in the Greek magical papyri (*PGM* XXII.a.11–14 (Betz); Scarborough 1991: 158–9). As well as magic, people may have used non-fertile sexual positions. As Keith Hopkins (1965) argued for the Roman empire, if one's neighbour was avoiding pregnancy there was little way of discovering her secret if she was simultaneously using a barrier contraceptive – such as a sponge soaked in vinegar or oil, or cedar resin applied to the mouth of the womb, which could have acted as spermicides – while also taking herbs and jumping up and down after intercourse, while her partner was wearing an ivory tube round his left ankle (Hopkins 1965: 139).

Against this sort of approach, Riddle argues that ancient herbal drugs contained oestrogenic substances which would have been highly effective either as contraceptives in our sense of the word,[3] or as early-stage abortifacients which, by ending a pregnancy before the seed was considered to have 'set', would have been considered 'contraceptive' in the ancient world. In modern pharmacology, conception may be defined as 'the successful implantation of a blastocyst in the uterine lining'; a contraceptive is an anti-fertility agent that prevents ovulation and/or fertilisation; an interceptive prevents implantation of the fertilised ovum in the womb; and an abortifacient acts after implantation has occurred (Farnsworth *et al.* 1975a: 539, 541). These categories would be entirely alien to Hippocratic medicine. In *On Generation/Nature of the Child*, conception is an extended process in which 'from beginning to end, the process of growth in plants and in humans is exactly the same' (*NC* 27, L 7.528; Lonie 1981: 18). Here, in contrast to the alternative Greek tradition in which only men produce seed while women contribute raw material (Introduction), both sexes contribute seed (*gonê*). After 'mixing', the seed must acquire breath (*pneuma*); then it inflates, forming a membrane on the surface like that which forms on bread rising in a warm place. Only then does it draw in menstrual blood to enable it to 'become a living thing' (*to mellon zôon*, *NC* 14, L 7.492; Lonie 1981: 7). This last phrase implies that the seed is not yet 'a living thing': and it becomes a *paidion*, a 'little child', only after the formation in turn of bones, head, limbs and sinews, mouth, nose and ears, eyes, sexual organs, entrails, respiratory organs and, finally, excretory organs. 'Formation' takes a maximum of 42 days for a girl, 30 days for a boy, the differential being because female seed, being weaker and thinner, takes longer to 'set' (*NC* 18, L 7.504; Lonie 1981: 9–10). The completion of formation is followed by the further stages of 'branching' – in which the fingers and toes appear like twigs at the tip of a branch (*NC* 19, L 7.506; Lonie 1981: 11) – 'rooting' of the nails and hair, and movement of the embryo. *Nutriment* 42 (Loeb I, 356) gives 35 days for formation, and 70 for movement. In *Nature of the Child*, movement occurs after three months for a boy, but after four for a girl, because males are stronger than females (*NC* 21, L 7.510–12; Lonie 1981: 12–13). In this rich account, it is impossible to find a simple translation for our concept of 'conception'.

Since conception was a gradual process taking place over several months, the line between abortion and contraception was also drawn at a point different from our own (Hopkins 1965: 136, 150). In the early Roman empire, Soranos (*Gyn.* 1.60; T 62) distinguished a contraceptive – *atokion*, literally 'not-breeding' – from an abortive – *phthorion*, literally destruction, 'murder'. But the view that the seeds needed to mix, set, branch, and move meant that contraception extended several months into pregnancy.

To add to our problems of interpretation, in the ancient world it was assumed that the most fertile time of the month was just after a menstrual period, when the womb was emptied of blood but remained open to receive semen;[4] for example, *Nature of the Child* 15 states, 'The most favourable time for conception is just after menstruation' (L 7.494; Lonie 1981: 8). If, on the contrary, it was your intention to avoid pregnancy, the best time for intercourse would be about fourteen days into the cycle, because the womb would then be firmly closed. Any attempt to avoid conception would thus have led to intercourse at what Western biomedicine considers to be generally the most fertile days of the month. By our standards, the ancient 'safe period' is our fertile period, and vice versa.

Riddle further suggests that knowledge of the drugs which would stop conception occurring was based on rational observation by women, later recorded by men, forming a reservoir of knowledge which went underground during the Renaissance as medical training shifted to the universities and medical practitioners lost touch with the female, oral tradition which had kept alive knowledge of the classical contraceptive recipes. Riddle identifies so many substances, particularly pot herbs (1992: 155), as contraceptives and/or early stage abortifacients that even he shows signs of concern at the implications of his work, marvelling that the Mediterranean world is populated at all (1992: 38). Some substances were taken orally, others used as pessaries; those which Riddle considers would have been particularly effective include pomegranate skin, pennyroyal, willow, and squirting cucumber.

I will be investigating his claims for these ingredients at the end of this chapter, but before considering specific substances and their possible efficacy we need to ask more fundamental and culturally specific questions: what was the social and cultural context within which the recipes were given? Is there any evidence that contraceptive knowledge before, during or after the Hippocratic period was kept by women and transmitted within female networks? Even more fundamentally, by what standards can we judge the efficacy of ancient remedies and, in particular, contraceptives?

What do women know?

There are, in general, two ways of finding 'women's knowledge' in the Hippocratic texts. One is to argue from silence, perhaps using parallels from our own or other societies: the other relies on taking at face value the Hippocratic writers' own statements about women as informants.

Arguing from silence is dangerous, but widespread. For example, Blundell writes, 'Female wisdom concerning childbirth was doubtless handed down by word of mouth. Consequently, we possess very little information about normal deliveries' (1995: 111). In fact, the reverse is true; it is because we possess little written information about normal deliveries that we assume there was some unrecorded female tradition concerning them.

Arguing for a female tradition from Hippocratic statements about what women say is equally problematic. The main knowledge which women were accepted as having – or, perhaps, were imagined to have – concerned pregnancy (above, p. 32). A woman was thought to 'know' when she had conceived by a sensation of closure in her womb or by observing that the seed did not leave her body after intercourse; however, as we saw in Chapter 2, not all women 'know', and this knowledge is in any case not always accepted by Hippocratic writers. On several occasions *iatroi* say that they know because women or, more specifically, certain women, have told them. In *Fleshes* 19 (Loeb VIII, 160), the writer attributes his information on the formation of the foetus to public *hetairai*, 'common prostitutes'. This immediately makes it problematic; *hetairai* would have been unlikely to have had the same attitude to pregnancy as other women, since their professional value depended on remaining attractive to customers. Another Hippocratic writer supports this suggestion. In the famous passage *Nature of the Child* 13 (L 7.488–90), a slave woman employed as an entertainer 'had heard the sort of thing women say to each other, that when a woman is going to conceive, the seed remains inside her and does not fall out. She digested this information, and kept a watch' (trans. Lonie 1981: 7; cf. 160–2). The Hippocratic writer encouraged her to jump up and down so that her heels touched her buttocks, until she aborted what was thought to be a seven-day-old conceptus. This passage is often used to demonstrate 'the sort of thing women say to each other', but it should be pointed out that the entertainer is hardly a standard Greek woman; neither are the women she meets in the course of her work. There also appears to be a contradiction between the entertainer's lack of knowledge on what to do when the seed does not fall out, and the knowledge attributed to the public *hetairai* in *Fleshes*, who not only 'know when they have become pregnant' but can then destroy the child so that 'it drops out like a piece of flesh' (*Fleshes* 19, Loeb VIII, 160). The difference may be that the latter are explicitly labelled here as 'experienced' women.[5]

The anonymous writer of the tenth book of *History of Animals* notes several times that women emit what he calls 'seed' at the end of erotic dreams (*HA* 634b29–31; 635a34–6). How does he 'know' what women dream or feel? Rousselle asserts that he 'must have received his accounts of the sensations they experienced from women themselves' (1988: 28); in a sophisticated analysis of the different Hippocratic claims for the origin of their knowledge, Hanson (1996a: 166–7) argues that the writer of *Fleshes* openly admits that he has discussed these matters with midwives and prostitutes, while the author of *Generation* often prefers to cover up the dubious origins of his information by a general appeal to 'women as a group'. But a further possibility must be that this is all male bluff, comparable to the manufacturers of methods of birth control in the 1930s couching their claims in the voices of female 'experts' sharing their expertise 'woman-to-woman' (Tone 1996: 496; cf. King 1995a). Greek men both insist on the public silence of women while creating fictional women who are highly voluble (Halperin 1990: 290). In the field of erotic dreams as much as in physiology, where there is no way of proving that your explanation is superior to that offered by someone else, claims like those of the Hippocratics and the writer of the tenth book of *History of Animals* could be made up to trump a previous card in the game, without any reference whatsoever to real women. In the same tradition, Aristotle says that many women have 'choking feelings' and 'noises in the womb' immediately before a period begins, as well as a particular feeling in the flanks and groin which tells them they are pregnant (*HA* 582b10–12; 583a35–b3; cf. 584a2–12). The Hippocratic idea that the womb is a reversed jar with its own neck (Latin *cervix*), mouth (Latin *os uteri*) and lips (Latin *labia*), in sympathetic relationship with the corresponding parts of the upper female body, so that the loss of virginity changed the timbre of a girl's voice (Hanson and Armstrong 1986), made 'choking feelings' a perfectly plausible response as the mouth of the womb prepared to open and shed its monthly burden of blood.

A further type of source material sometimes brought into the debate at this point consists of more general statements made by men in the ancient world concerning what women talk about among themselves. A careful reading of this material calls into question the apparently positive evaluation of women's knowledge by the Hippocratic author of *On Generation/Nature of the Child* and by Aristotle. Lesley Dean-Jones (1994: 28 and n.85) gives what she describes as two positive and two negative examples of ancient Greek authors' assessments of women's transmission of knowledge. The two 'negative' examples are not controversial; they are Simonides' picture of the virtuous bee-woman, who does not enjoy sitting around among women where they tell stories about love (*aphrodisioi logoi*, 90–1), and the attack in Euripides' *Andromache* (943–6) on women who lead each other on to wrongdoing, in which women are called 'teachers of evil'. The examples claimed as 'positive' are however far from straightforward. In Aristophanes' *Ecclesiazusae* (526–50) Praxagora explains to her husband that her absence from home at night was due to going to help a friend in labour, not – as he suspects – a visit to a clandestine lover. There is no specific reference here to the transmission of knowledge, only to practical support; and, far from giving a positive evaluation of women's knowledge, its suggestion of a concern that women's 'support networks' may really be a cloak for adultery recalls the *Andromache* passage.

The second example claimed as 'positive' by Dean-Jones is even more complex. It is the passage from Chariton's novel *Chaereas and Callirrhoe*[6] in which the steward's wife, Plangon, notices that Callirrhoe, who at this point in the story has been sold into slavery, is two months pregnant by her absent husband Chaereas. Here Plangon is not, however, simply a confidante of the inexperienced younger woman; she is acting on behalf of Callirrhoe's love-struck master, Dionysios, who is trying to make use of Plangon's knowledge of women in order to win Callirrhoe for himself. When Plangon offers to help Callirrhoe to abort the child, this is really only pretence; she knows talk of abortion will instead serve to push Callirrhoe into wanting to keep the child, and will thus further her own plans to help Dionysios (2.8.4–11.6). Plangon's offer of knowledge which will cause an abortion is only the prologue to the central part of the section, where Plangon suggests that, since Callirrhoe is a mere two months pregnant, her best option is to marry her master Dionysios and to pass the baby off as his (premature) son (2.10.5). Callirrhoe decides that to live as Dionysios' wife will at least give the child a chance of life. At the end of the novel it is clear that Dionysios still believes that this is his true son, a situation which in turn makes Callirrhoe's assurances to Chaereas, after their eventual reunion, that she has remained faithful to him alone, seem hard to believe; she must have slept with Dionysios for him to believe that the child could be his (Goldhill 1995: 127–32). Far from this being a positive evaluation of the sort of knowledge women pass on to each other, we could instead read this passage as a depiction of women's knowledge being used to achieve a lasting deception of the male.

Callirrhoe's initial innocence and Plangon's knowledge recall an important distinction made in the Hippocratic corpus between two types of women, with implications for their reliability. The trustworthy 'woman of experience', discussed in Chapter 2, is the type claimed as the source for women's oral tradition. When *Diseases of Women* (1.62, L 8.126) lists youth, inexperience and embarrassment as the factors which not only prevent women from knowing what is wrong with them but also keep them from telling a doctor when they suspect something may be wrong, it is 'experience of the diseases arising from menstruation' and age which are seen as the main ingredients of the 'woman of experience'. Callirrhoe, like Pliny's third wife Calpurnia, is in Hippocratic terms an 'inexperienced' woman who does not even realise that she is pregnant: Plangon has the knowledge which will enable her to detect and, if required, to end Callirrhoe's pregnancy. The ancient medical writers thus accept women's knowledge, but we should add the important provisos that it may be a knowledge which they have constructed *for* women, and that they reserve to themselves the right to judge exactly *whose* knowledge they will accept. Also relevant here is Patricia Crawford's warning (1994: 99) in connection with the period 1500–1750 in English history:

> In practice, women's knowledge must have been less effective than people believed, otherwise there would not have been so many unwanted pregnancies outside marriage.

What do women want?

Plangon tells Callirrhoe that she knows how to end a pregnancy at two months. Several naturally occurring chemicals induce cramps and convulsions which can include uterine contractions, thus causing abortion; for example, ergot, a fungus growing on rye. They can also have serious side-effects; ergot can cause gangrene, and many other such substances risk damage to a foetus if it is not expelled. Abortifacients marketed in the nineteenth century worked on the basis that anything which produces 'a horrible shock in the lower digestive tract might so disrupt the uterus that a miscarriage would result', but such interventions frequently failed, so that a mechanical abortion had to be sought (Olasky 1988: 5). In a discussion of the dangers to pregnant women in *Diseases of Women* 1.25 (L 8.64–8), diarrhoea when the embryo is still small is considered to cause miscarriage; but so is severe constipation, thought to cause overheating and to place excess pressure on the embryo.

Ending pregnancy was permitted in all classical cultures, although there was sometimes social disapproval of women whose motive was merely to keep their looks (e.g. Ovid, *Amores* 2.14; Soranos, *Gyn.* 1.60; T 63); the famous 'prohibition' on it in the Hippocratic Oath only seems to rule out abortive pessaries, leaving mechanical intervention and orally administered drugs as possibilities,[7] while the equally famous description of the slave-entertainer in *Nature of the Child* (13, L 7.488–90), mentioned above, shows that abortion by certain means at certain stages of the process of pregnancy was perfectly acceptable to a Hippocratic doctor. Soranos, writing in the early Roman empire, does not condemn what he chooses to call 'abortion': he simply notes that it is safer to prevent 'conception' happening in the first place (*Gyn.* 1.60; T 63), which should perhaps be understood to mean that early-stage abortifacients are preferable to late abortion. By the third century AD, however, abortion by any means could result in criminal charges in the Roman world: but only if the woman died, or if she carried out an abortion without the consent of her husband, thus depriving him of heirs (J.F. Gardner 1986: 158–9).[8]

How is ancient knowledge of drug effects – therapeutic, contraceptive or abortive – supposed to have developed, bearing in mind that there were no experiments at the time of the Hippocratic corpus? As we saw in the previous chapter, the ancient Greeks and Romans attributed the development of remedies to observation of the animal kingdom, but obvious problems of time-scale are introduced by the suggestion that this route can be used to gain knowledge of effective plant contraceptives, in a modern sense of 'contraception'. Yet even in the twentieth century this sort of transmission has been claimed for contraceptive materials. Work on plant oestrogens was the result of economic losses to Australian sheep farmers in 1946 after sheep grazing on clover became infertile (Biggers 1959: 51; Farnsworth *et al.* 1975b: 718). Writing on claims in world-wide folklore for the contraceptive effects of a wide range of plants, Brondegaard argued that in several cases at least this was 'undoubtedly . . . based upon practical experiences' (1973: 167). He then speculated that, in using the plants for 'various diseases', their additional contraceptive effects would gradually have become apparent.

Much recent scholarship on the Hippocratic corpus concentrates not on the theme of drug knowledge being passed from animals to humans, but on oral transmission from women to women. Riddle sees Hippocratic early-stage abortifacients not as violent remedies based on delivering a shock to the digestive system, but as 'women's secrets' (1997: 6), passed down from mother to daughter, which male medical writers somehow appropriated. He argues that ordinary women carried out 'countless experiments' (1992: 87) and then passed on their knowledge orally, 'just as one would learn recipes for cooking' (1992: 156).[9] Is there any direct or comparative evidence which can be used to support such a claim, or is there simply sloppy arguing going on here?

The problems can best be illustrated by examining how one scholar, consciously positioning herself in the feminist reappraisal of classical texts, approaches some of the gynaecological recipes. How can we identify a 'traditional women's remedy' when we meet one? Sue Blundell lists various Hippocratic treatments intended to cure infertility; designed to soften and open up the womb, the closure of which was seen as the root of the problem, these comprised ointments, pessaries and fumigations (1995: 105). The ingredients included animal products and plant extracts, such as juices and seeds. Blundell does not rate these highly; she suggests that they allowed the classical Greeks to make 'little progress in their treatment of infertility', and explains that medical writers of the fifth century BC were 'greatly handicapped' by their 'ignorance' of the existence of the ovaries.

It seems odd to condemn the Greeks for their ignorance of the ovaries. Herophilos 'discovered' the ovaries in the third century BC, but did not share our view of their role (above, p. 38). Even by the early nineteenth century, many experts thought that menstruation and ovulation occurred at the same time. In 1865, echoing Plutarch's imagery of 'wounding' as essential for conception (*Mor.* 769e), Ernst Pflüger argued that the purpose of menstruation was to make an endometrial 'wound' to which a fertilised egg could more easily be attached, and it was not until 1901 that Josef Halban demonstrated the endocrine origin of menstruation (Simmer 1977). Odder still is the contrast between Blundell's negative assessment of how women would have responded to these ancient fertility drugs, when set beside her enthusiasm for ancient contraceptives as 'women's wisdom'. The absence of any specifically Hippocratic contraceptive drugs, with one notable exception which will be discussed shortly, means that Blundell has to look ahead to Soranos for some idea of what a contraceptive recipe would look like. She finds Soranos' recipes 'homely and straightforward' (1995: 108), so much so that she says 'it is hard to believe that they were not the product of a long tradition of women's wisdom'. She then argues from silence, stating that the absence of such contraceptive recipes from the Hippocratic corpus means that in this period contraception, although being practised by women, must have been used without men's knowledge (107–8).

But the ingredients of Soranos' 'homely and straightforward' recipes, described in such affectionate terms, are no different from the fertility drugs which Blundell's imagined Hippocratic woman rejected in favour of 'more mystical methods': namely, plant and animal substances administered orally or as pessaries. Is it therefore correct to admire Soranos' contraceptives, seen as originating in the 'women's wisdom' responsible for the (lost/unwritten/invisible) Hippocratic contraceptive recipes, while rejecting Hippocratic fertility drugs as the product of male ignorance, and in the process to present women as the keepers of contraceptive remedies, men as the proponents of fertility remedies?[10] Riddle of course goes further still, asserting that women's contraceptive recipes 'worked' while men's fertility recipes did not.

This identification of contraception as women's concern, fertility as men's interest, has the whiff of anachronism; it is a feminist reading creating Greek women in the image of women of the post-Pill era, able to exercise – preferably without men's knowledge – their 'right to choose'.[11] In Hippocratic medicine, it is true that the emphasis was placed firmly on helping women to conceive; the signs of fertility should be identified, and women of a less promising physical type enabled to conceive regardless. For example, *Prorrhetic* 2.24 (Loeb VIII, 270) begins:

> This is how you can tell which women are more likely, and which less likely, to conceive. First, their appearance. Small women are more likely to conceive than large, thin more likely than fat, white than red, black than livid, those with prominent veins than those without. In older women, well-nourished flesh is bad, but stately large breasts are good. These things are obvious at first sight. You should enquire about her menstrual periods, if they appear every month, and if they are sufficiently heavy, a good colour, the same amount each time, and on the same days each month. For these things are the best. The place in which conception occurs, which we call the womb, should be healthy, dry and soft . . .

The third book of *Diseases of Women*, also called *On Sterile Women*, states in its opening chapter:

> Now I will reveal by what causes women are completely sterile, and why they do not give birth until they are cured. I say the cause is this: if the mouth of the womb is tilted completely away from the external sexual parts, the woman does not conceive; for the womb does not receive the seed, which falls out immediately.
>
> (*DW* 3.213, L 8.408)

This condition, like the state of fertility described in *Prorrhetic*, can be detected from the menstrual cycle; here, menstruation will be entirely absent or, if the deviation of the mouth of the womb is not as severe, it will be difficult and painful.

The Hippocratic texts are male constructs, and here they support the thesis that there was a male interest in ensuring female fertility. Once pregnancy is established, they regard it as a delicate condition because 'it requires much careful attention and much skill to bring an embryo to full term, to nourish it in the womb, and to survive bringing it into this world in childbirth' (*DW* 1.25, L 8.68).[12] But would a woman's own views be any different, when her position within the household depended on producing legitimate heirs for her husband's family? Dean-Jones argues that 'The models of the female body in the Hippocratic Corpus are the product and the common property of society, women as well as men . . . Women must have acquiesced in the model to the extent of providing data to support it and acceding to therapy based upon it, but this need not mean that women were relinquishing a positive for a negative image' (1994: 37–8). Culturally, as we saw in the previous chapter, childbirth was to a woman as war was to a man; Hippocratic anatomical explanations of how the process of becoming an internally 'complete' woman was dependent on bearing children would have encouraged women's interest in fertility drugs. Within marriage, fertility was a concern shared by women and men.

But fertility at what level? Even if women in the ancient world had access to effective plant-based contraceptives, we may question whether their intention in using these would have been to limit completed family size. Infant mortality was high in antiquity; in the Roman world, for example, for which we have more evidence, probably 50 per cent of children died before the age of 10 (Bradley 1994: 143). The best evidence for ancient demography comes from Roman Egypt (Bagnall and Frier 1994), where it has been estimated that married women would need to have given birth five or six times in order simply to maintain the population at a stable level. 'If the Total Fertility Rate had fallen by just one child, from 5.7 to 4.7, then Egypt's population, when it stabilized, would have halved every century' (Frier 1994: 330). In these circumstances, even if reliable contraceptives were available, widespread use of them in marriage in order to limit completed family size would have been equivalent to 'a culture of suicide' (Frier 1994: 331).

But 'birth control' is not the same as 'family limitation' (Frier 1994: 329 n.41). There are two other, complementary, scenarios for the use of contraceptive methods in ancient culture which do not affect completed family size: seeking to space the same number of births more widely in order to extend the period of lactation, and avoiding pregnancy outside marriage.

Lactation, which delays the return of ovulation, is usually seen as a contraceptive in itself, rather than as a motive for using other forms of contraception. But literature on ancient breast-feeding is perhaps unduly optimistic about the contraceptive effect of lactation alone. One problem is that, in élite Roman society at least, breast-feeding was carried out by a hired wet-nurse, not by the mother (Parkin 1992: 129–32). But even where it is the mother who breast-feeds, a summary of the literature by the demographer

Gigi Santow (1995: 24) shows that breast-feeding has a 'failure rate' of 50 per cent in a twelve-month period: 'the effect is neither indefinite nor predictable in the individual case'. In order to maintain lactation effectively, if this is perceived as desirable for child health, it is therefore necessary to use some other form of contraception.

Without our theory of ovulation, why should people in the ancient world have considered breast-feeding to have contraceptive effects? In Hippocratic medicine, as we saw in Chapter 1, there are connections between the chest and the reproductive organs in both women and men; *Epidemics* 2.1.6 (Loeb VII, 22) says that there is *koinônia*, 'fellowship', between chest, breasts, genitals and voice, so that the breasts wither in women who are about to miscarry (see also *Aph.* 5.53, Loeb IV, 172), while a chronic cough stops when a testicle swells up (Dean-Jones 1994: 215). Furthermore, breast milk and menstrual blood are the same fluid in two different forms, and it is impossible to have both at the same time. The appearance of breast milk in a woman who is neither pregnant nor has recently given birth signifies menstrual suppression (*Aph.* 5.39, Loeb IV, 168), while milk flowing freely from the breasts of a pregnant woman indicates that the unborn child is unhealthy (*Aph.* 5.52, Loeb IV, 170).

What are the implications for the use of contraception of these links between breasts and womb, and breast milk and menstrual blood? In Hippocratic logic, the continuation of breast-feeding should mean that no menstrual blood is left in the womb to provide the raw material for the formation of a new foetus, making breast-feeding – on its own – a contraceptive. But in which direction does the menstrual blood prefer to flow: to the womb, or to the breasts? Its natural exit is via the womb; the route via the breasts is a diversion. This is why medical texts state that pregnancy *may* occur while breast milk is still flowing, meaning that at least some of the fluid has been drawn back to the womb; Aristotle says that normally there will be no menstruation and no conception during lactation, but adds that, if conception does take place, then the milk will dry up (*GA* 777a13–19). Parkin (1992: 130–1) argues that two references in Roman literature may imply that breast-feeding was thought at least to reduce the chances of becoming pregnant. The first is Soranos' recommendation of a wet-nurse in order to help the woman 'with a view to her own recovery and to further childbearing'. In fact the passage cited here (*Gyn.* 2.18; T 90), which expresses a preference in most cases for mother's milk, seems rather to envisage breast-feeding as a tiring activity which can lead to premature ageing; 'the expenditure for the nourishment of the offspring necessarily makes her own body quite emaciated'. A more promising passage is from the *De liberis educandis* (*Mor.* 3d5) traditionally ascribed to Plutarch, which again recommends maternal breast-feeding as superior to wet-nurses, unless the mother is unable to breast-feed 'either because of bodily weakness (for such a thing can happen), or because they are in a hurry to have more children'. The possibility of spacing births in order to preserve the health of a woman is, however, mentioned explicitly in Soranos, but he recommends abortives, rather than breast-feeding, if childbirth would be dangerous due to abnormalities of the womb (*Gyn.* 1.60; T 63).

The use of other types of contraception in order to space births and preserve lactation is thus a possibility in the ancient world. Frier (1994: 333) has argued that an even more urgent scenario for the use of contraception would have been extra-marital sex. Santow (1995) shows that this is where people are most likely to learn contraceptive behaviour, carrying it into their marriage when it is needed; for example, to preserve lactation. As caretakers of information about such behaviour, Frier (1994: 333) suggests midwives, who may have picked it up from their clients and passed it on; this is questionable, since ancient midwives may have had very small constituencies (see below, Chapter 9, pp. 176–7), but a similar argument was made by Conway and Slocumb (1979: 243) for abortive and emmenagogue information in Spanish New Mexico. A further possibility, and one with more support in the ancient sources, is that the information was kept by prostitutes (Scarborough 1991: 144–5; Frier 1994: 331); the problems raised by the sources for this route of transmission will be discussed further below.

So it is possible that, despite the Hippocratic writers' interest in encouraging conception, and their view of childbirth as a thorough purge with health benefits for a woman, their patients would have been interested in contraceptive information. However, amidst all the advice on keeping the womb healthy and achieving pregnancy in the Hippocratic texts, the only explicit contraceptive given is a substance called *misy*, possibly copper ore,[13] taken orally and recommended as having the power to prevent conception for a year (*DW* 1.76, L 8.170 and *NW* 98, L 7.414). Riddle speculates that this would work, in terms of chemical efficacy; if traces of copper were excreted in the urine and faeces, this could contaminate the vagina, then be absorbed into the lining of the womb and prevent implantation (1992: 74–6). However, even on this highly optimistic reading, it still would not work for a year.

This brings us back to the important issue of efficacy. Regardless of the origins of the gynaecological recipes, as women's traditional remedies, men's new inventions or a combination of male theory superimposed on female tradition, would they work? Riddle is doubtless correct to argue that some of the remedies given in Hippocratic gynaecology would have been abortive in effect, but he says more than this. By using laboratory studies of the effects on small mammals of some of the plants used, Riddle argues not just for effects which are 'contraceptive' in ancient terms while being 'early-stage abortifacient' in ours, but also for knowledge of materials which were, in our terms, contraceptive. Riddle's books raise in an acute form the question of the validity of applying modern research – in this case, on pharmacology – to the ancient world. In chemistry, has Riddle found a universal language which can be applied to every human society, everywhere?

When is a purge not an abortion?

Restricting ourselves for the moment to interventions which in our terms are early abortions, comparative historical work demonstrates how a substance which leads to abortion may be given under the rubric 'To bring on a late period'. Crawford (1981: 69) documents for seventeenth-century England the practice of seeking an abortion by asking to have a 'suppressed' menstrual period induced, Astruc (1761: 37) demonstrates a fear that women who deny the possibility of pregnancy may be lying, and recommends that the wise doctor should always start with the most gentle emmenagogues, while P.S. Brown (1977) and Angus McLaren (1994: 267) discuss the code-words 'removing "obstructions"' in nineteenth-century medical advertisements.[14] However, as McLaren (1984: 102) asks, 'was every woman whose periods had stopped and who employed a herbal potion seeking to abort?'

For Riddle, everything expulsive becomes an abortifacient; 'bringing on a period' is always to be read as Hippocratic code for 'causing an abortion'. Certainly, many of the remedies given as multipurpose gynaecological cures in the ancient medical tradition are general purges, listed as being good to expel a dead foetus or retained placenta, bring on labour, or cause retained menstrual blood to be expelled. But Riddle consistently translates as 'uterine abortifacient' Greek phrases which actually state 'Able to expel the afterbirth' (Riddle 1992: 78 on *DW* 1.78) or simply 'an expulsive' (*ekbolion*).[15]

By reducing all of Hippocratic gynaecology to abortion advice, Riddle fails to appreciate the importance of menstruation in its model of the female body. The most common disorder in Hippocratic gynaecology is indeed a late period, so what was envisaged as action to bring on a delayed period could in our terms have been an early abortion. But the Hippocratics insist that women's diseases are caused by retained menstrual blood; for them, bringing on a period may simply be bringing on a period.[16]

The problems may be illustrated by the implications of my statement that 'the most common disorder in Hippocratic gynaecology is a late period'; even this apparently straightforward diagnosis glosses over an immense cultural gap between the Greeks and ourselves. A late period is *not* the 'same' symptom regardless of the culture in which it occurs. At the simplest level, what are the parameters; how late is late? In the Introduction I briefly discussed anthropological literature, which includes examples of societies in which it is 'normal' to menstruate only every two months, so that monthly menstruation is a worrying symptom requiring medical treatment. A passage of Aristotle's *History of Animals* states that 'in some women the menses come regularly each month – in the majority every third month' (582a34–b5). Even counting inclusively, as the Greeks did, this implies that he expected the majority to bleed at greater than 28-day intervals (Dean-Jones 1994: 96 n.181). In contrast, the Hippocratic texts expect relentlessly regular monthly bleeding, and medical intervention is expected if the bleeding does not occur. They define 'lateness' far more strictly than does Aristotle.

When we consider the *significance* of a late period, a further level comes into play. In our culture we assume that the most common reason is pregnancy. Although this was also a possibility for Hippocratic medicine, theories about the anatomy and physiology of women radically different from those of Western biomedicine meant that it was not always the first response. As we have seen, in Hippocratic gynaecology a woman was composed of a fundamentally different kind of flesh from a man, needing to purge excess fluid every month to prevent it from rotting and causing disease (e.g. *DW* 1, L 8.12–14; on rotting, *DW* 2.156, L 8.332). Her womb could also move around her body.

These aspects of Hippocratic knowledge about the female body – spongy flesh, excess blood and wandering womb – prevent any neat correspondence between the diseases diagnosed in Hippocratic gynaecology and the disease categories of biomedicine. For the latter, it is possible to 'miss' a period: for the Hippocratics, it was not. This is because we believe in ovulation; we believe in hormonal messengers travelling round the body, with luteinising hormone freeing an egg from an ovary, a subsequent rise in levels of follicle-stimulating hormone, and the cyclical withdrawal of oestrogen causing the lining of the womb to shed itself. If the balance between these messengers is upset, there will be no shedding, and no period. In our system, the absence of menstruation can mean pregnancy, or can imply some other sort of hormonal disturbance. In the *Diseases of Women*, menstruation occurs not because of hormones but because of women's spongy, wet flesh, seen as part of their fundamental nature. It is therefore absolutely essential for health that the blood comes out each month without fail, because it is always building up in the body as a result of normal eating and drinking encountering spongy flesh. Indeed, there is no Greek term for a 'missed' period; the Greeks say instead that the blood is 'hidden', lurking somewhere within the body (the verb *kryptomai* is used in *DW* 1.2, L 8.14; *DW* 1.3, L 8.22, etc.). If the blood is not being used to form a baby then it must be exerting pressure on the internal organs, causing symptoms around the body.

It would thus appear somewhat perverse to impose our diagnostic labels, or to use chemical efficacy to judge how therapies 'worked', while rejecting the Hippocratic anatomy of a woman and the whole medical theory which made the treatment appear necessary. If we are confronted with a Hippocratic text in which a fumigation – a lengthy treatment in which hot vapour is passed up the vagina through a reed – is prescribed (e.g. *DW* 2.133; L 8.284–6; see Chapter 11 pp. 218–9), can there be any point in analysing the chemical constituents of the substances burned to create the vapours, when we do not believe in the movement of the womb for which that fumigation was prescribed?[17]

Testing folk remedies

If we cannot always take references to late periods and purges as coded messages for abortion, can we at least say that the recipes given in the classical texts would either have caused abortion if a woman was indeed pregnant, or would have prevented pregnancy occurring? Riddle's work makes much use of ethnopharmacological contraceptive research, based on testing plants with a reputation in world folklore for alleged contraceptive effects; Farnsworth *et al.* (1975a: 541–6) identified and listed 225 such plants. This is an area being actively encouraged by the World Health Organisation in its search for new, effective plant agents which interfere with fertility by acting on sperm production, ovulation, fertilisation or implantation of the ovum in the womb (Farnsworth *et al.* 1975a: 535–6). Most such work looks at oestrogens, which can cause the ovum to be retained in the oviduct or, alternatively, to be expelled from the uterus (Farnsworth *et al.* 1975a: 539). It is not known why – in terms of their value to the plant – oestrogenic substances are produced in plants (Harborne 1993: 106).

Laboratory experiments on animals, using these plants, can be challenged from two main directions: first, is it acceptable to generalise from laboratory animals to people, bearing in mind that there are considerable variations in their reproductive cycles so that 'Different species can vary in their response to different types of compounds' (Farnsworth *et al.* 1975a: 536)? Second, are the materials given to laboratory animals prepared in such a way that, even if the leap from small mammals to people was considered reasonable, the effects on animals from the concentrated essence of the plant cannot be considered equivalent to the effect on humans taking the plant in an infusion? For example, tests on coriander seeds – chosen because of their traditional use by women in Saudi Arabia to limit fertility – demonstrated an anti-implantation effect in rats, but 1 kilogram of coriander seeds was needed to generate 6 grams of the dried extract administered to the rats, who were then given 500 milligrams per kilogram of body weight (Al-Said *et al.* 1987: 166). It is not easy to see how this amount, projected for a woman, fits in with Riddle's optimistic scenario in which 'The woman's salad may have been her control over her own life and her family's life, while the men and nonchildbearing women ate from the same bowl and saw it as simply a nourishing, tasty meal course' (1992: 155). In a recent study carried out on plants claimed as abortifacients in Indian traditional medicine (Nath *et al.* 1992), the plants were chopped up, air-dried in the shade, ground to a 60-mesh powder, soaked in 90 per cent ethanol or distilled water, filtered, soaked again, and filtered once or twice more. The residue was discarded and the filtrates dried in a Rotavapor at 45–50 degrees C. The material was then stored at –40 degrees C, before being given to pregnant rats. The use of these plants in traditional medicine cannot possibly replicate this purity and concentration.

In this last study, moreover, most of the plants investigated were still less than 50 per cent effective in causing the rats to miscarry, but two were judged to be 100 per cent effective. It is difficult to know whether the 'ineffective' plants were simply being tested at the wrong point during the reproductive process; Farnsworth *et al.* (1975b: 741) suggest that some of the tests performed to date have not followed through the stages sufficiently to cover contraceptive, interceptive and abortifacient properties. If extrapolation from laboratory rats to humans is considered valid, then it is also worth noting that many of the less 'effective' plants caused serious birth defects in those rat foetuses which were not aborted (Nath *et al.* 1992). An earlier study of nine indigenous Indian drugs which were reputed to have an anti-fertility effect concluded that seven were ineffective, among them the seeds of *Vitex agnus-castus*, a plant also claimed to have anti-fertility effects in ancient Greek and Roman drug lore, and already discussed in Chapter 4 (pp. 86–8). Of the two effective plant materials in this study, one was the skin of *Punica granatum*, the pomegranate (Gujral *et al.* 1960).

Riddle (1992: 25–6) notes that Soranos gave five vaginal suppository recipes which involve pomegranate peel. These occur at *Gynaecology* 1.62 (T 64–5). In Soranos' terms, these are seen as contraceptive either because they are cooling and clogging, preventing the male seed from entering the womb, or because they are heating and irritant, driving out the seed. The recipes are:

> Grind the inside of fresh pomegranate peel with water, and apply.
>
> Grind two parts of pomegranate peel and one part of oak galls, form small suppositories and insert after the cessation of menstruation.
>
> Moist alum, the inside of pomegranate rind, mix with water, and apply with wool.
>
> Of unripe oak galls, of the inside of pomegranate peel, of ginger, of each 2 drachms, mould it with wine to the size of vetch peas and dry indoors and give before coitus, to be applied as a vaginal suppository.
>
> Apply pomegranate peel with an equal amount of gum and an equal amount of oil of roses.

It should be noted that all of the above are to be inserted into the vagina. Yet the Indian research Riddle cites with such confidence was carried out on oral administration, not of straightforward pomegranate rind, but of dried and powdered material. Riddle claims the following results in his summary of Gujral's Indian research: 'female rats fed pomegranate and paired with males not treated with the plant showed only 72% as many pregnancies as the control group; in testing female guinea pigs under the same conditions, none became pregnant' (1992: 25; cf. 1997: 42). In fact, the results obtained by Gujral were based on 25 pairs who managed only 20 matings; in 20 per cent of pairs, therefore, the 'contraceptive' effect is simply that the rats did not mate.[18] This does not appear to be a type of contraception envisaged by Soranos, although the five pairs who did not even mate are included in Riddle's figure of 72 per cent (i.e. 18 pairs) which proved infertile. Riddle does not point out that his emphasis on this 72 per cent (he does not say 72 per cent *of what*) gives a number of other misleading impressions. For example, his emphasis on pairs of treated females with untreated males may suggest that pomegranate is only a 'female' mode of birth control for rats; but when pairs of rats were mated in which both the male and the female were treated, out of ten pairs six matings were infertile and four were fertile. Riddle's omission of this material raises the suspicion that he is deliberately skewing the data so that contraception can be made to seem a female matter. When the experiment was repeated on guinea pigs, Riddle says, 'none became pregnant'; in fact, this apparently impressive 100 per cent result was derived from only four pairs of guinea pigs. Furthermore, Riddle states that 'forty days after drug withdrawal, the fertility of both rats and guinea pigs was restored to normal' (1992: 25–6; cf. 1997: 42). This is simply not a fair summary of the laboratory results; after treatment 16 per cent of the rat pairs with an untreated male and a treated female, and 25 per cent (i.e. one) of the guinea-pig pairs, remained infertile (Gujral *et al.* 1960: 50).

In discussing pomegranate, Riddle makes much of the point that the experiments on rats and guinea pigs were only successful when the fruit *skin* was used: extracts of the seed, roots and whole plant had no effect, and 'The fruit skin is precisely what Soranus prescribed' (1992: 26). In *Eve's Herbs* he modifies this to 'only the fruit skin around the seed was found to lower' fertility (1997: 42), so that he can elide this with the ancient sources which 'usually name the seed of the pomegranate as the agent that affects fertility' and then 'assume that their term for seed would include what we identify as pulp or seed covering' (1997: 43). This is an interesting sleight-of-hand, but it does not convince. In 1992 he did not draw attention to the fact that pomegranate was given to small mammals orally, whereas Soranos used it in a pessary. Instead, he moved on to myth for confirmation of his ideas, citing the story of Persephone, who was carried off by the God of the underworld, Hades, and offered a pomegranate to eat. She was then doomed to stay underground, with the earth above condemned to sterile winter, for one month for every seed she ate. He then writes, 'Curiously, modern scholars have not made the connection that the pomegranate was the substance that kept the virgin goddess Persephone from being fertile' (1992: 26). But, if only the peel has any effect, why in the myth was she said to have eaten the seeds? The neat, consistent picture Riddle is looking for, with myth recording information only now capable of confirmation in laboratory conditions, is simply not to be found here.

Riddle later cites 'A textbook authority (Harborne 1977)'[19] as stating that pomegranate seeds have oestrogenic properties (1992: 51–2). But – as Harborne himself stated – even this point is disputed in pharmacological research. Heftmann *et al.* (1966: 1339) argued that pomegranate seeds were 'the richest plant source of estrogens yet found', yielding 17 milligrams of oestrone per kilogram. However, when Dean *et al.* (1971) subsequently reinvestigated this result they were unable to replicate it, instead managing to extract only 4 micrograms per kilogram: their findings thus differed from those of the earlier study by a factor of 4,000 (1971: 2216). They suggested two possible reasons for the discrepancy. Either levels of oestrone varied dramatically from year to year – for example, the oestrogenic effects of clover depend on the phosphorus levels in the soil (Biggers 1959: 63–4) – or, more worrying, the earlier experiment had wrongly registered as oestrone substances which in fact were not oestrone. Later in his book, when discussing the development of the pharmacological tradition in the Roman writer Oribasius (*fl.* AD 360), who does not mention pomegranate, Riddle writes, 'Some drugs that were considered less effective drop out or seldom appear, such as pomegranate' (1992: 89). Here we have a further oddity: in one chapter pomegranate is highly successful, and in another it is so ineffective that it is dropped. To confuse matters further, the sixth-century AD writer Aetius recommends pomegranate *flowers* (Riddle 1992: 94). In Dioscorides, the flowers were used as an astringent mouthwash (1.110), while both Pliny (*NH* 23.59.110) and Dioscorides mention that swallowing the flowers can prevent eye trouble (Riddle 1984: 421–4). Yet Riddle says, 'the prescriptions are being refined and improved' (1992: 97) in the thousand years between Hippocrates and Aetius. Riddle's own evidence, on the contrary, makes it difficult to perceive an empirical, developing tradition: parts of pomegranates come and go, sometimes the 'right' parts, sometimes not.

Another plant mentioned with approval by Riddle is willow (*salix*). In 1933, Skarzynski obtained from female willow *flowers* a substance, trihydroxy-oestrin, chemically resembling a human female hormone (1933: 766); according to the research summarised by Harborne (1993: 105–6) the flowers have female steroids. It is however willow *bark* which is traditionally supposed to interfere with ovulation. Aetius (cited in Riddle 1992: 97; 1997: 61) recommends as a contraceptive a decoction of willow *bark* with honey (to reduce the bitter taste), to be drunk 'continually', and also gives a male contraceptive drink consisting of the burned testicles of castrated mules drunk with a willow decoction. The eleventh-century AD text of Constantine the African has the juice of willow *leaves* to be drunk so that a woman will not conceive (Riddle 1992: 119; 1997: 61). Thus flowers, bark and leaves all feature in the ancient pharmacopoeia.

World-wide, the main traditional abortifacients are tansy (*Tanacetum vulgare*), pennyroyal (*Hedeoma pulegioides*), rue (*Ruta graveolens*), apiol (*Petroselinum sativum*) and oil of savine (*Juniperus sabina*) (Farnsworth *et al.* 1975a:

582). However, tests on human uteri in laboratories found no effect from the volatile oils of pennyroyal, savine or tansy; it is possible that 'when abortion does occur after the use of these volatile oils, it occurs only following toxic doses; fatal doses are not always abortifacient' (Farnsworth *et al.* 1975a: 583). Taken with the point already made, that foetal damage may result from plants taken as abortifacients, this does not give a very encouraging picture of women's traditional lore.[20] Furthermore, since the population curves for traditional societies do not show the patterns of fertility associated with effective methods of birth control (Frier 1994: 332–3), if such plants were being used one could argue that they were either killing those who took them (P.S. Brown 1977: 299; Beagon 1992: 220), or being totally ineffective, or carrying serious risk to the foetus.

The pharmacological research on traditional abortives and emmenagogues is thus very far from being as straightforward as Riddle suggests. It is easy to find examples of plants which are ascribed powerful effects in folklore but are shown to be remarkably ineffective in laboratory tests; for example, Saha and Kasinathan's disappointing results on *Artemisia vulgaris*, garlic and onions (1961: 1097). Dewy-eyed nostalgia for the good old days of herbal medicine is as misleading as the belief that every substance named in folk traditions of other cultures carries a coded message about efficacy. This is demonstrated particularly well by the use of the plant derivative chaulmoogra in leprosy therapy in Western biomedicine for a period of fifty years, from the late nineteenth century onwards. In the absence of any effective treatment for leprosy, medical workers in the colonies looked at indigenous medical traditions. James Mouat (1815–99) discovered an Indian story in which King Rama of Benares was isolated in a jungle cave because he suffered from this disease (Feeny 1964: 105–7). While there, the king ate the fruit and leaves of the kalaw tree, and was completely cured. Raw chaulmoogra oil was given to leprosy patients from the 1850s onwards, but caused gastric irritation. Researchers argued that the substance was effective; the problems lay with incorrect use (e.g. Phillippo 1890: 71). Laboratory work in England separated out from the tree chaulmoogic acid and hydnocarpic acid (Tansey and Milligan 1990: 100), and injections meant that the side-effects of raw oil could be avoided. Burroughs Wellcome then marketed Alepol and Moogrol which became the standard treatments for leprosy. But, by the 1930s, it became clear that the painful injections were in fact having no beneficial effect at all. Myth and folklore may be poor guides to efficacy.

The efficacy of the placebo

Our judgement of the efficacy of ancient ingredients is additionally complicated by the placebo factor. In its original, nineteenth-century, use, the term placebo (literally, 'I will please') was used because the substance given, while thought to be of no real use, kept the patient happy. The definition of a placebo thus focused on its *in*efficacy (Sullivan 1993: 220).

Contemporary drug research has an ambivalent relationship with the placebo. Double- and triple-blind tests, in which a new drug is compared with a placebo, are part of the way in which medicine demonstrates its scientific neutrality (Sullivan 1993: 214). In the course of such tests, it has become apparent that the patients on the placebo pill may not only feel better, but may also experience measurable or visible changes in such things as heart rate and blood pressure (White 1985: 52–3). Subsequent studies of the placebo effect have shown that apparently biologically inert substances can not only relieve symptoms, but can also have toxic side-effects. Furthermore, even if a patient is explicitly told that the pill given contains no medicine and is composed purely of sugar, if he or she is also assured that others have been helped by this treatment and that the doctors think it will help here, the placebo effect will still operate (Brody 1980). Research thus relies on placebos but, if the placebo has an 'effect' which can be measured, this cannot be accepted as a physicochemical one, because the fundamental point about the placebo is that, by very definition, it is chemically inert. Instead, the effect has to be defined as in some way psychological. In the 1950s the effect was explained with reference to a 'suggestible' personality: only the impressionable and immature could possibly be taken in by placebos (White 1985: 54–5). By the late 1970s, psychology was replaced by biochemistry with the discovery that the body produced its own painkillers, endorphins (Levine *et al.* 1978: 654–7). However, the placebo effect is not just experienced as pain relief, but also affects angina and even seasickness (Moerman 1992: 70–1); the placebo should be recognised as 'a drug of significant potency' (Adler and Hammett 1973: 598). Furthermore, work on contemporary British patients suggests that, for them at least, the placebo effect of medication can depend on factors such as its colour (coloured is more powerful than white, while multicoloured is more effective than monochrome), its type (capsules are more powerful than tablets, and injections are perceived as the most powerful of all), and how many pills are given (Moerman 1992: 72–4).[21]

The Hippocratic *Places in Man* 46 (Loeb VIII, 92–4) insists that 'real drugs' do not depend on luck (*tychê*) for their effects, but instead rely on the sound principles discovered by the medical *technê*. It is possible for us to give what, in our terms, are rational explanations for many items in the Hippocratic pharmacopoeia, but we cannot know, for all the reasons already stated, whether their efficacy was due to entirely different considerations. Cantharid beetle pessaries feature in the Hippocratic gynaecological pharmacopoeia, and they would have an irritant and purgative effect; wild cucumbers are used as a purge, and they would have a laxative effect; urine is used in many recipes, and has antiseptic qualities; rubbing animal fat or oil on to sore skin would ease it. However, we cannot always reconstruct the reason why a substance was used in a particular context, and it is perfectly possible that a physician was doing what we would see as the 'right' thing for the 'wrong' reason. Shape, colour, smell or a myth associating substance and symptom may have been more important to many early doctors – and patients – than chemical constituents; all natural matter carries rich cultural values (von Staden 1992b) not best determined by laboratory tests, so that the presence of items in the ancient pharmacopoeia 'clearly owes more to the symbolic associations of the substances in question than to their objective efficacy' (Lloyd 1983: 83).[22] *Ecballium elaterium*, the squirting cucumber, is said to inhibit ovulation in mice if taken as 100 milligrams per kilogram of body weight (Farnsworth *et al.* 1975a: 549). In ancient gynaecology, however, the salient point may be its 'homeopathic' quality of forcefully ejecting its seeds, thus making it appropriate for ejecting an unwanted conception, a retained afterbirth or a suppressed menstrual period.

Heinrich von Staden has drawn attention to one aspect of ancient drug therapy with an interesting gender division: the Hippocratic restriction of therapy involving excrement to female patients. In the nineteenth century, in order to preserve the view of the corpus as the rational precursor of modern medicine, the passages in the Hippocratic corpus in which this therapy occurs were dismissed as 'interpolations'. There is still a tendency either to pass over these passages in silence or to suggest that they are from an earlier chronological level, or another culture. In Chapter 1 I mentioned Longrigg's description of coprotherapy as 'this nauseating practice' (1993: 9), and it is significant that even this outburst occurs in a discussion, not of Hippocratic medicine, but of the ancient Egyptian papyri; when he comes to the Hippocratics, Longrigg is silent on the continued use of excrement.[23] Yet as von Staden (1991b: 43) has pointed out, faeces and urine were used in ancient medicine up to the time of Paul of Aegina in the sixth century AD. The dismissal of such substances as the choice of ignorant women healers by Nathaniel Hodges in his discussion of the therapies used in the Great Plague of 1666 is also worth noting as an example both of the continued use of dirt and of its eventual rejection by the learned tradition (Hodges 1672). What is particularly noteworthy in the Hippocratics is not however the *use* of such substances, but their *restriction* to curing the female body. This is not a question of a different cultural evaluation of substances which we now regard as 'dirty'; von Staden assembles a wide range of sources to demonstrate that the Greeks felt much as we do about excrement (1991b: 44 n.6). Yet these substances were not only used in fumigations, where they would be burned and the vapours allowed to enter the vagina, but were also inserted into the vagina or the mouth in order to disperse blockages thought to be preventing menstruation or conception. Von Staden links recipes involving excrement to religious practices of purification, showing that, from the third century BC onwards, purity laws governing cults saw intercourse, menstruation and childbirth as progressively more 'polluting' (1991b: 52); but 'dirt' was also used in magical practices, because that which pollutes is also that which is magically powerful (Parker 1983: 233). He also points out that the Hippocratic gynaecological fumigation has its parallels in the sphere of religion; in particular, in a source from the fourth century BC, the madness of the daughters of Proitos was treated by fumigation (Diphilos fr.125, *PCG*). In our terms, the use of excrement in therapy would have caused iatrogenic disorders, due to the risk of serious infection: in Greek terms, it made sense to use it for women because only a strongly 'dirty' substance could successfully purge the dangerous 'dirt' of suppressed menses.

Beyond drugs

Interrogating ancient medical texts to discover whether or not the drugs contained effective ingredients may also be criticised as giving undue weighting to just one aspect of the medical encounter: drug therapy. The introduction of Western biomedicine – *our* drugs – to cultures in the developing world has not only shown the importance of making our drugs acceptable in terms of other cultural constructs of disease and recovery, but has also led to some rethinking of how drugs work for us. One important quality of drugs is their 'thinginess' (van der Geest *et al.* 1996: 154): they are material substances, and part of making dis-ease into something visible and tangible. Far more important than chemical efficacy may be the shared cultural matrix of doctor and patient which enables the drug to make sense.

Furthermore, the ritual of prescribing or administering the drug – in our culture, the white coat and the prescription pad – can affect its efficacy. Even in Western biomedicine, it has been argued that the central healing act is the pronouncing of a diagnosis and the subsequent issuing of a prescription, 'the doctor's most therapeutic act' because it shows concern and legitimises the illness (van der Geest *et al.* 1996: 160); taking the prescribed medication is less important than giving meaning to the patient's experience of illness (Adler and Hammett 1973; Brody 1980: 119–20; Brody and Waters 1980). Sullivan (1993: 230) too has argued that diagnosis and treatment should not be seen as different stages. Patient non-compliance – failing to take the medicine – is understandable according to this model, because 'healing' has already happened in the diagnosis and prescription; non-compliance may also represent the patient trying to regain some sense of control by extending the intervals between doses (van der Geest *et al.* 1996: 166). Moerman argues that 'by far the most significant element in this process is the character of the physician and the display (I usually think of it as a dance) he or she produces for the patient' (1992: 72). In the ancient medical tradition words were very important; practitioners were expected to present their theories and explanations fluently, either in the context of a public debate with a rival, or in the more private context of a bedside consultation when the client – or potential client – needed to be persuaded of the healer's skills. Actions too were important in treatment, so that many therapies involved an element of dramatic display. Some, like succussion on a ladder (see Chapter 2, p. 44), were such good theatre that they would be carried out in public.

In such public therapies, the patient's illness is acknowledged and displayed to the onlookers. There is no trace here of the individualism of contemporary Western society, which encourages keeping one's ill-health to oneself. Where the family and community have greater roles, one purpose of the therapy is to stimulate them to acknowledge the illness of the patient and to care for him or her. The use in the gynaecological texts of a very wide range of substances – from the everyday, cheap cabbage-water to the exotic, expensive scents such as Egyptian perfume, myrrh and narcissus oil – would suggest that what is of prime importance is not what 'works', but perhaps a combination of what the patient can afford, and how far the doctor needs to go in impressing her or her husband. Because Hippocratic doctors are in open competition, the third healer called in will be under considerable pressure to think of something a little *different* after the usual remedies have already failed (Lloyd 1987: 68–9, 96, 110); it is to this, perhaps, that we owe one of the recipes in the Hippocratic corpus, in which turtle liver, removed while the turtle is still alive, is ground up and served in human breast milk, in order to encourage the flow of the lochia (*DW* 1.78, L 8.172).

Drug use thus occurs within a wider cultural context; just as it is hard to talk about contraception in our sense where conception is seen as a slow process of coagulation and setting, so it is hard to judge whether a drug worked when, first, we do not believe in the disease diagnosis for which the drug is being given, and secondly, we do not share the culture, with its beliefs about the animals and plants used in drugs and the symbolism associated with them.

Even if some attempts at contraception occurred in extra-marital intercourse or to protect lactation, it should be noted that plant- and animal-based drugs were not the only possible methods available in the ancient world. Not only did the ancient 'safe period' method recommend sex at what we would regard as precisely the least safe time of the month, but non-fertile sexual positions and practices were widespread (King 1994) and infanticide – which could be seen as a very late, and sex-specific, abortion – was practised, although it is difficult to know how widely it occurred. A newborn child had to be formally accepted by the father before being recognised as a person, so it is of interest that this method was in the hands of the *father*, not the mother.

There remains considerable debate about the use in antiquity of *coitus interruptus* (Frier 1994; Santow 1995); this is almost never mentioned by our sources, but does this mean that nobody did it or – entering the dangerous realms of argument from silence – that everybody did it, but failed to mention it because it was so obvious?[24] The one non-medical literary reference occurs in a poem by Archilochos, a seventh-century BC writer.[25] This poem survives only in a damaged papyrus, so reconstruction is not easy. However, it seems mostly to consist of the words of a man who is trying to persuade a girl into taking part in a sexual act. She advises him that if he is really 'in a hurry' he should try another member of her household, 'a lovely tender girl who really wants to'. He is not convinced: the girl in question is 'overripe, twice as old as you; her maiden blossom is fallen away'. Instead, he says, if she is reluctant, they need not go all the way and 'do the divine thing'; he will 'land in the grassy meadows'. Since meadows and gardens are common euphemisms for the female pubic hair (Henderson 1975), he seems to be saying he will withdraw before ejaculation. It is not clear from the remainder of the poem whether or not he managed to keep his word.

As for Hippocratic literature, to my knowledge the sole reference which has ever been interpreted as a description of *coitus interruptus* occurs in *On Generation* 5 (L 7.476),[26] which states that, 'When a woman has intercourse, if she is not going to conceive, then it is her practice to expel the sperm from both partners whenever she wishes to do so' (trans. Lonie 1981: 3). The initiative here rests with the woman, not the man, and may perhaps be interpreted as a reference to washing the seed out after intercourse (Hopkins 1965: 130–1 n.18). In the early Roman empire, Soranos recommended a form of withdrawal by the female partner, in order to prevent the ejection of semen deep into the womb, alongside sneezing after intercourse, washing the vagina and drinking cold water (*Gyn.* 1.61; T 63–4). In general, though, like infanticide, *coitus interruptus* is a *male* method.

I would argue that it would make more sense in terms of ancient culture to see the dominant modes of birth control as likely to be male. In one popular version of conception theory, he plants the seed; the woman is only the field in which it grows. It may therefore be seen as his right to decide if the growing plant is to be uprooted. Men make decisions over life and death; men pay the Hippocratic doctor, and men decide when to call him to a member of the household. Riddle not only sees oral contraception as the main method being used in the ancient world, but argues that early contraceptive drug knowledge was part of a female, orally transmitted tradition. But when male writers say that women have ways (unspecified) of preventing conception, this may be more appropriately seen as part of a wider fear in ancient culture that women have knowledge of drugs, herbs, and spells which are potentially damaging to men. The Greek for healing drug, *pharmakon*, also means poison, and as we will see in the next chapter the great poisoners of antiquity tended to be women. The myth of effective plant-based contraceptives may thus be a male expression of a fear that women hold the knowledge which could enable them to control the fertility of the household.

8

GENDER AND THE HEALING ROLE

The discussion of contraception in the previous chapter raised the issue of the gendering of knowledge through examining some of our assumptions about contraception and abortion in the ancient world. In this and the following chapter I will be discussing the ways in which later readers of the Hippocratic works have used these texts in defining the roles of nurse and midwife as naturally 'feminine'. In the process, I will be putting forward models for the role of women in healing which, I will argue, are more appropriate to the social context of Hippocratic medicine. In our culture, the roles of nurse and midwife are so firmly feminine that exceptions need to be qualified as 'male nurse' and 'male midwife'; in the seventeenth century, many writers deplored both the word and the concept of a 'man-midwife' (e.g. Douglas 1736). I will be arguing that, where Hippocratic materials have been used to support the role of nurse as one linked particularly closely to feminine qualities, the history of midwives demonstrates that more complex connections are possible between Hippocratic texts and subsequent debates. Midwifery has been a contested field since at least the seventeenth century, and as such it has seen more than its fair share of versions of reconstructions of the past.

As I showed in Chapter 3, a major obstacle in studying the Hippocratic corpus today is formed by the ways of reading it which have developed from its uses in the centuries since the texts were first written down. The dominant image of the texts today remains the one presented by orthodox medical works in the biomedical tradition, in which Hippocrates is seen as the 'Father of Medicine', becoming a superb doctor by whatever criteria for superb doctors are currently in fashion. It is interesting, however, that the need to demonstrate a pedigree going back to Hippocrates is not unique to physicians, nor even to biomedicine. Historically less powerful branches of the medical profession have also asserted their true descent from the same Father as their overbearing brother, while even 'alternative' therapies such as homeopathy, aromatherapy, chiropractic and osteopathy have felt the need to play the medical profession at its own game, trying to climb into the same family tree.[1] The multiple images of Hippocrates and of Hippocratic medicine which have resulted from these different quests for historical roots stand as testimony to the sheer variety of the Hippocratic corpus; almost any type of therapy can find a bloodline amongst the conflicting theories of the ancient texts.

In this chapter I will concentrate on attempts to find a Hippocratic pedigree for one branch of the health care professions: nursing. In our own recent medical history, the division of labour between doctors and nurses articulated by Florence Nightingale has essentially been that 'The physician or surgeon prescribes . . . – the nurse carries out' (Gamarnikow 1991: 117). Diagnosis and prescription rest within the sphere of the doctor, while the nurse observes the patient and reports her observations to the doctor (Gamarnikow 1991: 116). A further, and related, opposition is that the nurse cares, while the doctor cures (e.g. Achterberg 1991: 100–1).

Nursing has unique historical problems. It has had to work even harder than the other ancillary medical fields to be accepted as a profession at all, rather than being presented as an extension of naturally feminine qualities of passivity, obedience to men, self-sacrifice and caring. Nurses encapsulate the unstructured and invisible roles of women, acting as daughters to administrators, wives to doctors and mothers to patients (Muff 1988: 201). The history of nurse training, in particular, has had to fight against the idea that no training was necessary because nurses merely do what comes naturally to women by virtue of their sex alone. Even the desire to train as a nurse was, at least in the Victorian period, viewed negatively; the surgeon Isaac Baker Brown, whose attempts to claim a Hippocratic origin for clitoridectomy were discussed in the Introduction, suggested that patients suffering from hysteria had 'a great disposition for novelties' which, in women of the relevant social class, made them 'fond of becoming a nurse in hospitals' (1866a: 15).

The dominant model of the nursing past, constructed by doctors but colluded in by nurse trainers, is a highly negative one, so that histories of nursing aimed at nurses have traditionally tended to start in the mid-nineteenth century and to gloss over anything before Florence Nightingale. Only in the last two decades has the emergence of a new anthropology and history of nursing begun to question the traditional model of 'progress out of the dark ages to the present, modern times'.[2]

How has the ancient Greek past been used in traditional histories of nursing, including not only those which appear in textbooks for nurses but also those aimed at doctors? How have the two professional groups' perceptions of themselves – and each other – been formed by the histories written for them? Both professions receive highly schematic, 'broad brush' accounts of their past (Davies 1980: 11), based on the idea that the professional position of the *iatroi*, the healers of the Hippocratic corpus, was not unlike that of physicians today. Histories of medicine for medics give a highly selective picture of ancient Greek medicine in which the emphasis is placed on the development of empirical, rational medicine out of a background of superstition, religion and irrational practices. Histories of nursing tend to continue this positivist slant; as a standard history of nursing puts it: 'Hippocrates . . . stands out as a real person. The chief contribution of his school was to render the magic of medicine into a science' (Jensen 1943: 35).[3]

Histories written by nurses for nurses stress the position of nursing as an independent occupation with its own identity, and therefore emphasise difference from other health workers (Maggs 1987: 3–4), so that their Hippocrates may veer away from the positivist Hippocrates shared with medics. The 'nursing Hippocrates' is praised in particular for his powers of careful observation of the course of a disease, translated as his discovery of 'patient-centred medicine' (Dolan 1978: 34).[4]

As we have seen throughout this book, in contrast to the traditional feelings of kinship between modern biomedicine and Hippocratic medicine, recent work on the Hippocratic corpus by classical scholars has illuminated the nature of the difference between then and now, between them and us. Such work follows in the tradition of the eminent classicist Edelstein, who in 1931 ended his influential article on 'The Hippocratic physician' with the statement that 'ancient and modern medicine are far removed from one another. And the difference is one not only of detail, but of fundamental outlook' (Edelstein 1931: 110). An essential aspect of this outlook derives from the social position of the medical practitioners whose writings form the Hippocratic corpus, and from their conscious attempt to set themselves apart from the other types of healer practising in their world (Lloyd 1979: 37–49). Their image of their own medicine is that it is a coherent system of cause and effect rather than an *ad hoc* combination of unexplained remedies. They place what they do within the context of a divinely ordered universe but, although they are not opposed to religious systems of healing, they see no particular deity as being responsible for the cures they effect.[5]

The main claim they make for the sort of medicine which they practise is that it constitutes a *technê*. This claim, discussed in Chapter 6, is part of a more general fifth-century Greek investigation in which attempts were made to isolate those features of human culture which had raised mankind above the level of the beasts. Any *technê* has both a practical and a theoretical side and, by producing written texts, the *iatroi* demonstrated the intellectual side of their specific *technê*. Relevant here is the comparison between the *technai* of medicine and writing made by the author of *Regimen*, discussed in the Introduction, in which writing puts together the symbols of the voice, while medicine puts together the signs made by the body. For medicine's claim to be one of the *technai* separating humanity from the beasts – particularly in view of stories of animals who can heal themselves or each other – it is significant that the voice is presented in early Greek anthropology as one of the defining characteristics of humanity (Vegetti 1979: 102). Specifically, man has the faculty of speech (*phônê*) while the beasts do not (e.g. Plato, *Protagoras* 322a; Xen. *Mem.* 1.4.11–12; Diod. Sic., 1.8.3–4 and 9; Eur. *Suppl.* 201–8). However, *phônê* can also be used of animal cries (e.g. Hes., *Erga* 448);

this leads Aristotle to argue that although some animals possess the power of speech, only man has *logos* (*Pol.* 1253a10–15), so that even animals with a *phônê* cannot produce an organised language (*On Interpretation* 16a28–9).

The combination of *phônê* and *logos* is essential to the ancient Greek concept of medicine, since the ability of the healer to diagnose correctly rests not merely on observing the patient, but also on questioning him or her and listening to what is reported (*Prog.* 2, Loeb II, 8). This feature comes out most clearly in Roman discussions of veterinary medicine, seen as an inferior form because 'just as animals are inferior to humans, so the veterinary art is to medicine' (Vegetius, *Mulomedicina* preface 1; Mudry 1982: 183), but also because it is not possible to question dumb animals (Celsus, *De medicina*, preface 55 and 65). Only human beings can produce language; only they can extend the uses of that language by writing it down in symbols, so only they can have the medical *technê*.

The Hippocratic doctor is thus both writer and reader of the symbols of human communication. He must 'study correctly what has been written' (*Ep.* 3.16, Loeb I, 256), while also reading the patient's body through the seven Greek vowels which are the senses (*Regimen* 1.23, Loeb IV, 258–60).

As we have already seen, the Hippocratics were also adept in the art of speaking (Edelstein 1931: 99–100; Jouanna 1984: 26–44), in order to persuade patients of the value of their treatments; this element of persuasion extended further to practical, public displays, with spectacular therapies such as succussion on a ladder (see Chapter 2, p. 44). In the treatment of women, tying the patient head down was used to cure prolapse of the womb by shaking the womb back inside (e.g. *DW* 3.248, L 8.462), while tying her with her head up was thought to induce labour (e.g. *DW* 1.68, L 8.142–4). One writer in the Hippocratic corpus appears to trace the disease of 'Simos' wife' to this very practice when she was giving birth, suggesting that it was seen as a potentially dangerous therapy not only in fractures but also in labour (*Ep.* 5.103, Loeb VII, 216).

The ethical treatises of the Hippocratic corpus, discussed in Chapter 2, imply that the effectiveness of a doctor should be apparent from the simplicity of his self-presentation, with quackery being implied by 'theatrical' bandages, extravagant dress and elaborate perfume, so that the Hippocratic healer is not only writer, reader and orator, but also actor.[6] While accepting the 'well-defined rules' of his *technê* (Ferrari and Vegetti 1983: 202), he feels free to innovate within these and to disagree with other practitioners of the same *technê* over points of theory and practice, including how far one should go in playing to the crowds. The important point here is that there is no individual or corporate body to enforce standards or to lay down the rules. No system of training exists to authorise practitioners, so that anyone who looks and acts the part can find clients willing to pay.

What of nursing within Hippocratic medicine? Wet-nurses and children's nurses certainly existed in the ancient world (Greece: Herfst 1922; Rome:

Joshel 1986), but hospital nurses did not, for the simple reason that there were no hospitals. It is however possible to look at the role of sick-nurse within the context of the home. In his article on doctors in the Daremberg and Saglio encyclopaedia of antiquity published in 1904, Reinach devoted just one sentence to nursing in the ancient world: 'It goes without saying that women, being so to speak born sick-bed attendants and nurses, have at all times carried out these functions' (Reinach 1904: 1682–3). This echoes the assumptions made by Florence Nightingale, whose reforms of nursing were made in the belief that, because giving care to sick members of the family is a natural female role, it followed logically that every woman must be a nurse at some point in her life (Maggs 1985: 173–4). In his introductory material for the second volume of the Loeb edition of Hippocrates, published in 1923, W.H.S. Jones put the same sentiment more cautiously: 'The conclusion we are tempted to draw . . . is that the task of nursing fell to the women, whether slaves or free, of the household' (W.H.S. Jones 1923: xxx). This is also the view given by nursing history; for example, Deloughery assumes that, in the ancient Greek world, nursing was 'an incidental household duty' (Deloughery 1977: 8–9). The assumptions about the division of medical labour which lie behind these statements, and the cultural differences which they ignore, need to be further examined.

Sections on ancient Greece in traditional histories of nursing may open with perfectly accurate remarks on the absence of nurses from the Hippocratic corpus – such as 'Hippocrates does not refer to nurses as such' (Guthrie 1953: xi) – but nevertheless invariably manage to identify some aspect of Hippocratic medicine which can be used to supply an origin for the profession. For example, the feminist social reformer Lavinia Lloyd Dock, who aimed to provide nurses in the first decades of this century with 'a sense of their own identity' (Roberts and Group 1995: 84), wrote with Adelaide Nutting *A History of Nursing*. On the subject of Hippocrates, they informed their readers,

> few nurses know with what perfection and minuteness he has described all that they are taught of symptoms and the meaning of every shade of expression, change of position . . .
>
> (Nutting and Dock 1907: 76)

and, in a clearly political bid, claimed that Hippocrates stated that 'the assistant was the co-worker with the physician' (1907: 78).

In Dock and Stewart's *A Short History of Nursing*, first published in 1920 and quickly established as the standard work, this approach is continued, so that the absence of nurses from the Hippocratic corpus becomes merely an issue of terminology; Hippocrates detailed the technique of 'what we now call nursing' (Dock and Stewart 1938: 32; repeated by Donahue 1985: 76).

In a more recent history of nursing the Greeks are assigned the distinction of being

> the first Western group to become conscious of the need for a trained nurse. Though they met this need with apprentices and attendants rather than a separate occupational group, merely that the need was recognised is extremely important in the history of nursing.
> (Bullough and Bullough 1979: 19; cf. Dolan 1978: 33–4)

I will return to the role of apprentices shortly, but what assumptions about the gender of medical attendants lie behind claims such as these? One view found in histories of nursing is that there must have been nurses of some sort in the ancient world, because who else could have performed those tasks which we now associate with the nurse? A doctor would not have had time to bandage, bathe, mix drugs, sponge the patient and apply poultices (Robinson 1946: 20; cf. W.H.S. Jones 1923: xxx). 'Women doubtless did much noble, if unnoticed work among the sick' (Pavey 1938: 61).[7] Where they did, however, it was not always appreciated. A passage of the Hippocratic *Epidemics* describes a boy who developed a fever twelve days after being hit on the head with a potsherd by another boy; the writer declares that this was because the woman who washed the wound 'rubbed the area around it and it took a chill' (4.11, Loeb VII, 98, trans. W.D. Smith). Thucydides' description of the plague which hit Athens in 430 BC, a valuable – if over-used – source for many aspects of ancient medicine, has the friends of the sick person as the main carers (Thucydides, *Peloponnesian War* 2.51); the *Oikonomikos*, the fourth-century list of advice given by Ischomachos to his young wife on household management, includes the assumption that it is the responsibility of the wife to ensure that sick slaves receive care, although she is not apparently expected to care for them herself ([Xen.], *Oik*. 7.37). In a military context, the commander was similarly supposed to ensure care for his soldiers (e.g. Velleius 2.114.1–2). In situations where care for the sick is provided by friends or household members, it may thus be the case that the carer is female; but is there any evidence to suggest that there was ever a preference stated for a woman to occupy this role?

A famous example of a woman in a 'nursing' role within the household comes from a legal case of the fourth century, pseudo-Demosthenes' *Against Neaira*. A sick man, Phrastor, who has quarrelled with his own family and has no children, is eventually cared for by his estranged wife and her mother. In the speech from which we know him, the women are described as coming to his home bringing with them 'things suitable for the illness', and they 'watch over' him. The speech does not mention any healer being called to attend Phrastor; Lloyd (1983: 79 n.78) argues that we should understand from this that 'no doctor is available'. Phrastor is so ill that 'his sickness, his childlessness and the care (*therapia*) of the women and his enmity towards his own kin' persuade him to recognise as legitimate his son by his estranged wife. The central phrase for the subsequent history of nursing is: 'You yourselves know how valuable a woman is in illness, being there to help a sick person' (pseudo-Demosthenes 59, *Against Neaira* 55–60).

How should we interpret this statement? To an extent, the presence of any member of the family or friend is better than being ill alone; this comes across clearly in many texts (e.g. Thuc. 2.51; Isoc. 19, *Aegineticus*). Here, however, we have a statement aimed at the jury of male fellow-citizens, which is intended to explain to them how the sick man came to recognise the child as his legitimate heir. The verb used to describe how the women achieved this is far from neutral in tone; it is *psychagogeô*, literally meaning 'to lead the soul' and thus 'to persuade' or 'to delude'. Women who persuaded men to act were to be feared (Vial 1985: 53–4); it could thus be argued that the reference to the value of women in illness is not to be read as straightforward praise of their nursing abilities, but on the contrary is designed to remind the jury that when a man is weakened by illness even a woman can prevail over him.

In the law court speeches of fourth-century Athens illness is presented as a very dangerous time when you find out who your true family and friends really are. Another law court speech from the late fourth century has the speaker describe how he cared for a man now deceased, because no relatives came to help, with the exception of the dead man's mother and sister who were themselves ill (Isoc. 19.11–12). The dead man adopted the speaker as his son and heir and gave him his sister as a wife. Here the carer is adopted, and it is he who addresses the jury; it is therefore in his interests to make his adoption a natural result of the situation. In contrast, in the speech *Against Neaira*, the speakers are not those who benefit from the situation, and hence the adoption is presented negatively, as a result of undue influence by scheming women.

Furthermore, there is a strong tradition in both Greek and Roman culture of associating the administration of drugs with women. Nursing histories pick this up (e.g. Nutting and Dock 1907: 82), but do not note its negative tone, mentioned in the previous chapter. In Homer, Agamede, the daughter of King Augeas, knows 'all the *pharmaka* of the earth' (*Il.* 11.739; cf. Seymer 1932: 13) while Helen of Troy has a famous *pharmakon* which can dispel grief (*Od.* 4.220–32). For Baas' history of medicine, first published in German in 1876, this makes Agamede and Helen 'female physicians' (1889: 86). However, as the description of Helen makes clear, *pharmakon* can mean both healing drug, and poison (Eur. *Medea* 718: cure for sterility, but also 385, 789 and 806: poison). Such a tradition may thus tell us more about fear of death at a woman's hand than about the division of labour in healing in the Greco-Roman world (Johns 1995). Taking a Roman example, the emperor Claudius was alleged to have been poisoned by his wife Agrippina, aided by the famous female poisoner, Locusta, and the doctor, Xenophon (Suet. *Claudius* 44, cf. *Nero* 33–4; Tac. *Annals* 12.66–7). After an unsuccessful attempt was made on her life, Tacitus' Agrippina showed another side of women's knowledge of *pharmaka*: not only had she already taken antidotes to stop poison affecting her, but she also treated herself for her wounds (Tac. *Annals* 14.5–6).

Two important points for the history of nursing emerge from this. First, the connection of women with nursing the sick and administering drugs does not necessarily stem from a belief that caring and gentle qualities are somehow 'feminine'; instead, it may owe more to the image of woman as dangerous outsider taking advantage of a man's weakness due to illness in order to further her schemes. Secondly, the tendency to imagine that there must have been women attendants by a patient's bed, which takes as natural a division of labour between busy male doctor and noble, unnoticed female nurse, is simply a reading of the past in the image of the present. The absence of images of women nursing the sick in the visual arts of Greece and Rome, remarked on by Kampen (1988), may be due to a cultural unease about women in such roles; when compiling an illustrated history of nursing, Donahue (1985) avoided the issue by using classicising images of the past from artists such as Rubens and Alma-Tadema.

A further slant on ancient Greek medicine used by nursing history is to abandon any search for women in nursing roles and instead to suggest that, until modern times, there was 'little formal distinction between what were thought of as "doctoring" and "nursing" tasks' (Versluysen 1980: 187–8). This is a more helpful approach than to assume that female 'nurses' have always existed, because it is true in Hippocratic medicine that not just diagnosis, prescription and complex medical procedures constituted 'medicine'; the application of the prescribed treatment and the monitoring of the patient's environment, areas we would today classify as 'nursing', were under the control of the *iatros*. There is, however, a very good reason for this: it was essential to the Hippocratic doctor's authority that he should impress the patient and the rest of the household with his total control over the case. *On Decorum*, a treatise widely used by histories of nursing to demonstrate not only that Hippocrates had already taught all the principles of nursing (Nutting and Dock 1907: 78) but also that he 'paved the way' for the use of 'trained attendants on the sick, who would have been the equivalent of nurses' (Mellish 1984: 16), shows the ideal here:

> You must practise these things with all reserve, in the matter of palpation, anointing, washing, to ensure elegance in moving the hands, in the matter of lint, compresses, bandages, ventilation and purges . . . bear in mind your manner of sitting, reserve, arrangement of dress, decisive utterance, brevity of speech, composure, bedside manners, care, replies to objections, calm self-control to meet the troubles that occur, rebuke of disturbance, readiness to do what has to be done . . . The bed also must be considered . . . Consider also noises and smells . . . Perform all this calmly and adroitly, concealing

> most things from the patient while you are attending to him. Give necessary orders with cheerfulness and serenity, turning his attention away from what is being done to him; sometimes reprove sharply and emphatically, and sometimes comfort with solicitude and attention.
> (extracted from *On Decorum* 8, 12, 15 and 16, Loeb II, 290–8)

By the definitions as familiar to Lavinia Lloyd Dock as to us today, much of this careful creation of an environment conducive to healing comes into the sphere of 'nursing'. However, the observation that much of Hippocratic medicine was, in our terms, nursing should not prevent us from noting the very different cultural context within which these tasks were seen. Rather than being associated with a caring and submissive female assistant, they are part of the world of the male *iatros* who performs most of his recommended treatment himself in order to impress the patient and to attract as much of the glory of a successful cure as possible. As *On Decorum* puts it: 'Let there be no doubt about the points which will secure the success of your plan, and no blame will attach to you, but achievement will bring you *ganos*' (*Dec.* 17, Loeb II, 298). *Ganos* is literally 'brightness' and should here be translated as 'glory'.

Hippocratic healers thus performed what we would see as nursing tasks at least partly to ensure that they were credited with the cure. The issue of blame versus glory influenced further aspects of their behaviour. They avoided taking on hopeless cases, tended to blame the patient if anything went wrong, and made only limited and very specific use of any type of assistant.

An important aspect of prognosis in Hippocratic medicine is the identification of those patients who have no prognosis: the hopeless cases, since 'to restore every patient to health is impossible . . . men do die, some owing to the severity of the disease before they summon the physician, others expiring immediately after calling him in – living one day or a little longer – before the physician by his art can combat each disease' (*Prog.* 1, Loeb II, 7). This statement of apparent realism from the Hippocratic *Prognostics* should not necessarily be read as an acknowledgement of the limits of the medical *technê*; a closer reading will show that the grounds for despair lie not with the art, but with either the disease or the patient. This is also the position taken in the definition of medicine in the treatise *The Art*, where the writer states, 'Medicine . . . is to do away with the sufferings of the sick, to lessen the violence of their diseases, and to refuse to treat those who are overmastered by their diseases, realising that in such cases medicine is powerless' (*The Art* 3, Loeb II, 193; Edelstein 1931: 93–4). If patients realised how sick they were and called the physician sooner, they would perhaps survive. What we have here are let-out clauses which can be invoked to cover the *iatros* in the event of failure. In the triangle of doctor, disease and patient, the fault generally lies with the latter two, not with the doctor.

Although their model of doctor/patient interaction included the doctor asking questions and the patient responding (e.g. *Dis.* 1.1, Loeb V 98–100), some texts show that the Hippocratics simultaneously operated with a low opinion of the patient's reliability as a witness to his or her own body. But not only patients were sometimes regarded with a certain unease. *Precepts* supports the idea of calling in 'others' for two reasons; because additional opinions are helpful if the doctor is finding a case particularly difficult, and because fellow-workers (*synergoi*) can provide valuable assistance (*Precepts* 8, Loeb I, 323). It is not clear here whether the 'others' are fellow *iatroi*, other types of healer, or lay people; although there is the possibility of some co-operation between fellow followers of the medical *technê*, occasional criticism of the actions of other *iatroi* suggests that even these people may be seen as competitors. The writer of *On Joints* claims that some *iatroi* are too keen on impressing the crowds, while others who have manual skills lack intelligence (*On Joints* 33, Loeb III, 262). The case history of Tychon, struck in the chest by a catapult at the siege of Datum, includes criticism of 'the physician who removed the wood'; 'it appeared to me' and, indeed, to Tychon, that part of the shaft had been left in the diaphragm. This physician also administered an enema and another drug through the bowel. Although Tychon seemed to have improved the following morning, the writer's prediction was of convulsions followed by death, and this was proved correct on the third day (*Ep.* 5.95, Loeb VII, 213; *Ep.* 7.121, Loeb VII, 413).

The use of other healers as 'fellow-workers' has further relevance to the question of gender. Like the disease, the patient, and other healers who have charge of the case, those working under the direct authority of the *iatros* can also be blamed when a cure turns out to be impossible. The evidence on assistants in Hippocratic medicine is meagre, but it can be supplemented from later sources. There is no special word for 'medical assistant'; instead, the verb *pareimi*, 'to be present, to stand by', is used in a number of passages, the context often making it difficult to decide whether those 'present' are present in the capacity of helpers or simply happen to be in the room at the time. For example, when the wife of Theodorus had a fit of madness in the course of her illness, she railed at 'those who were there' (*Ep.* 7.25, Loeb VII, 331); bearing in mind not only that she has been talking deliriously for several days and has threatened her child, but also that her outburst towards 'those present' occurs in the night – indicated in the case history by the statement that, after this incident, she remained in what appeared to be a coma for 'the rest of the night' – she seems to have people with her at night to watch her condition. In a discussion of the *oikonomia*, or 'household management' of the sick person, 'things concerning those present/the attendants' are listed as one of the factors which the doctor needs to take into account (*Ep.* 6.2.24, Loeb VII, 235; cf. *Aph.* 1.2, Loeb II, 120). If the translation 'assistants' is used, such passages may imply people in a specific role, although not necessarily one for which they are formally trained; if, on the other hand, we translate as 'the other people present', we suggest that they are merely other members of the household who may have particular skills useful to the *iatros*.

Another relevant term is *therapeusontes*. In *Regimen in Acute Diseases* the writer, while recommending baths, notes that few houses have the equipment or the *therapeusontes* necessary for these (*Reg. Ac.* 65, Loeb II, 120). Jones' translation for the Loeb was 'attendants', and the connection of the Greek word with our 'therapy' may encourage us to see these as medical attendants with a specific role. However, the verb from which it is derived means 'to do service to' (Van Brock 1961: 138), and the best translation here may be 'household members', including both kin and slaves. It is significant that it is while Phrastor is without anyone to *therapeuein* his disease that his estranged wife and her mother arrive, while in another law court speech of the early fourth century BC the male speaker tells the court how he 'cared for' (*etherapeusa*) a patient for many months with the aid of a male slave, losing much sleep and suffering greatly (Isoc. 19.24–8). What we would classify as 'nursing', the observation of the patient and attention to the patient's needs, is not seen here as an exclusively female role; it does not require training and, in the absence of a *iatros* who has his own economic reasons for assuming control over all aspects of the case, the resources of the household are used rather than any professional groups.[8]

In the gynaecological texts, another role appears: that of the 'other woman' who assists in the examination of some patients. Is she a member of the household, an assistant associated with the *iatros*, or a healer in her own right? In most cases the term used translates as simply 'a woman' or 'another woman' (e.g. *DW* 1.21, L 8.60; 3.213, L 8.408, 410), and this should probably be taken to mean any experienced woman who happens to be present in the household. Jacques Jouanna (1992: 176–7) suggests that it is in the more recent parts of the Hippocratic gynaecological treatises that 'another woman' is used, with the male healer carrying out the examination himself in texts of an older date; however, as we saw in Chapter 2, the difference could instead relate to the male healer's perception of the patient and her level of experience and embarrassment. In *Excision of the Foetus* 'two women' take the legs of a patient who is to be shaken in order to speed up labour, and 'another two women' take her arms (*Excision of the Foetus* 4, L 8.514–16). Shaking the patient is also performed in order to remove a dead foetus; in a description of the procedure given in *Diseases of Women*, 'two men' are present helping to shake the patient while a 'female healer' (designated by *iatreousa*, from the same root as *iatros*) removes the foetus and the placenta (*DW* 1.68, L 8.144). It is not clear whether men are preferred over women as helpers here because of their strength (Hanson 1994: 170), because it would be distressing to women to assist in this procedure or because just as men are the ones who decide whether a newborn is to be accepted as a member of the household, so it is appropriate that they assist in this distortion of birth.

These examples from Hippocratic gynaecology show how 'the other people present' can be enlisted to help the *iatros*; they support the suggestion that these are mostly untrained members of the household, used as required to supplement the resources of the *iatros* who has charge of the case. Where a *iatros* is not employed, they watch over the patient and provide what is necessary. Where a *iatros* is used, they help in procedures which require more than one person to perform them – baths, succussion on a ladder, shaking a bed – or where they have a particular quality or skill needed by the *iatros*; for example, a boy or woman can help reshape a broken nose, because they have soft hands (*On Joints* 37, Loeb III, 270).

In histories of nursing, it is not only 'those present' who may be transformed into proto-nurses. A passage which occurs frequently in histories of nursing is *On Decorum* 17, which mentions apprentices (literally, 'those learning') who can be left in charge of the patient to carry out the instructions of the *iatros*, administer treatment and watch for any changes (*Dec.* 17, Loeb II, 298; cf. W.H.S. Jones 1923: xxxi; Robinson 1946: 21; Bullough and Bullough 1979: 17). As medicine is a *technê*, something which can be taught, one way to enter it is through working under a good practitioner (Edelstein 1931: 90). For the second century BC, a decree honouring Onasandros of Cos outlines his career, moving from apprentice to assistant to the healer Antipater, before branching out on his own (Jouanna 1992: 524–6). However, this is not the only possible route to becoming a healer; the Hippocratic texts demonstrate that an individual could always impress the crowds by less formal means. The success of an 'apprentice' only increases the reputation of his master, provided that the latter makes it clear who is giving the instructions and to whom any changes should be reported.

It is thus possible to show that, in the ancient Greek world, 'doctors' performed 'nursing' tasks for socially specific, institutional reasons. Rather than leaving such tasks to invisible but noble women driven by some biological imperative to nurture, the *iatros* had a strong incentive for carrying them out himself, since it was through successful and impressive treatment that he established his own authority and gained further cases. With the exception of the apprentices, who were already dependent on their master, assistants of either sex would have no fixed role and would not be trained, but would be brought in, as needed and as available, to further the glory of the doctor in his handling of the case.

There is one further set of reasons why the tasks we call 'nursing' would not have been fully entrusted to a female person, and this takes us away from the economic position of the *iatros* and into Greek philosophy of the person and Greek constructions of gender difference. The male–female relationship is central to the anthropology of nursing; nursing has been described as 'an excellent case study of males exploiting females' (Hoekelman 1975: 1150–2). Also important is the role of authority, since nurses have traditionally been seen as 'submissive and dependent on physicians for whatever authority they exercised' (Fitzpatrick 1977: 822). It has been argued that, cross-culturally, the definition of a 'good nurse' in any given society will reproduce that of the 'good woman' in general (Gamarnikow 1978: 98, 114–16).

Foucault brought together these themes of sexual difference and authority; his influence on the contributors to Celia Davies' *Rewriting Nursing History* (1980) is obvious, particularly the uses of his work on madness and on the prison system to provide a theoretical framework for the study of hospitals. In volumes 2 and 3 of his *History of Sexuality* (1985; 1986) Foucault turned to the ancient world, discussing the concept of moral behaviour. He argued that the Greeks defined moral behaviour in relation to self rather than in relation to an overriding code of action. Whereas a moral code in the Judaeo-Christian tradition lists what is permitted and what is forbidden, Greek morality worked by weighing up all the relevant variables – one's sex, age, individual nature – and the current conditions, such as the time of year, the location, the prevailing winds and other environmental factors, and only then assessing what would be the best course of behaviour. Foucault has been criticised for drawing his version of ancient morality exclusively from élite philosophical texts written for and about male subjects but, for Hippocratic medicine, his picture remains an accurate one. The image of the male citizen trying to maintain health by balancing food intake and exercise, hot and cold, wet and dry, bearing in mind the predominating features of his environment, is that of the Hippocratic *Regimen*. The key virtues are moderation and self-control; it is primarily for the individual to assess his condition and correct his habits accordingly (*Regimen* 1.2, Loeb IV, 226–30). An important philosophical text here is Aristotle's *Nicomachean Ethics*, which discusses the principle of 'the mean' and the dangers both of excess and defect (1104a25 ff.); it is following the mean which is the route to moral excellence, and this involves exercising the powers of choice and reason in all aspects of life (1106b37–7a8). In the *Ethics* and *De anima*, Aristotle contrasts the uncontrolled man (*akratês*) with the self-sufficient man (*enkratês*) in whom the intellect exercises power over the appetites (*De anima* 433a1–8; *NE* 1095a4–12, 1111b14–16, 1151a20 ff.). In Hippocratic terms, this recalls the idea that disease has to 'overpower' health (*krateesthai*) before the person becomes ill, and the good doctor is able to see the early signs of this battle commencing (*Regimen* 1.1, Loeb IV, 230).

What is applicable to moral health can also be used to achieve physical health; Aristotle explicitly argues from the physical consequences of ignoring the mean to the moral consequences of such action (Aristotle, *NE* 1104a11–17; Jaeger 1957). In this context I would suggest that disease shows that the patient is unable to control himself properly, and has made the wrong decisions. The doctor must therefore take over, assess the patient's condition and assert control on behalf of the patient. Indeed, *The Doctor* 1 (Loeb VIII, 300–2) explicitly states that it is by his own demonstration of self-control (*enkratês*) that the *iatros* proves himself qualified to assume control over another; he must have a well-ordered life, and look healthy, or no one will believe him capable of healing others. This point is also made in one of the fables of Babrios: once a frog claimed to be a *iatros*, but the fox mocked him, saying, 'How can you claim to heal others, when you can't even stop yourself from being so green?' (Babrios, 120). To the 'self-possession' exhibited by the doctor in *On Decorum* (12, Loeb II, 294), and recommended in Aristotle's moral philosophy, one must therefore also add self-control. If the doctor's self-control is sufficient, he can also take over control on behalf of the patient; otherwise, left to themselves, sick people give up and die (*Precepts* 9, Loeb I, 324).

I have deliberately chosen here to refer to the patient as male; this is because, in classical Greek philosophy of the self, it is only the male who has the responsibility and the right to determine his actions according to the principles of moderation and self-control. Women are denied the possibility of being active agents in this sense. Moral excellence is shown by a man in commanding, but by a woman in obeying (Ar. *Pol.* 1260a20–3). The right of the male to exercise control in all other spheres rests on and derives from his ability to control himself. The patient is thought to be unreliable, unable to follow instructions and in need of constant surveillance precisely because he is no longer fully in control. The doctor, his healthy appearance bearing testimony to his orderly way of life and his ability to control himself, must comfort and cajole the patient back into a position from which he can again resume control over his own life. Phrastor is so ill that the women caring for him are able to persuade him to do what they want; such is the vulnerability of a sick man that even women – who cannot control themselves when in full health – are able to control him.

If we apply this model of the gender of control to the possibility of women as healers, it would suggest that, because a woman's self-control is always inferior to that of which a man is capable, a woman healer can only attend other women. For a woman to serve as *iatros* to an adult male is, at least theoretically, impossible. Where a woman is described as a *iatros*, she should rather be seen as a 'woman who treats women'; should one have treated a male patient, she would have become invisible in terms of the prevailing ideology in which only a man could demonstrate sufficient self-control in order to take over control on behalf of a sick adult male.

In a famous case in Galen's *On Prognosis*, the wife of Boethus was ashamed to consult the *iatroi* about her menstrual problems; instead, she called in the midwives (*maiai*). When there was no improvement, her husband summoned *iatroi*; among them was Galen, who eventually took control of the case. This presents an interesting pattern of successive levels of control over a sick woman, moving from female midwives, to the male head of household, and on to a male *iatros* (Galen, *On Prognosis* 8; Nutton 1979: 110–16). However, several female attendants remained present throughout; one is even commended by Galen as 'an excellent woman', although when the wife of Boethus fainted Galen dismissively described the female attendants as 'no use' because they 'simply stood around screaming'.

The sources on Roman child-nurses provide a parallel case in which we can trace the lines of control. A woman is an appropriate carer for a child, who is even lower than she is on the scale of control. Joshel (1986: 8) has shown that the 'good' child-nurse in Roman culture is portrayed as someone whose 'activities and physical routine must be carefully controlled and monitored'; she is 'either firmly under the control of her employer or she has a disposition that makes control of her unnecessary'. Like the doctor, then, the child-nurse should be capable of some control but, as a woman, she should simultaneously be under the control of a man, the head of the household.

The sources for ancient Greek medicine can thus be used to show the problems caused by reading ancient texts through modern filters. We have a clear image of the nurse as female, and we link her femininity to the qualities we expect her to show in her nursing role. In our culture, a woman's natural fitness for the nursing role still 'goes without saying' (Reinach 1904); indeed, current studies of medicine in the early modern period commonly insist on the role of women as the traditional healers in a much wider sense (e.g. Lingo 1986: 593). The Greek *iatros*, however, needed to demonstrate his self-control in order to prove himself (literally) fit to exert total control over a patient. For both cultural and economic reasons, and in order to ensure he received the credit for a cure, he needed to supervise as many aspects of the treatment as possible, only using assistants where specific procedures made them essential. A woman in a nursing role with a male patient is presented not as part of some natural order, but as deeply unnatural; the woman who prepares healing drugs for her husband's household may also prepare poisons, and the woman who cares for a sick man may be able to influence his behaviour to her own ends. The 'fundamental outlook' of the ancient Greeks is thus sufficiently different from our own to make them an inappropriate source for those trying to find direct precursors for the modern nursing profession; but it is precisely the nature of that difference which makes their medical world so valuable in demonstrating the role of culture in influencing the pattern of medical personnel.

9

IMAGINARY MIDWIVES[1]

In the previous chapter, the explanations given by medical and nursing histories for the absence of women as nurses in the Hippocratic texts were examined, and it was concluded that this absence was due not to Hippocratic silence about women in the role of nurses for the sick, but rather to cultural factors making it seem inappropriate and possibly even dangerous for a sick man to be nursed by a woman. In their attempts to gain control of cases, it would be in the interests of Hippocratic doctors to play on this imagery. When we turn to midwifery, another role within health care which we assume is naturally one for women, a far wider range of historical responses can be charted, because the proper gender for a midwife has been the topic of intense debate over the last three centuries, while – with the exception of specific areas, such as the care of the insane (Hughes 1994) – the female gender of a nurse has been taken for granted until far more recently. It was in England and the United States that 'man-midwives', in various forms, posed the most serious challenge to women in the role, so that it is within these countries that there have been the most significant attempts to reconstruct the ancient past in order to justify the present.

In England, from the seventeenth century onwards, attempts were made to shift the control of normal childbirth out of the hands of women and into those of men. This contrasts with the experience of the rest of Europe, where normal births continued to be supervised by midwives, who would call in a male surgeon only when difficulties were encountered (A. Wilson 1995: 5). Adrian Wilson (1995) has vividly described the traditional birth scene, set in a darkened and airless chamber, in which a close circle of friends surrounded the parturient woman and subsequently took over her household chores while she enjoyed her 'lying-in'. At the centre of this circle was the midwife. From the early sixteenth century she would be licensed by the bishop, having supplied testimonials to her morals and competence[2] and sworn an oath in which she agreed to baptise infants in emergencies. Midwives were expected to call in male practitioners when labour was not proceeding normally; surgeons' complaints about 'ignorant midwives' may therefore be because they saw only those cases in which things had gone badly wrong. The definition of a 'difficult case' was a matter of negotiation between those attending the birth, and the parturient woman herself; it was a social rather than a biological decision (A. Wilson 1985: 349–57).

Renate Blumenfeld-Kosinski argues that men had assisted in normal childbirth in the ancient and Arab worlds (1990: 94–5), and thus that their entry into this sphere in the early modern period should be seen as a regaining of control rather than a new development. Although they had continued to be used in the medieval period when it was necessary to extract a dead foetus, she suggests that it was through Caesarean sections that male surgeons once more entered obstetrics; the first Caesarean which was survived by both mother and child is alleged to have been performed by a Swiss pig gelder, Jacob Nufer, on his wife in 1500, with the assistance of two midwives (eleven others, too nervous to take part, waited outside) (Blumenfeld-Kosinski 1990: 42). François Rousset's *Hysterotomotokia*, published in French in 1581, and translated into Latin by Caspar Bauhin in 1582, argued that the operation could be performed with the loss of neither mother nor child, even retaining the woman's potential for childbearing; Rousset used the heroic image of Alexander cutting the Gordian knot to represent the male surgeon cutting to bring to a successful conclusion an apparently impossible birth. From Caesareans, Blumenfeld-Kosinski argues, men gradually moved back into the birth chamber for normal deliveries as well. However, there was no uniformity, even in England; 'man-midwives' were an urban, and particularly a London, phenomenon (Loudon 1986: 86), while turning the baby in the womb or removing it with the use of hooks and craniotomy were the preferred options over Caesarean section in difficult births, priority being given to saving the life of the woman rather than that of the child (A. Wilson 1995: 22). Nor was technology necessarily 'male'. The increased use of the forceps between around 1700 and 1770 did not correlate with the new 'man-midwives', as some men claimed that they could deliver difficult births by using manual pressure on the sacrum, while others – perhaps those who were called in at a later stage of such deliveries (Moscucci 1990: 49) – praised the forceps in certain situations.

By the nineteenth century, surgeon-apothecaries included man-midwifery in their job (Loudon 1986: 87–8), and some deliveries were taking place in hospital, although in his presidential address to the Obstetrical Society of London in 1865 Robert Barnes argued that the main characteristic distinguishing English midwifery from continental practice remained its basis in 'home or domiciliary practice' (*TOSL* 7, 1865: 38). Male obstetricians and female midwives continued to challenge each other's roles. One example was the debate over the 'puerperal week' versus the 'puerperal month'. In a presidential address delivered to the Obstetrical Society of London in 1864, Henry Oldham argued for the 'week', claiming that the traditional full month of 'lying-in' only became necessary if a patient was given opium, then put on to slops for up to a week, and prescribed bed rest for two weeks to prevent prolapse (*TOSL* 6, 1864: 18–19). In the absence of these practices which, he said, only served to make a patient feeble and risked inducing nervous disorders, a mere week would suffice. But this argument clearly had an economic basis. It concerned male practitioners' disagreements on whether further attendance on the patient in the first month was covered by their basic midwifery fee. Oldham said that it was not; only the 'puerperal week' was included, and anything after this would involve a further charge.

The manuals directed to midwives in the early modern period make it clear that the range of health problems on which they were consulted was much wider than the birth process and the care of the newborn, so that Wilson – who gives examples of eighteenth-century midwives who also practised medicine, surgery and bloodletting – proposes that 'The midwife was the women's doctor, and perhaps the women's confidante, of early-modern England' (1995: 38; cf. Pelling and Webster 1979: 187). In the United States, where midwifery was in economic competition with general practice, it was subject to attacks far more serious than anything experienced in England; for example, under a statute passed in 1894, the state of Massachusetts could charge midwives with the unlicensed practice of medicine, even in cases where they were fully trained as midwives, made no claims to general medical knowledge, and were meticulous in calling in physicians to assist in difficult births (Friedman 1987).

The debates arising from the early modern period and re-enacted in the nineteenth century are alive and well today. Should a male practitioner deal with normal childbirth? What is the proper scope of a midwife's practice? What should be the balance between theory and experience in midwifery training?[3] Should a midwife be permitted to prescribe drugs, and in what situations should she call in an obstetrician? Who decides when the progress of labour is 'abnormal'? In this chapter I will argue that our perception of the ancient Greek past continues to be heavily influenced by debates of this kind, and in particular by the assumption that midwifery in the past saw a real dichotomy between 'ignorant' midwives, superstitious and empirical, and 'learned' male experts (Moscucci 1990: 50).

A valuable new historical slant on all these questions has recently been provided by work on midwives in early modern Europe (Marland 1993a), which has built on earlier challenges to the stereotype of the 'midwife-as-witch' (Harley 1990) to re-examine assumptions that early midwives were 'ignorant'. Instead, although their methods of training differed from the dominant male models of university education and book-learning, early modern midwives had their own effective education system based around key texts read with an experienced midwife as guide (King 1995b); in London, they also attended deliveries in the capacity of 'midwife's deputy' for as long as seven years before applying for a licence to practise in their own right (Willughby 1863: 73; A. Wilson 1985: 136; 1995: 32). Even after this training period, midwives in urban centres remained in contact in order to discuss difficult cases and to learn from each other's experience (Evenden 1991).

So what was the origin of the persistent stereotype of the 'ignorant midwife' (Harley 1981)? Its roots lie in a combination of two sources: male attempts, from the late seventeenth century onwards, to take over control of the potentially lucrative field of obstetrics, and female support for medical men. For example, Pierre Dionis, whose instruments were displayed at the Obstetrical Society of London shortly before Isaac Baker Brown's trial, argued that midwives were ignorant, and that it was impossible to be a surgeon 'without being acquainted with all that relates to the Art of Midwifery' (1710: 155–6). In the mid-nineteenth century, the Norwich accoucheur John Green Crosse described midwifery as 'a practice which is shared by the most ignorant old women in the universe' (1851: viii–ix), while arguing that women could not be expected to learn the advanced midwifery of his own day because this would expose them to a topic 'which must necessarily be repulsive, indelicate, and peculiarly uninteresting to the sex' (1851: 2). Midwifery is 'more safe and efficient, and not more repulsive in a moral sense, in the hands of properly qualified gentlemen' (1851: 3). Such 'gentlemen' had a vested interest in persuading women to adopt their type of intervention, which often offered a medicalised birth in which the woman becomes the passive patient to whom drugs are given and on whose body surgical instruments are applied, in contrast to the midwifery model in which the labouring woman is the active centre of the process, her own body determining the speed of action.[4] Where they could afford the higher fees, it was eighteenth-century women themselves who chose male midwives (A. Wilson 1995: 7). Women were easily persuaded by male claims that female midwives were insanitary; the image of midwife as drunken bawd has a long history (King 1993b: 118) and, when suffering from urinary or gynaecological disorders after giving birth, women tended to blame inadequate midwives. This does not, of course, mean that we should accept their view uncritically; the fault may have lain with poor hygiene from a lack of sterile delivery procedures, which would have been a problem with any medical practitioner of the time. When the first women qualified as doctors, it became clear that identical training was not expected to erase the gender difference. During the 1874 debate on whether the bye-laws of the Obstetrical Society of London should be interpreted in such a way that Elizabeth Garrett Anderson could be admitted to the Society, Charles Routh stated, 'I do not think the women of England themselves – that is my experience of them – will go to female practitioners when they can get male practitioners' (*Obstetrical Journal* 2 (1874–5): 35).

Alongside the historical stereotype of the 'ignorant midwife', another persistent image of midwifery existed. This was the image of the 'excellent midwife', usually glimpsed as an ideal which real women persistently failed to match, and derived from Soranos' *Gynaecology*. Here we meet a woman who is one long series of superlatives: sober, discreet, free from superstition, literate,[5] knowledgeable, with a good memory, and trained in all three branches of medicine, namely diet, surgery and drugs (*Gyn.* 1.3–4; T 5–7). This ideal midwife, perhaps constructed as a guide to the Roman *paterfamilias* looking for a good midwife for his wife, was to have a very long history as a standard against which all real midwives could be compared, only – inevitably – to be found wanting (King 1995b; Hanson and Green 1994). For example, unacknowledged, she lies behind Wolveridge's 1671 statement that 'The best Midwife is she that is ingenuous, that knoweth Letters, and having a good memory, is studious, neat and cleanly over the whole body . . . ' (1671: 26–7).

It is possible to argue that the source problems for the history of midwifery in the ancient world and beyond are seriously skewed by the mere existence of Soranos' *Gynaecology*. This historical accident of preservation does not only affect our appreciation of Soranos himself, restricting our perception of him to being simply a 'gynaecologist', when in fact he is said to have written a total of perhaps twenty-one works on subjects as varied as etymology, biography, drugs, fevers, eye disorders, hygiene and acute and chronic diseases (Hanson and Green 1994; Hanson 1996b: 299). It also affects our reconstruction of the context within which the *Gynaecology* was produced, the very size and nature of the text encouraging a number of misleading assumptions. For example, the simple fact that we have a midwifery text from the second century AD may lead us to speculate that it was written in response to perceived inadequacies of midwives prior to that time. This thesis would then assume that a real development in women's health care took place in the early Roman empire. The names of twenty-five midwives are given in the CIL, and the imperial women of the early empire were served by slave- and freed-women in this role. Midwifery training may have been received from family members who were either doctors or midwives; Galen dedicated his treatise *On the Anatomy of the Uterus* to a midwife, and his description of the midwives consulted by the wife of Boethus for her discharge rates them as 'the best in Rome' (*On Prognosis* 8, Nutton 1979: 110). However, we know neither how good were 'the best', nor how poor were 'the rest'. Nor is Galen a transparent reporter; he needs to claim that Boethus' wife had the best midwives in Rome in order that his own light may shine more brightly after he succeeds where they failed.

In Latin materials, a further problem is the term *medica*, which tends to be translated as 'woman doctor'; but does *medica* necessarily mean a perfect replica, in all but gender, of a *medicus*? A number of funerary inscriptions from the first and second centuries AD describe women as *medicae*; for example, Julia Saturnina, 'the best *medica*' (CIL 2.497), and the freedwoman 'Secunda Livilla *medica*' (CIL 6.8711). From the later Roman empire we have the story of a midwife and barmaid who was called away from the second role to serve in the first (Eunapius, *Lives* 463; G. Clark 1993: 69). It is thus clearly inappropriate to think of midwifery in the ancient world as a 'profession' in the sense of a full-time employment, and being a *medica* would be little different. Comparative evidence from the Netherlands in the eighteenth century shows that it would have been impossible for a midwife in a rural area to make sufficient to live on; there were simply too many midwives for the population (Marland *et al.* 1987). But similar observations also apply to male doctors in the ancient world. An inscription from Metapontum in Southern Italy (SEG XXX 1175), dated to around 250 BC, shows that there were at least seventeen doctors in the city at a time when the population may have been no more than 7,000. One wonders in the light of this inscription how seventeen doctors for this number of people could have been financially viable, but there were also at least twenty-five 'sites of medical activity' at Pompeii (Nutton 1995a: 14–15 and n.64).

Putting aside for the moment the evidence of Soranos and of Roman inscriptions, and going back further, to the Hippocratic corpus, what model of midwifery can be reconstructed for the classical Greek world? For this period, the main non-medical source is Plato's dialogue *Theaetetus*, in which Socrates claims to be the son of a midwife in order to put forward his view of mental activity in which he acts as midwife to the ideas of other men. The statements he offers on the functions of the midwife are far from straightforward, since he is shaping his image of midwifery in order to fit his own activity. He presents the midwife as a woman past the age of childbearing, but barren due to age alone, as experience is necessary to develop any skill (149b–c). She can detect pregnancy, bring on labour and relieve pain by using both chants and drugs (149c–d; 157c–d), 'can bring a difficult birth to a successful conclusion' and can also cause a miscarriage 'if that is what seems best' (149d–e). She is also a match-maker, but here Theatetus claims that he was not aware of this aspect, a reaction which may suggest that Socrates is inventing material to fit his purpose in presenting himself as midwife of the soul (Nickel 1979: 516).

There is no Hippocratic treatise on obstetrics, so it is usually assumed that midwifery was 'a female activity that in general was taken for granted' (Demand 1994: 66) while Hippocratic healers 'were only called in if special difficulties were being experienced' (Blundell 1995: 110). This model of traditional midwives for normal labours, and male healers only when something went wrong, is deeply ingrained in our reading of the past (e.g. Nutton 1992: 25). But Plato's Socrates suggests that a midwife in the Hippocratic period 'can bring a difficult birth to a successful conclusion' (*Theaetetus* 149d), while comparative historical material suggests that the response to a difficult birth may be to call in a different midwife (Marland 1993b: 211 n.74). Even the arrival of a male *iatros* does not necessarily mean that the midwife departs. In the Hippocratic gynaecological texts, in addition to the women of the household who assist in procedures where extra pairs of hands are required, there is one occasion on which a woman healer appears, and works alongside the Hippocratic male *iatros* in a birth which has become 'difficult'; the use of the term 'female healer' (*iatreousa*) for this woman, who in *Diseases of Women* 1.68 (L 8.144) assists in removing a dead foetus and the placenta while two men shake the patient, suggests that this is a woman who is regarded as medically trained (Hanson 1996a: 169; cf. Jouanna 1992: 176). In another section of the same treatise a 'cord-cutter' (*omphalêtomos*) appears (*DW* 1.46, L 8.106), apparently the Ionic dialect word for *maia*, midwife (Hipponax fr.19 *GLP*;[6] Eust. *ad Il.* 14.118; Hanson 1994: 174). But she is the object of criticism; if she cuts the cord too soon, part of the afterbirth will remain in the womb, and a Hippocratic healer will have to use his skills to ensure its proper expulsion. Nor is she represented in these texts as having exclusive rights even over this part of the birthing process;[7] a male *iatros* could also be the one to cut the umbilical cord (e.g. *SF* 15, L 8.484). Further negative assessments of female practitioners appear from the early Roman empire. In his *Natural History* Pliny the Elder gives the opinions of both male and female practitioners, but this does not mean that he trusts women experts. Olympias of Thebes is mentioned three times, on the abortive powers of mallow (*NH* 20.84.226), on menstruation (*NH* 28.77.246) and on cures for sterility (*NH* 28.77.253). But the authority of the midwives Lais and Elephantis, who also feature more than once, is undercut by Pliny's remark that one gives a recipe to cure sterility, while the other says that precisely the same substance causes barrenness (NH 28.23.81); 'better not to believe them,' says Pliny (*melius est non credere*).

In the treatise *Fleshes*, female healers (here called *akestrides*) appear in a more positive light; they are mentioned as assisting women giving birth (*Fleshes* 19, Loeb VIII, 164), and the *iatros* is advised to ask them if he needs to be convinced that a child born in the seventh month can survive. Should we therefore construct a highly positive image of the ancient midwife, akin to Wilson's 'women's doctor, and perhaps the women's confidante, of early-modern England' (1995: 38)? Demand (1994: 66) goes further, arguing from one reference in *Diseases of Women* 1.34 (L 8.80) that midwives either listened to, or read for themselves, the material given by the Hippocratic *iatros*. The passage in question states that 'one must not use astringents (*ou chrê styphein*) as the *iatroi* do'. Demand interprets this as 'the doctor directly addresses the midwife, telling her not to do as male doctors do', but as the impersonal form is used there is no indication that the audience is supposed to be female. There are several other passages in *Diseases of Women* in which 'some doctors', 'many doctors' or simply 'doctors' are criticised by the writer for their ignorance,[8] and these should be seen as part of the generally competitive nature of Hippocratic medicine rather than as evidence for an audience of non-*iatroi*.

After the classical period, further female forms from the root *iatr-* are attested in Greek inscriptions, among them *iatreinê* or *iatrinê*, and the compound *iatromaia*, 'healer-midwife' (Robert 1964; Nickel 1979: 517). This last term is particularly problematic; does it mean that the *iatr-* healers did not normally cover midwifery? This could be supported from the late fourth-century BC funeral stele of Phanostrate, in which she is described as *maia kai iatros* (*IG* II/III 3^2 6873); the Greek *maia*, which means both midwife and 'old woman', does not appear in the Hippocratic corpus. Yet although the *iatreousa* in *Diseases of Women* 1.68 (L 8.144) assists in a birth, it is one defined as 'difficult'; it would therefore certainly be possible to argue that, while the *iatromaia* was a midwife as well as a healer, other *iatr-* healers did not cover normal labour. But this is only one possible option. Another is that women designated as Greek *iatreousa* – or Latin *medica* – treated all health problems of other women and, perhaps, children. In the previous chapter I suggested that the prevailing ideology meant that, ideally at least, their practice would not extend to male patients. By being interested in 'diseases of women' in general (Van Brock 1961: 66–7; Robert 1964: 175–8) they are not however 'gynaecologists' in our sense because, as we have seen, women's disorders were thought to affect the whole body. Soranos includes all diseases of women in his *Gynaecology* and, even if this text had not survived, the Hippocratic treatises show how disturbances of menstruation can affect the whole body by pressure on other organs. It is we who restrict 'midwifery' to childbirth, and 'gynaecology' to conditions of the womb and other genitalia; the Hippocratics saw gynaecology as all diseases affecting women, and childbirth as an event having a beneficial effect on the whole body, so that a *maia* may have been a female practitioner who assisted in childbirth but, because of the influence of the womb and menses on the whole body, could also be valuable in other disorders of women. This can be supported for the second century AD from Soranos, who states that 'the public is wont to call in midwives in cases of sickness when the women suffer something peculiar which they do not have in common with men' (*Gyn.* 3.3; T 129). Thus, when a recipe for dentifrice is ascribed to a female practitioner (as in Scribonius Largus, *Compositiones* 59), this does not mean that she was 'branching out' into dental care; teeth too could be under her remit, because of the view – Hippocratic in origin – that a woman's body consisted of a tube linking mouth and nostrils with vagina.

Hippocratic healers were certainly involved in 'difficult' births where no other healer, of either gender, is mentioned; in *Diseases of Women* (1.69, L 8.146), for example, the *iatros* tries to correct presentation by an arm or a leg, pushing the limb back inside and attempting to turn the baby so that it resumes the 'natural' (*kata physin*) position of head-first. However, various 'helpers' can also be used; this description occurs in a section describing a series of difficult births (1.68–70, L 8.142–8), in which the *iatros* helps to deliver babies – both dead and alive – who are too big or too weak to come out on their own. The Hippocratic model of normal labour put the onus on the baby to fight its way out (*NC* 30, L 7.530–2; *7MC* 1, L 7.437); as I noted in Chapter 6, the uterus was thought to play only a passive role in this process. To assist the baby, the Hippocratic doctor and his helpers shake the bed or turn the baby *in utero*. If the baby is dead, the doctor dismembers it and removes it by means of instruments called the 'squeezer' (*piestron*), the *osteologon* and the *helkystêr* (*DW* 1.70, L 8.148), procedures also discussed at greater length in *Excision of the Foetus* (L 8.512–18). Further discussion of difficult births occurs in *Superfoetation*, where a thumbnail rather than a knife was recommended for extracting a dead foetus (*SF* 7, L 8.480), and an ingenious method was discussed for the delivery of the afterbirth using counterweights (*SF* 8, L 8.480–2; Hanson 1994: 165–8).

But were Hippocratic healers involved in 'normal' births as well? Lesley Dean-Jones (1994: 212) argues from silence; she suggests that Hippocratic healers indeed observed normal birth, but that this 'was so routine that the Hippocratics did not bother recording those they observed'. There are passages in *Diseases of Women* which suggest observation of the entire process of labour, such as 1.34 (L 8.78–80), where the writer states 'I say that a woman who is about to give birth breathes rapidly, and when the purgation begins, the belly is full and hot to touch', before going on to list possible difficulties and their treatments: air in the womb, pain in the loins, difficulty in breathing, heavy blood loss, dry labour, inability to give birth, and swelling in the womb during or after birth. Following Jacques Jouanna (1992: 175), Nancy Demand (1994: 66) has argued that Hippocratic healers worked with female assistants not only in abnormal labour but also in normal labour, and further suggests that the women who worked as such assistants would have increased their own status as healers in their communities. Ann Ellis Hanson suggested that the presence of a Hippocratic healer was a matter of taste: 'those who were in the habit of turning to doctors' would have involved them in birth as much as in other health matters (1994: 158). She noted that nineteen of the thirty-three case histories in the *Epidemics* which involved pregnancy and birth gave details either of the birth itself, or of the period immediately after it, thus illustrating the presence of Hippocratic doctors at births (1994: 171–2). However, many of these births did not progress normally. Of the nineteen, five were explicitly labelled 'difficult' births; but in seven others it is clear from the description of symptoms that there were complications, such as a retained afterbirth or the absence of the lochia. Hanson has also looked at the evidence from the early Roman empire to suggest another model for the difficult birth: looking at the legally 'difficult' birth, in which the paternity of the child was at issue, she suggests that the norm in the medically 'difficult' birth too would have been the 'crowded scene', in which further midwives and medical men were added on as things became worse (1994: 175–6).

When we turn to Greek myth, other models of midwifery appear. The art is particularly associated with Artemis, who acted as midwife to her own brother Apollo. Who was the midwife for Artemis herself? Aelius Aristides says (37.18) that Athena acted as midwife to Leto when Artemis was born, and also crowned Apollo as healer of the Greeks; 'therefore Artemis is in charge of lying in for other women, but this goddess was in charge of lying in for Artemis at her birth'. It is Athena who taught Artemis 'both her art and her way of life'. In the birth of Erichthonios, conceived by Earth after

Hephaistos ejaculated on Athena's leg while pursuing her, Athena acts as midwife again (Loraux 1993: 111–43).

Artemis, as a young female goddess devoted to virginity with no personal experience of giving birth may, like Athena, seem an odd candidate for divine midwife. Guided both by the image of the Socratic midwife past the age of childbearing and by historical midwives in the early modern and modern periods, we tend to assume that the typical midwife has been an older woman who has given birth several times, like the seventeenth-century Quaker midwife Elizabeth Glidwell, who began to work as a midwife to support her young children while her husband was in prison (Hess 1993: 61), or the Frisian midwife Catharina Schrader, mother of six, who set up in practice a year after the death of her husband, a barber-surgeon (Marland *et al.* 1987: 7). But it is helpful to recall that midwives in eighteenth-century Paris were often unmarried (Gelbart 1993: 135), while the childless and probably unmarried eighteenth-century French midwife, 'Mme' du Coudray, who was employed by Louis XV to improve the population of France by travelling the country training midwives through demonstrations on mannequins, singled out very young women to teach (Gelbart 1993: 143; A. Wilson 1995: 5). In his attack on the 'man-midwives' of his day, John Douglas (1736: preface) notes that 'A Maid may be taught the art of delivering women, yet she is not a Wife.' In Soranos too there is explicit rejection of the idea that a midwife needs to have given birth herself; in this sense, the enlightened new midwifery of Soranos is returning to the 'mythical midwifery' of ancient Greece. In ancient tragedy and novels, the midwife tends to be an older widow; a woman without a *kyrios*, so free to travel. Why these two extremes? Is the midwife supposed to be a woman who herself is not bleeding, and therefore not able to be polluted by childbirth?

The model of the virgin midwife is also an element of a story which has had enormous influence on the history of midwifery, and which eloquently demonstrates how post-seventeenth-century debates about the gender and training of the medical personnel appropriate to childbirth have influenced our perception of the past. This is the myth of Agnodike, which occurs in only one ancient source, a list of discoverers and inventors given by the Roman writer Hyginus, *fabula* 274. The date of this section of Hyginus is uncertain, but it may be later than the rest of the work, which probably dates to the second century AD (Nickel 1981: 170); however, complicating the dating issue, the Latin text of Hyginus shows signs of being based on earlier Greek originals, one such sign being the name Agnodike, which should properly be Hagno-dikê, 'chaste before justice'.[9]

Agnodike is described as an Athenian girl who lived at a time when there were no midwives (*obstetrices*), because women and slaves were forbidden to learn the art of medicine. Sarah Pomeroy's discussion of Agnodike makes much of the use of *obstetrix* as the chosen term for 'midwife' here, following Mary Grant (1960: 176) in translating it as 'obstetrician' and suggesting that this denotes a medically trained childbirth attendant in contrast to the untrained – and, by implication, less effective – midwife. Pomeroy's choice means that she produces a novel answer to the question of how there could have been 'no midwives' in Athens before Agnodike; instead of being the first midwife, Agnodike becomes 'the first woman obstetrician' while 'the career of obstetrician is to be distinguished from that of midwife as requiring more formal education' (1977: 58–9).[10] If the story was originally Greek, however, all such explanations become irrelevant: there is no obvious Greek equivalent for *obstetrix* other than *maia*, and this would give a very different slant to the story.

By suggesting that there were no midwives because women and slaves were forbidden to learn the art of medicine, the story operates with an interesting and subsequently controversial assumption: namely, that midwifery requires training in medicine as a whole. This is indeed the position taken by Soranos, who expected his ideal midwife to be trained in drugs, surgery and diet, but it is by no means a common view. Due to women's modesty (*verecundia*), Hyginus goes on, they preferred to die rather than let a male practitioner attend them in labour. The scenario of a ban on midwives matches no known historical period, and we should not be seduced by the following description of how 'a certain Agnodike, a virgin girl (*Agnodice quaedam puella virgo*)' cut off her hair, dressed as a man and went to study medicine under 'a certain Herophilos' into thinking that the story is a genuine reflection of conditions in the third century BC when Herophilos of Chalcedon did in fact practise at Alexandria. The real Herophilos dissected humans, wrote a midwifery manual (*Gyn.* 3.3–4; T 130–1 and 4.1; T 176–7)[11] and is credited with the discovery of the ovaries (Galen; K 4.596), thus making him 'the ideal teacher for the would-be obstetrician' (Pomeroy 1977: 59); but his historicity cannot be used to prove that of Agnodike, as his name may well have been added to the story simply to make it sound convincing.[12] Interestingly, by learning from Herophilos Agnodike ceases to deserve her place in a list of 'Who discovered/invented what': she learned her art from a man.

After her medical training, Agnodike is supposed to have successfully attended Athenian women in labour. When they refused to let this apparently male doctor examine them, Agnodike performed the gesture of *anasyrmos*, lifting her tunic to expose her lower body.[13] When her jealous male rivals (the *medici*) lost business to her, they accused her of seducing her patients and the women of feigning illness, and brought Agnodike to court; here again she performed *anasyrmos*, but this time to prove that she was not a man, and so could not have seduced her patients. However, this revelation of her sex laid her open to the charge of practising medicine against the law excluding women from medical education. She was saved only when the wives of the leading men of Athens lobbied the Areopagus on her behalf, saying to the men, 'You are not husbands but enemies, for you condemn to death she who brought us life.' Hyginus then says that the law was changed so that free-born women could learn the art of medicine.

This story, variously argued to be an historical account, a novella (Grant 1960: 20) or a myth,[14] had enormous influence in the history of medicine from the publication of the first printed edition by Jacobus Micyllus, in 1535, onwards, particularly through its popularisation in Tiraqueau's *De nobilitate et iure primigeniorum* (1566: 314 no.357) and his *De legibus connubialibus et iure maritali*, where it appeared from the enlarged 1554 edition onwards (Brejon 1937: 54; Tiraqueau 1576: 57[r]).[15] It also appears in editions of Charles Estienne's *Dictionarium historicum, geographicum, poeticum* from the 1560s onwards (e.g. 1590: 25[v]). It was subsequently used to supply a precedent for many variations on medical personnel and practice: for male midwives, for a female monopoly on midwifery, for women doctors and, most surprisingly, since these do not even feature in the story, for medical abortion and for Caesarean section. Men could use it to show that women's control of midwifery was not always taken for granted; women could use it to argue that male midwives are not acceptable to most women; women trying to enter the medical profession found its conclusion valuable in showing that, in enlightened Athens, women had once been permitted to study medicine.

One of the earliest uses of Agnodike was by the French writer Catherine des Roches (1542–87), who includes a very personalised version of the story in *Les Oeuvres des Mes-Dames des Roches de Poetiers mere et fille*, first published in 1578. In her analysis of this text, Tilde Sankovich (1988: 66) argues that, for Catherine, the story was reframed to express the closeness of her relationship with her mother, and the struggles the two women experienced in asserting their right to a literary career in the face of male envy. In Catherine's version of Agnodike, women were not allowed even to read about the subjects they were forbidden to practise. Catherine's Agnodike becomes a herbalist who not only ministers to the physical needs of women but also restores their spiritual health (1988: 63).

A century later, when William Sermon published *The Ladies Companion, or the English Midwife*, Agnodike was already sufficiently familiar to be known as 'that famous Maiden' (1671: 2). For Sermon, midwives had existed 'from the beginning', and Agnodike was an example of women being forced, due to the embarrassment of telling men about 'distempers in their natural parts', 'to practise Physick, especially one with the other'. Sermon probably learned Agnodike's story from the 1612 English translation of Guillemeau's *Child-Birth or, the Happy Deliverie of Woman*, a book originally aimed not at midwives but at surgeons (King 1995b: 197 n.42). In the translator's preface to Guillemeau, women's modesty and the risk of divulging their private matters are explored; 'the virginitie of pen and paper' is seen to parallel 'the white sheetes of their child-bed'. For Guillemeau, the story of Agnodike ends with the Athenians 'giving Gentle-women leave to studie and practize Physicke' (1612: 81). Guillemeau was one of two midwifery texts recommended to the trainee midwife in an unpublished manuscript of the 1660s or 1670s, Edward Poeton's *The Midwives Deputie*, the second chapter of which describes the midwife who has read Guillemeau and *The Byrthe of Mankynde* as 'well furnished, if you understand what you read, and remember what you understand'.[16] This meant that Agnodike became familiar to late seventeenth-century midwives as a potential model for women in medicine. Among these midwives was Elizabeth Cellier, who put forward proposals for a College of Midwives in 1687. In her pamphlet *To Dr . . . an Answer to his Queries, concerning the Colledg of Midwives* (1688), Cellier produced another very personal version of Hyginus' story, in which her own experiences in the legal system were transferred to Agnodike, so that new characters, including witnesses being paid to give false evidence, entered the story (King 1986b: 58–9). She used Agnodike not only to argue for the antiquity of midwives, but also to claim that their organisation into professional bodies predated any corporate organisation of doctors (King 1993b). She insists that midwifery 'ought to be kept a Secret amongst Women as much as is possible' but – despite learning about Agnodike from Guillemeau – she does not push for a wider medical role for women, and she still believes that doctors should be called in for difficult births.

But other writers of this period firmly believed that Agnodike was in some way 'the first woman doctor'. This view is elegantly expressed by the fact that a woman quack healer practising in late seventeenth-century London chose to advertise herself as 'Agnodice: The Woman Practitioner, dwelling at the Hand and Urinal, next Door to the Blue Ball in Hayden-Yard in the Minories, near Aldgate'. The handbill she circulated, a copy of which survives in the British Library,[17] claims that she 'Travelled for many Years in Forreign Parts' – an echo of the suggestion that the original Agnodike had travelled abroad to learn her skill from Herophilos – and states that she can treat skin diseases and itches. She can also reshape eyebrows to make low foreheads appear high, whiten teeth and cure diseases of infants, children, and of her 'own Sex'. On the latter, she added 'the Diseases in particular I shall forbear to mention, they being not proper to be exposed to the public'. She states that she can cure venereal disease, test for pregnancy and aid conception. This range of talents is not dissimilar to those attributed to ancient practitioners; for example, the midwife Salpe, cited in Pliny, is supposed to have been able to provide aphrodisiacs (*NH* 28.80.262), cure weak eyes (*NH* 28.18.66), remove excess hair (*NH* 32.47.135) and stop dogs barking (*NH* 32.51.140). Even in the late nineteenth century Agnodike manages to provide a parallel, if not an exemplar, for women doctors; the 1889 English translation of Baas' history of medicine states that she 'practised midwifery in Athens under the same difficulties at the hands of her male colleagues as those which meet our doctresses at the present day' (1889: 121). In 1903 Mary Breakell used Agnodike's story to suggest that, while 'our sober-minded lady doctors of to-day' should not go so far as to don male clothing, they should learn from this ancient example the benefit of wearing a special uniform which signifies their 'proved efficiency and ability in every fold' (1903: 825). After all, 'the fact remains that . . . Agnodike triumphed' (820).

The suggestion that Agnodike was an early supporter of abortion and Caesarean section is perhaps even more surprising than her role as a woman doctor. This view of Agnodike has been spread by the work of Kate Hurd-Mead, who claimed that women had been midwives before the Athenian law excluded them, then imagined that their subsequent exclusion had been because they were performing abortions, and finally wrote of Herophilos,

> From him Agnodice must have learned how to perform embryotomy, using a boring and cutting instrument before crushing the child's head. She also performed Caesarean section on a dead mother and did other operations as taught by her master.
>
> (1938: 45)

The subtle shift in the above passage from presenting this entirely imaginary material as informed speculation – 'must have' – to stating it as fact – 'she also performed' – has, not surprisingly, encouraged subsequent midwifery historians to treat all the additional details in Hurd-Mead's account of Agnodike as true. For example, Towler and Bramall (1986: 14) wrote, 'Another charge against her was that she procured abortions. She is said to have successfully performed Caesarean sections'; Alic (1986: 28) stated, 'In Athens in the fourth century BC women doctors were accused of performing abortions and were barred from the profession'; and, most recently, Jeanne Achterberg's *Woman as Healer* (1991: 32) simply copies Hurd-Mead to state that 'she was well trained in the tradition of her master teacher Herophilus. From him she learned how to perform Cesarian sections, embryotomy, and other medical procedures'.

The Caesarean section issue was, however, one in which Agnodike was invoked as a past precedent well before Hurd-Mead. In the eighteenth century she was used by the Parisian anti-Caesarean doctor Jean-François Sacombe (1750–1822), known as 'the Juvenal of French physicians', whose satirical poem *La Luciniade* describes her eloquence, rather than her physical display, as convincing the court of the Areopagus of her innocence on the charge of seducing her patients:

> On la traîne au Sénat, mais grâce à la nature,
> Agnodice en trois mots confondit l'imposture:
> Je suis femme, dit-elle . . .
>
> (Sacombe 1792, Chant 3, 26–7)[18]

Agnodike has also been a model for women in science; the French midwife Marie Anne Victoire Boivin (1774–1841) was addressed by Daniel

Wyttenbach, the professor of Greek literature at Leyden, as 'the French Agnodike', on account of her 'mérite scientifique' (Delacoux 1834: 42). In some of the more imaginative rewritings of the story, Agnodike recapitulates the stages through which Hippocratic medicine was thought to have passed, moving from religion to science. In Delacoux's *Biographie des sages-femmes* (1834: 26) Agnodike devotes herself to the cult of Artemis Eileithyia before deciding to learn medicine, while Mary Breakell imagined Agnodike 'sacrificing her long hair on the Altar of the Goddess of Health' (1903: 819–20).[19]

In all the above cases, Agnodike is used as a positive role model, whatever side of whichever debate she is supporting. However, not everyone wanted her on their side; sometimes she becomes an example of the sort of midwifery which should be left behind in the past. Furthermore, the idea that the Greeks had once 'enacted a law prohibiting women from undertaking the practice of physick' could become a good reason for continuing to keep them out (J.M. Adair 1790: 77). In 1851, during the period when the movement for women's education was beginning to question the exclusion of women from the medical profession, an American doctor, Augustus Gardner, delivered a lecture entitled 'A history of the art of midwifery'. His purpose was to show 'the past inefficiency and present natural incapacity of females in the practice of obstetrics', and he attacked midwives in the ancient world as being characterised by 'gross empiricism' and 'superstitious practices', adding that 'during the many centuries when the practice of midwifery was in female hands, literally, no improvement was made'. He describes the ancient midwife as

> a remarkable busybody . . . She busied herself about everything which interested women . . . She made marriages,[20] procured abortion, and cured sterility; in short, the Cleopatras, Aspasias and Agnodices of Ancient Greece, were very similar and probably more ignorant than the infamous Restells and Costellos of our day.
>
> (1852: 26)

It is noteworthy that Agnodike is so well known that the mere mention of her name is sufficient, but here she is keeping very strange company. Cleopatra is known in midwifery history not only as the seductive Queen of Egypt, but as the alleged author of a compilation text, cited by Galen (K 12.403 and 12.492), covering women's diseases and also discussing skin disorders and cosmetics. Aspasia was a writer on women's diseases in the second century AD; the English translation and enlarged edition of Baas' history of medicine claims that Aspasia was concerned with 'cosmetics and free-love' (1889: 95). Madame Restell was Anna Lohman, a notorious midwife-turned-abortionist in mid-nineteenth-century New York. Her 'Female Monthly Pills' were advertised from 1839 onwards, and contained ergot and cantharides; if these failed, she carried out surgical abortions in her back room. It was her contention that her remedies derived from those used by her grandmother who, she claimed, had been a midwife and female physician in Paris (Browder 1988; Olasky 1988: 4–13). Madame Catherine Costello was her New Jersey rival, who like Restell advertised herself as a 'female physician' (Olasky 1988: 14–16), perhaps suggesting that this was shorthand for an abortionist.

Where the positive Agnodike supports a wide range of possibilities for women in medicine, the negative Agnodike is thus associated primarily with illegal abortionists. As one of a number of 'imaginary midwives' from the ancient world she has travelled further and to more effect than her sisters because she carries the hint of historicity. It makes no difference to midwifery history that there are no *maiai* in the Hippocratic corpus; Agnodike – her origins obscure, her story unclear – will perform any function which may become necessary. Perhaps the most surprising example of her uses is the widely found statement in midwifery histories up to the present day that three midwives were officially in control of midwifery in classical Athens (e.g. Towler and Bramall 1986: 14).[21] As if her story did not already include enough possibilities, this claim derives from a typesetting error in an edition of Potter's *Archaeologia Graeca*, a work first published in 1728; whereas the Latin of Hyginus' story ends with free-born women (*ingenuae*) being permitted to study the art of medicine, the 1764 edition of Potter reads 'three' for 'free' to produce the statement that the Athenians 'permitted three women to undertake this employment' (324–5).

One more possibility exists within the variations on the theme of Agnodike. This is the approach taken by John Stevens in his attack on man-midwifery, first published in 1849. When outlining his view of the midwifery of the past, in which he insists that 'The Greeks invariably employed midwives' and 'The Romans also employed women only' (1849–66?: 4), he compresses Hyginus' account to the extreme, writing that

> It is said the Athenian doctors procured a legal enactment, transferring the practice of midwifery to themselves; but at the very attempt the women rose *en masse*, and declared they *would die, rather than submit to such an outrage* upon common decency.
>
> (1849–66: 4)

Here even Agnodike has disappeared; she has moved from the imaginary to the invisible.

10

GREEN SICKNESS

Hippocrates, Galen and the origins of the 'disease of virgins'

The seventeenth-century female quack healer who called herself 'Agnodice: The Woman Practitioner' included among the list of disorders she could cure 'Green-sickness'. When examining the ways in which Hippocratic gynaecology has been used by the medical profession, green sickness – like Isaac Baker Brown's 'procedure' – stands out as an example of the use of Hippocratic texts to give the authority of an ancient precedent to something which, in fact, is new. Something called *morbus virgineus*, 'the disease of virgins', 'the white fever', 'green-sickness' or chlorosis was discussed from the sixteenth century until it dropped out of medical textbooks in the beginning of the twentieth century; although its disappearance has been well documented in recent years,[1] there remains little consensus on what exactly it was, or on why it is no longer found (Siddall 1982: 254). In 1587, it was listed in Mercado's *De mulierum affectionibus* as 'the most frequently and most commonly found' disease affecting virgins.[2] Irvine Loudon has argued that, in certain historical periods, 'any sickly but normal girl in an irritable mood' was likely to be diagnosed as having it (1984: 32). The target population was thought to consist almost exclusively of young girls, so that in the late nineteenth century it came to be known as 'the special anaemia of young women'.[3] In the eighteenth century, there were outbreaks of what was diagnosed as 'mass chlorosis' in girls' boarding schools, with works such as John Coakley Lettsom's *Hints Respecting the Chlorosis of Boarding-Schools* (1795) offering advice on the regimen to be adopted to prevent such incidents occurring. In later stages of its history the category grew and was subdivided to embrace forms such as male chlorosis and late chlorosis or chlorosis tarda, but the new categories only throw into relief the profile of the typical sufferer as young and female.[4] The list of eleven symptoms given by Sydenham in the mid-seventeenth century would have been recognised throughout the history of chlorosis; in a mid-eighteenth-century translation this reads as follows:

> This indisposition is attended with (1.) a bad colour of the face, and whole body; (2.) a swelling of the face, eyelids and ankles; (3.)

> heaviness of the whole body; (4.) a tension and lassitude of the legs and feet; (5.) difficult respiration; (6.) palpitation of the heart; (7.) pain in the head; (8.) feverish pulse; (9.) drowsiness; (10.) an unnatural longing for such things as are noxious, and unfit for food; and (11.) a suppression of the menstrual discharge.
>
> (1753: 658)

This final feature, absence of menstruation, is fundamental to the diagnosis, especially in the sixteenth and early seventeenth centuries. In the diaries of Richard Napier, an English astrological priest-physician working in the south-east Midlands in the early seventeenth century, case histories in which the diagnosis ' green sickness' is given were subsequently amended to 'obstruction of the spleen' if the patient menstruated (Sawyer 1986: 491 n.41).[5]

Much remains unclear about this supposedly once common condition. Even the patient's skin colour, which Sydenham described merely as bad, is open to debate. Some medical writers suggested that the patients visibly turned green, but the English name ' green sickness' may simply allude to the youth of the typical sufferer, rather than to a green hue (Loudon 1980: 1672). Another sixteenth-century usage of 'green' in a medical context which does not refer to actual skin colour occurs in the notes Simon Forman (1552–1611) made of his medical practice from 1597 onwards; he uses the term 'grene' for 'newly delivered of a child' (Traister 1991: 441). Astruc wrote that the skin is 'like wax or candle grease' but can be 'the yellow of a dead leaf, or a yellow tending towards green, or towards black' – a wide range of hues (1761: 4). In the sixteenth century, sufferers were more likely to be described as 'pale' – hence the 'white' fever – and in the mid-nineteenth century, when the development of blood testing led to the identification of chlorosis with the low haemoglobin levels of hypochromic anaemia, the alleged green colour was rarely noted by medical practitioners (Loudon 1984: 27). Stengel (1896: 343) suggested that even the hair might become 'light coloured in spots'.

Within medical history, most attention has been paid to the disappearance of chlorosis in the early twentieth century. This medical mystery has been explained by assuming a simple 'one-to-one equivalent' (Brumberg 1982: 1469) between current Western biomedical categories and those of the early modern period, and then seeing the disorder purely as a form of iron-deficiency anaemia, remedied by an improved diet,[6] or by examining changes in female dress and their supposed effect on the internal organs (Hansen 1931: 184; Vertue 1955; Hudson 1977: 457–8), or by seeing chlorosis as learned behaviour, expected by physicians and duly produced by their young female patients (Brumberg 1982).

My interest lies in examining the historically and logically prior question: why was chlorosis first described in the mid-sixteenth century? Where did it come from? In the course of its history, chlorosis has been linked by writers contemporary with its peaks to causes ranging from 'love and other passions of the mind' (Cullen 1803: 362) to constipation (Fox 1839: 53; F. Taylor 1896: 720); Sir Andrew Clarke proposed a theory of 'auto-intoxication by faecal products' (E.L. Jones 1897: 42). Whatever the fashionable 'vice' – from drinking sweet coffee (James 1743–5 s.v. chlorosis) to tight-lacing (Lettsom 1795: 17) to masturbation (Hudson 1977: 457; Loudon 1984: 31) – it was likely to be implicated. I will trace the origin of green sickness to an apparently more prosaic – but no less extraordinary – event, namely the re-discovery of *On the Diseases of Virgins* in the early sixteenth century. This would suggest that attempts at retrospective diagnosis of early modern medical conditions are unhelpful; it is not in observed reality, but in the rediscovery and chosen modes of reinterpretation of ancient texts, that we will find the solutions to the problems which chlorosis poses for medical history.

What is the origin of the classical-sounding name 'chlorosis'? The term for this combination of symptoms was not coined until 1619, when Varandal of Montpellier wrongly claimed that it was a Hippocratic word.[7] The point that the word does not in fact appear anywhere in the Hippocratic corpus was recognised by some eighteenth-century medical writers, such as Astruc, who noted that Varandal was the source of the error (1761: 5, 7). But why 'chlorosis'? The Greek word *chloros* is often translated into English as 'green', or 'yellowish-green', suggesting a simple equation with the English vernacular green sickness. Beecher and Ciavolella (1990: 119) suggest that the appropriate colour is a 'greenish yellow tint of the skin'. But *chloros* has itself been the object of considerable scholarly discussion. In the most detailed study of its uses in Greek literature, Eleanor Irwin argued that it changed its meaning from 'green' in the eighth century BC to 'pale' or 'blanched' in the fourth century BC (1974: 31–79). In Homer, it was closest to 'green', and was seen as the colour appropriate to fear; in *Iliad* 7.479, for example, the Greek troops waiting outside Troy are affected by *chloron deos*, 'green fear' (Cyrino 1995: 164 n.69). Irwin suggests that the physiological rationale was that frightened people produced more bile from the liver, the organ in which fear was centred (1974: 62–4):[8] by the fourth century BC those who were afraid were thought to become pale, because blood was believed to rush to the heart, away from the surface of the body (Irwin 1974: 63–4; Ar. fr.243).

One usage of *chloros* in Greek literature has proved particularly influential; this is in Sappho 31, a poem known to medieval and Renaissance writers through its preservation in pseudo-Longinus, *On the sublime* 10.1–3, where it was used as an example of Sappho's excellence (*aretê*) in selecting the most important aspects of the symptoms of love's madness (*tais erôtikais maniais*; Weinberg 1950).[9] It was this poem which led to *chloros* being linked with the condition of love-sickness; one of the causes of chlorosis, too, was thought to be unrequited love. From the twelfth century onwards, love-sickness was a recognised medical condition in the Western medical tradition; Mary Wack has argued that this was due to the influence of Constantine the African's

Viaticum, an adaptation of an Arabic text, al-Jazzar's *Kitab Zād al-Musāfir*, which included 'passionate love' as an autonomous disease category (1990: xiii and 35). The *Viaticum* was a central text in the medical curricula of many European universities from the early thirteenth century onwards. The medical construction of love-sickness in Western medicine drew on representations of desire in classical Greek and Latin texts such as Sappho 31, while setting these in a physical context of humoral disturbance supplied by al-Jazzar, who was himself influenced by Galen's medical theories. Jacques Ferrand, a practising physician whose treatise on love-sickness was published in 1610, went so far as to say that Sappho had already identified all the signs of love; it was left to later physicians only to classify these (Beecher and Ciavolella 1990: 41, 271–2; Beecher 1988).

In the partially preserved poem 31, Sappho describes the sensations she experiences when seeing the girl she loves talking and laughing with a man. The man who hears the girl's sweet voice and lovely laughter seems to Sappho to be in a situation 'equal to the gods'. When Sappho looks at the girl 'even for a moment', her heart trembles in her breast, her senses are affected, and she is near death; unable to speak, she feels a fire beneath her flesh, her sight fails, her ears hum, she sweats and trembles and says, 'I am more *chloros* than grass' (*chlorotera de poias emmi*, 13–14). Are these sensations the result of watching the beloved in animated conversation, or of having been supplanted in her affections by the man in the poem?

The most common translation of the key phrase is 'greener than grass', and this translation has been used to support a reading of the poem which diagnoses what is affecting Sappho as jealousy, or as an 'anxiety attack'. Scholars – mainly male, and uncomfortable with the female homoeroticism of the poem – who put forward this argument suggest that the girl Sappho loves is to be married; seeing the beloved relaxing in the company of the man who is to replace her causes Sappho to feel jealousy. The 'jealousy thesis' can be traced back to the 1850s, but the idea of an 'attack' of this kind was put forward by the psychiatrist George Devereux in 1970. In responding to Devereux, Marcovich (1972: 21, 25) pointed out that this is not a sudden attack, but a chronic problem; Sappho's use of the subjunctive *idô* in line 7 should be understood as '*each* time I look at you . . . ', while Sappho marvels at the nameless man who can 'keep sitting right opposite you and keep listening', implying that she herself can only see the beloved for a moment before she is overwhelmed by her beauty.

But jealousy is far from being the only possibility. The spectrum of meanings of *chloros* also associates it with paleness and moisture; Irwin argued that the core meaning was liquid/fresh, so that flowers or dew could be described as *chloros* (1974: 33–56). For her, the best translation of Sappho's words would be 'more grassy than grass', thus making *chloros* 'not . . . a symptom of exhaustion, but of excitement' (1974: 65–7). Snyder followed up the idea that the main use of *chloros* was in connection with 'youth and life';

she therefore suggested that 'more *chloros* than grass' 'anchors the speaker's experience firmly in the natural world, a world of freshness, growth and moisture' (1991: 13–14). This would make the expression contrast strongly with the next line, 'I seem to be little short of dying.' This reading of the poem is consistent with pseudo-Longinus' explanation of why he cited it in *On the Sublime*; he praised Sappho's ability to capture the contradictory sensations central to the feeling of being in love, and found her picture entirely plausible.

Sappho 31 was a highly influential poem in the ancient Roman world. The Latin poet Catullus produced a heterosexual 'creative translation' of it (Catullus 51; Gaisser 1993: 163), in which he stopped in mid-phrase, in order to end with a reminder to himself that these fantasies of another man with his beloved are only the result of too much leisure (*otium*). Catullus' version stops before he feels the sensation of being 'more *chloros* than grass'. Echoes of Sappho's poem also appear in Theocritus 2.106–10, Lucretius 3.152–8 and Longus Pastor 1.17.4. This last work, from the third century AD, is a Latin imitation rather than a translation; Longus Pastor develops 'more *chloros* than grass' into 'more pale in the face than summer grass', grass thoroughly bleached by the hot summer sun (Irwin 1974: 65–6). This interpretation of Sappho removes the sense of contrast between this line and the following one, 'It seems to me I am little short of dying.'

Another important classical text for discussions both of love-sickness and of chlorosis is Ovid's *Art of Love* 1.729, which states that it is fitting that a lover becomes pale (*palleat*), because paleness is the colour most appropriate for a lover.[10] The definition of *pallens* given in the *Oxford Latin Dictionary* is 'Pale, wan', from illness, death or emotion; however, the entry goes on to suggest that, in Mediterranean populations, we should understand this as involving a yellowish or greenish tint, making the colour close to the Greek *chloros*. This denial that *palleat* means simply 'pale' is also found in sixteenth- and seventeenth-century writers; in Shakespeare's *Love's Labour's Lost* (I.ii.81; *c.* 1595), the 'fantastical Spaniard' Armado seems to have Ovid in mind when he remarks 'Green indeed is the colour of lovers', while Ferrand calls the colour of lovers one 'blended of white and yellow, or of white, yellow and green', and cites Galen as evidence that pale (*ôchros*) and *chloros* are equivalent terms for a certain complexion.[11] Here Ferrand is using Giovan Battista della Porta's influential work, *De humana physiognomonia libri IV* (1601: 200, 201–5), which discussed the significance of different colours of the face and body; Ovid's comment on pale lovers is repeated, and *chloros* is described as sometimes meaning 'pallid'. This text furthermore suggests that, in women, a white colour is associated with excessive sexual appetites (1601: 198).

When would these classical texts have been available to writers of the early modern period? Pseudo-Longinus' *On the Sublime* was known in the fifteenth century, but received little attention until Francesco Robortello published an edition in 1554. A few months later, in October of the same year, Marc

Antoine de Muret brought out his commentary on Catullus, in which he was the first to identify in print Catullus 51 as a translation of Sappho 31 (Muret 1554: 57; Gaisser 1993: 163–4, 147). In his treatise on love-sickness, first published in 1610, Jacques Ferrand not only cited Sappho (through Longinus), using Sappho as evidence that all the symptoms of love classified by later physicians were already known to her, but also quoted from Catullus and Ovid (Beecher and Ciavolella 1990: 271–2, 41). Green sickness could perhaps be seen as a form of love-sickness, but one in which there is no love object.

So the precise colour connotations of chlorosis are not easy to recover; however, Sappho's use of *chloros* encouraged its connection with love-sickness. As the poem was only available from 1554, what are we to make of 'green' sickness in English vernacular texts? The earliest use of ' green sickness' as a distinct condition which I have been able to trace dates to 1559, when it is explicitly called 'a new disease' but is not yet linked to menstrual suppression, nor seen as a condition found only in young girls. Since this makes vernacular usage considerably earlier than 1608, the date proposed by Sawyer (1986: 490–1 and n.42) and followed by Loudon (1984: 29), we need to look at the precise details of the relevant text. This is William Bullein's *A newe Boke of Phisicke called ye Government of Health*, which refers to onions helping 'the grene sickness' (1559: 124), mentions 'greene sicknes' as a possible consequence of eating too much pepper (1559: 217), and in a discussion of the uses of Mithridatum recommends it 'for women whiche have a newe disease peraccidentes called the greene sicknes' (1559: 228). Even earlier, in 1547, Andrew Boorde's *Breviary of Helthe* used 'grene sicknes', but as the direct equivalent of 'grene jaundis', one of three types of jaundice mentioned. The green variant was seen as the result of the corruption of blood from a mixture of yellow bile and phlegm. Boorde, however, does not suggest that this condition is unique to any age-sex group, nor does he regard it as 'new'.[12] Somewhere between 1547 and 1559, green sickness becomes a condition in its own right, rather than a form of jaundice; references to it are brief and inconclusive in English vernacular literature in the mid- and late sixteenth century, but the remedies recommended would suggest that it is already seen as exclusive to women, and is associated with digestive problems or blockages and with a bad colour in the face. For example, Bullein's *Bulwarke of Defence* (1562) includes a section on the use of onions:

> They doe make thyn the Bloude . . . [they] bee hoat in the thyrd degree, but they warme and cleanse the Stomacke, brynge good Colour to the face, and then they muste be good for the neewe Greene Sycknesse.

So much for the main names of the condition; what of its alleged classical origins? Many writers on chlorosis have claimed Hippocratic antecedents for the clinical description of the condition. For example, in his *History of Physick* Daniel Le Clerc mentions '(g) Virgins, the Diseases of Virgins' but adds: 'This disease is described by Hippocrates, but he gave it no particular name' (1699: 248). At the end of the nineteenth century, Stengel claimed that 'the ancient writers, beginning with Hippocrates, looked upon chlorosis as a disease in some way dependent upon disturbance of menstruation. Hippocrates attributed it to the retention of blood in the uterus' (1896: 330–1). Among recent writers on the history of chlorosis, Hudson states that there are 'descriptions of what could be chlorosis dating back to Hippocrates' (1977: 448). But this has always been a disputed point; Astruc (1761: 5) felt that it was only mentioned in passing in *On the Diseases of Virgins*.

The first full clinical picture which fits what came to be seen as the basic symptomatology of chlorosis simply calls the disorder 'the disease of virgins'. This Latin text, published in 1554, but probably composed in the 1530s, is Johannes Lange's *Medicinalium epistolarum miscellanea*.[13] Lange, born in 1485 in Löwenburg in Silesia, and educated at the universities of Leipzig, Ferrara and Pisa, was a highly knowledgeable writer, familiar with the medical debates of his day; he used the letter format, popular in medicine in this period, and was immersed in the classical tradition (Fossel 1914; Nutton 1984a; 1985b). From similarities of wording, it is clear that he owned a copy of the 1525 Latin translation of the Hippocratic corpus by Marco Fabio Calvi.[14] Although he prefers to cite Hippocratic treatises from this rather than from the Aldine Greek text of 1526, he could read Greek when necessary; he cites Galen's commentary on *Regimen in Acute Diseases* in Greek, and in some of his Hippocratic sections it may be possible to see him comparing the Greek and Latin texts before reaching his own version.[15]

Lange's 'letter' is ostensibly directed at a friend whose first-born daughter, Anna, a girl of marriageable age, has fallen ill. A section is a direct translation of the Hippocratic text *On the Diseases of Virgins*. In contrast to the main Hippocratic gynaecological treatises, the three volumes of *Diseases of Women*, this short text survived in the Arabic tradition, having been translated from Greek in eighth- or ninth-century Baghdad; it is mentioned in about AD 900 by Rhazes (*al-Hawi* 9.67, 69; see Rhazes 1505), and in the thirteenth century by Ibn Abi Usaibi'a (1.32).[16] In the West, however, its fortunes were very different; unlike sections of *Diseases of Women*, it does not feature in manuscript compilations of gynaecological knowledge.[17] Its inclusion in Calvi's Latin edition in 1525 thus brought it back into the Western medical tradition for the first time in many centuries; in 1526 it was also included in the Greek Aldine edition of the Hippocratic corpus.

Lange explicitly names the newly available *On the Diseases of Virgins* as his source for the advice given. Lange commends his friend for sending him details of all the symptoms affecting Anna, the first of which is paleness of the cheeks and lips 'as if bloodless', *velut exsanguia pallescere*. Later in the letter Lange cites Ovid on the appropriate colour for lovers, *quum palleat omnis amans, et color sit aptus amanti*. There is no mention here of green skin colour, either for lovers or for sufferers from the 'virgins' disease', but unfortunately this does not settle the question, since in *Epidemics* 2.2.12 (Loeb VII, 34) it is said that loss of blood makes the skin green.

In general, Lange – like Niccolò Leoniceno (1497) before him – believed that all diseases were known to the ancients, and thus that an entirely new disease was impossible, any which appeared to be new being properly understood as transformations of other diseases (Fossel 1914: 248). In stating this, he was taking up his position in a medical debate of the time, stimulated by such apparently new diseases as syphilis and the English Sweat; another of his letters is 'On new diseases'.[18] If Anna's set of symptoms form a distinct disease, he believes, then it must be possible to find this specific disease somewhere in the classical medical corpus, and Lange believes he has done so in *On the Diseases of Virgins*. He names Anna's condition 'the disease of virgins' in order to underline this claim of identity.

The relationship between Lange's letter and its alleged Hippocratic source is, however, far from straightforward. Despite the enormous confidence in its Hippocratic origins found in the works of medical writers throughout its history, no Hippocratic or other classical medical text either names or describes green sickness/chlorosis. The condition in *On the Diseases of Virgins* is far from being a perfect match; Schwarz (1951: 146) goes so far as to say that *On the Diseases of Virgins* 'does not contain the faintest hint' of chlorosis. But it is also misleading to suggest, as did Starobinski (1981: 460), that Lange simply combined two or more other Hippocratic texts to produce the 'disease of virgins': the Hippocratic passages usually cited in this connection are *Coan Prognoses* 333 (L 5.656), a discussion of a disorder affecting children at the age of seven, involving paleness, breathing difficulties and eating earth, and *Prorrhetic* 2.31 (Loeb VIII, 280), a disorder identified as 'Chlorose' by Littré, explicitly found in 'both men and women', with symptoms of a bad colour, headaches, piles, and eating stones and earth.[19] Furthermore, although Lange explicitly cites *On the Diseases of Virgins*, not all the passages he assigns to this text are in fact found there. On some occasions this is simply due to carelessness in specifying when a quotation ends and Lange's gloss on it begins; on others, however, Lange's interpretation can help us see how and why the version of the text he was using differs from the published versions available today.

As we saw in Chapter 4, *On the Diseases of Virgins* describes – or threatens – the medical risks faced by young girls at menarche if they do not marry, despite being 'ripe for marriage'. An excess of blood, due to 'food and the growth of the body', is unable to escape because 'the mouth of exit' is closed. It therefore moves up the body, becoming stuck at the heart and diaphragm, where the internal channels through which it must pass are believed to be 'at an angle'. It then exerts pressure on the heart, presented here as the seat of consciousness. This causes mental disturbances; in particular, seeing ghosts and desiring death as a lover, sometimes resulting in suicide by hanging or drowning. Relief comes when there is no obstacle to the flowing out of the blood; the recommended therapy is marriage, 'for if they become pregnant, they will be cured'.

Although this text has been neglected by classical scholarship and, until very recently, by Hippocratic studies, in other areas of scholarship and in earlier historical periods it has enjoyed great popularity and influence. The number of editions published from the sixteenth century onwards (L 8.465; see also Celli 1984) gives only a hint of this; more significant is the large number of references to it, some direct quotations, others not acknowledging their source, in medical writing of the sixteenth and seventeenth centuries. Its role in the creation of chlorosis is only one aspect of this popularity.

In his letter based on this text, Lange describes how his friend's first-born daughter Anna, of the age for marriage, is pursued by wealthy and noble suitors. His friend has had to turn down their offers because of Anna's weakness. No doctor has been able to explain the disease, or to prescribe treatment. In his confusion, Anna's father is supposed to have turned to Lange. The symptoms are listed as follows: her face is pale, as if bloodless; her heart trembles severely at any bodily movement, and the arteries of her temples pulsate with feeling; and she has laboured breathing when dancing or climbing stairs. We can see how Lange's letter set the tone for all subsequent clinical descriptions of chlorosis, with even very minor details of much later clinical descriptions being heavily dependent on it, by noting how this appears to be echoed by John Pechey in 1694; when describing the behaviour of 'a gentlewoman of 28' after being cured of green sickness, he writes that she 'could with pleasure run up four pair of stairs at a time' (1694: 10). Lange goes on to say that Anna avoids food, especially meat; her legs – in particular near the ankles – swell at night. Lange says that, from this list, the diagnosis is obvious. It is a disease which lacks a name, but does not lack a treatment; he calls it 'the disease of virgins'.

Lange then moves straight into a version of the Hippocratic text *On the Diseases of Virgins*; sometimes his terminology is taken directly from it, but on other occasions there is a more Galenic ring to his words. This condition, he says, often attacks virgins when they are ripe for a man, as the menstrual blood flows down from the liver to the pockets and veins of the womb.[20] This blood cannot break through because of the narrow mouths of the veins, which are not yet open and which are additionally obstructed by viscous and unconcocted humours and, finally, because of the thickness of the blood itself. Here, Lange is moving away from Hippocratic explanations to Galen, who in *On the Causes of Symptoms* 11 (K 7.264 ff.) gave narrowness of the channels supplying the womb with blood, the presence of excess humours and thick, sticky blood as three of the possible causes of menstrual retention. The approach taken to disease in general in *On the Causes of Symptoms* may be summarised as follows. Food in the form of chyle is taken from the stomach to the liver; from there, having been converted into blood, it is attracted to the rest of the body. Each part has the power of pulling to itself what is needed. A part may be too weak or too strong, pulling in less or more than it needs; the channels through which the nutriment passes may be too narrow, as a result of disease or an obstruction, or the blood may be too thick or sticky. The fault may also rest with the quality of the food which has been consumed (Galen, *On the Causes of Symptoms* 3.3; K 7.221–2).

Quoting directly from Calvi's 1525 translation of *On the Diseases of Virgins*,[21] Lange goes on to describe how the retained blood flows backwards to the heart, liver, diaphragm and the veins of the praecordia; much is taken to the head, and severe symptoms are also caused around the viscera. He then reverts once more to a Galenic model, in which the heart, stomach and liver are linked to each other, so that all become crammed and blocked with coarse blood and vapours. The heart tries to drive these out, and it trembles all over with palpitation. At this point the patient lies as if dead. Here again Lange cites Galen; *On Difficulty in Breathing* 3.12 (K 7:954), available in new printed Latin translations in the 1530s,[22] and the commentary to the Hippocratic *On Regimen in Acute Diseases*, where in 4.78 (CMG V. 9,1, p. 336) Galen discusses the possibility of asphyxiation if an obstruction forms in an artery rather than in a vein. Hippocratic writers use *phlebs* or 'channel' to cover what we distinguish as arteries and veins; the distinction between two types of channel was probably not made until Praxagoras of Cos in the late fourth century BC. Even then, the difference had nothing to do with the circulation of the blood, but was related to the belief that blood and *pneuma* travelled through different systems (Duminil 1979: 156; Furley and Wilkie 1984: 22). The roles of arteries and veins in Galenic physiology remain very different from those envisaged in a post-Harveian model of the body; for Galen, veins transport 'venous blood' from the liver as part of the nutritive faculty, while arteries carry the superior form, 'arterial blood', from the heart in order to transmit the vital faculty (Whitteridge 1971: 41–5).

Lange ends with his advice on Anna's marriage, which he claims is taken straight from 'the divine Hippocrates'. The patient is cured of this disease by bloodletting, if there are no contraindications, or alternatively the afflicted virgin should marry. If she conceives, she will recover. Lange then adds what he says is his own advice but which is actually standard Galenic practice: medicines for provoking the menses and for opening up obstructions, to refine the coarse blood.[23] We may note here that Galen used mint, pennyroyal, savin and dittany (Galen, *On Treatment by Bloodletting* 18, K 11.304; Brain 1986: 93); Lange does not specify. Lange's letter ends, 'So therefore, take courage, betroth your daughter: I myself will gladly be present at the wedding. Farewell.'[24] The origin of the medical advice given in this letter is thus presented in a highly misleading way. Lange claims his own advice as 'Galenic', and the Galenic norm as 'Hippocratic', merging the anatomy of *On the Diseases of Virgins* with standard Galenic anatomy, with no attempt to discuss where the two differ.

Lange lists three treatments: bloodletting and marriage, both claimed as Hippocratic, and emmenagogue drugs, which he says he has added. What most writers from the sixteenth century onwards pick up from Lange, however, is the only therapy of the three to derive directly from the Hippocratic text: the recommendation of marriage as the best cure for green sickness (e.g. Astruc 1761: 63–4). Ballads of the late seventeenth century provide some examples: 'A remedy for the green sickness' (*c.*1683) includes the verse:

A handsome buxom lass
lay panting on her bed.
She look't as green as grass
and mournfully she said
Unless I have some lusty lad to ease me of my pain
I cannot live
I sigh and grieve
My life I now disdain.[25]

In another ballad, 'The maid's complaint for want of a Dildoul', the speaker, aged 16 and a virgin, has a condition 'which many maides do call the sickness green' and will do anything 'for a dill doul, dil doul, dil doul doul'.[26] It was only in the nineteenth century that sex as therapy for this condition came to be questioned; Andrew Fogo, writing in 1803, challenged the accepted wisdom of his day by which both doctors and lay people recommended 'indulgence in venery' as a cure, as being far from practical or desirable for a girl with green sickness; and there was also a serious obstacle in the way of such therapy since, if a girl was pale and breathless, 'there is never a man will look at her, except to laugh and make a jest of her' (1803: 81).

Whereas the curative powers of sex for chlorosis can be seen to derive from the Hippocratic *On the Diseases of Virgins*, Lange's second remedy, bloodletting, has a more complex relationship to the text. It is not found in the best Greek manuscripts, although it makes sense if we project back a Galenic reading, and see Anna's blood as thick and obstructive. But bloodletting does feature in Calvi's 1525 Latin translation of *On the Diseases of Virgins*, to which Lange evidently has access. The original Greek translates as, 'But there is a deliverance from this when nothing prevents the flowing out of the blood'; there is no suggestion here of taking action to remove blood from elsewhere in the body. Some Greek manuscripts, however, have an extra word inserted (*therapeia*) which would make the first part, 'The treatment for this deliverance', a reading which makes rather less sense, hence its rejection by Littré. It is this tradition which Calvi uses, reaching the translation 'But the deliverance from this, and the cure is – if nothing prevents it

– bloodletting.'[27] This moves the meaning away from the natural release of blood through defloration, menstruation and, in due course, childbirth, towards the artificial release of blood by bloodletting. Twenty years later, Cornarius' Latin translation (1546: 286) gave very similar wording.[28] These shifts towards suggesting deliberate removal of blood lie behind Lange's 'Deliverance from this disease is by bloodletting, if nothing prevents it.' By the time of the publication of de Baillou's study of the condition in 1643, the Hippocratic remedies are simply summarised as 'Bloodletting is a cure, but the best medicine is marriage' (1643: 67).[29]

The relationship between chlorosis and bloodletting is thus a complex one. Bloodletting is actually very rare in the Hippocratic corpus, and there are few cases in which it is performed on women.[30] As Peter Brain (1986: 118–19) showed, although Galen gives the impression that bloodletting was a common therapy in the Hippocratic texts, it is in fact found only about seventy times in the entire corpus: even in the seventeenth century it had been noticed that bloodletting is nowhere near as common in the Hippocratic corpus as it is in Galen. It was Galen who saw it as the remedy of choice for menstrual suppression, but he was reluctant to let blood in anyone under age 14 (*On Treatment by Bloodletting* 13, K 11.290; Brain 1986: 87). Since, in the classical tradition, menarche is linked with the fourteenth year – that is, age 13 – it would be very unwise to take blood from girls at menarche, yet 'ripeness for marriage' in the ancient Greek context of the Hippocratic *On the Diseases of Virgins* suggests precisely this stage of life. In addition, Galen explicitly forbids bloodletting if 'the complexion of the whole body lacks the colour that indicates an abundance of blood' (*On Treatment by Bloodletting* 9, K 11.279–80; Brain 1986: 81). Since Anna is 'pale as if bloodless', she is hardly an ideal candidate. Trying to read a Hippocratic text in a Galenic tradition encourages the recommendation of this cure, yet the age group of the sufferers and the key symptom of paleness are contraindications. This is understood by de Baillou, who was practising medicine at the end of the sixteenth century. He sees the condition of green sickness as resulting from a dietary defect, an obstruction or the presence of unconcocted humours; in any case, he says, the problem is insufficient 'good' blood, so in most cases one should purge the bad humours or remove any obstruction rather than bleed the patient (1643: 87). An earlier indication that not everyone agreed on the universal use of bloodletting to relieve menstrual suppression comes in Simon Forman's account of his London practice from 1597 onwards; he found that many of his female patients had 'stopped menses' as a symptom, but avoided bloodletting for this (Traister 1991: 438).

Another aspect of Lange's description which has interesting implications for reading a Hippocratic text through Galenic filters is the symptom of changed skin colour, to 'pale, as if bloodless'. Changed skin colour can be demonstrated as having both Hippocratic and Galenic referents. On the Galenic side, a text Lange clearly knows well is *On the Causes of Symptoms*.

Immediately after Galen's account of menstrual suppression in this text, he goes on to discuss how skin colour will be affected by the presence of corrupt humours; the humours will either flood the skin, or will sink to the depths of the body (*On the Causes of Symptoms* 3.12; K 7.267). In this tradition, de Baillou's long discussion *De foedis virginum coloribus* opens with the statement that the colour of the body comes from the humours (1643: 57). On such a reading, the internal turmoil Lange describes, with blood moving from the womb to the heart, diaphragm and liver, could either imply that there will be insufficient blood remaining to tint the skin, or that the change is due to other, corrupt, humours moving to the surface.

But there is also a possible Hippocratic reference to altered skin colour in *On the Diseases of Virgins*. In Chapter 4 I argued that, in the original context of this text, the symptom of feeling strangled and the attempts at suicide by hanging were significant because they showed how the medical construction of the disease drew on beliefs about the role of Artemis in the female life-cycle. Lange does not translate the part of *On the Diseases of Virgins* which says that 'the patient hangs herself, as if this were better or useful' or perhaps '. . . or appropriate behaviour'. The Greek word being translated here as useful or appropriate is *chreios*. In his Latin translation of the whole text Calvi, however, followed an alternative manuscript tradition which reads *chroia* here; *chroia* means the skin, and, in particular, the colour of the skin. Calvi thus translated the Greek into Latin as *coloremque crebro variat et mutat*, thus getting 'and her skin colour frequently changes and alters'. I would suggest that Lange's interest in changed skin colour derives from his familiarity with this Latin translation, one which, in general, he seems to prefer to the second translation of the same text appearing later in the Calvi Hippocrates. He is then assuming that the 'change' must be from a healthy pink to a paler complexion. The second, inferior, translation in Calvi derives from the same manuscript tradition, but here gives *quidam varios trahit colores*, 'indeed she draws to herself various colours'. In texts written in the later sixteenth century, a distinction is made between loss of colour, and bad coloration due to the presence of corrupt humours; for example, de Baillou (1643: 84–5) discusses the difference between *achroia*, which he takes to mean paleness, and *kakochroia*, bad coloration coming from the presence of bad humours. The improved Latin translation in Cornarius' version of the Hippocratic corpus, *et strangulari, tanquam meliora sint haec, et omnem vitae utilitatem excedentia*, which is clearly based on a manuscript favouring *chreios* over *chroia*, did not act to correct the emerging picture of green sickness (1546: 286). Paleness, with other variations on an altered skin colour, therefore enters the disease picture as the result of Calvi's choice of Greek manuscripts when translating the Hippocratic corpus into Latin for publication.

In order to understand the development of the disease picture of chlorosis, it is therefore necessary to read the Hippocratic *On the Diseases of Virgins* in a context which is based partly on the Galenic theory dominant in the early sixteenth century and partly on significant reinterpretation of the Greek text. In addition to paleness, chlorosis includes three major symptoms which are found in Lange but not – or, at least, not on first reading – in the Hippocratic *On the Diseases of Virgins*. These are difficulty in breathing, dietary disturbance and swelling. Lange says that Anna 'has an attack of dyspnoea when dancing or climbing stairs; her stomach turns away from food, above all from meat; her legs – especially near the ankles – swell at night'. These three symptoms feature in all later descriptions of green sickness. Dyspnoea may be a way of giving a medical interpretation to the Hippocratic references to feeling strangled and to suicide by hanging. Later in the letter Lange describes how veins blocked with blood put pressure on the diaphragm, causing rapid, shallow breathing. 'Strangulation' is seen here as a medical symptom with an organic cause, rather than as a preferred mode of suicide. Swelling of the lower limbs which, with lassitude in the feet and legs, is characteristic of later descriptions of chlorosis such as that of Sydenham quoted at the opening of this chapter (cf. Astruc 1761: 4), could be derived from misinterpretation of another section of the Hippocratic text, in which an analogy is drawn between the oppression of the heart due to the misplaced menstrual blood, and the numbness caused in the feet if a person should sit still for a long time. If the feet 'go dead' in this way, and swell, the Hippocratic writer explains, this is due to excess blood collecting in them, and can be reversed by immersing the feet in cold water to just above the ankles. It should be underlined that the writer never says that the feet and ankles swell in a case of retained menstrual blood: he merely compares the ease with which excess blood in the feet can be dispersed with the difficulty encountered in reversing a flow of menstrual blood in the more critical and more complex area of the heart.

Dyspnoea and swollen feet can thus be seen to derive – indirectly, at least – from *On the Diseases of Virgins*. Lange's description of Anna turning 'away from food, especially meat' is far more complex. Such dietary symptoms too may originate in the Hippocratic text, which refers to 'food and the growth of the body' causing the excess of blood which leads to menarche; the ancient Greek idea is that, as food makes blood (e.g. Homer, *Il.* 5.341–2; Aristotle, *PA* 650a34–5, 651a14–15; Longrigg 1985) so too much food can cause too much blood. De Baillou cites the Hippocratic *On Generation* 2 (L 7.472–4) to show that a girl at puberty has naturally narrow channels, while the completion of maturation means there is suddenly an excess of blood in her body which is not needed for growth (1643: 68; Lonie 1981, 1–2). The combination of narrow channels and a surplus of blood can also affect the mind; the explanation of the risks of female puberty in the 1694 edition of *Aristotle's Masterpiece* is that the blood 'which is no longer taken to augment their bodies, abounding, incites their minds and imaginations to Venery'. The only solution is matrimony, otherwise girls will develop 'a Green and Weasel Colour, Short Breathings, Tremblings of the Heart, and c.' (*Masterpiece* 1694: 2–3).

In sixteenth- and seventeenth-century texts, avoiding foods which produce a large amount of blood was therefore logically recommended for women who want to make the minimum amount possible of both menstrual blood and seed. For example, the midwife Jane Sharp advised unmarried women and nuns to avoid meat and eggs (1671: 326). Discussing the late nineteenth century, Brumberg argued that the rejection of meat was seen as 'a positive social virtue' for 'good' girls to exhibit (1982: 1473–4). In Galenic theory, meat is the food which is most completely converted to blood, leaving least residue (e.g. *De alimentorum facultatibus* 3.26; K 6.714). If Anna's aversion to food, especially to meat, is seen in these terms, then her symptoms could be seen as a deliberate attempt to resist a natural process.

Both the natural excess of puberty, and deliberate restriction of the diet to halt the production of this excess, are thus linked to the onset of green sickness. Another possible food connection is Sydenham's 'unnatural longing for such things as are noxious, and unfit for food'. This idea was also found in sixteenth-century descriptions of the virgins' disease. Mercado argues that green sickness can affect pre-pubertal girls who eat 'juicy or perverse foods' (1587: 216, 219). Juicy here means blood-producing; foods which can lead to surplus blood even in a girl who should be too young to have such a surplus. Perverse foods occur in many descriptions from the sixteenth to the nineteenth century, their consumption being either a symptom or a cause of green sickness. Such descriptions envisage the sufferer ceasing to eat meat, but instead consuming earth, chalk, slate pencils, tobacco pipes and other 'non-food' substances (*Masterpiece* 1694: 72; Sharp 1671: 263; cf. Stengel 1896: 348). To complicate the picture a little more, some sixteenth- and seventeenth-century writers add that these perverse substances are consumed deliberately, in order to acquire the pale complexion seen as socially attractive; for example, Bullein's *Government of Health* (1559: 217) describes women who 'would fayne be fayre' deliberately eating food which dries up their blood, and as a result falling into 'greene sicknes . . . and oftentimes sodain death'. Here again it is the patient who is to blame for the disorder.

Turning 'away from food, especially meat' is thus a Langian statement open to a variety of subsequent interpretations: as a poor diet, as fasting leading to thick blood, or as the consumption of unsuitable foods which block the veins. In all three the condition can become a deliberate attempt by Anna to defy her destiny as a mature woman.

For most of its history, green sickness is a 'women's disease'. Many writers are adamant that men cannot have it, and the earliest of its many names – *morbus virgineus* – ties it firmly to women. In classical medical thought, women are more likely than men to suffer from an excess of blood, because not only is their flesh of a wet and spongy texture but their sedentary way of life encourages the accumulation of a plethora. Chlorosis can reinforce sexual difference and the roles which are assumed to follow from it. Mercado argues that sufferers are unable to work, and if they are made to work then their minds will fail due to insufficient heat (1587: 217). But in the history of chlorosis there is no such word as 'can't' and, by Varandal's discussion of 1619, housework has been elevated to the status of a cure (98–9). This is not a new idea; the sixth-century writer Aetius of Amida suggests that women who have ceased to menstruate, a condition he attributes to too much leisure, 'must be put to work' (16.61) while Fontanus opened his work *The Womans Doctour* with the words, 'Women were made to stay at home, and to looke after Household employments' (1652: 1).

Chlorosis thus uses Hippocratic and Galenic texts to support ideas of women's innate weakness and proper roles. It does this by addressing the problems of young unmarried women, seen as an anomalous category. Tardy's commentary to *On the Diseases of Virgins* is instructive here: 'Certain virgins are, in fact, the most exposed to disorders of the womb, because their wombs grow feeble or very weak on account of their being exempt from, and deprived of, their own characteristic functions' (1648). The message of green sickness could thus be summarised as 'if you've got it, use it'. Anna's father's question to Lange is simple: should his daughter marry? Yes, answers Lange; marriage will most probably cure her. Marriage remains the issue, until the end of the history of chlorosis; while in 1839 Samuel Fox protested that the idea that marriage was the only cure was 'an absurdity, and I must say, obscenity' (117), the 1905 English translation of von Noorden's essay on chlorosis notes that 'The only important point is whether chlorotic girls should be allowed to marry' (523–4). Being a woman is inherently unhealthy, but the best way to remain as healthy as possible is to marry, have children and keep up with the housework. The social role appropriate to a woman is the means by which her physical health is assured.

It also becomes clear, in the history of gynaecology, that a woman's health can never be fully guaranteed. Following the Hippocratic texts, female existence is represented as a precarious state. If a young girl on the brink of womanhood stops eating, her blood will thicken and move sluggishly. If she eats too much, or eats juicy foods, she will cause an excess of blood. If she eats perverse foods, she will block her veins. Her virginity is both socially desirable and medically dangerous: her pale complexion is seen by some writers as erotically stimulating, and by others as ugly.[31] A further variation, the idea that chlorosis is 'the anaemia of good looking girls' (Tait 1889: 282–3), an idea also found in the early sources (e.g. Mercado 1587: 215–16), means that, to an extent, the diagnosis reinforces one's value as a potential marriage partner, and almost becomes a diagnosis worth seeking. Whatever she does, the young girl is at risk because of the natural process of puberty.

She is also at risk because of the chlorosis tradition itself. Loudon has noted that 'the clinical descriptions (at least up to 1850) were remarkably consistent' (1980: 1669). Having drawn attention here to some of the remarkably minor details which were retained to the end of its history, I would argue that this consistency is due to their close reliance on each other, and should not be used as evidence for a single 'real' disease behind the texts. The chlorosis tradition is a literary tradition, in which symptoms are developed in reference to textual authorities rather than to observed reality. The early modern medical texts derived from *On the Diseases of Virgins* act to legitimise changes to the ancient Greek picture – such as the introduction of bloodletting – which later authors have inserted. Where the desired symptoms or therapies do not already exist in the developing chlorosis tradition, the subsequent contributors to that tradition show no hesitation in creating them. Chlorosis is thus both an example of the rigidity caused by adherence to classical texts, and a case in which we can chart innovation and development within the classical paradigm.[32]

In Lange's invention of a 'disease of virgins' we can see what was happening in the crucial years immediately after 1525–6, when 'the humanist Hippocrates hit the market' (Nutton 1989: 426). When he read Hippocrates, Lange interpreted the texts through the dominant Galenic paradigms, and through the versions given in published Latin translations. In the process of reading about Hippocrates' women, he created a version of the disorder described in *On the Diseases of Virgins* which was to influence the gynaecological approach to the bodies of young women for centuries to come.

11

ONCE UPON A TEXT

Hysteria from Hippocrates

Labels and origins: a name without a disease?

Throughout this book we have seen the powerful influence of the concept of 'Hippocrates, father of medicine', as the hero who freed the emerging science from the chains of superstition and introduced empirical observation, while incarnating the eternally correct doctor/patient relationship in his bed-side manner. In 1922, Charles Singer visualised Hippocrates as 'Learned, observant, humane . . . orderly and calm . . . grave, thoughtful and reticent, pure of mind and master of his passions'.

Green sickness is not the most significant of the diseases of women for which Hippocratic origins have been claimed as a way of validating the diagnosis. I now want to turn to another, even more important, disease category which has waved the banner of Hippocratic origins for much of its recent history: 'hysteria'. By looking at the ancient precursors claimed for it, and at their interpretations over time, I will argue not only that hysteria is a label totally inapplicable to Hippocratic medicine, but also that its use positively hinders our understanding of Hippocratic gynaecology as a medical system. The value or otherwise of the label 'hysteria' has been the object of much debate in medical literature, and medical writers are aware of the role of tradition in its use; for example, in his Shorvon Memorial Lecture delivered in 1964, Eliot Slater argued that 'the justification for accepting "hysteria" as a syndrome is based entirely on tradition and lacks evidential support' (1965: 1396). What is not appreciated is the flimsiness of the alleged origin of the diagnosis of hysteria in the Hippocratic corpus, and it is only by reclaiming the relevant texts from their use in the tradition that we can understand and challenge the diagnosis in later centuries.

In 1892 a physician, Hunter Robb, published translations of sections on the *Diseases of Women* under the title 'Hippocrates on hysteria'. A few decades earlier, when translating the corpus into the medical French of his own day (Sournia 1983: 264), Emile Littré had had no hesitation in retrospectively diagnosing several sections as 'hystérie'. However, the authority cited to support the claim of Hippocratic hysteria by more recent medical historians, psychologists and physicians is, almost without exception, the history of hysteria published by Ilza Veith in 1965 (Micale 1989: 227). Born in Germany, Veith studied medicine in Geneva and Vienna; she emigrated to the United States in 1937, and in 1947 was awarded the first American doctorate in the history of medicine. While writing *Hysteria*, she suffered a severe stroke which paralysed her left side; despite suffering symptoms in the weeks before this, she had not sought medical help for fear that she would be diagnosed as 'hysterical'. After the stroke, she tried to convince herself that her paralysis must be hysterical and would therefore go away (Showalter 1993: 328, 331).

Veith recognised the power of the diagnosis of hysteria, a power seen more recently in the media responses to Elaine Showalter's *Hystories* (1997) with its claims that Gulf War Syndrome and Chronic Fatigue Syndrome are our modern 'hysterias'. Yet her work has been used to give this diagnosis even greater power, by associating it with the name of Hippocrates. On the origin of the label, she wrote:

> In the Egyptian papyri the disturbances resulting from the movement of the womb were described, but had not yet been given a specific appellation. This step was taken in the Hippocratic writings where the connection of the uterus (*hystera*) with the disease resulting from its disturbance is first expressed by the term 'hysteria'. It appears in the thirty-fifth aphorism, which reads: 'When a woman suffers from hysteria . . .'
>
> (Veith 1965: 10)

These points have achieved canonical status since the publication of *Hysteria*. Medical writers confidently state that 'the name, hysteria, has been in use since the time of Hippocrates' (Woodruff *et al.* 1974: 118), refer back to 'the time of Hippocrates, who coined the name' (Bart and Scully 1979: 354), and cite Veith as the sole source for the 'information' that 'disorders diagnosed as hysteria have been encountered for about 2,500 years' and furthermore that 'as everyone knows, the term hysteria originated in Greek antiquity' (Guze 1967: 491, 493). This confidence extends beyond the origin of the word 'hysteria' to the very essence of ancient Greek gynaecology. Satow, a psychotherapist and sociologist, asserts that

> 'hysteria' has been a label used for a pot-pourri of female ailments and non-ailments alike since antiquity . . . The Greeks and Romans called almost all female complaints hysteria and believed the cause of all these female maladies to be a wandering uterus . . . In various Hippocratic texts the term hysteria is applied to a large variety of female complaints.
>
> (1979/80: 463–4)

What 'everyone knows' is, however, not necessarily true. The earth is not flat, although once 'everyone knew' that it was. Even leaving aside the attempt to use Egyptian evidence, which has already been challenged,[1] Veith's claims for Greek medicine are seriously flawed. As only one recent writer on the history of hysteria, Trillat (1986: 14), has recognised, the 'various Hippocratic texts' applying the term 'hysteria' to many complaints simply do not exist;[2] moreover, to suggest that Hippocratic gynaecology calls almost everything 'hysteria' is a gross over-simplification. A total revision of our understanding of the tradition is long overdue.

Returning to the text claimed by Veith as the inaugural moment of hysteria, the 'thirty-fifth aphorism', this is a significant choice since *Aphorisms* is one of the most widely translated and best-known works of the Hippocratic corpus (see Chapter 3, p. 58). But there is no 'thirty-fifth aphorism'. Rousselle criticised Veith for reading back contemporary ideas into antiquity (1980: 1115 n.27), but a greater problem is that Veith took at face value the translations available to her.[3] What she was referring to here was, in fact, *Aphorisms* 5.35 (L 4.544), which does not use the noun 'hysteria' at all; instead, using the plural form *hysterika*, it begins *Gynaiki hypo hysterikôn enochloumenei*, and it may be translated as 'In a woman troubled by *hysterika*, or having a difficult labour, a sneeze is a good thing.'

What are these *hysterika*, and what is so good about a sneeze? Such questions plunge us directly into the heart of the hysteria debate. *Hysterika* looks as though it should mean 'hysterics', but we need to examine the term more closely. In his commentary on the *Aphorisms*, Galen noted the difficulties of translating *hysterika* (K 17b.824–5). It could refer to all diseases of the womb,[4] or only to a particular condition called *hysterikê pnix* (best translated as 'suffocation of the womb') described by a number of post-Hippocratic writers,[5] or to problems with the afterbirth, also known as *ta hystera*. He favours setting the aphorism in the context of *hysterikê pnix*, for the following reasons. First, *hysterika* cannot refer to the afterbirth, because *hystera* and *hysterika* are not the same word. Secondly, it cannot refer to all diseases of the womb, because Hippocrates says that it is helped by sneezing. Clearly, not all diseases of the womb are helped by sneezing and, since Hippocrates cannot be wrong, Galen concludes that the passage must refer to *hysterikê pnix*.

There is, however, no reason why we must follow Galen's line of argument since, despite his objections, there is nothing to prevent us translating the phrase as 'When a woman suffers from things to do with the womb.' A sneeze was believed to expel various kinds of matter that may cause disorders; in a specifically gynaecological context, mustard, black or white hellebore, and castoreum were widely recommended in the ancient world to promote menstruation or expel the afterbirth.[6] Since retained menses were thought to cause many female disorders, the expulsive value of a sneeze could be beneficial in many 'things to do with the womb'.

In a passage of Pliny the Elder (*NH* 20.87.238), written a century before Galen, mustard is used to cause sneezing in the narrower context of 'suffocation of the womb', 'suffocation' being the Latin translation of *pnix*. Mixed with vinegar, it roused women suffering from an epileptic fit or *vulvarum conversione*[7] *suffocatas*, translated in the Loeb edition as 'fainting with prolapsus', but more literally meaning 'suffocated by the turning of their wombs'. In 'suffocation of the womb', it was difficult to tell whether a sufferer was dead or alive; in a case repeated in the later literature of hysteria, Pliny describes a woman who lay as if dead for seven days with *conversio vulvae*, turning of the womb (*NH* 7.52.175). In such cases, it was necessary to test for life by holding a feather or a piece of wool at the nostrils. A sneeze was welcomed as evidence of the presence of life.

Sneezing, due to its expulsive powers, can thus be 'a good thing' for many disorders affecting women, but by the first century AD it had come to be seen as particularly valuable in 'suffocation of the womb'; as Galen put it, a sneeze was both a 'sign' (*sêmeion*) that the patient has revived and a 'cause' (*aition*) of recovery, since in itself it revives the patient (Galen, *In Hipp. Aph.* K 17b.824).

Regardless of how we choose to translate the passage, it should be noted above all that this is not what Veith calls 'a specific appellation': a disease label.[8] Veith admits that the form *hysterikos*, 'from the womb', 'connected with the womb', or, when applied to a woman, 'liable to disorders of the womb' is 'more frequently used' (1965: 10),[9] but she does not acknowledge that it is in fact used exclusively, and moreover that the *Aphorisms* example is only a further case of this general type.

It is not difficult to find the source for this particular misconception by Veith. The idea that it is in the Hippocratic corpus that hysteria is not merely described, but also named, can be traced back beyond her to Emile Littré's edition of the corpus published from 1839 to 1861; the gynaecological volumes, numbered 7 and 8, appeared in 1851–3. Littré provided not only a French translation, but also chapter headings which have no analogue in the Greek manuscripts (Rousselle 1980: 1090). Since Littré – like Galen – 'read Hippocrates in his own image and in the image of the medicine of his time' (W.D. Smith 1979: 31), it is not surprising that nineteenth-century medical categories made their way into the *Diseases of Women*, where several sections are labelled 'Hystérie'. When Robb looked for 'Hippocrates on hysteria' in 1892, he translated into English not only the text of Littré's edition, but also the confident chapter headings which had not existed in the Greek.

Littré's chapter headings go further than simply labelling certain sections as descriptions of hysteria. He also distinguishes between imaginary movement of the womb, which he classifies as hysteria, and real movement, which he calls displacement, making comments such as, 'This section appears to be a confusion of imaginary with real movements of the womb' (L 8.275, on *DW* 2.128); 'This appears to be some displacement of the womb rather than hysteria' (L 8.327, on *DW* 2.150); and 'there is confusion between imaginary and real displacements' (L 8.309, on *DW* 2.137). He believes that the Hippocratic texts do not make sufficiently clear the distinction he seeks, in contrast to Veith, who – equally wrongly – claims that 'the Hippocratic physician was aware of the importance of a careful differentiation between hysterical symptoms and those of organic disease' (1965: 13). The writers of these texts made no such distinction. They described what was, for them, a real and organic condition: the movement of the womb to other parts of the body.

The origin and process of transmission of the error in translation should now be plain. Littré read the Hippocratic corpus in the context of his time, when hysteria was a recognised condition of disputed aetiology. He expected to see hysteria, duly found it, and drew it out in the headings he wrote for the various sections. Robb translated into English the passages headed by Littré as hysteria, and subsequent readers of the Hippocratic corpus have accepted Littré's categories. In some passages hysteria slides inexorably from adjective into noun, from headings into text; looking in particular at the *Aphorisms* passage used by Veith, Littré translated as 'Chez une femme attaquée d'hystérie', Adams gave 'Sneezing occurring in a woman with hysterics' and Chadwick and Mann have 'When a woman is afflicted with hysteria' (1950: 166). In giving 'When a woman suffers from hysteria' Veith simply follows the widely available Loeb translation (IV, 167).

Thus the diagnosis of hysteria is one made not by the ancient authors of the texts, but by a nineteenth-century translator. Does this matter? The tradition may be wrong to claim that the Greeks invented the name and thus the diagnostic category of hysteria, but, if the Hippocratic texts nonetheless contain the first clinical descriptions of hysteria, should we be unduly fussy about the origin of the name? To answer this objection, we must look at the term 'hysteria' and its implications when applied to a disease description. When a translator reads the diagnosis into a text, this action – like all acts of retrospective diagnosis – implies that there is a single fixed entity called hysteria, constant over time and place. If this is the case, then it may not matter that the name 'hysteria' is not Hippocratic. A concept can exist without being named; the ancient Hebrews had no word for what the Romans were to call *lex talionis*, the law of retribution in kind, but they did say 'An eye for an eye and a tooth for a tooth' (G. Lewis 1980: 71–2). The universality of hysteria is often asserted; Charcot stated that 'L'hystérie a toujours existé, en tous lieux et en tous temps' (Trillat 1986: 272) and Abse that 'east and west, hysteria continues unabated in various guises' (1987: 91).

If hysteria is constant, found throughout history, world-wide, it should be possible to talk about whether or not Hippocratic medicine recognised it, regardless of whether or not the Hippocratics named it, just as we can talk about whether tuberculosis, epilepsy and gonorrhoea were recognised. Furthermore, if it is a historical constant, one would expect a body of text as long as the Hippocratic medical corpus to contain some cases. By deciding that hysteria is a constant, we thus prejudge the question of whether or not it existed in ancient Greece; by definition, it must have done, and it remains only to find those sections in the text which provide a more or less accurate match with our chosen clinical picture.

An alternative approach would be to say that hysteria cannot be an historical constant, because it has apparently disappeared in this century. This would mean that we could search the Hippocratic texts for it without prejudging the issue; if there was no hysteria there, this would simply mean finding a later start date for the condition and explaining why it emerged then. The 'death of hysteria', however, like the 'death of God', is often asserted – for example, Trillat says 'L'hystérie est morte, c'est entendu' (1986: 274) – but the rumours of its death may have been exaggerated.

This is suggested by Abse's throwaway remark about hysteria's 'various guises', which introduces one of the key features of modern discussions of hysteria: that it is a mimic, able to pose as other diseases (Wright 1980: 233; Mitchinson 1986: 92). Instead of disappearing, it could have donned a new disguise. Making matters worse, in contrast to tuberculosis, epilepsy and gonorrhoea, hysteria is a disease for which medical practitioners in our society find it hard to agree a list of symptoms.

Contemporary medical writers on hysteria fall into two groups. One group accepts that hysteria is 'a valid, independent syndrome' (Woodruff 1967: 1119) and uses the Perley-Guze criteria, which list over fifty symptoms in ten areas; exhibiting twenty-five symptoms in nine out of ten areas qualifies as hysteria, in the absence of any other diagnosis (Guze 1967: 494–5). The position of the second group is conveniently summarised by the eloquent quotation marks of the title of Slater's 1965 lecture, 'Diagnosis of "hysteria"'. Picking up the Perley-Guze point that the hysteria label is applied 'in the absence of any other diagnosis', Slater concludes that the diagnosis merely indicates the 'absence of any other clinical findings'; it is 'a disguise for ignorance and a fertile source of clinical error . . . not only a delusion but also a snare' and 'a way of avoiding confrontation with our own ignorance' (1965: 1399; 1976: 40). Shorter has suggested that hysteria was a diagnosis covering undetected uterine infections (1984: 208), while Marsden noted that many patients diagnosed as suffering from hysteria turned out to have an underlying organic disease, concluding that 'there can be little doubt that the term "hysterical" is often applied as a diagnosis to something that the physician does not understand' (1986: 282–3). As Merskey put it, 'Whenever we are at the margin of our ability to decide on a diagnosis, hysteria is a possibility' (1986: 24). This is by no means a new approach; at the end of the nineteenth century John Russell Reynolds wrote that 'The employment of the word "hysterical" may sometimes be found indicative of the state of mind of the practitioner rather than of that of the patient's health. It simply conveys a doubt as to what is the matter' (1880: 631); Sir James Paget stated: 'it is desirable that this name [hysteria] should be abolished. For it is absurdly derived and, being often used as a term of reproach, is worse than absurd' (1873: 73; cf. M.J. Peterson 1986: 578). Yet hysteria fought back; it was in this period that Isaac Baker Brown claimed that a surgical cure for it was possible, writing that 'hysteria, instead of being a term of reproach, does truly represent a curable disease' (1866a: 20).

Slater argues that 'the justification for accepting "hysteria" as a syndrome is based entirely on tradition and lacks evidential support' (1965: 1396). Responding to Slater, Walshe significantly kept the title but omitted the quotation marks, defending 'the concept of hysteria as a nosological entity in its own right' (1965: 1452). The debate in medical circles has continued, for example in Alec Roy's collection of essays, *Hysteria* (1982). Mayou gave a fair summary of the medical situation: there is at present 'no agreement about diagnostic criteria' for hysteria (1975: 466).

In the midst of such uncertainty, almost the only feature of hysteria which is widely accepted is the suggestion that it can mimic the symptoms of any other disease (Paget 1873). In this case, how can hysteria itself be a disease, and what is there to prevent it from taking such radically different forms in different epochs as to be almost unrecognisable as the same condition? The corollary is also true; as Shorter puts it, 'every organic disease imaginable . . . has at one time or another been classified as hysteria' (1986: 551). Does a condition with such indistinct and shifting borders exist in any meaningful sense? As Trillat puts it, hysteria is 'une maladie qui n'en est pas une, tout en l'étant . . . ' (1986: 54).

When we write about hysteria today, the particular manifestation in our minds is often the highly dramatic image of nineteenth-century medical literature, its ideal type being Charcot's 'grande hystérie' involving violent muscular contractions culminating in an arched posture (the 'arc-en-cercle'), paralysis, loss of voice, retention of urine, anaesthesia and blindness.[10] But in his study of admissions for hysteria to the Edinburgh Royal Infirmary in the late eighteenth century, Risse (1988) found that only a minority of those attracting the diagnosis had fits of this kind; most women so labelled had loss of appetite or other digestive problems, menstrual difficulties and fainting spells, symptoms suggestive of many organic diagnoses. Yet one relatively constant feature of the diagnosis of hysteria in modern times is that it implies that the physical symptoms so labelled, whether dramatic or not, have no recognised organic cause. It should now be clear why hysteria has been described as 'that most unsatisfactory of psychiatric syndromes' (Mayou 1975: 466).

Marsden's discussion (1986: 279) shows the widest possible extent of the definition of 'hysteria':

> Physicians use the term to describe the symptom (conversion disorder or disassociation state), the illness (somatization disorder or

> Briquet's syndrome), the personality (histrionic), a form of anxiety (phobic anxiety after Freud), an epidemic outbreak (mass hysteria) and irritating patients (if female they are hysterical; if male they are psychopaths).

The irritation felt by physicians towards hysteria patients was eloquently expressed by a doctor writing in 1908, a time when the contracture or 'drawing up' of a limb was a common symptom:

> As Vance cut off the plaster cast from a 14-year-old girl whose leg had 'drawn up' a year previously, she cried, 'It is going to draw up; it is going to draw up', at which Vance said severely, 'If it does draw up, I will break your d ____ d little neck.'
>
> (Shorter 1986: 578 n.51)

Confronted with the breadth of the category of hysteria, some contemporary writers have sought to restrict the definition, excluding the syndrome and the personality type, and using hysteria only for a universal reaction comparable to anxiety or depression (Mayou 1975: 466–8; Shorter 1984: 205; 1986: 550–1; Abse 1987: 23–5). Shorter's suggestions are helpful here, permitting a degree of universality while incorporating variation across cultures. He accepts that hysteria 'is a real psychiatric disease, in addition to being an epithet with which men have stigmatized women across the ages'. However, he goes on, 'the presentation of "hysterical" symptoms tends to be molded by the surrounding culture' to a greater extent than, for example, the symptoms of schizophrenia. A major question to ask therefore concerns the social construction of the disease: why is it that, from a wide repertoire of the possible, 'certain symptoms are selected in certain epochs' (Shorter 1986: 574, 549; 1984: 202)?

Definitions: the textual tradition

Hysteria thus raises many contradictory questions. Is it another word for ignorance, or the perfectly adaptable mimic? Is it a dramatic performance, or a minor gynaecological disturbance? Is it caused by the womb, or has it no organic cause? Is it a wide-ranging category, 'a commonplace reaction' (D.C. Taylor 1986: 40), a 'non-verbal language' (Critchley and Cantor 1984: 1788), or something universal but highly specific? Beneath these questions lies a central one for anybody trying to write the history of hysteria: that is, what level of definition should be used for the purposes of the present work? One way around the problem would be to restrict this study to those sections of the corpus traditionally seen as descriptions of hysteria; for example, those so labelled by Littré. But the difficulty here is that Littré imposes his own distinction between 'real' and 'imaginary' movements of the womb, a distinction alien to the Hippocratic writers. An alternative would be to study all sections of the corpus in which the womb is described as moving to another part of the body, but this only reiterates the point that later writers use hysteria for symptoms with no organic cause, whereas the Hippocratics regard womb movement as something entirely organic.

The difficulties of deciding what constitutes hysteria for the purposes of an historical study are by no means unique. In his study of the disease concept 'asthma', Gabbay concluded that we cannot assume that all writers in the past who used the term were referring to the same thing (1982: 29). With hysteria, of course, the problems are greater, because our sources do not even use a common name. Gabbay raises the question whether a diachronic study of a disease concept investigates a constant natural entity, or a vast range of different concepts (1982: 33), and shows how this question all too easily leads the historian to 'historical paralysis' (1982: 42).

Like Medusa's head, the question 'What exactly are we studying?' turns the onlooker to stone. But it must at least be addressed, even in a negative way. To clarify: I am discussing here neither all texts in which the writers name the condition they describe as 'hysteria', nor all texts mentioning a particular combination of symptoms that I choose to label hysteria. Instead, I am concentrating on a set of early texts conventionally linked by subsequent writers: a finite series of texts, each drawing on an increasingly fixed group of those written by earlier writers, yet each simultaneously – at least to some extent – incorporating the ideas of its own age. I am thus studying hysteria from the perspective of a developing tradition of reading the Hippocratic corpus, a textual tradition that culminated in Littré.

Before turning to a more detailed study of those Hippocratic texts which have come to be used as evidence of hysteria in ancient Greece, it is worth considering the implications of the label 'hysteria' for Littré and for other writers. The Greek adjective *hysterikos* means 'from the womb'; a purely physical description of cause, showing the part of the body from which other symptoms emanate. In a woman, as the Hippocratic *Places in Man* 47 puts it, 'the womb is the origin of all diseases' (Loeb VIII, 94), so it would be fair to say that, in Hippocratic gynaecology, all diseases are hysterical. But the word cannot have the same nuances for us as for an ancient author.

Littré uses hysteria in a rather different way. In his *Dictionnaire de la langue française* (1863–77) he defines hysteria as follows: 'Hystérie: maladie nerveuse qui se manifeste par accès et qui est characterisée par les convulsions, la sensation d'une boule qui remont de la matrice dans la gorge et la suffocation' (Hysteria: nervous disorder which manifests itself in the form of a fit and is characterised by convulsions, by the sensation of a ball rising from the womb into the throat, and by suffocation). To understand Littré's position, we must first understand the debate within which he is situating himself. Before about 1600, the 'hysteric affection' was, as the name implies, attributed to the womb. In the early seventeenth century hysteria was linked not only to the male condition known as hypochondria, in which the spleen was thought to give off vapours, but also to melancholy, found in both sexes (Boss 1979). Robert Burton saw hypochondria and hysteria as forms of melancholy: Sydenham believed that both sexes could suffer from hysteria, but that in women it was the most common condition next to fever (Mitchinson 1986: 89). Thus there was a shift in 'the limits of hysteria, as it united with hypochondria and annexed parts of melancholy's crumbling empire' (Boss 1979: 232). At the same time the origin of hysteria shifted to the brain, or the whole person. In the eighteenth century, hysteria was increasingly defined as a 'neurosis'; excess blood naturally present in the female body led to increased nervous irritability, especially under the influence of too much meat, coffee or tea, or insufficient exercise (Risse 1988: 2–4). At this time, 'According to the conventional medical wisdom, hysteria was a chronic, quintessentially feminine, disease resulting from the peculiar constitution and physiology of women' (Risse 1988: 17).

By the mid-nineteenth century, when Littré was writing, some doctors believed that the cause of hysteria was a physical disorder of the womb: others did not (Merskey 1979: 12 ff.; Ey 1964: 3–19). For most writers of this period, however, hysteria 'was rooted in the very nature of being female' (Mitchinson 1986: 90) and marriage was an important aspect of a cure;[11] in a treatise on hysteria published just before Littré's translations of Hippocratic gynaecology were issued, Landouzy posed the critical question for the men involved, namely 'Peut-on épouser avec sécurité une hystérique?' (1846: 303). Pierre Briquet rejected the idea that the womb was responsible, in favour of a 'neurosis of the brain' in someone of the 'hysterical type'; the hysterical personality became a necessary part of the development of the disorder (Mai and Merskey 1981).

The label hysteria may thus imply a physical condition originating in the womb, or in being a woman, or may represent a claim that the symptoms have no organic origin. Littré's dictionary shows that he follows writers such as Brodie who said that 'hysteria . . . belongs not to the uterus, but to the nervous system' (1837: 46).

Hippocratic hysteria: the womb and its destinations

For the Hippocratic writers, however, the texts that have subsequently been used in the construction of hysteria described something resulting from a firmly organic cause, the movement of the womb. It is to the role of the womb that we must now turn. Throughout this book we have met the womb as an organ liable to move in situations of menstrual suppression, exhaustion, insufficient food, sexual abstinence, and excessive dryness or lightness of the organ itself. Hippocratic texts ascribe to womb movement a wide range of symptoms, depending on the part of the body to which it moves. In searching for Hippocratic hysteria, we could identify some combination of symptoms which so closely resembles the picture of hysteria in later historical periods that the problem of the absence of the name, or label, could be dismissed. But which historical period's image of hysteria should we take as our ideal type against which to measure the Hippocratic texts: the mild hysteria of the eighteenth-century Edinburgh Royal Infirmary? Or the dramatic hysteria of the mid-nineteenth-century Salpêtrière made famous by Charcot? It may be more productive to start from the opposite end, asking which Hippocratic texts have traditionally been used to prove that hysteria was found in ancient Greece. Robb's 'Hippocrates on hysteria' translated the *Aphorisms* passage and five chapters of the gynaecological treatises – *Nature of Woman* 87, *Diseases of Women* 1.7 and 2.123–5 – with brief summaries of *Diseases of Women* 2.126–7.

It is significant that these chapters are among the very small group of Hippocratic texts used in recent discussions of hysteria; the other major chapter usually brought into the debate is *Diseases of Women* 1.32.[12] Robb also cites the appendix to *Regimen in Acute Diseases* (68, Loeb VI, 326), which distinguishes between *pnix* – the breathing difficulty usually translated as 'suffocation' – caused by the womb, and that caused by spasm or convulsions. If the patient feels pressure from the fingers, the symptoms come from the womb: if not, then it is a convulsion. It is somewhat surprising to see this particular text being used as evidence of 'Hippocratic hysteria', because the reverse is usually seen as being the case, with sufferers from hysteria experiencing 'local loss of sensation' (Wright 1980: 233). However, close study of the passages used from *Nature of Woman* and *Diseases of Women*, so often the only examples of 'Hippocratic hysteria' given in contemporary discussions, reveals that they have in common only two points: some reference to the womb moving to another part of the body, and the symptom of pnix. The affinity between these two is not, however, constant. For example, the womb may move in the absence of *pnix*, as in *Diseases of Women* 2.127 (L 8.272–4), a section headed 'Hystérie' by Littré. Such features of modern hysteria as grinding the teeth, loss of voice, cold extremities and limb pains or paralysis do feature in Hippocratic texts, often in the company of movement of the womb and suffocation, but they may be found in the absence of either or both, and may be attributed to a named organic cause; for example, in *Diseases of Women* 2.110 (L 8.234–8) they arise from a red flux.

The difficulties of finding a passage in the Hippocratic texts to serve as a paradigm for Hippocratic hysteria increase when we look at Littré's classifications and at the texts themselves. Of the six texts used by Robb, only four are in fact headed 'Hystérie' by Littré: one chapter from *Nature of Woman*, 87 (L 7.408), and three from *Diseases of Women*, 2.123–5 (L 8.266–70). Not only do they give largely different combinations of symptoms and prescribe different remedies, but in none of them does even the adjective *hysterikos*, 'from the womb', appear.

Neither the category of hysteria nor the later disease label of *hysterikê pnix* has a place in Hippocratic medicine, although *pnix* exists as a symptom and *hysterikos* as an adjective. Any attempt to impose the diagnosis of hysteria on to the Hippocratic gynaecological texts risks distorting their approach to illness, as Hippocratic medicine emphasises description rather than diagnosis (Bourgey 1953: 149–52), rarely trying to fit collections of symptoms into pre-existing categories. The Hippocratics tend to distinguish different combinations of symptoms according to cause and treatment, rather than subsuming symptoms under a single disease label that 'covers over all the clinical detail' (G. Lewis 1976: 88). Not all Hippocratic texts name diseases; they may present a disease as 'another disorder', as 'if' or 'when' followed by one or more symptoms, as 'if' or 'when' followed by the name of a disease, or by giving the name of the disorder at the very beginning of the section (di Benedetto 1986).

When Hippocratic texts do give a specific name to a disorder, it may be taken from the affected part; from the way in which the disorder presents itself; from the specific sensation caused; or from something occurring in the course of the disease. Although there is no name given to the disorder, or disorders, in the texts usually seen as 'Hippocratic hysteria', their opening words are relevant here. These fall into two categories. Some start by describing the movement of the womb: 'When the womb turns to the head', for example, opens *Diseases of Women* 2.123 (L 8.266). Others start with the symptom of suffocation: the opening of *Diseases of Women* 1.32 (L 8.76) is 'If *pnix* suddenly seizes a pregnant woman'. The later name hysteria comes from the part believed to be affected: the womb. However, in the Hippocratic texts being considered here, the focus is either on the womb as the part that causes symptoms elsewhere, or on the symptom which occupies a central position: *pnix*.

The first description of womb movement with *pnix* in *Diseases of Women* is in 1.2 (L 8.14–22), a discussion of menstrual suppression in a childless woman. The preceding section, *Diseases of Women* 1.1 (L 8.10–14), explained why this is dangerous, presenting woman as wet and spongy, absorbing more fluid from the digestive process, and needing to have her flesh broken down by childbirth to achieve the necessary space in her body to ensure painless menstrual bleeding. *Diseases of Women* 1.2 suggests that, even in the soft, wet recesses of the female body, the womb may find itself short of fluid. If a woman abstains from the moistening activity of sexual intercourse, the womb may become 'dry and light', and go elsewhere to find dampness. It will 'turn around'[13] and move up the body; menstruation will cease, and if it does not occur for three months then there will be intermittent *pnix*, fever, shivering and pain in the limbs. If there is still no menstrual bleeding by the fourth month, the symptoms will worsen and will be joined by those of thick urine, a swollen abdomen, grinding the teeth, loss of appetite and difficulty in sleeping. In the fifth month all symptoms will be even more severe; if the condition persists and there is a sixth month without menstruation, the condition will have become incurable, and the woman will vomit phlegm, and suffer from extreme thirst, discomfort if touched, gurgling sounds from the blood in the womb which is unable to come out, loss of voice or difficulty in making herself understood, and irregular breathing. Finally, the abdomen, legs and feet will swell: death is near.

The disorder described in *Diseases of Women* 1.7 is similar, but does not follow this month-by-month pattern. The symptoms experienced here depend on the location to which the dry womb moves. The affected group is described as women not having intercourse, but older rather than younger women because their wombs are lighter in weight. Elsewhere in these texts it is explained that the younger the woman, the more blood she has in her body (e.g. *DW* 2.111, L 8.238–40). If a woman's vessels are emptier than usual and she is more tired, the womb, dried out by fatigue, turns around and 'throws itself' on the liver, because this organ is full of moisture. By interrupting the route of the breath through the body, this causes sudden *pnix*, during which the whites of the eyes are turned up, the woman is cold, and her complexion is livid; she grinds her teeth and has excess saliva, like a sufferer from Herakles' disease, another name for the condition that the Hippocratics usually call the sacred disease and which we would probably call epilepsy. Sometimes phlegm will run down from the head, causing the womb to leave the liver and return to its proper place, and the *pnix* will stop because the womb is now full of fluid, and heavy. If the womb stays on the liver or in the area of the hypochondria for a long time, however, the sufferer will be choked; if it moves to the mouth of the bladder, she will be unable to urinate; or it may go to the limbs or side.

Diseases of Women 1.32 gives an almost identical aetiology for *pnix* and a very similar picture of symptoms, but here the sufferer is pregnant. Not only fatigue but also insufficient food can cause the womb to move; the womb itself is described as being overheated as well as dry. As in 1.7 phlegm – described as cold – may run down from the head and cause the womb to return to its proper position; if it does not return quickly, there is danger to the foetus.

The so-called hysteria texts in *Diseases of Women* 2.123–5 are much shorter than those so far discussed and give little information either on the women most likely to be affected or on the mechanisms by which the symptoms are produced. Instead, they start by naming the location to which the womb has moved (without saying why it has travelled there), then give a short list of 'signs', and finally outline the treatment. 2.123 (L 8.266) opens: 'When the womb moves to the head and the *pnix* stops there, the head is heavy.' The signs are that the patient says she has pain in the channels in the nose and under the eyes: there is lethargy and foaming at the mouth. The first treatment is to wash her with warm water; if this does not work, cold water or cooled boiled laurel or myrtle water should be put on the head, and the head anointed with rose oil. Sweet-smelling fumigations should be applied below, foul-smelling substances to the nostrils; she should eat cabbage and drink cabbage-water.

Diseases of Women 2.124 (L 8.266–8) has an identical format but concerns movement to the heart; *Diseases of Women* 2.125 (L 8.268–70) and 2.126 (L 8.270–2) cover movement to the hypochondria, for which drinks of castoreum (beaver-oil) and fleabane are among the recommended remedies. As is usual in these texts, a range of different substances is given. 2.126 (L 8.272) describes a womb moving to the hypochondria; the most effective treatment for this location is fumigation (cf. 2.203, L 8.390). The fullest account of this therapy occurs in 2.133 (L 8.284–6), where forty days of pessaries and fumigations are performed when the womb moves to the hip joint, the mouth of the womb is closed and tilted, and menstrual blood, unable to leave by its usual route, instead travels to the breasts. It is worth translating in full, not only because the fumigation was performed for many centuries to treat hysterical suffocation,[14] but also because it is one of many chapters demonstrating womb movement in texts the hysteria tradition chose to ignore. Littré, in fact, diagnosed the condition described not as hysteria but as 'Obliquité latérale devenant chronique'.

The description of the fumigation in this long section reads as follows:

> First give a fumigation to the womb. Take an earthenware pot with two-sixths capacity, put on it a dish, and fit them together so that no air can get in. Then pierce the bottom of the dish and make a hole. Put in the hole a reed, about a cubit long. The reed must be properly inserted in the dish so that no vapour escapes. When you have prepared this, place the dish on the pot and plaster it round with clay. When you have done these things, dig a hole in the ground, two feet deep, large enough to make room for the pot. Then burn firewood, until you have made the hole red-hot. When it is red-hot, take out the wood and the biggest and hottest pieces of charcoal, but leave the ashes and embers in the hole. When the pot is heated and vapour rises, if the vapour is very hot, hold back: if not, she is to sit on the end of the reed, and pass it into the mouth [of the womb], then fumigate. If it cools, throw on red-hot charcoal, taking care that the fumigation is not too fiery. If, by adding the charcoal, the fumigation becomes more fiery than it should be, take away the charcoal. One should construct the fumigation in fine, still weather, so that she is not too cold: she should be covered with garments. In the pot you should put dry garlic, and pour in water so that it rises two digits above, and soak it well, and pour in seal oil too. Heat this. The fumigation must go on for a long time. After the fumigation, if she is able, she should wash her whole body as she pleases, the lower back and below the navel in particular. Give for dinner barley cake or wheat bread, and boiled garlic. On the next day, if she is weak from the fumigation, intermit that day; if not, go back to the fumigation. If, while she is being fumigated, she is able to examine it, order her

> to touch the mouth [of the womb]. The fumigation itself inflates the womb, makes it more upright and opens it. It is because it is like this, and can do such things, that you should use a fumigation.

This is clearly not a 'painting by numbers' format in which the *iatros* has his book beside him as he works; if a reader were to try to carry out the instructions in the order given, the jar would be sealed before the garlic and seal oil went in. The combination of what we interpret as firmness ('order her') and consideration ('hold back', 'if she is weak . . . intermit that day') is characteristic of Hippocratic gynaecology; other warnings about the dangers of exhausting the patient occur at 2.181 (L 8.364), 3.230 (L 8.442) and 3.241 (L 8.454). Using garlic as a form of scent therapy, again, is typically Hippocratic (Byl 1989). Yet despite combining womb movement and menstrual suppression, this text was not used in the construction of the hysteria tradition.

Returning to those texts which have been used by the tradition, *Diseases of Women* 2.127 (L 8.272), like 1.7, involves movement of the womb to the liver, but it defines the affected group differently. In 1.7 the woman most likely to be affected was the older woman not having intercourse, but 2.127 suggests that movement to the liver is more common in older unmarried women and young widows, especially the childless and the barren, who lack the beneficial purging of childbirth and the lochia. Here the argument is more reminiscent of 1.2. Section 2.128 (L 8.276) discusses movement to the hypochondria, recommending a fumigation followed by intercourse, and 2.129 (L 8.276) covers movement to the ribs, which can cause a cough, pain in the ribs, and what feels like a ball in the side. Section 2.130 (L 8.278) concerns movement to the hips or flanks, and 2.131 (L 8.278) movement to the middle of the waist, in which the drawing up of the limbs is mentioned as a symptom.

A further set of texts concerning womb movement may be found later in *Diseases of Women* 2. Two significant therapeutic points for the later history of hysteria occur at 2.201 (L 8.384), where the patient's groin and inner thighs are rubbed with aromatics to cure movement of the womb to the diaphragm, and 2.203 (L 8.388) which advises, 'When the womb causes *pnix*, light a lamp and snuff it out under the nostrils' and 'Take a lamp, throw on it a little oil, light it, and when it is extinguished hold it near the nostrils.' The first therapy is used in a famous passage of Galen, which will be discussed shortly: the second occurs in many later discussions of hysteria. It is also found in one of the texts used by the hysteria tradition, *Nature of Woman* 87 (L 7.408), which reads

> In suffocation caused by movement [of the womb], light up the wick of a lamp then snuff it out, holding it under the nostrils so that she draws in the smoke. Then soak myrrh in perfume, dip wool in [so

that it is thoroughly impregnated] and insert. Also give her a drink of resin dissolved in oil.

Examining these texts confirms that they operate by describing symptoms rather than by giving a single disease name and that, where they group symptoms and therapies together, they do so according to the part of the body to which the womb is believed to have moved.

Lack of sexual intercourse is only one of the causes given: marriage/ pregnancy is only one of the therapies listed, and is restricted to womb movement to the hypochondria. *Diseases of Women* 2.128 (L 8.276) ends by saying that, after fumigation, the patient should sleep with her husband: 'release from this disease, when she is pregnant'. Nevertheless, it is this treatment for womb movement that has received most attention in the secondary literature, above all in the work of the psychoanalyst and classicist Bennett Simon, in his book *Mind and Madness in Ancient Greece*. This includes a chapter entitled 'Hysteria and social issues' which opens with the familiar error, 'Hysteria, the disease of the "wandering uterus", was given its name by the Greeks' (1978: 238). Simon's overall approach to hysteria combines that of Ioan Lewis' study of spirit possession, trance and shamanism, which presents the possessed state as an indirect mode of protest used by powerless and peripheral members of society (I.M. Lewis 1971; Mayou 1975: 467), with a Freudian model. According to what Simon calls a 'psychodynamic understanding of hysteria', 'a hysterical symptom, for a Greek woman, permitted a safe expression of certain unmet needs', as a result of which expression the doctor would intervene on the woman's behalf as the 'wished-for good father' (1978: 242, 251). To summarise the 'culturally-sanctioned dumb show' (1978: 243) envisaged by Simon, an unmarried or widowed woman is supposed to express her (apparently inevitable) sexual frustration by hysteria; the doctor then legitimises her wish by announcing that the cure consists in letting her have what she wants, since it is precisely marriage and childbirth that will make her healthy again.

This approach is inadequate because it shows little understanding of the social conditions of women in antiquity, centred on ideals such as universal marriage at a young age. It also fails to come to terms with the fact that, in most of the texts labelled as 'Hystérie' by Littré, the marital status of the sufferer is not given,[15] or she is explicitly described as married.[16] In his entire discussion, Simon cites only one Hippocratic passage, *Diseases of Women* 2.151 (L 8.326), in which the woman patient is said to suffer in the same way as those who are struck with the sacred disease. In another passage on this last disease, Simon reveals that – like Veith – he has not read the Greek text of the Hippocratic corpus in sufficient detail. After a brief discussion of the 'madness of Heracles' which 'was considered by some to be a case of epilepsy'[17] Simon states: 'To my knowledge, the Hippocratic corpus contains no mention of the mythical characters who went mad and were portrayed so vividly on the

Athenian stage and in vase painting' (1978: 222). However, as mentioned above, the writer of *Diseases of Women* 1.7 (L 8.32) states that women with the condition he describes resemble sufferers from 'Herakles' disease'.[18]

It is, furthermore, perverse to describe hysteria as a 'safe expression' of a woman's needs when loss of voice, grinding the teeth, and movement of the womb to the liver may be the signal for the Hippocratic healer to tie bandages around the patient's waist, place foul-smelling substances under her nose, insert beetle pessaries, inject hot oil into the womb, or shower her with cold water. Despite being common therapies in Hippocratic gynaecology as a whole, marriage and childbirth are rarely the prescribed remedies for this combination of symptoms.[19] It is also unusual for the remedy to consist of something that could be seen as indirect sexual gratification: fragrant ointments rubbed on the vulva, as in *Diseases of Women* 2.150 (L 8.326; cf. 2.20, L 8.384), or the vaginal insertion of objects specifically described as resembling a penis, as in *Diseases of Women* 3.222 (L 8.430). Finally, it is inappropriate to use Simon's 'psychodynamic model' when in Hippocratic medicine there is no line drawn between psychological and organic illness (di Benedetto 1986: 4).

A similar approach to that of Simon is taken by Rousselle, who states that

> Greek women had no legal right to make any decision regarding their own marriage: they could not ask a man to marry them, or even decide that they wanted to be married or to accept an offer of marriage, so it is perhaps not surprising that their impotent anger should take the form of a disease in which their womb was literally suffocating them.
>
> (1988: 69)

Gourevitch (1984: 119) has traced the disappearance of 'the hysterical virgin from medical literature' between the Hippocratics and the Roman empire; she attributes this to institutional change since, if the age at first marriage falls further, fewer girls are left to become hysterical.

However, all such approaches are rooted in our own society's views on what is normal for a woman, on the nature of hysteria, and on the relationship between medicine and sexuality. Yet for the writers of the Hippocratic texts – and, probably, for the patients they treated – intercourse and pregnancy rightly belonged to the domain of the pharmacopoeia, due to the dramatic and beneficial effects they were believed to have on the body. Since all disorders of women ultimately originate in their soft and spongy flesh and excess blood, all disorders of women may be helped by intercourse and/or childbirth, to which marriage and pregnancy are the necessary precursors. There is thus nothing remarkable about the prescription of these in cases of movement of the womb.

But womb movement more commonly calls up a battery of other therapies, many of which use sweet- and foul-smelling substances. These therapies lie behind the assertion made by later writers – but not by Soranos and Galen – that the Hippocratic womb was regarded as an independent living being, fleeing from foul smells but moving to seek out more agreeable odours. We must now decide whether any such belief is necessarily implied by the use of scent therapy.

Plato and Aretaeus: the wild womb?

Another important passage in the hysteria tradition is Plato's *Timaeus* 91a–d, presenting the womb as a living creature desiring union which, if it remains unfruitful (*akarpos*) beyond its proper season, travels around the body blocking passages, obstructing breathing, and causing diseases. Colin Turbayne asserts that 'Plato's account follows that of Hippocrates who, in his *Sicknesses of Women*, coined the word "hysteria" and ascribed hysteria to the wandering womb' (1976: 132); Veith is cited in a footnote (1976: 140 n.11). Kudlien too assumes that Plato's link between womb and animal lies behind what he calls the 'well known ancient concept' of uterine suffocation (1968: 330; cf. Byl and de Ranter 1990: 321). As we saw in Chapter 1, Mark Adair has recently denied that the womb physically wanders in Plato; instead, he has argued that Plato was more sophisticated and enlightened than the Hippocratics so that, 'ahead of, not behind, his times', he provided a psychological explanation to replace the 'physiologically absurd' Hippocratic theories (1996: 153).

Plato, living from about 428 to 347 BC, was writing at the same time as the authors of *Diseases of Women*, or shortly after. Most commentators have therefore thought it valid to merge his theories with theirs, and to conclude that Hippocratic scent therapy too implies an animate womb with a sense of smell, 'a living thing inside another living thing' as the second-century AD medical writer Aretaeus wrote. The difficulty with this approach is that there are clear differences between the gynaecology of the *Timaeus* and that of the Hippocratic corpus, and there is ample evidence that the idea of the womb being – or being like – an animal was disputed even in antiquity. Its best-known expression, apart from the *Timaeus* passage, is in Aretaeus, who states that movement of the womb mostly affects younger women, whose way of life and judgement are 'somewhat wandering' so that their wombs are 'roving' (*rhembodês*). Older women have a 'more stable' way of life, judgement and womb. This already varies from the Hippocratic theories, which tend to link womb movement with *older* women, whose wombs are lighter. It is in the same section that Aretaeus asserts that 'the sum of the matter is that the womb in the female is *hokoion ti zôon en zôôi*' (2.11; CMG 2.32.28–33.1), usually translated as 'like some animal inside an animal', but which could be less emotively rendered as 'like a living thing inside another living thing'.

It has been suggested that the words of Aretaeus are based on a recollection of having read *Timaeus* at school.[20] But Soranos, writing in the same period, demonstrates that an animate womb could be considered very outdated in second-century medicine. He explicitly rejects the claim of 'some people' that the womb is an animal, although he admits that in some ways it behaves as if it were; for example, in responding to cooling and loosening drugs (3.29; T 153). He reinterprets the success of scent therapy, saying that it works not because the womb is like a wild animal (*thêrion*) emerging to seek pleasant smells and fleeing from foul ones, but because the scents cause relaxation or constriction. Galen, writing shortly after Soranos, discusses and rejects what he regards not as Hippocrates' but as Plato's theory of the womb as a living creature. After quoting from *Timaeus* he writes:

> These were Plato's words. But some [physicians] added that, when the uterus during its irregular movement through the body touches the diaphragm, it interferes with the respiratory [movements]. Others deny that the uterus wanders around like an animal. When it is dried up by the suppression of menstrual flow, it extends quickly to the viscera, being anxious to attract moisture. But when it makes contact with the diaphragm during its ascent, it suppresses the respiration of the organism.
>
> (*On the Affected Parts* 6.5)[21]

Soranos and Galen show that, at least by the second century AD, medical opinion was split on whether a belief in womb movement necessarily meant assigning to the womb the status of 'living thing' or 'wild animal'. It may further be questioned whether Plato's account owes anything to *Diseases of Women*.[22] In general, *Timaeus* has a humoral theory of disease, linking the four humours to the four elements: earth, air, fire and water. In contrast, the use of humoral theory in *Diseases of Women* is minimal, perhaps because the female body is so heavily dominated by blood.

The description of the womb in the *Timaeus* should be read in the context of the text as a whole, where analogies comparing certain parts of the body to living creatures are common. That part of the soul concerned with bodily desires is tied up in the body *hôs thremma agrion*, 'like a wild creature' (70e); a disease is like a *zôon*, in that it has a natural span of life (89b–c). At the start of the second generation of mankind, all who proved cowardly or unjust in the first become women; it is at this point that the gods put into *all* human beings a *zôon* desiring sexual union. In males, the penis has a disobedient and self-willed nature, 'like a *zôon*' and, like the savage part of the soul, it does not obey reason, the *logos* (71a, 91a–b). When the womb is described, the only difference is that it is no longer put beside the *zôon* in a simile, but appears in a metaphoric relationship; not 'like a living thing', but 'a living thing desiring to bear children' (91c).[23] In both cases, what is significant is that the organ moves independently of the will, in an uncontrolled way.[24] Since Plato/Timaeus has already mixed apparently non-figurative uses of *zôon* (the gods put a living creature in all humans) with obvious similes (the penis is like a *zôon*), it would be unwise to make too much of the way in which the womb is described. It should also be noted that animal analogies for the organs are used elsewhere in other philosophical texts; in Aristotle the heart is like an animal, and this is further compared with the genitals (*PA* 666a20–3; 666b16–17; Byl 1980: 124).

In men, the *zôon empsychon* that makes the penis behave 'like an animal' is in the seed, which comes from the spinal marrow (*Timaeus* 73c ff.). This theory of the origin of semen is consistent with Hippocratic anatomy, which traces its path up the spinal cord, behind the ears and to the head (*Gen.* 2, L 7.472; *NM* 11, Loeb IV, 30–2). In the description of the corresponding part in woman, the womb, there are however obvious differences from Hippocratic theories. Timaeus says that in coitus minute invisible and shapeless *zôa* are sown in the womb, where they grow to maturity. Apart from the very general sowing analogy (DuBois 1988), this does not correspond to anything in the corpus; indeed, in *Generation* 6 and 8 (L 7.478–80), both male and female contribute seed, the sex of the child being determined by the strongest seed.

Both Galen and Soranos mention the belief of some people that the womb is not just like an animal, but is an animal, yet Galen ascribes this to Plato and not to Hippocrates. Soranos apparently thinks that the use of scents in therapy tends to go with the belief that the womb is an animal (*Gyn.* 3.29; T 153) but, as his own explanation of why scent therapy works demonstrates, it is possible to use this technique in an entirely different conceptual framework; Soranos manages to reject foul-smelling substances on the grounds of their harshness, but supports sweet-smelling substances because they relax the uterine ligaments, and therefore can be used at the nostrils of a woman with uterine prolapse (*Gyn.* 4.38; T 205).[25]

There are thus two issues to be decided. First, did the Hippocratics believe in the womb as an independent being? I would deny this, not because I regard the suggestion as absurd and the Hippocratics as far too sensible to fall for it, but because I find nothing in the corpus to compare to Plato's discussion in *Timaeus*. Secondly, taking up Adair, did Plato himself believe in it? Here I would answer that Plato adds something new to the basic mobile womb of the Hippocratics; instead of the womb moving according to mechanical principles of wet and dry, it possesses something close to 'a mind of its own'. I would also question whether we would so readily read back ideas of the womb as an animal into Hippocratic medicine, were it not for the lasting influence of the imagery of the *Timaeus* on Aretaeus and on other writers, to the extent that Galen finds it necessary to refute this theory.

Our own medical theories play a major part in this discussion. It is self-evident to us both that the womb is not a living creature, and that it cannot move around the body, so that any suggestion that it does so move is startling, demands explanation, and may be given more weight than it deserves; it is, after all, only one element in Hippocratic gynaecology. In the case of Adair on Plato, we can clearly see the reluctance of a lecturer at Dartmouth Medical School to face the otherness of classical Greece. Adair argues that, in Plato, it is only the sensation of desire to procreate, rather than the womb itself, that moves through the body; while 'the rude and superstitious minds of poorly schooled ancient Greeks' could accept the mobile womb, he finds it hard to believe that anyone sensible – especially 'a brilliant ancient Greek' like Plato – would believe in it. Adair dismisses the wandering womb as 'preposterous' and 'ridiculous' (1996: 160). Since the womb 'has mass and position, both verifiable', 'sophisticated Greeks' would have realised that it could not move through the body without damaging the tissue through which it passed (1996: 158). But there is no reason why the Greeks should have put together womb movement and tissue damage; they could have kept two different areas of thought apart for practical purposes.

Stifling and suffocation: the development of the textual tradition

In my discussion of the ways in which the Hippocratics classified disease, I have tried to emphasise that the disease label hysteria, far from being applied in these texts for the first time, is a much later invention. The developing hysteria tradition uses only a selection of the Hippocratic texts on womb movement and, even within this selection, it ignores disagreement on matters as fundamental as the category of woman most likely to be affected, and the variation in symptoms according to where the womb travels in its quest for moisture. It also takes and merges distinctive images and therapies from these texts.

In the texts used to support this developing tradition, the symptom that stands out is the one which is sometimes used to introduce the disease description: *pnix*, or suffocation. What is the significance of this symptom for the Hippocratics? Rejecting our fascination with womb movement – which was, after all, seen as unproblematic by classical Greek writers – we should now consider the implications of *pnix* for Hippocratic medicine (cf. Shorter 1986: 574, 549).

In his history of hysteria, Trillat (1986: 16) posed a pertinent question: is it the womb, or the woman, who suffocates in these texts? He suggests that the answer is left open by the Hippocratic texts but, unlike the Littré translation, the Greek is actually relatively straightforward on this subject, partly because the Hippocratic writers often used plural terms for the womb. This means that, although in some cases it is the woman who suffers from *pnix* (e.g. *DW* 1.2, L 8.32, use of *hê gynê*), it is more commonly the womb that 'stifles'; for example, 'When the womb (singular) stifles' (*DW* 2.201, L 8.384) or 'If the womb (plural) arrives at the heart and stifles (plural)' (*DW* 2.124, L

8.266). I am proposing the translation 'stifles' rather than 'suffocates' for reasons that will shortly become clear.

In order to grasp some of the implications of *pnix*, the stifled womb that in turn stifles the woman, it is necessary to return to the question of what the Hippocratic writers – and the culture within which they practised – understood by the nature of woman. As we have already seen, whether women are represented as hotter or colder than men, the womb is associated with the heat necessary to 'bake' an embryo to maturity. The Hippocratic writers are therefore working with a traditional and powerful image of the womb as an oven; if nothing is cooking in it, its excess heat may spill out and affect the rest of a woman's body. The womb itself can suffer from stifling, with the woman's extremities feeling cold as all her heat centres on the womb, while an overheated womb-oven travels to find moisture to put out its fire.

Pnix is thus far more than 'difficulty in breathing', but one Hippocratic passage seems to suggest that the movement of the womb can physically obstruct the route of the breath through the body. This is *Diseases of Women* 1.7, the description of the desiccated womb 'throwing itself' upon the liver. When subsequent writers try to account for *pnix*, it is this aetiology of actual physical pressure which they take up. However, heat continues to play an important role even when *pnix* becomes simple obstruction of respiration.

Of course, like veins, arteries and pulse (Chapter 10, p. 197), the term 'respiration' has changed its meaning considerably since the Hippocratics. When we use it today, we may mean breathing in a general sense, but beneath this casual use lies our knowledge of the process by which oxygen is taken in and carbon dioxide given out. Translating the title of Galen's treatise *De usu respirationis* as 'On the use of respiration' rather than as 'On the usefulness of breathing', glosses over the implications of the term in the science of the second century AD and before. What we do not share with the ancients is their theory of 'skin-breathing', used in one of the immediately post-Hippocratic writers most relevant for the hysteria tradition: the fourth-century BC philosopher Heracleides of Pontus (*c*.390–310 BC).

In the mid-fifth century BC, the philosopher Empedokles proposed that all living creatures breathe through the pores of their skin (DK 31B100; Furley and Wilkie 1984: 3–5). Plato preserves a version of skin-breathing that also explains the movement of blood in the body: air enters through the skin to replace that exhaled through the nose and mouth, while also entering through the nose and mouth to replace that exhaled through the skin. It is the resulting movement, rather than the heart, which sends blood to those parts of the body needing nutriment (*Timaeus* 76b1–e9; Furley and Wilkie 1984: 7–8). Galen argued that breathing occurs 'for the sake of the innate heat' and that 'the use of breathing is the conservation of the innate heat';[26] breathing regulates the innate heat, either by fanning it or by cooling it.

Skin-breathing and innate heat play an important role in Galen's theory of 'hysterical suffocation', especially in relation to a story that existed in a number of versions and which went on to become a key part of the developing hysteria tradition: the treatment of an apparently dead woman, whose revival was described in a lost work by Heracleides (Diogenes Laertius 8.61 and 8.67). Discussing the most severe form of hysterical suffocation in *On the Affected Parts* 6.5 (K 8.415), Galen refers to this story as follows:

> For [Heracleides] says that that woman who had neither breath nor pulse could only be distinguished from a corpse in one way: that is, that she had a little warmth around the middle part of her body.

After Heracleides, Galen says, doctors developed tests for the presence of life: wool held at the nose, or a vessel of water on the navel. As I have already mentioned, in the later tradition a deep concern remains over the ability of hysteria to mimic death. One of the symptoms is the absence of any pulse, and stories are told of women mistaken for dead who revive on the edge of the grave (Grmek 1987; Debru 1992). This particular story from Heracleides' lost work 'On the absence of breath', *Apnous*,[27] is repeated in several other ancient writers. Closest to Galen in both date and wording is the third-century AD Diogenes Laertius, who states that the woman was *apnoun kai asphykton*, 'without breath or pulse', for thirty days (8.61). As well as this detail, he adds further information about the circumstances, which is duplicated in other writers. The hero of the story was apparently the 'show-man' Empedokles (Lloyd 1987: 101), who later told his friend Pausanias that he had realised the woman still lived by observing her innate heat. Amazed onlookers thought that Empedokles had performed a miracle, but in fact the woman recovered because she had continued to breathe through her skin alone. In Galen's discussion, her state is akin to hibernation; the key to her survival is the coldness of her body, which means that it can survive by skin-breathing preserving the innate heat (Debru 1996: 206–9).

This story was very popular in the sixteenth century; medical writers who used it included Pieter van Foreest (1599) and Nicolas de la Roche (1542: 65^{r-v}). Instead of following Diogenes Laertius, who said that the woman was without breath or pulse for thirty days, they used an earlier version, given by Pliny (*NH* 7.52.175) in the first century AD.[28] This set the story within a discussion of souls that leave the body and return to it, followed by accounts of people who recovered from apparent death. Pliny wrote, 'This topic is the subject of a book by Heracleides, well known in Greece, about a woman who was seven days without breath but was called back to life.'

Van Foreest (1599: 167–8) repeated the 'seven days' as well as Pliny's remark that 'the female sex seems particularly liable to this disease, since it is subject to turning of the womb' (*conversio volvae*). In his *scholia* on this section, van Foreest followed Galen's theory on the innate heat, which is also used to account for the coldness of the extremities. He then stated that all learned authorities agree that patients with this condition should not be buried until the *third* day. This seems odd, when the two ancient versions of the story gave seven and thirty days, but it may represent an elision with Christian beliefs. Origen (*c*. AD 185–254) uses Heracleides' story as a way of persuading unbelievers of the real possibility of Christ having risen from the dead (*Against Celsus* 2.16, 402; Heracleides fr.78 Wehrli 1953); he does not say how long Heracleides' woman lay as if dead, but the figure of three days may drift into the story from this analogy between her and Christ.

Galen was thus not the only ancient writer to associate the story in Heracleides' *Apnous* with a condition of the womb but, where Pliny merely stated that women were more likely to suffer in this way because their wombs move, Galen gave a full aetiology accepting the theories of innate heat and skin-breathing.

Galen and his influence: winners and losers in the textual tradition

So far, this chapter has covered the Hippocratic origins of the hysteria tradition in detail, while also mentioning the distinctive contributions of a small group of other writers: notably Plato and the second-century AD writers Aretaeus, Soranos and Galen. But what happened to womb movement and suffocation between Plato and the second century AD? This is not an easy question to answer; literary medical sources are sparse, and surviving fragments must be read through the hostile eyes of opponents. Apart from Plato, the only fourth-century BC writer to be incorporated into the tradition is Heracleides of Pontus. Other writers of this period enter the tradition only to be dismissed from it; for example, Soranos describes and criticises the therapy used for hysterical *pnix* by Diocles of Carystos as follows:

> He pinches the nostrils, but opens the mouth and applies a sternutative; moreover, with the hand he presses the uterus toward the lower parts by pressing upon the hypochondriac region; and applies warm fomentations to the legs.
>
> (*Gyn*. 3.29; T 153)

In the third century BC, Herophilos of Chalcedon is said to have described the ligaments – which he called 'membranes' – anchoring the womb in the abdominal cavity. In a positivist science, this last discovery would have proved false the theory that the womb is capable of movement around the body. But no discussion by Herophilos of suffocation caused by the womb survives. His follower Mantias, who lived around 165–90 BC, wrote on pharmacology, and one of the two surviving fragments of his work with a gynaecological theme concerns hysterical suffocation. This fragment, too, is preserved by Soranos, who tells us that Mantias recommended playing flutes and drums when an attack was imminent, and giving castoreum and bitumen with wine when the attack was over (fr.11: *Gyn.* 3.29; T 153).[29] It is interesting that the discovery of the 'membranes' does not appear to have significantly changed the therapy.

A further source for the period from the third to the first centuries BC consists of papyri from Greco-Roman Egypt, which give many recipes which originated in the Hippocratic corpus. One very ancient recipe collection, largely based on *Diseases of Women* and dated to the third or second century BC, mentions 'suffocation of the womb' but recommends dried otters' kidneys in sweet wine – the only time this recipe occurs in Greek literature (Marganne 1981 no.155; P. Ryl. 3.531, Pack² 2418). A further recipe is given for a cough after the suffocation. Another papyrus dated to 260–230 BC is too fragmentary for any reconstruction of the recipe, but concerns a 'hysterical woman' (*gynê hysterikê*); in the following line it is possible to read the word *pnigmos* (Marganne 1981 no.93; P. Hibeh 2.191, Pack² 2348). An even less legible papyrus from the early first century BC has been reconstructed by its editor to include the words *hysterikai* and *hysterikais* (Marganne no.8, Pack² 2394). Papyri therefore suggest that recipes found in the Hippocratic corpus and variations on them continued to circulate in the ancient world; taken with the fragment of Mantias, they give further support to the proposal that the disease category *hysterikê pnix* existed as a diagnosis in the second century BC.

A further literary account survives from the Roman Celsus, writing in the early first century AD. Book 4 of his encyclopaedia is arranged by the parts of the body, and includes a chapter on diseases of the womb. It begins with a description of an unnamed but violent (*vehemens*) illness coming from the womb, an organ here regarded as second only to the stomach in its influence on the rest of the body. The condition described takes away the breath, so that the woman falls down as if she has epilepsy; however, in contrast to epilepsy, the eyes are not 'turned', there is no frothing at the mouth, and the sinews are not stretched. Instead, the patient sleeps. Some women suffer from this throughout their lives. Celsus does not investigate the causes of the condition, but recommends treatments: bloodletting, cupping-glasses, an extinguished lamp wick or other strong-smelling material held to the nostrils, cold water poured over the patient, hot wet poultices, and massage of the hips and knees. To prevent further attacks he recommends that the woman should abstain from wine for a year, be massaged regularly, and put mustard on her lower abdomen daily so that the skin reddens. He adds suggestions for emollients, drinks (including castoreum), purges and fumigations.

Some of this material is familiar: the cold water, lamp wick and castoreum, for example, are no different from the Hippocratic recommendations, nor is the concern to differentiate the condition from epilepsy. Other suggestions are new: in particular, the possibility of a chronic version, and bloodletting as a treatment. Although employed in the Hippocratic corpus, bloodletting is not known to have been used previously for this condition; it was Galen who elevated bloodletting to the remedy of choice in menstrual suppression (see Chapter 10, p. 199).[30]

Of the three medical descriptions of hysterical suffocation surviving from the second century AD, Galen's was the most influential, although his triumph was not complete until after the eleventh century, when the translation of Arabic texts into Latin returned Galenic medicine to the West. I now propose to look in turn at the texts of Aretaeus, Soranos and Galen, establishing their contribution to the tradition, before turning to their use in antiquity and beyond.

The description of *hysterikê pnix* in Aretaeus' *On the Causes and Symptoms of Acute Diseases* is today best known for its image of the womb as being 'like an animal inside an animal', or 'like one living thing inside another'. Like the Hippocratic writers, Aretaeus not only believes that the womb can move within the body but also advocates scent therapy, with foul odours such as pitch, burned hair, an extinguished lamp, or castoreum applied to the nose and fragrant substances rubbed into the external genitalia (6.10.3, CMG 2, 140.17–19); unlike them, however, he knows of the membranes – which he calls *hymenes* – anchoring the womb in place (2.11.5, CMG 2, 33.29; 4.11.9, CMG 2, 1.28; 6.10.1, CMG 2, 139.27). We may find the combination of scent therapy and membranes contradictory: Aretaeus does not. He describes the womb – 'the seat of womanhood itself' – as being 'all but alive', moving of its own volition up to the thorax, or to left and right within the lower abdomen. It is when it moves upwards and remains there for a long time, pressing violently on the intestines, that the patient experiences *pnix*, described as being like epilepsy without the spasms.[31] Pressure is put on the liver, diaphragm, lungs and heart, causing a heavy head, loss of sensation, and deep sleep. Aretaeus then mentions a similar condition, characterised by *pnix* and loss of voice, which does not arise from the womb; the two differ in that only cases arising in the womb are helped by scent therapy, and in only these cases do the limbs move.

When the womb moves up the body there will be 'hesitation in doing her tasks, exhaustion, loss of control of the knees, dizziness, and her limbs are weakened; headache, heaviness of the head; and the woman feels pain in the channels (*phlebes*) at either side of her nose' (2.11.4, CMG 2, 33.15–17). The pulse will be weak and irregular, breathing imperceptible, and death follows suddenly; it is difficult to believe that it has occurred, since the patient has such a lifelike appearance. Recovery is equally sudden; the womb rises up very easily, and just as easily returns to its place. Here Aretaeus uses another vivid image: the womb sails high in the water (*akroploos*) like a tree trunk floating, but it is pulled back by its membranes (2.11.5, CMG 2, 33.29). Those which join the neck of the womb to the loins can distend and contract, like the sails of a ship (4.11.9, CMG 2, 81.31; 6.10.1, CMG 2, 140.3–4). The condition is more likely to affect young women, whose way of life and understanding are 'wandering', less firmly based.

Aretaeus thus combines womb movement with anchoring membranes, while continuing to explore key themes in the hysteria tradition; for example, the difficulty in telling whether a sufferer is dead or alive, and the resemblance to epilepsy. Although much of his therapeutic material is Hippocratic, in particular the scents, fumigation and sneezing, he follows Celsus rather than the Hippocratics in recommending letting blood from the ankle, while adding that one should pull out hairs from the patient in order to rouse her (6.10.3, CMG 2, 140.14; 6.10.6, CMG 2, 141.14–15). He goes beyond *Aphorisms* 5.35 to state that sneezing, if accompanied by pressure on the nostrils, can make the womb return to its place (6.10.5, CMG 2, 141.7–9). He introduces the idea of 'sympathy' in order to explain how the highest parts of the body can be affected by the womb; although the membranes prevent it from travelling that far, the womb can still exert its influence on these parts.

The main influence on gynaecology in late antiquity was Soranos. In the Latin West, sections were translated from Greek into Latin by Caelius Aurelianus in the fifth century and – more important still in terms of his later influence – by Muscio in the sixth century (Drabkin and Drabkin 1951; Pigeaud 1982). In the Greek East, Soranos was used in the gynaecological sections of the encyclopaedias of Aetius of Amida in the mid-sixth century and Paul of Aegina in the seventh century, making him 'la bible de la gynécologie et de l'obstétrique jusqu'à la Renaissance' (Gourevitch 1988: xxxi; Hanson and Green 1994). What did Soranos contribute to the textual reservoir drawn on by the hysteria tradition?

Soranos followed the Methodist 'method' (see Chapter 1, p. 38), although he was far from being a slave to it (Gourevitch 1988: xlv). He rejects the Hippocratic idea of extensive womb movement, believing instead that the womb is held in place by membranes (Green 1985: 34; Lloyd 1987: 164–5), and attributing uterine *pnix* to inflammation of these anchoring membranes causing tension, a *status strictus*. While rejecting any suggestion that the womb is an animal – it 'does not issue forth like a wild animal from the lair, delighted by fragrant odours and fleeing bad odours' (*Gyn.* 3.29; T 153) – he believes it can respond to certain agents by stricture or relaxation. As for treatments for the condition, he completely rejects the foul-smelling substances traditionally employed in scent therapy (they cause torpor and upset the stomach), together with sneezing (too violent) and sex (how can it cure disease when it has such bad effects on even healthy bodies?). Blood-letting is acceptable, however, after the patient has been warmed and rubbed with olive oil in order to relax her. The condition exists in both an acute and a chronic form, and treatment should take account of this (*Gyn.* 3.28; T 150–2).

Although Soranos' gynaecology dominated both East and West, in the Greek East medicine as a whole remained under the influence of Galen. In his treatise *On the Affected Parts* Galen described *hysterikê pnix* or *apnoia hysterikê*, 'absence of breath caused by the womb'. Aretaeus managed to combine anchoring membranes with womb movement; Soranos rejected womb movement and attributed symptoms to inflammation of the membranes; but Galen offered a new aetiology which eclipsed all that had gone before. Accepting that the womb was the cause of the symptoms, he suggested that this was due not to movement or inflammation, but to the retention of blood or 'female seed'. Depending on what was retained, symptoms ranged from contracture of the limbs, to weakness while remaining conscious, to lying motionless with an almost imperceptible pulse (6.5; K 8.414–37).

A much-quoted section of *On the Affected Parts* reads: 'I myself have seen many *hysterikai* women, as they call themselves and as the *iatrinai* call them' (6.5; K 8.414; see Allbutt 1921: 344). *Iatrinai*, literally 'female healers' (see Chapter 9), has also been translated as 'midwives': *hysterikai* is usually translated as 'hysterical', but a more accurate translation is 'suffering from the womb'.[32] Further evidence for the suggestion that women of the early Roman empire described themselves as *hysterikai* comes from one of Martial's *Epigrams* (11.71), where Leda tells her elderly husband that she is *hysterica* to trick him into calling young doctors to carry out what has – at least in satirical verse – become the standard treatment: sexual intercourse. But Galen distances himself from both the word *hysterikos* – he prefers 'the so-called hysterical symptoms' – and *pnix*, saying that *apnoia*, 'absence of breath', is a more appropriate term.[33]

However, Galen does regard sexual intercourse as beneficial for sufferers, and moves it to the centre of his new aetiology of the condition. Those most vulnerable to the disorder are 'widows, and particularly those who previously menstruated regularly, had been pregnant and were eager to have intercourse, but were now deprived of all this' (6.5; K 8.417, trans. Siegel 1976: 184). This passage is interesting, not only because it omits the childless, seen as particularly susceptible in several Hippocratic texts, but also because it points Galen towards the cause of the problems. He does not accept the Hippocratic aetiology of womb movement in search of moisture, since dissection shows this is impossible; the womb 'does not move from one place to another like a wandering animal, but is pulled up by the tension' of the anchoring membranes (6.5; K 8.426 and 430, trans. Siegel 1976: 189).

Why do these membranes become tense? He suggests that it is because they are filled with menstrual blood unable to move into the womb either because of the blood's thickness or because the orifices through which it passes into the womb are closed. So one cause of the condition can be menstrual retention. However, the most severe form of *hysterikê pnix* is due to the retention of another substance, 'female seed'. Galen, like the Hippocratic authors of the treatise *On Generation/Nature of the Child*, believed that women produced a seminal fluid, but he did not consider that this elevated the female to a position equal to that of the male. If retained in the womb, this seed could rot, causing noxious humours to affect the rest of the body through 'sympathy' (*Loc. Aff.* 6.5; K 8.420, 424, 432–3), that convenient concept used by Aretaeus, able to claim Hippocratic antecedents through texts such as *On Joints* 57, which described the 'brotherly connections' existing between parts of the body.[34] On the model of a minor bite or sting from a poisonous creature causing possibly fatal symptoms, the effects of retained seed could be dramatic (*Loc. Aff.* 6.5; K 8.421–4; Debru 1996: 239). By suggesting that symptoms depend on the nature of the matter retained, Galen departs from the Hippocratic classification of womb movements according to the part of the body reached; this is consistent with Galen's general humoral model, in which specific fluids cause specific symptom combinations.

As Monica Green (1985: 50–2) pointed out, it is noteworthy that, despite his rejection of the belief that the womb is a wandering animal, Galen nevertheless retains scent therapy. His treatise *On the Method of Healing*, to Glaucon (1.15; Daremberg 1856: 735) includes a brief reference to its use in treating a 'rising' womb, while *On Compound Medicines, According to Site* (9.10; K 13.320) lists substances – including castoreum and burned hair – to be placed at the nose of a woman with this condition. In a passage from *On the Affected Parts* (6.5; K 8.420) taken up by the hysteria tradition, Galen describes the case of a woman who had been a widow for a long time and who was told by a midwife that her symptoms were due to her womb being 'drawn up'. The woman applied to her external genitalia the 'customary remedies' for this condition and, feeling the 'pain and at the same time the pleasure' associated with intercourse, passed a quantity of thick seed; if we assume that these remedies are the aromatics to be rubbed on the thighs in *Diseases of Women* 2.201 (L 8.384), then the suggestion seems to be that rubbing in the traditional scented ointments causes orgasm, releasing retained seed. For Galen, both menstrual blood and seed must be evacuated, or they will become toxic and poison the body; scent therapy survives, but its rationale is altered. This passage describing the widow and the midwife was influential in the later history of medicine, and not only in discussions of hysteria; as noted in the Introduction, it was also used by nineteenth-century supporters of clitoridectomy.

We know little of the period after Galen in terms of the development of the hysteria tradition. A spell to cure the 'rising up of the womb' is preserved in a papyrus from Greco-Roman Egypt which has been dated to the third or fourth century AD (PGM VII 260–72, trans. Scarborough, in Betz 1986: 123–4). It calls upon the womb to

> return again to your seat, and that you do not turn into the right part of the ribs, or into the left part of the ribs, and that you do not gnaw into the heart like a dog, but remain indeed in your own intended and proper place.

This fascinating glimpse of popular belief shows the persistence of the idea of a mobile, animate womb; its gnawing 'like a dog' recalls Greco-Roman ideas of the insatiable sexual appetites of dogs – and women (see Chapter 1, pp. 24–5). In this spell we are not far from the womb of the *Timaeus*, running through the body when its desire to conceive is thwarted.

A different type of source from the later fourth century AD makes explicit the identification of the Greek *hysterikê pnix* and the Latin *suffocatio*. This is Marcellus of Bordeaux' *Book of Medicines*, which includes the disorder in a section on acute and chronic diseases of the head (1.25; CMG 5, 60.35–61.3).[35] It identifies only two symptoms – severe head pains and suffocation – which, if originating in the womb, 'the Greeks call *hysterikê pnix*'. Except for its organ of origin, the condition is considered comparable to epilepsy, frenzy, and dizziness.

Further contributions to the tradition: the Greek East

Returning to the set of connected texts which makes up the hysteria tradition, the Byzantine empire preserved many medical ideas of antiquity through the work of encyclopaedists such as Oribasius, Aetius, and Paul of Aegina.[36] Such writers, often dismissed as 'the medical refrigerators of antiquity', working in 'une époque de stagnation' (Meyerhof and Joannides 1938: 6), are now increasingly recognised as more than 'dumb copyists' whose labours have preserved for us works of earlier writers which would otherwise be lost (Nutton 1984b: 2–3). According to the needs of their audiences, they selected, paraphrased, added and cut the material available. They may add little new to our picture, but they standardise remedies for *hysterikê pnix*, while combining elements of Soranos and Galen in different ways. Both Aetius and Paul, for example, use Soranos but – like Galen – they bring back the scent therapy that he had so forcefully rejected. Both use Galen's idea of retained matter that must be expelled, while Aetius repeats the story of the widow applying the traditional remedies and ejecting thick seed.

Oribasius's fourth-century, seventy-volume compilation, derived from Galen, Soranos, and a number of lost works, relied on Soranos for the anatomy of the womb and other female sexual organs (*Collectiones medicae* 24.31, CMG 6, 2.1, 41–6). For his discussion of *hysterikê pnix* (*Synopsis* 9.45, CMG 6, 3. 305.10–28), however, Oribasius used the lost work of Philumenos of Alexandria, which recommended bandaging the extremities, rubbing the lower limbs, and scent therapy using foul odours at the nose and sweet oils to be injected into the womb.[37] Shouting at the patient and provoking sneezing were also acceptable, with bloodletting once she regained consciousness. Castoreum was also recommended; even alone, it may cure. In an earlier chapter Oribasius gives further remedies, including the by now familiar list of foul-smelling substances, here given as bitumen, castoreum, gum resin, pitch, cedar resin, extinguished lamp wicks, burnt hair, rue, asafoetida, onion and garlic (*Synopsis* 9.41, CMG 6, 3. 301). This closely resembles the list of substances criticised by Soranos and, of course, Soranos also disagreed with using loud noises to rouse the patient. It thus appears that Oribasius – and hence Paul – mixes Soranos' anatomy with the remedies used by the very traditions which Soranos most despised.

In the Byzantine world, medical education was largely textual, traditional and classical. We know of very few teaching centres in the fifth to seventh centuries AD; those students who neither came from a medical family nor were apprenticed to a physician were obliged to rely largely on texts for their instruction in both theory and practice (Kollesch 1973: 14; Duffy 1984). The sixteen-volume compilation made in the sixth century by Aetius of Amida was based on Oribasius and other writers. For his description of *hysterikê pnix* (16.68),[38] Aetius merged Galen's *On the Affected Parts* with the Philumenos material preserved by Oribasius. He accepts that the womb, which only *seems* to move, causes the condition, affecting the higher organs through 'sympathy'. Using the Galenic model of the body, he describes how spasms reach the head via the arteries, the brain through the spinal marrow, and the liver through the veins (Z 96.1–3). As a means of discovering whether or not the patient lives, he repeats Galen's test in which a woollen thread was placed at the nostrils or a bowl of water balanced on the navel. However, even if no movement was perceptible in the wool or water, he warned – again, following Galen – that it was possible that life yet remained. He sees the disorder as seasonal, happening mostly in winter and autumn, especially in young women who use drugs to prevent conception (Z 97.14). Although recalling Plato's image of the womb deprived of offspring running wild through the body, this appears to reflect a special concern on the part of Aetius. For Aetius, as for Galen, the symptoms are caused by the decay in the womb of seed or other material, which then cools down; the coldness is passed on to the brain and heart (Z 97.26–8). He cuts out the story from Heracleides but repeats – indeed, claims as his own eyewitness account (Z 98.1)[39] – Galen's story of the widow who felt 'pain and pleasure' before expelling the corrupt seed; here, however, Aetius adds extra details, explicitly telling us that the remedies were sweet ointments such as marjoram and iris oil rubbed into the genitalia by a midwife, and recommending these again later in this passage (Z 98.1–8; 99.18–22). Like Philumenos and Oribasius, Aetius recommends shouting at patients and repeats word for word the advice of Philumenos-Oribasius that castoreum alone may cure (Z 100.7; 101.1–3; cf. Oribasius *Synopsis* 9.45.6): the status of scent therapy is reinforced, even increased.

The seventh-century encyclopaedist Paul of Aegina based his work largely on the work of Oribasius, contributing 'practically no original material of his own' (N. Wilson 1983: 48); but his work circulated widely (N. Wilson 1983: 85–6), and the choices he made strengthened certain elements of the hysteria tradition. His description of *hysterikê pnix* closely follows that of Aetius, but states that the womb itself 'rises up'[40] to affect by sympathy the carotid arteries, heart and membranes. The patient loses her senses and her power of speech, the limbs being 'drawn together'. The cause – as in Galen – is the womb being full of seed or of some other substance that becomes rotten (3.71, CMG 288.19–20). Most sufferers die suddenly during the spasms; the pulse becomes frequent and irregular, and breathing, at first faint, is cut off. The condition is most prevalent in winter and autumn, most commonly affects the lascivious, and – in almost the exact words of Aetius – those who use drugs to prevent conception (CMG 288.24–7; cp. Z 97.12–14). During the attack the extremities should be bandaged and the patient rubbed all over. Foul-smelling substances – including stale urine – should be placed at the nostrils, and cupping and anal suppositories used. Sweet-smelling substances draw the womb back to its proper place. To rouse the patient, one should shout at her roughly and induce sneezing with castoreum, soapwort and pepper (CMG 289.6–8; cp. Z 99.8–10). Like Soranos and Oribasius, Paul separates treatment for the fits, or *paroxysmoi*, from treatment for the whole body; the latter begins with bloodletting and goes on to purging, exercise and baths (CMG 289.16; cf. Soranos *Gyn.* 3.28; T 150–2).[41]

In Byzantine medicine, then, a composite picture of *hysterikê pnix* was built up, incorporating the Galenic belief in retained substances poisoning the body, Soranos' anchoring membranes, Hippocratic scent therapy, Celsus' bloodletting, and a belief in the value of sneezing derived from the Hippocratic *Aphorisms* and Galen's commentary on them. Although the main authorities, Soranos and Galen, had vigorously denied that the womb could move, this idea came close to being reinstated by Paul of Aegina. Aetius preserved the Galenic tests to determine whether or not the patient still lived, while writers with otherwise divergent views agreed on the therapeutic value of castoreum.

The Latin West

In the West, meanwhile, the picture was in some ways very different. Although the *Aphorisms* circulated widely, few works of classical medicine survived, especially after knowledge of Greek declined during the fifth and sixth centuries. Although in Northern Italy some commentaries and encyclopaedias were adapted into Latin during the sixth century – among them, the work of Oribasius – most 'new' medical texts were short works based on Soranos (Green 1985: 135; 174–5 nn. 5 and 6). The fifth- or sixth-century version of Soranos by Muscio circulated widely; it plays down Soranos' attack on the idea that the womb moves around the body, going so far as to add to Soranos' introduction to the condition a new phrase claiming that the womb rises up towards the chest,[42] so that the 'Western' Soranos included womb movement from an early date.

The late fourth-century *Euporiston* of Theodorus Priscianus was originally written in Greek, but its author translated it into Latin (ed. Rose 1894: 228–30; Temkin 1932: 174). The Latin version contains a section entitled *De praefocatione matricis*, which follows the constriction/relaxation approach of Soranos, omits womb movement, but includes scent therapy. In AD 447 Cassius Felix compiled an encyclopaedia which he claimed was based on Greek medical writers of the logical, or dogmatic, sect; although he has a very Hippocratic description of hysterical suffocation, incorporating not only scent therapy but also womb movement, his work in fact owes much to Soranos as translated by Caelius Aurelianus (ed. Rose 1879: 187–9; Temkin 1932: 174–6; Green 1985: 167).

Other Latin texts surviving from this period may be more representative than these of medicine in the West after the fall of Rome. A dialogue set between Soranos and a midwife, apparently designed as a midwives' catechism, is preserved in a ninth-century manuscript but may date to the sixth century; this is the *Liber ad Soteris* (Rose 1882: 131–9; Baader 1984: 251). Another short text from the same period is the *Gynaecia* attributed to 'Cleopatra' (Green 1985: 153). This mentions a condition called *suppressiones vulvae*, the main symptom of which is difficulty speaking and which may thus be identified with *hysterikê pnix*; however, it neither mentions womb movement nor recommends scent therapy.

The ancient Hippocratic theories were not, however, entirely lost to the West (Kibre 1945; 1980: 347 n.1). Between the fifth and seventh centuries AD many Hippocratic works were translated into Latin at Ravenna (Müller-Rohlfsen 1980), among them *Aphorisms* and extracts from *Diseases of Women* (1.1, 1.7–38, and parts of 2). Several passages describing womb movement and suffocation are included in such translations (Mazzini and Flammini 1983; Vázquez Buján 1986; Irigoin 1973). Also translated was Galen's *On the Method of Healing, to Glaucon*, with its reference to scent therapy for a moving womb; the Ravenna commentator considers that, by using scent therapy, Galen appears to be endorsing the wandering womb theory (Palmieri 1981: 288–9, discussed Green 1985: 151–3).

It is, however, as misleading to regard the work of the scholars of Ravenna only as 'translation' as to dismiss the Byzantine writers as 'mere compilers'. In both cases we need to understand why they used the texts in a particular way, since these uses influenced what was translated. The Ravenna translations were made for practical and instructional purposes, so they are manuals rather than academic editions. More theoretical or speculative Hippocratic texts were neglected, and those translated were adapted according to the different moral and historical contexts in which they were to be used (Green 1987: 311; Mazzini 1985: 385). To make them more appropriate in a teaching context, extracts from some texts were set out in question-and-answer form, as dialogues, calendars, visual representations or letters. The *Letter to Maecenas*,[43] which survives in two ninth-century manuscripts, includes two passages of *Diseases of Women* used in the hysteria tradition: 1.7, on movement of the womb to the liver, and 1.32, on womb movement in a pregnant woman. The late eighth-century or early ninth-century manuscript Leningrad

Lat. F.v.VI.3 is a handbook including Latin translations of sections from *Diseases of Women*, one of which is our 2.127, a further description of movement of the womb to the liver. In the recipes given, substitutions are made in the pharmacopoeia according to what was available in this period (Diepgen 1933: 228–9; Walter 1935).

The Arab world

Another route of transmission of Hippocratic ideas to the West was through the Arab world,[44] where versions of Hippocratic texts, based on several manuscripts, were produced from the ninth century onwards. By about AD 800, such key Galenic works in the hysteria tradition as *On the Affected Parts*, *On Difficulty in Breathing*, and the commentary on *Aphorisms* already existed in Arabic or Syriac (Meyerhof 1926; Meyerhof and Joannides 1938: 6; Ullmann 1978: 11; Lippi and Arieti 1985). Where the Latin West concentrated on translating Hippocratic texts of immediate practical value, the Arab translators also covered the more theoretical and speculative treatises, so that both the 'Arabic Galen' and the 'Arabic Hippocrates' were fuller than their Latin equivalents (Durling 1961: 232; Lippi and Arieti 1985: 401).

However, neither *Diseases of Women* nor *Nature of Woman* was translated into Arabic, although two Byzantine commentaries on *Diseases of Women* 1.1–11 circulated in the Arab world before the eleventh century, together with Byzantine medical encyclopaedias (Ullmann 1977; 1978: 11–12; Green 1985: 303 n.15; 305 n.22). Hippocratic gynaecology was mainly transmitted through new encyclopaedic works. The *Firdaws al ḥikma (Paradise of Wisdom)* of 'Ali ibn Rabbān aṭ-Ṭabarī (810–861), completed in 850, includes approximately 120 quotations from the Hippocratic corpus, a large amount of Galenic material, and extracts from other Greek and Islamic writers (Meyerhof 1931: 13–15; Browne 1921: 37–40). Aṭ-Ṭabarī believes that the essential wetness of woman leads to menstrual loss; retained moisture sinks to the lowest part of the body and then comes out, 'just as in a tree the excess moisture comes out as gum' (*Firdaws* 2.1, ch.16; Siggel 1941: 242). In his section on uterine disorders, he includes suffocation of the womb, writing, 'Sometimes, through damming-up of menstrual blood and lack of sexual intercourse, vapours develop.' He explains that the retained blood becomes thick, and produces vapours that then affect the whole body, causing such symptoms as painful breathing, palpitations, head pain and suffocation of the womb.

A further discussion of suffocation occurs in the context of womb movement. The womb can lean to one side, but sometimes it actually rises up until it reaches the diaphragm, causing suffocation. 'Then the woman loses consciousness, with the result that her breath is stopped. Then one puts a bit of wool under her nostrils in order to see whether she is alive or dead.' The cause here is not menstrual blood, but accumulated seed; if there is an 'excess, lack or absence' of intercourse, seed will build up in the womb, rot, and become poisonous and thick. The womb then moves to the diaphragm and the woman suffocates (*Firdaws* 4.9, ch.17; Siggel 1941: 244–5).

Here womb movement is being combined with a Galenic aetiology of retained seed or menses, with the addition of aṭ-Tabarī's own contribution in the explanatory device of 'vapours'. Like the Greco-Roman concept of 'sympathy', these account for the womb's effects on distant parts of the body; and, when texts were translated from Arabic to Latin from the eleventh century onwards, 'vapours' travelled with them.

Another Arabic example of the transmission of Galenic theories of hysterical suffocation occurs in the work of Muḥammad ibn-Zakariyya' al-Rāzī (Rhazes), who collected excerpts from Greek, Arabic and Indian writers in twenty-four volumes and wrote a practical textbook of medicine,[45] which includes a chapter on uterine suffocation (1534: ch.87). Here Rhazes includes retained menses and seed, the patient falling down as if dead, and scent therapy, as well as the recommendation that a midwife should rub the mouth of the womb with a well-oiled finger. He does not state that the womb moves, but describes a sensation 'as if something is pulled up'.

'Alī ibn al-'Abbas al-Majūsī, Haly Abbas, wrote in the tenth century (Browne 1921: 53–7; Meyerhof and Joannides 1938: 7), combining Hippocratic aetiologies with a predominantly Galenic approach. He plays down the membranes anchoring the womb, saying that the womb can move around the body, and includes both sympathy and vapours. He explains that suffocation of the womb is dangerous because the vital organs – the brain and heart – are affected through sympathy. If a woman does not have intercourse, a large quantity of seed collects and will 'stifle and extinguish the innate heat'. Retained menstrual blood has similar effects (Kāmil I 9.39; Gewargis 1980: 43). As for treatment, he retains Hippocratic scent therapy, but explains its success partly in terms of vapours. Bad smells administered to the nose rise to the brain, 'warming, dissolving and diluting the cold vapours', but also driving the womb back down (Kāmil II 8.12; Gewargis 1980: 76). The womb is 'more or less an independent living being', yearning for conception, annoyed by bad odours and leaning towards pleasant odours; Plato's description of the womb as an animal desiring conception was known to the Arab world through Galen (Gewargis 1980: 18; Weisser 1983: 146–7; 1989). Al-Majūsī also recommends sexual intercourse as a cure, particularly for virgins, whose strong desire for sex and thick menstrual blood predispose them to the condition (Gewargis 1980: 44, 80).[46] If this is not possible, then he suggests the Galenic therapy of instructing a midwife to rub sweet-smelling oils on the mouth of the womb; this has the same effect as intercourse, warming and thinning the seed so that it drains away and the woman 'finds peace' (Gewargis 1980: 77).

Another writer working in Arabic in the tenth century was Ibn al-Jazzār, whose main work was the seven-volume *Kitab Zād al-Musāfir*.[47] The chapter on suffocation of the womb (book 6, Chapter 11) describes loss of appetite and chilling of the body arising from retained seed rotting, something to which widows and young girls of marriageable age are particularly liable. From the seed a *fumus* – a smoke, or vapour – rises to the diaphragm, because the diaphragm and the womb are connected; then, since further connections link the diaphragm to the throat and vocal cords, suffocation ensues. Similar symptoms may arise from retained menses; scent therapy, particularly the application of fragrant oils to the mouth of the womb, is recommended. Repeated here is a version of the story given by Galen of the woman who lay as if dead but was known to be alive by the presence of innate heat; here, however, it is Galen rather than Empedokles who becomes its hero!

The final Arabic writer to transmit and transform the classical texts on hysterical suffocation was Ibn Sīnā (Avicenna, b. AD 980), who included the condition in his *Qānūn* (III 21.4.16–19).[48] Cures include bloodletting, rubbing scented oil into the vagina, and placing foul odours at the nose. The explanation is based on Galen as interpreted by Aetius, with sympathy favoured over vapours; Avicenna includes the test for life with a piece of wool, and the story of the widow.[49]

So the distinctively Hippocratic features of womb movement, scent therapy, and the belief in the therapeutic value of sexual intercourse survive even when Galenic theory is taken up by Islamic culture. Despite the rejection of the moving womb by both Soranos and Galen, it was resurrected in explanations of hysterical suffocation in both East and West. In the Arab world, Soranos' *Gynaecology* may not have been translated, so his attack on the theory of the mobile womb may have remained unknown; as for Galen, although he explicitly rejects Plato's womb-as-animal theory in *On the Affected Parts*, he implicitly accepts it in *To Glaucon*, thus leaving later commentators free to reinstate it. Such elements of the hysteria tradition as the wool test for life and the story of the widow and the midwife, retained by the Byzantine encyclopaedists, continue in Arabic medicine; the story of the woman raised from apparent death by Empedokles is found in Ibn al-Jazzār but plays a minor role, perhaps because the short reference to it in Galen is insufficient for it to be properly reconstructed.

In terms of the most likely victims of the condition, it is interesting that Galen's prime target is ignored: widows who, deprived of regular intercourse, build up too much seed. Instead, virgins become the focus of medical interest. This is not a return to Hippocratic aetiology, as the Hippocratic texts on womb movement cover a range of female types, favouring the childless (whose flesh is not 'broken down'), older women not having intercourse, and young widows. The Hippocratic text that may lie at the root of this interest in virgins is *On the Diseases of Virgins*, cited twice by Rhazes (*al-Ḥāwī* 9.67; 69, see Rhodes 1505). The condition it describes in girls 'ripe for marriage' does not involve womb movement, but its explanation of symptoms being caused by excess blood unable to leave the body, and its recommendation of sexual intercourse, suggest that it is the origin not only of al-Majūsī's statements about the thick menstrual blood of virgins but also of al-Jazzār's target population of girls of marriageable age. Finally, in these writers, a new explanatory device comes into play to account for the effects of the womb on other parts of the body: vapours.

The meeting of three worlds

In Western Europe, where most of Galenic medicine was lost, Soranos dominated gynaecology as a whole (Green 1985: 132–3). His work was seen as shorter and more practical than that of Galen, and was preserved in abridged Latin versions which persistently reinstated the womb movement he had so vehemently rejected. Hippocratic medicine fared worse, although Latin translations of *Aphorisms* and some sections of *Diseases of Women* that described womb movement continued to circulate. Some Galenic treatises, too, were translated; however, whereas 129 works of Galen were translated into Arabic, only four existed in Latin before the end of the eleventh century. One of these was the practical work *On the Method of Healing, to Glaucon* but, as has already been discussed, this can be taken as a further reinstatement of the wandering womb. The third volume of Paul of Aegina's encyclopaedia, which includes his largely Galenic description of *hysterikê pnix* plus details of scent therapy, was translated into Latin, but probably not before the tenth century (Heiberg 1912: xiii, cited by Green 1985: 184 n.82).

The emphasis in the West lay firmly on the instructional and practical aspects of ancient medicine, so that the traditional therapies for hysterical suffocation were transmitted when discussions of its causation were not. The category of suffocation of the womb appears in several anonymous collections of texts from the eighth to the twelfth centuries. The eighth- or ninth-century manuscript Leningrad Lat. F.v.VI.3 contains several short texts on gynaecology, all of which show some resemblances to the Hippocratic *Diseases of Women* 2 (Egert 1936). Of these, *De causis feminarum* gives practical advice on what to do *si vulva suffocantur*, 'if the womb is suffocated', giving the Greek name for the condition as 'styrecersis': perhaps a garbled form of *hysterikê pnix* or *hysterika*?[50] The patient is given burned and pulverised stag's horn in wine or in hot water (Egert 1936: I 26). Another text in this collection, *De muliebria causa*, claims that 'uribasius' – Oribasius, the only authority named in these texts – recommends one drachma of agaric for suffocation of the womb (Egert 1936: II 16). This is repeated in a section of the following text, *Liber de muliebria*, which later gives a more complex recipe for suffocation of the womb when the patient is choked at the neck, so that it is turned back to the chest (Egert 1936: III 23).

Galenic treatises were returned to the West in the eleventh and twelfth centuries, through translations from Arabic to Latin made by Constantine the African in the late eleventh century at Salerno and Monte Cassino: a few were translated directly from Greek into Latin in the twelfth and thirteenth centuries, and these translations are usually of higher quality (Kristeller 1945; Schipperges 1964; Green 1987; Baader 1984: 259). The effect of Constantine on the history of medicine cannot, however, be overemphasised; his arrival in Italy with a cargo of books of Arabic medicine returned classical medical theory to the West. For my purposes here, what is most significant is that his translations included Galen's commentary on the Hippocratic *Aphorisms*, as well as the *Kāmil* of al-Majūsī, and an abbreviated form of the *Kitāb Zād al-Musāfir* by Ibn al-Jazzār (Ullmann 1978: 53–4; Green 1985: 220; 1990: 49 and 62 n.7).

What effect did these texts have on the hysteria tradition in the West? We have already seen the wide range of variations that can be played on the theme of womb movement. In the Hippocratic texts, a dry, hot, light womb rises in search of moisture; Soranos believes the anchoring membranes prevent any upward movement, while for Aretaeus the womb shifts but is pulled back by the membranes, affecting the higher body only by 'sympathy'. In Galen the problem is seen as being a womb filled either with retained seed or with menstrual blood, rotting to produce coldness. In Arabic medicine a Hippocratic mobile womb acquires Galenic contents, and vapours as well as sympathy explain its effects on the higher parts. In the Latin West the focus on Soranos had been combined with acceptance of womb movement.

The return of Galenic medicine from the Arabic world led to yet another variation on the theme of womb movement and its mechanisms. In twelfth-century Salerno the texts of the Hippocratic corpus, Soranos and Galen finally came together after their varied travels through the Latin West, the Greek East, and the Arab world (Kristeller 1945; Baader 1978; Green 1985: 234). The result was not a critical comparison of these traditions, but instead the decline of Soranos in favour of the Galenic medical system of humoral balance. In the description of suffocation of the womb in the twelfth-century encyclopaedia and textbook *De aegritudinum curatione*, Johannes Platearius, one of the 'masters' of the school of Salerno, combined Galen and Paul of Aegina with Ibn al-Jazzār's claim that the symptoms were caused by vapours rising from retained substances. However, Platearius went a step further than this, suggesting that it was not the vapours, but the womb itself, filled by these vapours, that rose up in the body and put pressure on the organs of breathing.

Monica Green has argued that, since the Latin translations of al-Majūsī's *Kāmil* omitted the section in which he describes the womb as an animal annoyed by foul smells and seeking pleasant scents, this particular merger of the mobile womb with Galenic theory may come, not from Arabic medicine, but from the survival of the idea in popular thought in the West (Renzi 1853: 338–9; Green 1985: 263–6 and pers. comm. 16 November 1991). Other features of Platearius' description are more familiar, showing the overall dominance of Galenic material; he recommends the Galenic tests of the woollen thread or the flask full of water, and among his suggested cures one finds sneezing provoked with castoreum or pepper, and the use of foul smells at the nose and sweet smells at the vulva. However, here too Green points out that non-Galenic ideas resurface; although Galen never categorically recommended marriage as a cure, Platearius advocates it if the cause is retained seed. Al-Majūsī did explicitly prescribe sexual intercourse as a cure; but, again, this was omitted from the Latin translation of his work (Green 1985: 267–8). It seems that the survival of Hippocratic theories – the wandering womb from *Diseases of Women* and the therapeutic value of intercourse from sections of that work and from *On the Diseases of Virgins* – should not be underestimated.

Another writer associated with Salerno in the twelfth century is the female physician Trota, associated with a number of treatises found in at least 122 Latin manuscripts from the thirteenth to fifteenth centuries (Green 1996a: 123 and forthcoming). The printed edition known as the *Trotula* merged examples of three medieval text-groups, adding in sections of Vindicianus' *De semine* and Rhazes' *Ad Almansorem* (Green 1996a: 145–6). Of the three earlier groups, Green argues that the more empirical *De curis mulierum* derives 'from Trota's *Practica* and perhaps Trota's own oral dictation' (1996a: 154). The more theoretical and Galenic *Liber de sinthomatibus mulierum* merges recipes from earlier medieval Latin treatises on women (Egert 1936) with a simplified version of chapters of the Latin translation of Ibn al-Jazzār's *Kitāb Zād al-Musāfir* made in the 1070s or 1080s (Green 1985: 274–5). Here it is not made clear whether suffocation results from vapours, or from the womb itself, rising up the body. Scent therapy is recommended by the *Liber de sinthomatibus mulierum* texts, which repeat the story of the woman who lay as if dead but was known to be alive through the presence of the innate heat; as in Ibn al-Jazzār, it is Galen rather than Empedokles who becomes its hero.[51]

The influence of Galen grew in the West, with Soranos becoming 'virtually obsolete by the thirteenth century' (Green 1985: 316); the gynaecological treatises of the Hippocratic corpus languished in the wings until their publication in the sixteenth century. However, one Hippocratic text stayed at centre stage, due to its role in medical education: the *Aphorisms*, containing the alleged origin for the label/diagnosis 'hysteria' with which this chapter opened, 'In a woman suffering from *hysterika*, or having a difficult labour, a sneeze is a good thing.' It circulated not only in the Latin West, but also in the Arab world, where it was coupled with Galen's commentary. This commentary, probably written in AD 175 (D.W. Peterson 1977), pushed for the very specific translation *hysterikê pnix*, but was only restored to the West by Constantine's translation in the eleventh century.

But, as I have shown elsewhere (King 1993a: 57–61), it was not until Galen's commentary was read by sixteenth-century humanists that the aphorism came to be understood as something more specific than a general comment on all disorders of the womb. Latin translations of the *Aphorisms* which can be traced back to fifth/sixth century Ravenna are very literal, and do not associate 5.35 with suffocation of the womb, instead giving 'In a woman troubled by the womb, or giving birth with difficulty, a sneeze coming on unexpectedly is best.'[52] Subsequent Latin translations kept the aphorism within a very general gynaecological context, even when editions from 1476 onwards reinforced 'the unity between Galen and Hippocrates' (Nutton 1989: 425–6) by printing Galen's commentary beside the Hippocratic text. Despite Galen's conclusion that *hysterika* is equivalent to *hysterikê pnix*, the connection with the translation of the Hippocratic aphorism was not made.

Tradition or truth?

Before the sixteenth century, the hysteria tradition slowly accumulated descriptions, explanations and remedies. Some features, such as scent therapy at both ends of the body, the use of an extinguished lamp wick to rouse a patient, and the application of aromatic oils to the sexual organs, went back to Hippocratic medicine, as transmitted by Galen. Others, although deriving from the Hippocratics, were transformed by Galen's reinterpretation; for example, Hippocratic *pnix* concerns a hot womb seeking moisture to douse its fire, yet after Galen it becomes 'obstruction of respiration' and the womb is seen as being filled with cold and corrupt substances rather than being hot and light. Other features remained in the tradition despite all that could be said to condemn them, most notably the wandering womb, which co-existed happily with apparently contradictory elements such as anchoring membranes.

By the mid-sixteenth century, the hysteria tradition was complete: the translation into Latin of Arabic and Greek texts made available virtually all the authors discussed here. Every commentator on suffocation of the womb knew which ancient authorities to consult for a description. Since these ancient authorities had themselves known and used the work of many of their predecessors, it is not surprising that the result was often merely further repetition. Latin and Middle English treatises from the thirteenth to the fifteenth centuries tend to be heavily dependent on the Arabic writers' versions of Galen, and retain scent therapy, sneezing as a cure, bloodletting, and therapeutic intercourse.[53] However, in the mid-sixteenth century something new does occur: as hysteria comes to feature in physicians' case-books and recipe books, and in women's recipe collections (Williams 1990), we increasingly find a desire to compare authorities, not only with each other, but also with 'reality'.

As an example of this we may take Pieter van Foreest's *Observationum et curationum medicinalium* (1599), book 28 of which concerns women's diseases. As the title suggests, rather than simply repeating the authorities, he also presents cases which he himself has seen. Observations 25–34 involve suffocation of the womb, due to retained seed or menses in pregnant women, widows and others. Rhazes, Ibn Sīnā and Galen are cited; Galen is particularly favoured and, although he is a supporter of the Hippocratic revival, van Foreest accepts Galen's attack on the Hippocratic theory that the womb dries out and seeks moisture (1599: 154–5). He notes that the ancient authorities believed that the womb itself travelled through the body, whereas 'more recent writers' think it is only vapours that rise. The motif of the woman who uses hysteria to manipulate men is reintroduced, echoing Martial's epigram on women who announce they are *hysterica* in order to have intercourse with a young doctor; van Foreest states that some women simulate hysterical suffocation by imagining sexual intercourse, and he cites the 'notorious poem' mocking this (1599: 167).

His use of his own observations is first suggested when, after repeating Galen's statement that the symptoms from retained seed are worse than those from retained menstrual blood, he adds, *Et hoc est verum*, 'And this is true' (1599: 167). Even Galen must be tested against experience. Observation 27 repeats the story of the woman who lay as if dead, here based on Pliny, and gives the standard tests for life, adding that a sneeze is more reliable than the wool and water tests. Observation 28 includes Galen's story of the widow who was cured after passing some thick seed. In Observation 30, on hysterical suffocation in pregnancy, appear two cases van Foreest has seen for himself, one dated to October 1589, while in Observation 31 he gives the case of Eva Teylingia, who was married in 1561 and was related to his own wife. She was unsuccessfully treated by several named doctors for suffocation, and 'on the third day I myself was called'. Van Foreest's therapy – based on foul-smelling substances placed in the navel – was successful.

Works such as this were used by Edward Jorden in his 1603 *A Brief Discourse of a Disease Called the Suffocation of the Mother*. What is most striking about this work, in which he sets out to show 'in a vulgar tongue' that symptoms 'which in the common opinion are imputed to the Divell' are in fact due to the suffocation of the womb, is not the use of authorities such as Hippocrates, Galen, Pliny and Ibn Sīnā, but his citation of recent cases seen and reported by men such as van Foreest, Amatus Lusitanus and Andreas Vesalius.

Is this, then, the triumph of experience over tradition? It is not. As Thomas Laqueur put it, 'Experience, in short, is reported and remembered so as to be congruent with dominant paradigms' (1990: 99).[54] As in the history of green sickness, so in the hysteria tradition we find that certain elements have an extraordinary vitality, continuing to be repeated well into the nineteenth century. To take one example, Jorden himself repeats the story of the woman who lay as if dead but was known to be alive by the presence of innate heat; he uses the version of Pliny (Jorden 1603: 10^{v}). This story has inordinate staying power, turning up many times in seventeenth-century literature; for example, Guillaume de Baillou (1538–1616) claimed that many women were being buried alive because it was wrongly being assumed that the absence of a pulse indicated death (1643: 206). In the nineteenth century, Thomas Laycock's *Treatise on the Nervous Diseases of Women* has a section on 'Apparent Death', citing Diogenes Laertius' version of the same story, here diagnosed by Laycock as hysteria. As a general rule, Laycock recommends delaying burial in such cases until there are signs of decomposition (1840: 317–18; based on Le Clerc 1702: 85).

Such powerful motifs as apparent death weave in and out of the medical accounts of suffocation of the womb and, later, of hysteria. Do such elements survive simply because they make such good stories? Or is the persistence of certain parts of the tradition evidence for the *accuracy* of that tradition, and thus for the accuracy of the diagnosis of hysteria?

In the Hippocratic corpus, neither the diagnosis of *hysterikê pnix* nor that of hysteria is made. The womb moves, causing a range of symptoms according to its eventual destination. At an unknown date, possibly – from the medical papyri – in the second century BC, a disease category of 'suffocation of the womb' was created by the merger of a number of discrete Hippocratic texts giving symptoms, causes and therapies. Galen challenges the label, but keeps the concept and develops a different explanation based not on womb movement but on retained blood and seed. In the early Roman empire, further stories were added to the disease picture, surviving in the different cultural climates of the Latin West, Greek East, and Arab world. Particularly resistant to change proved to be two of the original Hippocratic components, womb movement and scent therapy: most powerful of all was the need to give the concept antiquity by tracing it back in its entirety to the father of medicine.

I would suggest that what we hear in such texts as these is not the insistent voice of a fixed disease entity calling across the centuries, but rather what Mary Wack has called 'the rustle of parchments in dialogue' (1990: 292 n.6). Indeed, it is rarely even a true dialogue. As in the creation of green sickness/chlorosis the texts, deaf to pleas from anatomy and experience, continue to tell one another the traditional stories. The language may shift – the womb travels, vapours rise, sympathy transmits symptoms up the body – but the message remains the same: women are sick, and men write their bodies.

CONCLUSION

By looking both at the cultural context in which Hippocratic gynaecology was created, and at the subsequent uses of that gynaecology in medical history, this book has explored two different senses of 'reading the female body in ancient Greece'. I have shown how heavily the things said to women by gynaecology in the Western biomedical tradition have relied on the uses of Hippocratic texts and of an idealised classical past. With the history of hysteria we have come full circle, and return to Isaac Baker Brown who thought that, in clitoridectomy, he had at last discovered a simple, surgical cure for the condition. The full irony of his strategy now emerges: by misreading one Hippocratic text on the excision of warts, he was finding the cure for a condition that depended, for its very existence, on reading other Hippocratic texts by a process of selection and omission that significantly altered the meanings they had originally carried.

Throughout the periods discussed here, within the tradition of learned medicine, a particularly strong inequality in the patient/doctor relationship has made gynaecology an area acknowledged by its male practitioners as exceptionally perilous to their reputations. Seymour Haden's statement of the basis of mid-nineteenth-century gynaecology remains not only a powerful image of the gender division central to this branch of medicine, but also an idealising version of the superiority of the male healer:

> We are the stronger, and they the weaker. They are obliged to believe all that we tell them. They are not in a position to dispute anything we say to them, and we, therefore, may be said to have them at our mercy. We, being men, have our patients, who are women, at our mercy.
>
> (*BMJ* 1867: 396)

One factor contributing to this inequality was the doctor's presentation of self, a conscious process of persuading the patients who were expected to read the messages carried by the body. Hippocratic medicine had its own versions of the fresh flower in Isaac Baker Brown's buttonhole. In both cultures, the construction of a medical self-image needed to persuade the patient both of the healer's structural superiority and of his curative powers.

In the nineteenth century a number of factors threatened this position of power. Gynaecology was not just socially marginal, in its combination of intellectual and manual skills spanning medical and surgical activities; the nature of its interests also involved risks to the reputation of the male practitioner as a gentleman. The process of being the object of gynaecology could also damage the female patient in terms of the prevailing values of her culture; the diagnostic use of the speculum was thought to encourage her sexual appetites. In ancient Greece, where methods were being developed to enable the body to be read systematically, the senses were also being questioned as reliable guides to such reading. The body could deceive its readers.

For Hippocratic medicine, it was Pandora's separately created and inherently deceptive body that most strongly argued for the need for a separate medicine for women. She made necessary man's *ponos*, in agricultural labour: she released diseases into the world from her jar. Yet her merger of *parthenos* and *gynê*, and her failure to match 'inside' to 'outside', also risked undermining all that Hippocratic medicine asserted about understanding the body. In this difficult situation, menstrual blood came to the rescue of the Hippocratic reputation; the 'sacrificial blood' of menstruation and the lochia was interpreted as a sign enabling the female body to speak more loudly to the trained reader, even while doubts were being expressed about the quality of information given orally by the female patient. The body imagery which stressed the analogies, from the point of view of therapy, between the top and bottom of the internal tube within the female body, reinforced this move. By breaking down the category of 'woman' through classifying the women they met as experienced or inexperienced, *gynê* or *parthenos*, the Hippocratics tried to control what they saw as the unstable nature of the female body, its soft wet flesh collecting, hiding, and pouring out the blood which made possible the continuation of human life itself. In particular, they problematised female puberty, the time when a *parthenos* began to become a *gynê*, because it raised the fear that the two kinds of woman could merge in one person – as they did in Pandora – and therefore raised the fear that a *gynê* could revert to being a *parthenos* once more.

Gynaecology is both about underlining women's difference and about healing women patients. Hippocratic 'gynaecology' covered far more of the female body than we would now expect. The model of the female body dominant in the Hippocratic *Diseases of Women* argued that its 'difference' resided not in the mere presence of some special organs, but rather in every piece of its flesh and in the movement of fluids within that flesh. This model expected what we would now consider abnormally heavy bleeding, and intervened to encourage bleeding when it did not occur on cue; its remedies included material substances which we would now see as carrying the risk of infection, but also explained symptoms in a way which linked Hippocratic accounts of the womb and therapies for its disorders to Artemis, releaser and strangled goddess. The Hippocratic texts should always be read with caution; their formats, as confident statements of fact, case histories or personal opinions, are rarely straightforward accounts of reality. Medical statements accepting women's knowledge of their bodies, citing it as the source for male knowledge, and linking women with a tradition of drug use could be cards played in a male game of control, in which – since nothing could be independently verified – 'women' can be pulled in as supporters for some male theories, even while being rejected as inferior guides by the Hippocratic physicians who claim to read the body. Although we cannot know how many women would have experienced Hippocratic gynaecology in the ancient Greek world, this book has suggested how the models of the body held out by gynaecology could have affected women's lives and has explored some of the situations in which images of the classical past have gone on to influence the later history of women and medicine.

The Hippocratic corpus includes so many types of text and variations in theory that it has been a rich source for those seeking the authority of the past for any new medical development. Changing fashions in the history of medicine have tried to manage this diversity by dividing the Hippocratic texts into Coan and Cnidian, genuine and spurious works, rational and irrational; they have made the texts the object of retrospective diagnosis, and forced Hippocratic therapies into becoming the origins of our science. The Hippocratic corpus – or an image of what it contains – is equally available to physicians, nurses, midwives, and practitioners of alternative medicine. The construction out of Hippocratic gynaecology of the disease labels 'chlorosis' and 'hysteria', their deliberately classicising names, and their subsequent clinical application, suggests how real women have been constrained by the authority gained by citing the classical texts. Green sickness and hysteria both argue strongly that marriage is the proper destination of every woman, while gynaecological surgery could be used to make a woman into a 'good wife' (I.B. Brown 1866a: 30). The history of the uses of the myth of Agnodike to support variations on the theme of the proper personnel for midwifery and the proper scope of that role demonstrates how professional groups and individuals coped with the paucity of Hippocratic references to midwives. The later history of Hippocratic medicine can also change the way we see the Greek past. It encourages us to question whether midwives would have been restricted to 'normal' births and male healers to 'difficult' births. Looking at the attempts to create a Hippocratic pedigree for nursing helps us to appreciate further the cultural imperatives which made Hippocratic doctors perform tasks we now classify as 'female'.

By the selective use of comparative materials, and the interrogation of the Hippocratic tradition, I have tried here to explore a Hippocratic gynaecology that can be replaced in its context of production rather than being judged by what have, historically, been the dominant standards of Western biomedicine. I have also argued that current trends towards seeing the *Diseases of Women* texts as women's traditional lore, allowing us a rare glimpse of women's lives preserved in men's words, risk allowing nostalgia for an imagined past to cloud our judgement of Hippocratic gynaecology. It is a gynaecology that puts a new spin on the concerns articulated in myth and ritual, working by a complex dance involving rhetoric and self-presentation in the creation of authority, telling a story about what is hidden, and building up a narrative designed to move the patient towards the conclusion which is health.

NOTES

INTRODUCTION

1 In the report of the same meeting given in *The Lancet* for 6 April 1876, this is less felicitously expressed as 'We have our patients, who are women, we being men, at our mercy.'

2 This definition comes after the statement, 'Wicked or wonderful, women are in the very centre of the human scene, and whatever may be thought about their performance in the play of life it can scarcely be ignored. In the etymological sense this is what gynaecology, the study of women, is all about. But, in fact, the meaning of the word is much narrower . . . '

3 Peterson argues that gynaecology and obstetrics were two of the last subjects to be established as specialities; the peak period for setting up specialist medical periodicals in gynaecology was not until 1870–79 (1978: 270–1) and special departments in hospitals were not set up, nor diplomas in gynaecology and obstetrics offered, until even later (1978: 279). See also Moscucci 1990: 50.

4 *TOSL* 7, 1865: 42. Aveling, in *Obstetrical Journal* 1 (1873–74): 806, made reference to this mixture of surgery and medicine in his comment, 'He who would treat the complaints peculiar to women with success must use his hand as well as his head.' See also Loudon 1986: 90.

5 The OSL felt that the development of obstetrical instruments was one of its main roles (*TOSL* 6, 1864: 17–18), and took pride in viewing the use of the obstetric forceps as defining the nature of English obstetrics (*TOSL* 7, 1865: 40). One of the presidents of the Society, Robert Barnes, regarded instruments as superior to books when trying to understand the history of obstetrics, saying that 'A book speaks only one language, an instrument speaks an universal language, and needs no translation' (*TOSL* 9, 1868: 22).

6 For the *Oath*, see L 4.628–33 and Loeb I, 298–301. The most up-to-date bibliography on the classical context is given in von Staden 1996; for a summary of the subsequent history of the *Oath*, see Nutton 1995b and 1997, and for its place in ancient medical ethics Flashar and Jouanna 1997.

7 Where these exist, references to the Loeb Classical Library translations, with Greek or Latin on the facing page, are given for Hippocratic texts. Where there is no edition in this series, I give references to the Littré edition, in the form L volume.page.

8 It is surprising that cross-cultural comparison remains so controversial, despite

years of dialogue between classics and anthropology. Gourevitch 1994 criticised the cautious use of cross-cultural comparison in Dean-Jones 1994 by asking, 'What does it matter here what happens in this or that American Indian tribe?' The debate is far from new; in his preface, Dodds 1951 noted that the use of 'recent anthropological and psychological observations' was 'generally received by the learned with apprehension and often with active distaste'.

9 For example, Girard 1983 suggests that Hippocratic medical texts provide 'a concrete idea' of 'the daily life of women', telling us about women's diet, family life, sexual habits, domestic activities and diseases, while Rousselle 1988: 2 claims that 'the little we know from ancient doctors' writings about women's bodies is precious, particularly their reports of the questions women asked and their ideas about their own bodies'.

10 *Contra* Pearcy 1992: 615, 'If nothing else, we share with them the facts of our bodies and their limitations.' There are some species-wide universals, such as a 40-week gestation period, but even these can be perceived in different ways across cultures (Browner *et al.* 1988: 682). For a summary of the argument for the co-construction of the natural and the social, see Moore and Clarke 1995: 257–8. See also A. Young 1980: 107: 'it is necessary to reject the positivist faith that Western medical beliefs reflect and describe the universal nature of medical events'. Annoni and Barras 1993: 189 argue that it was not until Hippocratic medicine that the Greeks came to see 'the body' as an autonomous object. On the history of the body, see Turner 1990; Porter 1991.

11 Cf. Riddle 1987: 33 who asserted that 'there is no serious challenge to the assertion that the writers of these nascently scientific works founded a rational medicine different from folkish ways'. On defining rationality, see B. Wilson 1979; Tambiah 1990.

12 On coprotherapy, see Carson 1990, von Staden 1991b and 1992a, and below, Chapter 7, pp. 153–4.

13 When Laqueur quotes this poem, he only gives the first two lines of the section reproduced here, thus avoiding the disturbing implication that men 'are' really women. On the *Masterpiece*, see further Porter 1985; Bullough 1972–3: 241 notes that the work contains approximately three to four times as much information on women as on men, and argues for its 'erotic' value.

14 Lonie 1981 discusses the arguments for regarding this treatise, with *Diseases IV*, as the work of one author.

15 Föllinger 1996: 21–3 gives a summary of the pre-Socratic philosophers' interest in the question of sex determination.

16 All references to Soranos' *Gynaecology* are followed here by the page numbers in Temkin's English translation, published in 1956 and reprinted in 1991. For the Greek text, see the Budé edition by Paul Burguière, Danielle Gourevitch and Yves Malinas, *Soranos d'Éphèse. Maladies des femmes*, issued from 1988 onwards.

17 See further Chapter 1, p. 21 below.

18 Cunningham 1997: 121 discusses Vesalius' vocabulary of body and text, arguing that Vesalius privileges the body over Galen while simultaneously seeing himself as being truly 'Galenic' in so doing. Cunningham does not, however, investigate Hippocratic imagery of reading the body as the source for Vesalius' emphasis shifting from that of preceding anatomists.

19 The original drawing is in the Hunterian Collection, Glasgow (Az. 1.4); in the

published version, table XXVI, figure 1, the book was omitted. See J.L. Thornton 1982, plate 8.

20 This was the 1526 *Hippocrates de foemina natura* published by Claudius Chevallonius in Paris.

21 Brown's innovatory role in gynaecological surgery in this period is clear from his frequent presentations to the Obstetrical Society of London; see their *Transactions*, from 1859 onwards, where he described successful ovariotomies and surgery for vaginal atresia.

22 *Proceedings of the Seventh Annual Meeting* . . . (1865: 15).

23 *Ibid.* (1865: 17).

24 I am deliberately not discussing here the uses of clitoridectomy in female initiation in many societies today, since Brown's use of the operation was as a cure for a perceived disease, rather than a practice carried out automatically to transform girls into women. There are, of course, parallels; for example, the ritual use of clitoridectomy can be phrased in terms of making women 'clean', and of bringing out their procreative potential. See further Hayes 1975; MacCormack 1977: 98 and van der Kwaak 1992.

25 Revd J.P. Gell and Mr Victor de Méric in *Proceedings of the Seventh Annual Meeting* . . . (1865: 20 and 31).

26 In the introduction to volume 8, which contains the *Diseases of Women*, Littré wrote, 'Ce tableau des affections utérines qui affligeaient les femmes grecques, il y a plus de deux mille ans, est tout à fait semblable à celui que nous avons présentement sous les yeux; et il est évident que rien, dans leur existence, ne les mettait, plus que nos femmes, à l'abri de ces malades si fréquentes et si pénibles' (2).

27 On coagulation, see further Chapter 4, p. 89.

28 For discussion of the history of the idea that masturbation has dire physical and mental effects on both sexes, see Gay 1984: 295–310. Peterson 1986 argues that Gay and others have only looked at one side of the medical debate.

29 For a feminist analysis of the excision of the clitoris from anatomy texts from 1900 to 1991, a manoeuvre possible only by defining it as a non-reproductive part in an otherwise reproductive system, see Moore and Clarke 1995.

30 *Proceedings of the Seventh Annual Meeting* . . . (1865).

31 He certainly referred to the Home as 'my child, this Institution'; see *ibid.* 33 and 38.

32 Tanner 1867 gave a number of cases in which Brown's operation had apparently failed, from his own practice and from among those patients treated by Brown himself; in the discussion which followed Tanner's paper, the surgeon Robert Greenhalgh listed further cases in which patients treated by Brown showed no lasting improvement (Tanner 1867: 378–9). Tanner 1867: 383 noted that 'There could be no doubt that so long as the wound remained unhealed, and even for some few weeks afterwards, no improper practices could be resorted to, as the parts were left very tender'. See also Hare 1962: 22 n.24.

33 *Lancet*, 6 April 1876: 396 gives 'we have constituted ourselves the true guardians of their interests, and in many cases, in spite of ourselves, we become the custodians of their honour. We are, in fact, the stronger, and they the weaker. They are obliged to believe all that we tell them. They are not in a position to dispute anything that we say to them. We, therefore, may be said to have them at

our mercy. We have our patients, who are women, we being men, at our mercy.' On the 'exaggerated anti-feminism' of Victorian gynaecology, see A. McLaren 1994: 276.

34 The full record of the meeting appears in the *British Medical Journal* for 6 April 1867, 395–410 and in the *Lancet* for the same year, 427–41; where the two versions differ, I have noted the discrepancies.

35 Aveling's interest in the clitoris included exhibiting to a meeting of the Obstetrical Society of London in January 1874 an unusually large specimen, 'symmetrically hypertrophied'. See *Obstetrical Journal* 1 (1873–4): 810–11.

36 *BMJ* 1867: 401 gives 'an operation, as Dr. Haden showed, that has been practised from the time of Hippocrates, and has been mentioned by all writers since that period again and again. Why, at your own Society's meeting, there were instruments in the room, I think, of Dionis, invented on purpose for clitoridectomy [cries of Oh! Oh!].' On 28 March 1866 an exhibition of instruments was held under the auspices of the OSL at the Royal College of Physicians (*Catalogue and Report* . . . 1867; *TOSL* 8, 1867: 37–8). The catalogue does not list any belonging to Dionis, but Brown himself displayed his set of ovariotomy instruments in their box 'of polished coromandel wood, lined with silk velvet' (1867: 141–3) and the forceps and scissors used by him when performing clitoridectomy (1867: 113, 192).

37 On the cultural significance of *ponos* as 'pain necessary to the successful completion of the process', see below Chapter 6, pp. 123–6.

38 *Lancet* 1867: 434.

39 *Ibid.* 435 has for the second of these phrases 'it is not kind to interrupt me'.

40 In Eisenberg's celebrated formulation 'patients suffer "illnesses"; physicians diagnose and treat "diseases"' (1977: 11), so that illness designates the feelings of the patient, disease the cultural label which a medical practitioner applies to those feelings.

1 CONSTRUCTING THE BODY: THE INSIDE STORY

1 Langholf 1996: 113–14 on Xen. *Cyropaedia* 1.6.14–17, where the knowledge of medicine needed to be an effective general is presented as a romanticised and anachronistic version of Hippocratic theories on diet, exercise and location; I owe this reference to Ann Hanson.

2 Cf. Loraux 1993: 162 (= 1981: 174): *parthenos* is 'not so much the word for virgin as it is for a woman who is not yet married; it is less a physical state than a social status'. However, in the Epilogue written for this English translation, Loraux moves away from the social status to recover the role of *parthenos* as virgin (1993: 243–4); but this is virginity in the sense of Sissa 1990, a status linked not primarily to age or to the presence of a hymen, but instead to an attitude to sexuality. I will argue in Chapter 4 that the Hippocratic texts fear a slippage of the apparently mature woman, the *gynê*, back into the category of the non-bleeding, non-productive *parthenos*.

3 On interpretations of this phrase see Loraux 1993: 243 n.26, who argues against using it to read 'He received the virgin of Zeus as woman.'

4 Medical: *DW* 1.37, L 8.92; 2.119, 8.260; 2.133, 8.302 etc.; non-medical: Herodotus 3.32, Homer *Il.* 6.58.

5 Zeitlin 1996: 65 argues that the 'hope' in the jar is more positive, and should be understood to mean a child. However, this does not take into account the uncertainty of reproduction in Hippocratic texts, where phantom pregnancy or a uterine mole are also possible consequences of the closure of the womb-jar. The shapeless false pregnancy known as the 'uterine mole' is attributed to the mixing of excessive menstrual blood and inadequate male seed in *DW* 1.71, L 8.148–50.

6 In *Ep.* 5.19, Loeb VII, 170, a female patient produces bile and blood 'from both the top and the bottom'.

7 Rousselle 1988: 28 argues that the ideas of pseudo-Aristotle *On sterility* may predate Aristotle.

8 Dean-Jones 1994: 45 argues that 'from the earliest times ancient Greek science, in accounting for the difference between male and female bodies, focused on physiological processes rather than structure'. While I agree entirely with Dean-Jones about the primacy of menstruation in Hippocratic gynaecology, I consider that the structural differences in the nature of the flesh are of equal importance.

9 Farrell-Beck and Kidd 1996: 326–7 note that late nineteenth-century women's own estimates of loss were on the high side, due to the difficulty of measuring the amount; it was only in the 1920s that a figure of two fluid ounces for average loss was reached.

10 See Laws 1990: 150 on the range of estimates of blood loss in current gynaecology textbooks.

11 In this case, the absence of menstruation for two years is juxtaposed with 'piles, in winter', suggesting that the latter provide an alternative to the former.

12 Some manuscripts continue '. . . and because of this she is hotter than the man', but the better manuscripts suggest '. . . and because of this it comes after that of the man'. See the readings given by L 8.12. Föllinger 1996: 31–2 nevertheless argues that *DW* 1.1 is proposing that women are the hotter sex, since women have more blood and it is also hotter blood. Hanson 1992b argues that, in *DW*, women's heat varies over the month, hottest just before menstruation and coldest at its end.

13 Galen, *Loc. Aff.* 6.5; K 8.420–4, 432, discussed at length in Chapter 11, pp. 232–3.

14 Sarrazin 1921: 15 suggests that these 'mouths' should be seen, not as the internal os and the external os of the cervix, but as the consequence of the idea that the human uterus, like those of animals, is dual.

15 See L 5.126; some manuscripts of this section give 'of the womb', others 'of the vagina', so that Smith's edition for the Loeb chose to give simply *ho stoma*.

16 *Ta gynaikeia noseumata kaleumena*, Loeb VIII, 94.

17 For the continuation of this assumption in twentieth-century anatomy texts, see Lawrence and Bendixen 1992.

18 Dean-Jones 1994: 70 also regards *trapô/trepô* as the verb for a turning away accompanied by actual movement from its normal position.

19 I owe this suggestion to some material on witchcraft in the early modern period provided by Diane Purkiss 1996: 95-8 and 108.

20 See Galen, *On Anatomical Procedures* 9.10 (trans. Duckworth *et al.* 1962: 14) and 9.14 (1962: 25).

21 C. Singer 1923: 217 tries to deny that connections existed between sacrifice and Hippocratic medicine, partly on the grounds that the Hippocratic system is too

'scientific' to have been based on anything from the temples. Annoni and Barras 1993: 193–4 look at the details of sacrificial dissection in order to determine how the demands of sacrifice allowed the sacrificer to develop knowledge of specific areas of the body.

22 On the cultural reasons both for the absence of human dissection in classical Greece, and for its use in Hellenistic Alexandria, see Scarborough 1976; Potter 1976; von Staden 1992d.

23 On Soranos see Manuli 1982; Gourevitch 1988: vii–xlvi; on the difficulty of reading our main source for the 'sects', see Temkin 1935; Frede 1982; Lloyd 1987: 158–71; W.D. Smith 1989.

2 DECEITFUL BODIES, SPEAKING BODIES

1 Gleason 1995: 93 points out that intonation of the seven vowels was also a very common procedure in magical rituals; they were also written out, sometimes to form a triangular shape. See for example Betz 1986: 101–2 (PGM V.24–30); Betz 1986: 3 (PGM 1.15–19).

2 *On Decorum* is a relatively late text on medical etiquette, perhaps dating to after 300 BC. The Greek text of *Precepts* 10 suggests that the extravagant hats and perfume are worn in order to cure the patient; in his translation for Loeb I, 327 Jones finds this 'very strange', and therefore translates instead 'in order to gain a patient'. However, it may be wrong to reject the idea that the appearance of the healer can itself heal.

3 Parker 1983: 108 suggests that 'It is unlikely that the purifier had always been the degraded figure who appears in most of our texts.'

4 On public healing and its efficacy in the early modern period, see Lingo 1986.

5 The text here may be interpreted to mean either that they disobey the doctors, or that they abandon them.

6 The phrase *hôs ephê*, 'so he/she said', is not used of male patients in the *Epidemics*.

7 Reading here *ho drôn*, following Langholf 1990: 51 n.78.

8 W.D. Smith's translation for the Loeb gives, 'The task is to bring the body under consideration. Vision, hearing, nose, touch, tongue, reasoning arrive at knowledge.'

9 Phrontis occurs as a female proper name in *Il.* 17.40, and a male name in Paus. 10.52 and *Od.* 3.282, making it particularly appropriate for a woman who is to be trusted. Manuscript C however has 'If *phrontis* is present . . . '

10 *Our Bodies, Ourselves* was published by the Boston Women's Health Book Collective in 1971; see Moore and Clarke 1995: 276–7 for discussion of this and subsequent developments in feminist visual representations of the body.

11 Lloyd 1983: 71 n.51 suggests this is 'another woman', but this is less likely here.

12 The central text of the *Articella* group is Hunain ibn Ishaq's *Isagoge*, also translated from Arabic by Constantine the African; in addition to the *Aphorisms*, the nucleus also contains Galen's *Tegni* (the *Ars parva*), the Hippocratic *Prognostics*, Theophilus on urines, and Philaretus on pulses. On the *Articella*, see Kibre 1945: 382–4; Baader 1984: 259; Nutton 1989; Kristeller 1976: 66–7.

13 Lichtenthaeler 1963: 45 labels the apparent mismatch between the very general title and the specific contents as the 'false enigma' of this text, false because the point of the text is that such precise predictions can only be possible in the

limited field of the acute fevers (1963: 55). Kibre 1945: 387 argues that the text was chosen for translation into Latin in late fifth-century Ravenna because of the prevalence there of malarial conditions similar to those described in *Prognostics*.

14 On parallels from the poetry of Hesiod and Homer, where the poet or seer has the power to reveal the synthesis of past, present and future which constitutes the truth (*alêtheia*), see Detienne 1967: 130 n.101.

15 Edelstein 1931: 74 points out that an even more individualist approach to prognosis is taken in *Diseases* 1, where the age and gender of the patient and her previous medical history, as well as the time of year, are identified as factors making it difficult to predict how a disease will progress.

16 Demand 1994: 81–5 argues that descriptions such as this are best seen as malaria, of which nosebleeds are one of the secondary symptoms. While her insistence on the risks posed by malaria to pregnant women, due to the suppression of cell-mediated immunity in pregnancy, is very valuable, and accounts for the level of miscarriages in this *kausos*, here I am instead concentrating on how the Hippocratics would have made sense of the situation in terms of their models of the body.

17 Her case is discussed in more detail in Chapter 3, p. 70.

18 The *Epidemics* cases involving pregnancy are conveniently collected and translated by Demand 1994: 168–83.

3 THE DAUGHTER OF LEONIDAS: READING CASE HISTORIES

1 The distinction between notes and finished works was used as far back as Galen to classify Hippocratic texts; see Pigeaud 1988: 306 and 312, who shows how Galen's ideal of a genuinely Hippocratic work would need to demonstrate a particular kind of condensed style, believed to have been aimed at fellow doctors for whom it was not necessary to give every detail.

2 A hairy body and a beard are the features which the Christian saint Wilgefortis is granted by God in answer to her prayers that she may be able to avoid marriage. The variation in body hair between men and women is far from straightforward, however, the cultural line between 'masculine' and 'feminine' hair growth being drawn in a totally arbitrary way (Ferrante 1988: 231).

3 One of the best examples of the influence of the model of the Hippocratic *Epidemics* is the *Liber Epidemiorum et Ephemeridum* of Guillaume de Baillou (1640), in which constitutions and case histories are given for the 1570s. In the late eighteenth century, Sprengel claimed that 'the influence of the case-histories in the Hippocratic *Epidemics* was crucial to the development of sixteenth-century medicine' (Lonie 1985: 160). On Baillou, see the discussion by Lonie 1985: 169–74.

4 In a rare example of a medical writer dethroning the *Aphorisms*, Nutton 1989: 437 points out that the Paracelsian Petrus Antonius Severinus deliberately rejected them as part of his recasting of Hippocrates in a Paracelsian mould.

5 See Chapter, 2 p. 49.

6 Dean-Jones 1994: 139–40, 'In fact this syndrome (vicarious menstruation) does occur, though it is rare.'

7 It is used at *Ep.* 2.2.8, L 5.88, Loeb VII, 32; 3.16 (twice), L 3.122, Loeb I, 170.

8 In *Ep*. 2.1.7, a discussion of the diversion of bodily fluids to parts of the body far from their organ of origin, we read 'Violent nosebleeds cure many ills, as in the case of Heragoras. The physicians were unaware of it' (trans. Loeb VII, 26). The verb used here is *gignôskein*; LSJ (s.v.) suggests that *oida* implies 'I know by reflection', whereas *gignôskô* means 'I know by observation.' Another interpretation of the failure of the *iatroi* to observe/be aware of what happened to Heragoras may therefore be that they had already abandoned his case before the therapeutic nosebleed happened.

9 On the unsatisfactory attempts of the late nineteenth-century Hippocratic scholar Carl Fredrich to classify the texts of the Hippocratic corpus by intended audience, see Pigeaud 1988: 307–8.

10 Dean-Jones 1994: 140 proposes that the doctor failed to understand that a nosebleed is good when the menses are suppressed, and therefore wrongly continued his treatment after the healing nosebleed had occurred. On this reading too, the daughter of Leonidas is another black raven.

11 Edelstein 1939 conveniently summarises earlier scholars' claims for the authenticity of the works in the corpus.

12 See Edelstein 1939: 143: 'The longing to read Hippocrates' own writings, the difficulty of becoming reconciled to the fact that they are not extant, should at any rate be no reason for setting up the methodological postulate that they must have been preserved.'

13 Although Wellmann 1922, followed by W.H.S. Jones 1947, suggests Soranos.

14 The two aphorisms are considered together in the commentary of Theophilus (ed. Dietz vol.2: 462); cf. Aristotle *GA* 727a11–15; *HA* 587b31ff.; Byl 1980: 74.

15 Following the reading of Zeuxis, rather than Galen; cf. L 5.268–9; Manetti and Roselli 1982: 5.

16 The 'daughter of Teleboulos' in *Ep*. 1.16 (Loeb I, 170) dies on the sixth day after giving birth; the 'daughter who lived with the wife of Komes the market supervisor' conceived and had a difficult delivery (*Ep*. 4.24, Loeb VII, 116), while the 'sister of Harpalides' gave birth to a daughter (*Ep*. 7.6, Loeb VII, 306–8). I would argue that the mutual reinforcement of 'daughter of' and *pais* is another matter.

17 These texts use either *apethanen* (7.36–8, Loeb VII, 340; 81, Loeb 378; 109, Loeb 404; 116, Loeb 406) or *eteleutêsen* (7.10, Loeb VII, 314; 14–21, Loeb 322–4; 28–9, Loeb 334; etc.).

18 A comparable passage may be *Ep*. 4.49, Loeb VII, 144; the case of the daughter of Histaios, who died while young (*apethane, paidiskê*). As W.D. Smith points out, *paidiskê* is an ambiguous term, which could be translated as 'little girl', 'maid' or even 'prostitute'. Since the girl has been taking purgatives, which appeared to help, before her death, she too could be interpreted as being too young for her body to take such purging.

19 Littré 8.23 does not bring out in translation the point that the text separates blood loss by vomiting from blood loss through the rectum; it is only the latter which is thought to be something particularly affecting *parthenoi*, and this is consistent with the suggestion that the route to the head and nostrils is treacherous in younger women. Damascius comments on *Aph*. 5.33, 'Not only from the nostrils, but also from the rectum' (ed. Dietz vol.2: 462).

4 BLOOD AND THE GODDESSES

1 I am using the new edition of Flemming and Hanson (forthcoming) here.

2 An extensive literature exists on the bear rituals of Brauron and on the passage of Aristophanes, *Lys.* 641–7, which is our main literary source for them; Osborne 1985: 170 argued that, 'Brauron provides the structure within which adolescent sexuality can be comprehended.' On the symbolism of the bear, Perlman 1989 suggests that its hibernation is linked with the shy, retiring *parthenos*, while its nurturing and protective qualities are associated with the mature *gynê*. On the age of the young girls 'acting the bear', see Perlman 1983. On the myths of Callisto, who became a bear in order to give birth, see Sale 1965.

3 *NC* 30, L 7.538 and *DW* 1.1, L 8.10–14, discussed in chapter 1, p. 32.

4 Flemming and Hanson (forthcoming) note the large number of similarities between the vocabulary of *Sac. Dis.* and *Virg.*; Demand 1994: 97 points out that both texts see blockage of internal channels as the origin of the symptoms experienced.

5 Loraux 1984 (trans. 1995) emphasises the Greek linguistic equivalence of strangling and hanging (from a beam or tree): 'The essential lies within this constantly repeated equivalence, "hanging or strangulation"' (1984: 201; 1995: 104). This contrasts with Roman practice, which regarded as significant whether or not a person had remained in contact with the ground in death; this meant that those who were hanged could not be buried, while those who were strangled did not lose this right.

6 The same expression is used by Soranos, *Gyn.* 1.33; T 31; see also 1.17; T 15.

7 I owe this point to Geoffrey Lloyd. Lefkowitz 1981: 14 translates as '*After* the first menstrual period.'

8 The phrase is also used in *The Art* 7 (Loeb II, 200).

9 Demand 1994: 101 argues that 'it seems likely that the *manteis* who treated young girls suffering from the illness of maidens were often, like the traditional midwives, women'. I do not find her evidence for this persuasive, and have therefore taken them to be male.

10 Baumann 1939 suggests that the offering of garments is a substitute for the sacrifice of one's own body; however, the fact that it is the plural *gynaikes* rather than the singular *parthenos* making the offering renders this possibility unlikely here.

11 See above, Chapter 1, p. 28.

12 *Venit nunc mihi in mentem Milesianum virginum novum insaniae genus, de quibus Plutarchus scilicet. illae se vulgo suffocabant. aeris intemperiem nonnulli id malum attulisse putabant. qui sapientiores habebantur, Diis illud acceptum referebant; at noster auctor idem antiquissimus, ac prudentissimus horum malorum culpam omnem in menstruorum detentionem, ac suppressionem referendam semper censuit.*

13 Cf. *Mor.* 253e, in which the second of Kylon's daughters to hang herself ensures beforehand that her body will be modestly laid out after her death.

14 Baumann 1939 goes further, suggesting that maidens' natural 'Todes-Bereitschaft' leads to the fascination held by suicide for young girls, and states – as a point so obvious that it needs no support from footnotes – that women committing suicide have always preferred drowning or hanging over other options.

15 See Prince and Tcheng-Laroche 1987.

16 Loraux 1987: 61 argues for tragedy and gynaecology as separate universes, and suggests that, in tragedy, the noose is generalised as a womanly form of death and opposed to the sword as a manly mode (1987: 16). I would instead position Phaedra's death by the noose as a deliberate attempt to mimic the proper mode of suicide of a wronged virgin.

17 For the imagery of wounding in defloration and pregnancy, see Plut. *Mor.* 769e.

18 See the analysis of the Herodotus story in Vernant 1968: 15–16, where *parthenos* equals true warrior.

19 On the use of *agnos castus* in medical herbalism today, particularly for what are perceived as menstrual disorders, see Mills 1992, who suggests that it does not contain any hormones but can nevertheless cause hormonal changes.

20 Some of the text of Meuli 1975 represents a reconstruction of Meuli's views by Reinhold Merkelbach; the section on Artemis appears on 1043–7.

21 Calame 1977: 271–2 and n.189 notes that girls are typically changed into trees immediately before or after their first sexual experience, or in order to avoid it; in such cases, the tree is rarely a fruit-bearing variety.

22 On the 'plant code' see Detienne 1972.

23 This conclusion is similar to that of Kahn 1978: 103–4, but goes further in the parallels between womb and *agnos* and between the mode of operation of the goddess and the herb.

24 As Pigeaud 1988: 322 notes in connection with Laennec's use of analogies from 'everyday life' and from the natural world in order to describe the sounds he thought he could hear when using the newly invented stethoscope, one of the risks of using analogy is that the world of everyday life changes, and the once clear and helpful analogy becomes obscure: 'La référence à l'expérience commune risque de changer avec la société.'

25 On *hiereion* see Casabona 1966: 30–8; this passage of *DW* is noted by Lloyd-Jones 1983: 99 and n.80 in a brief discussion of female blood loss, but its implications are not drawn out. For the gynaecological literature, Fasbender 1897: 181 and n.2; 225 n.4.

26 This is also the modern medical view; menstrual blood cannot clot, since it has already clotted in the endometrial cavity and has then been reliquefied by enzymes. However, some clots are passed, because in a heavy flow some blood passes out too quickly to have undergone the clotting and reliquefying process. This means that both the Greek view (clots) and the Victorian view (no clots) are 'right'.

27 There is no other evidence for Amnias as a cult title of Eileithyia, although Hesychius (s.v.) gives Amnisia, 'of Amnisos'. An ancient sanctuary of this goddess in the caves at Amnisos on Crete is mentioned in *Od.* 19.188, supported by archaeological evidence. See Willetts 1958; T.H. Price 1978: 81 ff. According to Call. *Art.* (162, and scholiast), Artemis is associated not only with childbirth, but also with the nymphs of Amnisos, while Paus. 1.18.5 reports a tradition that Eileithyia was born there.

28 The reference to Hunain's note to *On Anatomical Procedures* 12.4 appears in Duckworth *et al.* 1962: 117, where the anatomical part of the translation team, Towers, added 'A foetus in its amniotic sac looks very like this.' In pseudo-Aristotle, *On Sterility* 635b14 and Soranus, *Gyn.* 1.57 (T 58) the foetal membrane

is known as the *chorion* or as the *angeion* because it 'encases the embryo like an *angeion*': the womb is seen as an *angos* or 'jar' in the Hippocratic corpus too, either by way of analogy (*Gen.* 9, L 7.482) or by saying that the womb 'is' a jar (*Ep.* 6.5.11, Loeb VII.258 with the commentary of Galen).

5 ASKLEPIOS AND WOMEN'S HEALING

1 Mikalson 1983: 22 and 122 n.24 distinguishes the functions of prevention and cure. On local healing cults around Athens, see Garland 1992: 132–3. Demand 1994: 95 distinguishes between 'establishment gods' such as Asklepios, with whom doctors had good relationships, and 'marginal religious healers', among whom she includes those attacked in *On the Diseases of Virgins*. Since both groups recommend dedications to the gods, I have here preferred to take them together in order to compare their methods with those of the Hippocratics.

2 The evidence is summarised by Demand 1994: 91–2. See further Aleshire 1989 and 1991.

3 Literary evidence for the cult in Edelstein and Edelstein 1945; for these examples, see the texts cited there as testimonia 423.3, 423.5, 423.4 and 9, 423.6, 423.12, 423.27 and 423.19. *Iamata* also survive from Rome, Athens and Lebena.

4 See for example the experiences of Aelius Aristides discussed in Chapter 6, pp. 128–9 (test. 408; Edelstein and Edelstein 1945: 154).

5 Formulations such as these are particularly problematic when we remember that Galen himself not only cited dreams sent by Asklepios as a way of avoiding serving on a dangerous army campaign, but also attributed the cure of his abscess to the god; see *On My Own Books* 2 (K 19.19), trans. P.N. Singer 1997: 8.

6 See Cunningham 1997: 202 on the influence of the nineteenth-century separation of religion from science on our understanding of Renaissance anatomy.

7 See Purkiss 1996: 77: 'The idea that belief in the supernatural is mistaken is taken to be necessary to histories of religion.'

8 See *ibid.* 78 on 'the hollowness at the centre of historical discourse on the supernatural . . . The supernatural must be transformed into something else so that it can be discussed.'

9 This inscription is given by Clement of Alexandria, *Stromateis* 5.1.13.3 (Edelstein and Edelstein 1945, test. 336) and Porphyry, *On Abstinence* 2.19.5 (test. 318).

10 The attempts of Herzog 1931 to explain these rationally, in terms of an extended period of amenorrhoea followed by a pregnancy, are discussed by Demand 1994: 93–4.

11 The *iamata* from Epidauros include a Spartan mother sleeping at the temple for her daughter (test. 423.21), and a father who dreams on behalf of a missing son (test. 423.24); see also Burkert 1987: 15–16 on Tibullus envisaging his beloved Delia sitting outside the temple of Isis in gratitude for his cure. See also Mikalson 1983: 22–3.

12 Dillon 1994: 240 suggests that patients would normally go to their nearest Asklepieion, but would travel to a major one if they thought it necessary. For an example see *Anth. Pal.* 6.330, discussed by Garland 1992: 133. Osborne 1985: 154–72, cited by Demand 1994: 90, shows that even at Brauron women travelled a considerable distance to make offerings to Artemis.

13 The meaning of the placebo effect will be discussed in Chapter 7.

6 WHAT DOES MEDICINE MEAN? THE PAIN OF BEING HUMAN

1 A. Young 1980: 102 suggests that 'Western society . . . uniquely gives some priority to preserving biological life even after social life has permanently ended.'

2 In terms of the illness/disease distinction, chronic illness can sometimes be seen as a set of experiences which have failed to find a disease label; in other cases, the label is applied, but carries with it none of the expectations of treatment and cure which normally characterise a disease.

3 Littré suggests that the appendix to *DW* 1 (92–109, L 8.222–32) is an extract from this lost work. See also Schöne 1924.

4 A *thêriakê* is literally an antidote to the bite of a venomous beast; Nicander wrote a poem, the *Thêriaka*, describing such antidotes.

5 Conway and Slocumb 1979: 248 point out that less volatile oils are produced in plants grown at high altitude; although Dioscorides was admirably aware of the effect of different sites, times of collecting and modes of storage on drug efficacy, he regarded drugs gathered from high places as being stronger (*Materia medica*, preface 6; Scarborough and Nutton 1982: 196).

6 See also *Places in Man* 41, Loeb VIII, 80–2; drugs do not always act in the same way, so that a laxative may even, on occasion, constipate.

7 See for these examples CML IV, tables I and II. I owe this reference to Ann Hanson.

8 Nearer to home, Helman 1978 has demonstrated how general practitioners working in Western biomedicine adapt their explanations to the patient to take account of folk beliefs about feeding a cold and starving a fever.

9 These 'conditions' include sexual intercourse; in *Loc. Aff.* 6.5, Galen's description of a woman suffering from symptoms caused by retained female seed, the warming effects of the remedies rubbed on to her external genitals makes her feel 'pain (*ponos*) and pleasure (*hêdonê*) just as in sexual intercourse'.

10 Voicelessness is a particularly common symptom in the *Epidemics*, usually taken as a very bad sign. See for example *Ep.* 5.63, Loeb VII, 196; *Ep.* 5.80, Loeb VII, 204; in *Ep.* 5.55, Loeb VII, 192 the patient is voiceless, until on the seventh day she speaks, the fever weakens, and she survives.

11 As argued by Hanson 1991: 94, followed by Demand 1994: 129. The version given by Littré *DW* 1.34, L 8.80, discussed by Dean-Jones 1994: 212, appears to suggest that the womb contracts around the baby; however, Grensemann 1982: 126 points out that the words *malista de tês hysterês* stating that 'above all, her womb' wraps around the baby, do not appear in 50 per cent of the manuscript tradition.

12 Cf. *Dis.* 1.14, Loeb V, 124; 1.20, Loeb V, 144 etc.

13 Greek: *odunê narkodês kai aporos pherein.*

14 Gleason 1995: 82–102 discusses the importance of voice in the Second Sophistic.

15 See Pearcy 1988: 380–2 on the relationship between the diaries and the *Sacred Tales*; Pearcy (379) describes the 'sophisticated narrative self-consciousness' of the *Tales*, while Perkins 1992: 248 shows how the latter is a 'shaped discourse'. Whereas the diaries contain 'facts', the *Tales*, by disordering events, represents 'truth'.

7 READING THE PAST THROUGH THE PRESENT: DRUGS AND CONTRACEPTION IN HIPPOCRATIC MEDICINE

1 Guthrie's article for nurses on the early history of their profession suggested that 'perhaps the earliest nurse in history was some wise old woman, skilled in the use of homely remedies' (1953: x). The view that women have, throughout history, been the keepers of drug lore for the benefit of the household is now a commonplace in contemporary historical studies, particularly for the early modern period, from which women's recipe/drug collections survive. William Withering's 1785 account of how he came to use the foxglove describes how he was given an old Shropshire woman's secret recipe for dropsy, made of over twenty herbs, of which the only active ingredient was the foxglove. He tried different ways of preparing the remedy, but states that the old woman 'overlooked' the diuretic effect and used the drug wrongly, to produce vomiting and purging (1785: 2). This story can be used to show male practitioners playing down their debts to women; but it could equally be used to show that women's knowledge was not as effective as they liked to think.

2 Indeed, Riddle himself has shifted away from the warning he issued in an earlier study of the *Materia Medica* of Dioscorides: 'If one searches the historical documents of medicine to find those drugs which appear in our modern medical guides, we distort the record' (1985: xxii).

3 The main problem of Riddle's recent work is that it uses 'contraception' simultaneously in a modern sense, to denote something used at intercourse to prevent pregnancy (as in the case of the testimony given by Béatrice to the Inquisition, where she inserts 'a certain herb' before intercourse, 1997: 10–34) and in a pre-modern sense, as intervention in very early pregnancy before the seed has set or the foetus 'quickened'.

4 For modern examples of this belief from World Health Organisation data, see Snowden and Christian 1983: 126–8.

5 *Haitines autôn pepeirêntai pollakis*, 'who have frequent experience of these things'.

6 The date of this novel is not known, but it is thought to be from the first century BC or the first century AD.

7 In the first half of the first century AD, the Roman physician Scribonius Largus (*Compositione*, preface, 5) understood the Oath in the wider sense; see Mudry 1997: 307–9.

8 The punishment was temporary exile; Justinian, *Digest* 47.11.4; 28.2.27, 28. A disputed fragment, attributed to Lysias (fr.10 Gernet), is the only evidence that abortion was a criminal offence in classical Athens; it suggests that a woman was forbidden to seek an abortion if her husband died while she was pregnant, because the heir must be allowed to claim the estate. As in the Roman case in the third century AD, the rights of the *kyrios* outweigh those of the mother. The rights of the child do not come into the calculation; the foetus was not regarded as being independent of its mother's body, and so it had no legal status.

9 Frier 1994: 328–9 has usefully collected the scattered references in Riddle which reveal his underlying hypothesis concerning the transmission of birth control information in antiquity.

10 These assumptions are also criticised by Scarborough 1991: 162.

11 The current readiness to do this recalls the valuable arguments of Diane Purkiss 1996: 20–2 on how the image of the healer-witch, popular today, 'offers nostalgic pleasures to anxious urban residents'.
12 This passage was brought to my attention by Ann Ellis Hanson, on whose forthcoming edition and translation of the text my version is based.
13 Dioscorides 5.100 gives this identification.
14 For China in the period 1600–1850, Furth 1986: 64–5 argues that lists of drugs to be avoided in pregnancy could be turned around and used as lists of abortifacients. I owe this reference to Monica Green. See also Porter 1994: 150 on *Aristotle's Masterpiece*. Conway and Slocumb (1979: 243) point out that, in a modern Roman Catholic community in Spanish New Mexico, treatment described as being for a 'late period' is morally preferable to 'abortion'.
15 The Greek phrase in *DW* 1.78 which he uses is *hysteron dynaitai ekballein*.
16 Cf. Porter 1990: 16, who argues for the long eighteenth century that 'We cannot dismiss the possibility that the traffic in female medicines to restore the courses was aiming to do precisely that.'
17 Cf. Browner *et al.* 1988: 684, where it is pointed out that an Aztec remedy for headaches can be analysed in terms of their claim that a headache can be caused by excess blood in the head, so that we need to discover whether the remedy would cause a nosebleed; or in Western bioscientific terms, so that we investigate whether the remedy cures a headache.
18 Farnsworth *et al.* 1975b: 739 also question, from a scientific viewpoint, the reliability of some animal studies of this kind, when there is no use of control animals to suggest 'the expected rate of successful pregnancies in the strains and species used had no plant extract been administered'.
19 Not given in Riddle's 1992 bibliography, this is presumably a reference to the first edition of Harborne's *Introduction to Ecological Biochemistry*. In subsequent editions, this material is given at 1982: 100 and 1993: 105–6. However, Harborne is merely quoting earlier work, such as the opposed findings of Heftmann and Dean, glossed over by Riddle.
20 Introducing a list of over 100 plants with a reputation as contraceptives or abortives, de Laszlo and Henshaw 1954: 627 warned that 'Some of the plants listed are known to contain poisonous substances – any indiscriminate use would be dangerous.'
21 The appendix to *Diseases of Women* 1 gives a formula for 'the black drug' (1.96, L 8.222–4), perhaps suggesting that colour was thought to be powerful in ancient compound drugs.
22 Cf. von Staden 1991b: 58–60 on the use of *skilla* (squill) in purificatory rituals, the expulsion of scapegoats, and treatments for the womb; von Staden 1992b and Chapter 4, pp. 86–8, on *Vitex agnos castus*.
23 In his review of von Staden (1989) for the *Society for Ancient Medicine and Pharmacy Newsletter* 17 (1989): 39–40, Robert K. Ritner detected bias against Egyptian medicine here too, with Greek culture being seen as 'pure' and Egypt being blamed for elements seen as 'barbarous'.
24 Hopkins 1965: 143–50 points out that it is not an 'obvious' method, and cites comparative materials indicating that it needs to be both explained and learned.
25 P. Colon. 7511 = *SLG* 478; the translation is from Bing and Cohen 1991: 54–6.
26 In his notes to Galen's *The Construction of the Embryo* 1, P.N. Singer 1997: 421

claims that the reference in the Hippocratic *Nature of the Child* 13 to women's gossip that one does not conceive if 'the seed comes out' after intercourse could be read as a further allusion to *coitus interruptus*. This would involve understanding *gonos*, 'seed', here to mean 'penis'. Singer's attribution of this idea to Ann Hanson should be discounted (Ann Hanson, pers. comm.).

8 GENDER AND THE HEALING ROLE

1 See, for example, Davis 1988: 158, where Hippocrates becomes 'the "Father of Holistic Medicine"'. The advantage of Hippocratic medicine is its sheer range, making it possible for almost any type of healing to find a precursor; thus in S. Moore 1988: 134–5, 'Hippocrates was the first physician to identify a link between spinal problems and ill health', while Chaitow 1982: 23 claims that 'Manipulative methods as part of medical treatment are known to date back to earliest times. Hippocrates wrote of their value.' MacEoin 1992: 8 makes homeopathy 'a concept which had existed from the time of Hippocrates'. In some alternative health guides for a lay audience, the orthodox biomedical image of Hippocrates as the ideal doctor is both maintained and challenged with a claim that the medical profession ignored his 'observations on cure by "similars"' for a millennium, during which the folk-medicine of ordinary people kept the principle alive; see Castro 1990: 3.

2 Davies 1980 (quotation, p.11) was the first collection of essays to criticise the dominant model, characterised by another contributor to the collection, Katherine Williams, as the Sarah Gamp to Florence Nightingale model. See also Summers 1988: 13–14, who points out that Dickens' Sarah Gamp is intended not as a historical portrait, but as a caricature.

3 This is repeated in the 8th edition of Deloughery 1977: 8–9.

4 Based on a 1958 rewriting of Goodnow 1961 (itself first published in 1919); but see Edelstein 1931: 88 n.3.

5 Most famously, *On the Sacred Disease* argues that the symptoms of the seizures described are due not to the gods but to the movement of phlegm in the body. However, when the writer states that these seizures are no more sacred than any other disease, he is not saying that no disease is sacred. Attempts to present Hippocratic medicine as an attack on religious healing can go too far, and give the misleading impression that the intervention of the gods is totally rejected; in fact *Decorum* 6 (Loeb II, 288) states that all cures are ultimately from the gods.

6 On the element of performance in Galen, set in the context of medicine as 'public acts of rhetorical staging' in the Second Sophistic, see von Staden 1994: 50, who argues that Galen's dissections too should be seen as rhetorical acts rather than as scientific experiments.

7 This sentence is based on Nutting and Dock 1907: 82 where it read: 'Women in Greece, as in all countries, doubtless did much noble if unnoticed work as nurses.' Nutting and Dock attribute this to the original German edition of Baas 1889.

8 It is, of course, clear that no group of healers in the ancient world could be seen as constituting a 'profession' in anything like the modern sense of the term defined by Goode 1960: 903, a definition which requires a licensing system, strong identification of members with their profession, and freedom from lay evaluation.

9 IMAGINARY MIDWIVES

1 I owe the title of this chapter to Angelos Chaniotis, who pointed out to me that the most prominent midwives of Greek antiquity tend to be 'imaginary' ones; the invisible midwives of the Hippocratic corpus, Artemis, Agnodike . . . See also Nancy Demand 1994: 66, who calls the Hippocratic midwives 'shadowy figures'.

2 Harley 1990: 11 argues that reputation, in the form of 'acceptability among respectable neighbours', was more important than technical expertise.

3 The 'Changing Childbirth' initiative currently encourages midwives to do academic research.

4 Physicians were not always as interventionist and arrogant as some feminist historians have argued; Kass found that the casebooks of nineteenth-century American physicians showed them feeling frightened and perplexed by childbirth, while worrying that their textbooks were 'vague and indefinite' (1995: 205). As a result, they acted according to the parturient woman's own assessment of her condition, and preferred to sit down and wait rather than intervene. This is also true of the seventeenth century, when Percival Willughby (1863: 209) wrote in about 1672 of the benefits of trusting in Dame Nature rather than 'too much officious doings'. See King 1995b.

5 Or perhaps 'with a basic education', translating *grammaton*; the Budé edition suggests 'possède une instruction élémentaire' (*Gyn.* 1.2.5–6).

6 M.L. West translates it in *GLP* as 'birthcord-snipper'.

7 Aristotle, *HA* 587a9 says that cutting the cord is the job of the midwife (*maia*; cf. Plato, *Theaetetus* 149d–e) but the need to specify this may suggest that other healers are present (Dean-Jones 1994: 213).

8 See *DW* 1.2, L 8.20; 1.65, L 8.134; 2.114, L 8.246.

9 Discussion of the textual problems in Matakiewicz 1932–33; Liénard 1938; Holzworth 1943; Schwartz 1957; Nickel 1981: 170. On the name, Sankovich 1988: 64 suggests that it derives from *agnôs*, and should mean 'the unknown'; this explanation does not account for the *dikê* element.

10 Cf. Bolton 1881: 5: 'the first female practitioner who received a medical education appears to be Agnodice'. Withers 1979, writing for an audience of American nurse-midwives, also follows the 'first obstetrician' route.

11 Withers 1979 produces a new connection between the elements of the Hyginus story and the historical facts about Herophilos by suggesting that the midwifery manual was written as a direct result of 'the stir one of his pupils had made in Athens'!

12 It is also possible to believe in Agnodike while dismissing the 'Herophilos connection' on the grounds that he is not known to have practised at Athens (Delacoux 1834: 26; cf. Nickel 1981: 171–2); however, the alternative reading, which progresses from Herophilos' absence from Athens to assume that Agnodike would therefore have had to travel to Alexandria to meet him, is equally valid.

13 For the uses of this gesture in antiquity, see King 1986b: 61–8.

14 Blundell 1995: 145 suggests that 'there is perhaps a grain of truth' in the story of Agnodike, but does not tell us which part this may be.

15 Hurd-Mead 1938: 45 cites Tiraqueau.

16 BL Ms Sloane 1954: 9v; see King 1995b: 192.

17 BL 551.a.32.199.

18 On Sacombe, see Dumont 1971 and Laget 1979: 180; on his context in French society of the seventeenth and eighteenth centuries, see Laget 1980.
19 On the inventions of 'historiens fantaisistes' dealing with Agnodike, see Baudouin 1901: 10–13.
20 This recalls the Socratic midwife of *Theaetetus* 149c–d.
21 Guillemeau 1612: 83 has three honest midwives in charge of detecting pregnancy and testing virginity.

10 GREEN SICKNESS: HIPPOCRATES, GALEN AND THE ORIGINS OF THE 'DISEASE OF VIRGINS'

1 See for examples of recent approaches to the condition, stimulated by the rise of anorexia nervosa, Figlio 1978; Loudon 1980; Starobinski 1981; Siddall 1982; Brumberg 1982; Loudon 1984. Artistic and literary aspects are discussed by Loudon 1980: 1669; cf. McFarland 1975: 250–8. Dixon 1995 reproduces a large number of images of sick maidens, mostly from seventeenth-century Holland, several of which are associated by title or by content with green sickness. However, she chooses to merge green sickness, love-sickness, hysteria, nymphomania and many other categories which sources contemporary with their alleged prevalence chose to distinguish. By glossing over attempts to separate them, and instead seeing them all as different labels for a single condition, 'a mysterious universal ailment of many names that has afflicted women throughout history' (240), Dixon fails to understand the rich range of ways in which medicine has historically claimed to hold the keys to the health of women of all ages and social classes. Her book is also littered with a series of serious factual errors. Hansen 1931: 182 discusses the absence of chlorosis not only from ancient medical literature, but also from ancient poetry and art, believing that anything adversely affecting the marriage prospects of young girls would have been the subject of 'long and lively discussion' by their mothers and would thereby have entered non-medical literature. This may be somewhat fanciful, but the point remains that a full history of chlorosis would need to take account of changes in the visual representations of the condition. De Baillou 1643: 58 describes the role of 'ignorant and complaining mothers' who are shocked by the speed with which their afflicted daughters appear to be wasting away.
2 Mercado 1587: 215; cf. Varandal 1619: preface, on the many pale and disfigured virgins of his own day as a result of cachexia, the 'pale colours' and the *foedi colores: . . . quibus plerasque virginum nostrarum hodie deturpari conspicimus*. All quotations are given with page numbers from the 1620 edition of Varandal.
3 The subtitle of Ernest Lloyd Jones' work of 1897, *Chlorosis: the special anaemia of young women*.
4 In the nineteenth and early twentieth centuries there was considerable debate over whether male chlorosis was possible; writers such as Samuel Fox 1839: preface, who regarded chlorosis as a liver disorder, argued that it also appeared in 'young and delicate' men. A summary of the debate is given by Cabot 1908: 641. When the English translation of von Noorden's essay on chlorosis appeared in a collection on the diseases of the blood, the editor, Stengel, 1905: 339, felt it necessary to correct von Noorden's statement that only females could contract the condition. On late chlorosis, see Stengel 1896: 351 and Hudson 1977: 452.

5 I owe the characterisation of Napier as an 'astrological priest-physician' to David Harley.

6 Hudson 1977: 452–5 points out that the magnesium salts often prescribed to counteract another supposed symptom of chlorosis, namely constipation, would have prevented the iron given to nineteenth-century chlorosis patients from having any beneficial effect.

7 Varandal 1619: 1: *quem vulgus pallidos colores sive foedos, icterum album, febrem amatoriam, morbum virgineum appellant, nos ex Hipp. chlorosin quae est species cachexiae.*

8 Eur. *Suppl.* 598–9, 'pale fear perturbs me below my liver'.

9 It is also preserved in a papyrus fragment from the third century BC; *PSI*, *Omaggio all'xi congr. internaz. di papirologia*, Florence 1965, 16 f.

10 *Palleat omnis amans, color hic est aptus amanti.* This is also cited, without attribution, by Luis Mercado, in his 1588 discussion of the 'white fever' which draws heavily on Lange's 1554 description of the disease of virgins. Mercado 1587: 215 uses the Ovid lines to support the identity of love fever, white fever and the disease of virgins. See also Varandal 1619: 5; Stengel 1896: 329.

11 Ferrand 1623: ch. 15, using the edition of Beecher and Ciavolella 1990: 274–5 and 448 n.5; for Galen, Ferrand uses the commentary on Hippocrates, *On Regimen in Acute Diseases* (CMG V.9, 1).

12 Boorde 1547: 75^{r} cited in Norri 1992: 336. Boorde 1547: 74^{r} also says that the 'grene sicknes' is 'named Agriaca' in Arabic texts.

13 Lange, *Medicinalium epistolarum miscellanes* was published at Basel in 1554, with a second and extended edition issued in 1560. It was popularised as case 256 of the fourth volume of Schenck von Grafenburg's *Observationum medicarum, rararum, novarum, admirabilium, et monstrosarum libri*, published in Frankfurt in 1600; the fourth book, on the reproductive organs of both sexes, was first published separately in 1596.

14 This can be seen by comparing *Epistula* 1.21 and the Calvi translation of the Hippocratic *On the Diseases of Virgins*.

15 For another sixteenth-century humanist, Gabriel Harvey, who appears to have read several books simultaneously, see Jardine and Grafton 1990.

16 Both Ullmann 1970: 32 and Sezgin 1971: 40–1 no.17 and 45 no.3, argued that *Diseases of Women* was translated into Arabic. Ullmann 1977: 248 however suggested that references to this work in Arabic authors derive not from direct knowledge of the text itself but rather from lists of Hippocratic works given in the order in which Galen recommended that they should be studied. He concluded that 'Das Buch ist – so darf mit Sicherheit gesagt werden – nicht ins Arabische übersetzt worden.' Two commentaries on the first eleven chapters of *Diseases of Women* 1 were, however, known in the Arabic world; see further Ullmann 1977: 245–62. It is possible that the availability of *On the Diseases of Virgins* in the Arabic world accounts for the interest in disorders arising from the 'thick menstrual blood' of virgins in the writers Ibn al-Jazzār and al-Mūjīsi (see Chapter 11, p. 239).

17 For example, *DW* 1.1 and 1.7–38 in Paris Bibliothèque Nationale Lat. 11219 (ninth century) and Leningrad Lat. F.v.VI.3 (eighth or ninth century), on which see Egert 1936 and Walter 1935. See also Mazzini and Flammini 1983. The *editio princeps* is given by Vázquez Buján 1986. Pearl Kibre 1980: 362 argued that no

Latin translations of *Diseases of Women* were made between the eighth and the sixteenth centuries.

18 Lange 1554: 2.13, which refers to the classical idea that there were 300 diseases afflicting mankind (cf. the emperor Tiberius contracting the apparently new disease of *colum* in Pliny, *NH* 26.6.9); is this not sufficient, asks Lange, without any new ones? The English Sweat appeared in 1485, with further outbreaks in 1508, 1517, 1528 and 1551; syphilis apparently arrived in Europe in 1495. On the subsequent history of the idea of 'new diseases', see Stevenson 1965 and Thorndike 1957.

19 The *Prorrhetic* passage is used by Varandal 1619: 4, in order to show that chlorosis is only a variant of cachexia. For de Baillou 1643: 66–7, the stated age of seven in *Coan Prognoses* is not a problem, since according to the Hippocratic principle by which age groups are formed, both seven and 14 – the age of puberty – are significant and potentially dangerous times of life.

20 *Sed hic morbus virgines infestat, quum viro iam maturae, ex ephebis excesserint. Nam id temporis, natura duce, sanguis menstruus ad matricis loculos, et venas ab epate defluit.*

21 Calvi gives *On the Diseases of Virgins* twice; Lange follows the first version, headed *De virginum natura liber*. The repeated phrases in these two translations may suggest that the process of translation involved the comparison of Greek manuscripts with an earlier, Latin, translation; the differences between the two versions in content, Latin style and knowledge of Greek suggest two different translators at work. The first translation is far superior on all counts.

22 Vassès 1533: 74, lines 28–30, gives *In totum siquidem, ut diximus, cum vel tumor, vel dolor in hypochondriis fuerit, parva de necessitate et frequens adest respiratio, ut nihil mirum sit, si in sequentibus, ubi hypochondrium hypolaparou, id est, subinane dixit, adiecerit spirituosum autem non valde.* See also Cornarius 1536: 96.

23 *Hippocratis . . . qui in libello de morbis virginum ait: Huius morbi liberatio est, venae sectio, si nihil obstiterit. Ego vero, inquit, praecipio, virgines hoc morbo afflictas, ut quamprimum viris cohabitent, et copulentur: si conceperint, convalescent: si vero in pubertate hoc morbo non corripientur, tum paulo post eas invadet, nisi viro nupserint . . . Hoc saluberrimo divini Hippocratis consilio, si medicamenta menses provocantia, et obstructionum aperitiva, sanguinis grossi subtiliativa adiunxeris, nihil his praesentius reperire et excogitare poteris.*

24 *Quare bono sis animo, filiam tuam elocato: nuptiis quoque libens interero. Vale.*

25 BL, C.40.m.10.(161.).

26 Ibid (163.).

27 *Sed huius liberatio, et medela est (nisi quid vetet) sanguinis missio.*

28 *Caeterum curatio ut hinc liberentur, est sanguinis detractio, si nihil fuerit quod impediat.*

29 *Curatio in venae sectione, optimum remedium viris cohabitare.*

30 Brain 1986: 93 is wrong to claim that there is only one case of bloodletting in the Hippocratic *Diseases of Women*; Dean-Jones 1994: 142 finds six examples in the three books, to which Hanson 1994: 187 n.81 has added two more (*SF* 23, L 8.488 and *DW* 3.241, L 8.454–6), both of them cases where it is performed 'as amplifier to menstruation'. Dean-Jones nevertheless argues that bloodletting is essentially regarded by the Hippocratics as 'a remedy for the male body'.

31 The alternative Latin disease name for the condition, *foedi colores*, 'ugly complexions', is significant here.

32 The specific example of green sickness thus modifies the general argument put

forward by Vivian Nutton that the sixteenth-century movement 'back to Hippocrates' only took place after the 1560s (1989: 435).

11 ONCE UPON A TEXT: HYSTERIA FROM HIPPOCRATES

1 The Egyptian origin of the concept of the wandering womb is asserted by Sauri 1973: 540–2, following Veith, and by Wesley 1979: 1–8; Wesley, however, shoots himself in the foot by attributing the words of Plato, *Timaeus* 91c to the Egyptian Papyrus Ebers. Lloyd 1983: 65 n.21 and 84 n.100 does not accept the implied link between Egyptian and Greek theories of the wandering womb. See further Hanson 1985 and Merskey and Potter 1989 who conclude, 'the wandering womb did not come from Egypt'.

2 M.J. Adair 1996: 153 n.1 accepts that 'the ancients never used the term "hysteria"', but nevertheless believes in the validity of the diagnosis today, writing of 'the physical distress and disease we know as "hysteria"' (163).

3 *Contra* Merskey 1985: 576, whose confidence in Veith's Latin – 'The Latin references . . . seem to be handled by Dr Veith as if she was fully in charge of that material in the original language' – could lead the reader to expect command of both classical languages.

4 It is used in this way by the second-century AD Aretaeus of Cappadocia; Chapter 11 of the fourth book of his *On the Causes and Symptoms of Chronic Diseases* is entitled 'Concerning *hysterika*' (CMG 2.79–82). A separate chapter of his work on acute diseases, 2.11, discusses *hysterikê pnix* (CMG 2.32–5).

5 The classic description of the symptoms which came to be collected under this label is Soranos *Gyn.* 3.26–9; T 149–54, on which see below.

6 Pliny's *Natural History* gives many examples of these uses: e.g. mustard, *NH* 20.87.237; black or white hellebore, *NH* 25.31.53; castoreum, *NH* 32.13.28. Cf. *Aph.* 5.49, Loeb IV, 170. After intercourse, sneezing could cause a miscarriage (*NH* 7.6.42).

7 'Conversion' here carries none of the later, post-Freudian implications of 'hysterical conversion', and simply means a physical turning. Beaver-oil is also used by Pliny as a fumigation or pessary for women suffering 'from their wombs' (*NH* 32.13.38); in other words, sneezing can expel from either above or from below, and thus return a womb to its correct position.

8 Since the noun is not used in this period, it is entirely irrelevant for Mary Lefkowitz, in a discussion of fourth-century BC medicine, to claim that 'the term hysteria means "wombiness"' (1981: 13).

9 Ar. *GA* 776a11 states that woman is the only *hysterikon* animal; A.L. Peck's translation for the Loeb edition gives here 'alone of all animals women are liable to uterine affections' (p. 467). Cf. *Prorrhetic* 1.119, Loeb VIII, 198, *CP* 343, L 5.658 and 543, L 5.708.

10 Showalter 1997: 30–7 summarises Charcot's work, and suggests that the diagnosis of hysteria had a certain appeal for the patients; in addition to being an explanatory label, it gave them 'a warped celebrity' (1997: 36).

11 On recommendations of marriage in seventeenth-century hysteria literature, see Williams 1990: 385 n.6.

12 Sauri 1973 uses *DW* 1.7 and 2.123–5; Palis *et al.* 1985 translate *NW* 3, L

7.314–16; 73, L 7.404; 75, L 7.404 and 87, with *DW* 2.123–5, while Veith 1965: 10 n.1 is 'primarily based' on *DW* 1.7, 1.32 and 2.123–5.

13 In Greek, *strephontai hai mêtrai*, close to the Latin *converto*.

14 Hanson (forthcoming) discusses the more sophisticated equipment used for fumigation of the womb in some Hippocratic discussions (e.g. *DW* 3.230, L 8.438–40), when a chair was used, apparently on the grounds of increased safety and comfort.

15 E.g. *DW* 2.126, L 8.270–2; 2.150, L 8.326; 2.203, 8.386–92.

16 E.g. *DW* 2.128, L 8.274; *DW* 2.129, L 8.276; *DW* 2.131, L 8.278–80.

17 Pseudo-Aristotle, *Problems* 30.

18 Greek *hypo tês hêrakleiês nousou*, translated by Littré as 'aux épileptiques'. On Herakles and representations of disease, see von Staden 1992c.

19 E.g. *DW* 1.37, L 8.92; *DW* 2.115, L 8.250; *DW* 2.119, L 8.260; *DW* 2.128, L 8.276; *DW* 2.133, L 8.302; *Gen.* 4, L 7.476.

20 Ann Hanson, pers. comm.; Adams 1834: 458 suggests that the *Timaeus* passage 'ought perhaps not to be taken in too literal a sense, considering that philosopher's well-known propensity to mystification'.

21 K 8.425–6; translation based on Siegel 1976: 187. Galen also quotes from this section of *Timaeus* in *On Anatomical Procedures* 12.2 (Duckworth *et al.* 1962: 113–14), where he notes the combination of singular and plural forms for the womb here.

22 It is by no means certain that the passage represents Plato's own views (Krell 1975: 404); Timaeus may be a historical figure, but historical figures in Plato usually utter views which have something of Plato in them.

23 Not *hoion zôon*, but *zôon epithymêtikon enon tês paidopoiias*.

24 M.J. Adair 1996: 157 rather misses the point when he argues that the womb 'translocates at will' while the penis 'does not migrate autonomously'; the essential similarity is that both move, independently of the will.

25 Discussed in detail in Hanson (forthcoming). A work entitled 'Select Aphorisms concerning the operation of medicaments according to the place', contained in BL Sloane 2117, has a section on 'Hystericalls' describing how the womb is drawn to aromatics and repelled by their contraries (121^{v}–2^{r}). Discussing how this mechanism works, the author roundly rejects the belief of 'some sotts' that the womb possesses 'the sense of smelling'.

26 Galen, *De usu respirationis* 3, K 4.492 and 4.508; Furley and Wilkie 1984: 109 and 131.

27 An alternative title is *Peri tês apnou*; if correct, this could mean 'The woman without respiration'; see Debru 1996: 207. Also known as 'On the causes of disease', the remaining fragments of this text are given in Wehrli 1953.

28 The *editio princeps* of Pliny was published in 1469, but book 7 was in circulation in manuscript from the early ninth century (Chibnall 1975; Reynolds 1983: 307–16).

29 Von Staden 1989: 517–18. On the effects of these discoveries on medical writing, see Gourevitch 1988: xxxiv–v.

30 *On Treatment by Bloodletting* 3, K 11.201; 13, K 11.290.

31 In his discussion of epilepsy itself, Aretaeus includes the symptom of '*pnix* as if strangled', 1.5.6, CMG 2, 4.27. For discussion of the content of Aretaeus, see Temkin 1932, especially p. 170. It is worth noting that Veith 1965: 22–3

wrongly asserts that Aretaeus makes a 'brief reference to male hysteria'; in fact, although he mentions an unnamed condition which affects both sexes and shares some symptoms with suffocation of the womb, in his discussion of satyriasis he explicitly denies that suffocation of the womb can affect men, since men do not have wombs (2.12.4, CMG 2, 35.11–12).

32 Trillat 1987: 28 argues from this passage that it is in Galen's work 'qu'apparait le mot d'hystérie', albeit in adjectival form. This is not particularly significant since, as I have already shown, the adjective *hysterikos* is also used by the Hippocratics, and he is wrong to argue that 'Hippocrate adopte la théorie populaire et rejette le nom. Galien rejette la théorie mais adopte le nom.'

33 In *Loc. Aff.* 6.5, K 8.424 he describes *tôn hysterikôn legomenôn symptômatôn*; see also the commentary on *Aph.* 5.35, K 17B.824.

34 Galen uses *sympaschei*, K 8.424; *On Joints* 57, Loeb III, 332 uses *adelphixia*, and names the womb as one of the organs the movements of which are affected by such connections with other parts of the body. In the sixteenth century, the Latin *communitas* was the preferred term.

35 The *edition princeps* of Janus Cornarius, *De medicamentis empiricis, physicis, et rationalibus liber* (Basel: Froben), published in 1536, has a note in the margin beside this chapter reading '*suffocatio de vulva*'.

36 On encyclopaedism, see Lemerle 1986: ch.10; medical treatises are mentioned only on p. 341.

37 Translated Bussemaker and Daremberg 1876: 539–40. Philumenos wrote a work on gynaecology, and another on venomous animals and remedies for their bites and stings; the latter is available as CMG 10 1, 1. He uses the same remedies for certain poisons as for *hysterikê pnix*, thus agreeing with Galen's view that retained seed and, to a lesser extent, menses act as poisons in the body. About Philumenos little is known; his dates are variously given as the first century AD, *c.* 180 AD, or the third century AD. He does not explicitly use Galen – which would support the earlier dates – but the view of *hysterikê pnix* as a sort of poisoning may well imply knowledge of Galen's ideas.

38 While the completion of the CMG Aetius is awaited, book 16 appears only in the unsatisfactory edition of Zervos 1901: 95 ff. Soranos is cited on p. 97.26. Ricci 1950: 70–6 provides an English translation based on this. See also Garzya 1984.

39 Debru 1992 argues that the readiness to use the first person when telling other people's stories is characteristic of this genre; Nutton 1991: 12–13 shows that the stories Galen had read or heard thirty years before were transformed into his own 'eyewitness' accounts in his later writings.

40 CMG 9.1, 288.8; Greek *anadromê*. For translation, see Adams 1834: 345–6.

41 One independent Greek text, probably from the sixth century, survives in a ninth-century manuscript: the *Book of Metrodora*, a practical treatise in many ways reminiscent of Hippocratic medicine (Guerra 1994). It includes some remedies for *hysterikê pnix*, which use the traditional foul- and sweet-smelling substances, specifically castoreum, rue with honey, and pig's dung with rose water (Guerra 1953: 41; 1968: 89).

42 Muscio should be consulted in the edition of Rose 1882, section 4.26–9 (pp. 58–61); compare with Drabkin and Drabkin 1951. The added phrase, *ascendente sursum ad pectus matrice*, occurs at Rose 1882: 58.9–10 and Drabkin and Drabkin 1951: 76.367–8.

43 Also known as the *De natura generis humani*, this comprises extracts from the first book of the Hippocratic *Diseases of Women*, with others from Vindicianus; see Vázquez Buján 1982 with Beccaria 1961: 36 and 38–9; Kibre 1980: 280–2; Agrimi 1985. The text is found in the manuscripts Paris BN Lat. 7027 and Paris BN Lat. 11219.

44 The terms 'Arabic medicine' and 'Islamic medicine' are misleading; many of those whose work is considered in the following section were not Muslims or were not of Arab extraction. Veith 1965: 94–7 paid little attention to the Arab world, saying merely that 'the three leading Muslim physicians [Ibn Sīnā, Rhazes and Haly Abbas] did not write much about hysteria'. The difficulty for a classical scholar studying the fortunes of the hysteria tradition in the Arab world is the paucity of texts available in European languages; however, since many of these works were translated into Latin, it is possible to make some provisional comments. A more detailed version of this section appears as King 1993a: 49–54.

45 Rhazes was probably born in 865, and died in 925 or 932; see M.J. Young *et al.* 1990: 370. The Kitāb al-Ḥawị fi't-Ṭibb, *The Comprehensive Book of Medicine*, known in Latin as the *Continens*), was written in around AD 900 (Ullmann 1978: 43; M.J. Young *et al.* 1990: 373). On al-Kitāb al-Mansuri fi't-ṭibb, known in Latin as the *Liber ad Almansorem*, Jacquart 1994.

46 This picks up Aetios (Z 97.13) on the susceptibility of the young to suffocation; see also Green 1985: 114.

47 Translated into Latin as the *Viaticum*, this was an important source for medieval European medicine, translated into Greek and Hebrew as well as Latin (Schönfeld 1974; Jazi 1986; 1987; Dols 1973: 67–9). I am using the Latin translation of the *Viaticum* published in 1515, an abbreviated form of the Arabic text; for an English translation, Green 1985: 249.

48 Known as the *Canon*, the Latin translation made in the twelfth century by Gerard of Cremona was highly influential, reprinted thirty-six times in the fifteenth and sixteenth centuries (Ullmann 1978: 46; Siraisi 1987). I am using the printed edition of 1564 here. On Avicenna in the Middle Ages, see Jacquart and Thomasset 1988: 174–5.

49 Meyerhof and Joannides 1938: 66 argue that rubbing oils into the mouth of the womb in imitation of intercourse is absent from Greek medicine, but of course it is found not only in Galen but also in the Hippocratic corpus.

50 Vivian Nutton (pers. comm.) suggests another possibility, *hysterikê krasis*.

51 Green 1996a: 185 lists the relevant section as *Liber de sinthomatibus mulierum* 45; see also Green 1985: 285 and n.91. For details of the complex rewritings and reworkings of the material in the three groups, see Green 1996a and 1996b.

52 *Mulieri de matrice laboranti aut difficulter generanti, sternutatio superveniens, optimum*; see Müller-Rohlfsen 1980: xviii–xix and 72; Beccaria 1961: 23.

53 For the thirteenth century see Walter Agilon ch. 42, on suffocation of the womb (Diepgen 1911: 149); heavily dependent on Ibn Sīnā, this includes a version of the woman who lay as if dead, with Galen as hero-narrator. See also Thomas of Brabant (Ferckel 1912: ch. 59).

54 For a more optimistic view of the relationship between science and experience in this period see Jacquart and Thomasset 1988: 46.

BIBLIOGRAPHY

Abse, D.Wilfred (1987) *Hysteria and Related Mental Disorders: an approach to psychological medicine*, 2nd edition, Bristol: John Wright.

Achterberg, Jeanne (1991) *Woman as Healer*, London: Rider.

Adair, James M. (1790) *Essays on Fashionable Diseases*, London: T.P. Bateman.

Adair, Mark J. (1996) 'Plato's view of the "wandering uterus"', *Classical Journal* 91: 153–63.

Adams, Francis (1834) *The Medical Works of Paulus Aegineta* vol. 1, London: Welsh.

—— (1849) *The Genuine Works of Hippocrates*, 2 vols, London: Sydenham Society.

Adler, Herbert M. and Hammett, Van Buren O. (1973) 'The doctor–patient relationship revisited: an analysis of the placebo effect', *Annals of Internal Medicine* 78: 595–8.

Agrimi, Jole (1985) 'L'*Hippocrates Latinus* nella tradizione manoscritta e nella cultura altomedievali' in Mazzini and Fusco 1985: 388–98.

Aleshire, Sara B. (1989) *The Athenian Asklepieion. The people, their dedications, and the inventories*, Amsterdam: J.C. Gieben.

—— (1991) *Asklepios at Athens. Epigraphic and prosopographic essays on the Athenian healing cults*, Amsterdam: J.C. Gieben.

Alfageme, I. Rodríguez (1995) 'La médecine technique dans la comédie attique' in van der Eijk *et al.* 1995: 569–85.

Alic, Margaret (1986) *Hypatia's Heritage: a history of women in science from antiquity to the late nineteenth century*, London: The Women's Press.

Allbutt, Sir T. Clifford (1921) *Greek Medicine in Rome*, London: Macmillan.

Al-Said, M.S., Al-Khamis, K.I., Islam, M.W., Parmer, N.S., Tariq, M. and Ageel, A.M. (1987) 'Post-coital anti-fertility activity of the seeds of *coriandrum sativum* in rats', *Journal of Ethnopharmacology* 21: 165–73.

Andò, Valeria (1990) 'La verginità come follia: il *Peri Parthenion* ippocratico,' *Quaderni Storici* 75: 715–37.

Annoni, Jean-Marie and Barras, Vincent (1993) 'La découpe du corps humaine et ses justifications dans l'antiquité', *Canadian Bulletin for Medical History* 10: 185–227.

Astruc, Jean (1761) *Traité des maladies des Femmes*, Paris: P.G. Cavelier.

Avicenna (Ibn Sina) (1564) *Liber Canonis*, trans. Geerard of Cremona, in *Libri in re medica omnes*, Venice: Valgrisi.

Baader, Gerhaad (1978) 'Die Schule von Salerno', *Medizinhistorisches Journal* 13: 124–45.

—— (1984) 'Early medieval Latin adaptations of Byzantine medicine in western

Europe' in John Scarborough (ed.), *Symposium on Byzantine Medicine, Dumbarton Oaks Papers* 38: 251–9.

—— and Winau, Rolf (eds) (1989) *Die Hippokratischen Epidemien: Theorie–Praxis–Tradition*, Verhandlung des Ve Colloque international hippocratique, Berlin 10–15.9.1984, *Sudhoffs Archiv*, Beiheft 27, Stuttgart: Franz Steiner.

Baas, Johann Hermann (1889) *Outlines of the History of Medicine and the Medical Profession* (first published as *Grundriss der Geschichte der Medizin*, 1876, trans. H.E. Handerson), New York: Vail.

Bagnall, Roger S. and Frier, Bruce W. (1994) *The Demography of Roman Egypt*, Cambridge: Cambridge University Press.

Bart, Pauline B. and Scully, Diana H. (1979) 'The politics of hysteria: the case of the wandering womb' in Edith S. Gomberg and Violet Franks (eds), *Gender and Disordered Behavior: sex differences in psychopathology*, New York: Brunner/Mazel, 354–80.

Baudouin, Marcel (1901) *Les Femmes médecins. Étude de psychologie sociale internationale. Tome 1: Femmes médecins d'autrefois*, Paris: Institut International de Bibliographie.

Baumann, Evert Dirk (1939) 'Die Krankheit der Jungfrauen', *Janus* 43: 189–94.

Beagon, Mary (1992) *Roman Nature: the thought of Pliny the Elder*, Oxford and New York: Oxford University Press.

Beccaria, Augusto (1961) 'Sulle tracce di un antico canone latino di Ippocrate e di Galeno, II. Gli Aforismi di Ippocrate nella versione e nei commenti del primo medioevo', *Italia Medioevale e Umanistica* 4: 1–75.

Beecher, Donald A. (1988) 'The lover's body: the somatogenesis of love in Renaissance medical treatises', *Renaissance and Reformation* 24: 1–11.

—— and Ciavolella, Massimo (eds) (1990) *Jacques Ferrand: a treatise on lovesickness*, Syracuse, NY: Syracuse University Press.

Behr, Charles (1968) *Aelius Aristides and the Sacred Tales*. Amsterdam: Hakkert.

—— (1981) *P. Aelius Aristides, The Complete Works. Vol. II. Orations XVII–LIII*. Leiden: E.J. Brill.

Benardete, Seth (1969) *Herodotean Inquiries*, The Hague: M. Nijhoff.

Bender, S. (1953) 'Symptoms of menstruation', *Nursing Mirror* 17 April: 159–60.

Berger, Peter L. and Luckmann, Thomas (1966) *The Social Construction of Reality: a treatise in the sociology of knowledge*, Garden City, NY: Doubleday.

Berndt, Ronald M. (1962) *Excess and Restraint: social control among a New Guinea mountain people*, Chicago: University of Chicago Press.

Berthiaume, Guy (1982) *Les Rôles du Mágeiros: étude sur la boucherie, la cuisine et le sacrifice dans la Grèce ancienne*, *Mnemosyne* supplement 70, Leiden: Brill.

Betz, Hans D. (1986) *The Greek Magical Papyri in Translation*, vol. 1: *Texts*, Chicago: University of Chicago Press.

Biggers, John D. (1959) 'Plant phenols possessing oestrogenic activity' in James W. Fairbairn (ed.), *The Pharmacology of Plant Phenolics*, London and New York: Academic Press, 51–69.

Biller, Peter (1992) 'Views of Jews from Paris around 1300: Christian or "scientific"?', *Studies in Church History* vol. 29: *Christianity and Judaism* (ed. Diana Wood).

Bing, Peter and Cohen, Rip (1991) *Games of Venus: An anthology of Greek and Roman erotic verse from Sappho to Ovid*, New York and London: Routledge.

Blackman, Janet (1977) 'Popular theories of generation: the evolution of *Aristotle's*

Works, the study of an anachronism', in John Woodward and David Richards (eds), *Health Care and Popular Medicine in Nineteenth-Century England*, London: Croom Helm, 56–88.

Blumenfeld-Kosinski, Renate (1990) *Not of Woman Born*, Ithaca, NY: Cornell University Press.

Blundell, Sue (1995) *Women in Ancient Greece*, London: British Museum Press.

Boddy, Janice (1982) 'Womb as oasis: the symbolic content of Pharaonic circumcision in rural Northern Sudan', *American Ethnologist* 9: 682–98.

Bolton, Henry Carrington (1881) 'The early practice of medicine by women', reprinted from *Popular Science Monthly* 18 (1880).

Bonnet-Cadilhac, Christine (1993) 'Traduction et commentaire du traité hippocratique "Des maladies des jeunes filles"', *History and Philosophy of the Life Sciences* 15: 147–63.

Boorde, Andrew (1547) *The Breviary of Helthe*, London: W. Middleton.

Boss, Jeffrey M.N. (1979) 'The seventeenth-century transformation of the hysteric affection, and Sydenham's Baconian medicine', *Psychological Medicine* 9: 221–34.

Bourgey, Louis (1953) *Observation et expérience chez les médecins de la Collection hippocratique*, Paris: J. Vrin.

Bradley, Keith (1994) 'The nurse and the child at Rome: duty, affect and socialisation', *Thamyris* 1: 137–56.

Brain, Peter (1986) *Galen on Bloodletting*, Cambridge: Cambridge University Press.

Breakell, Mary L. (1903) 'Women in the medical profession: by an outsider', *Nineteenth Century* 54 (2): 819–25.

Brejon, Jacques (1937) *André Tiraqueau (1488–1558): un jurisconsulte de la Renaissance*, Paris: Recueil Sirey.

Brelich, Angelo (1969) *Paides e parthenoi*, Rome: Edizioni dell'Ateneo.

Brisson, Luc (1976) *Le Mythe de Tirésias: essai d'analyse structurale*, Leiden: Brill.

Brodie, Sir Benjamin C. (1837) *Lectures Illustrative of Certain Local Nervous Affections*, London: Longman.

Brody, Howard (1980) *Placebos and the Philosophy of Medicine: clinical, conceptual, and ethical issues*, Chicago: University of Chicago Press.

—— (1987) *Stories of Sickness*, New Haven and London: Yale University Press.

—— (1994) '"My story is broken; can you help me fix it?": Medical ethics and the joint construction of narrative', *Literature and Medicine* 13: 79–92.

—— and Waters, David B. (1980) 'Diagnosis is treatment', *Journal of Family Practice* 10: 445–9.

Brondegaard, Vagn J. (1973) 'Contraceptive plant drugs', *Planta Medica* 23: 167–72.

Browder, Clifford (1988) *The Wickedest Woman in New York: Madame Restell, the abortionist*, Hamden, CT: Archon Books.

Brown, Isaac Baker (1866a) *On the Curability of Certain Forms of Insanity, Epilepsy, Catalepsy and Hysteria in Females*, London: Robert Hardwicke.

—— (1866b) *On Surgical Diseases of Women*, 3rd edition, London: Robert Hardwicke.

Brown, P.S. (1977) 'Female pills and the reputation of iron as an abortifacient', *Medical History* 21: 291–304.

Browne, E.G. (1921) *Arabian Medicine*, Cambridge: Cambridge University Press.

Browner, C.H., Ortiz de Montellano, Bernard R. and Rubel, Arthur J. (1988) 'A methodology for cross-cultural ethnomedical research', *Current Anthropology* 29: 681–702.

Brumberg, Joan Jacobs (1982) 'Chlorotic girls, 1870–1920: a historical perspective on female adolescence', *Child Development* 53: 1468–77.

—— (1993) '"Something happens to girls": menarche and the emergence of the modern American hygienic imperative', *Journal of the History of Sexuality* 4: 99–127.

Bullein, William (1559) *A newe Boke of Phisicke called ye Government of Health*, London: J. Day.

—— (1562) *Bullein's Bulwarke of Defence againste all sicknes, sorres and wundes*, London: John Kyngston.

Bullough, Vern L. (1972–3) 'An early American sex manual, or, Aristotle who?', *Early American Literature* 7: 236–46.

Bullough, Vern L. and Bullough, Bonnie (1979) *The Care of the Sick: the emergence of modern nursing*, London: Croom Helm.

Burford, Alison (1969) *The Greek Temple Builders at Epidauros*, Liverpool: Liverpool University Press.

Burkert, Walter (1966) 'Greek tragedy and sacrificial ritual', *Greek, Roman and Byzantine Studies* 7: 87–121.

—— (1977) *Griechische Religion der archaischen und klassischen Epoche*, Stuttgart: Kohlhammer; English trans. by John Raffan, *Greek Religion*, Cambridge, MA: Harvard University Press, 1983.

—— (1987) *Ancient Mystery Cults*, Cambridge, MA: Harvard University Press.

Bussemaker, Ulco and Daremberg, Charles (1851–76) *Oeuvres d'Oribase*, 6 vols, Paris: Imprimerie Nationale.

Byl, Simon (1980) *Recherches sur les grands traités biologiques d'Aristote: sources écrites et préjugés*, Brussels: Palais des Académies.

—— (1989) 'L'odeur végétale dans la thérapeutique gynécologique du Corpus hippocratique', *Revue Belge de Philologie et d'Histoire* 67: 53–64.

—— (1995) 'L'air géographique des médecins hippocratiques' in van der Eijk *et al.* 1995: 225–35.

—— and de Ranter, Anne-Françoise (1990) 'L'étiologie de la stérilité féminine dans le *Corpus hippocratique*' in Potter *et al.* 1990: 303–22.

Cabot, Richard C. (1908) 'Pernicious and secondary anaemia, chlorosis, and leukaemia', in Sir William Osler and Thomas McCrae (eds), *Modern Medicine: its Theory and Practice* vol. 4, Philadelphia: Lea and Febiger, 1907–10, 612–80.

Cadden, Joan (1993) *Meanings of Sex Difference in the Middle Ages*, Cambridge and New York: Cambridge University Press.

Cahen, Émile (1930) *Les Hymnes de Callimaque*, Paris: Éds de Boccard.

Calame, Claude (1977) *Les Choeurs des jeunes filles en Grèce archaique*, Part 1, Rome: Edizioni dell'Ateneo e Bizzarri; English trans. by Derek Collins and Janice Orion, *Choruses of Young Women in Ancient Greece: their morphology, religious role and social function*, Lanham, MD and London: Rowman and Littlefield, 1997.

Calvi, Marco Fabio (1525) *Hippocratis Coi medicorum omnium longe principis, Octoginta volumina . . .* , Rome: Franciscus Minitius.

Campese, Silvia (1983) 'Madre materia: donna, casa, città nell'antropologia de Aristotele' in Campese *et al.* 1983: 13–79.

—— with Paola Manuli and Giulia Sissa (1983) *Madre Materia. Sociologia e biologia della donna greca*, Turin: Boringhieri.

Carson, Anne (1990) 'Putting her in her place: woman, dirt, and desire' in Halperin *et al.* 1990: 135–69.

Casabona, Jean (1966) *Recherches sur le vocabulaire des sacrifices en grec: des origines à la fin de l'époque classique*, Aix-en-Provence: Éds Ophrys.

Castle, Sarah E. (1994) 'The (re)negotiation of illness diagnoses and responsibility for child health in rural Mali', *Medical Anthropology Quarterly* 8: 314–35.

Castro, Miranda (1990) *The Complete Homeopathy Handbook: a guide to everyday health care*, London: Macmillan.

Catalogue and Report of Obstetrical and Other Instruments: exhibited at the Conversazione of the Obstetrical Society of London, held by permission at the Royal College of Physicians, March 28th 1866 (1867), London: Longmans Green and Co.

Catonné, Jean-Philippe (1994) 'A nosological reflection on the *Peri Partheniôn*: elucidating the origin of hysterical insanity', *History of Psychiatry* 5: 361–86.

Celli, Blas Bruni (1984) *Bibliografía Hipocrática*, Caracas: Ediciones del Rectorado, Universidad Central de Venezuela.

Cellier, Elizabeth (1688) *To Dr . . . an Answer to his Queries, concerning the Colledg of Midwives*, London.

Chadwick, John and Mann, William N. (1950) *The Medical Works of Hippocrates: a new translation*, Oxford: Basil Blackwell.

Chaitow, Leon (1982) *Osteopathy. A complete health-care system*, Wellingborough: Thorsons.

Chalmers, Alan F. (1982) *What is This Thing Called Science? An assessment of the nature and status of science and its methods*, 2nd edition, Milton Keynes: Open University Press.

Chance, Burton (1930) 'On Hippocrates and the Aphorisms', *Annals of Medical History* 2: 31–46.

Chaniotis, Angelos (1995) 'Illness and cures in the Greek propitiatory inscriptions and dedications of Lydia and Phrygia' in van der Eijk *et al.* 1995: 323–44.

Chantraine, Pierre (1968–80) *Dictionnaire étymologique de la langue grecque: histoire des mots*, 4 vols, Paris: Klinksieck.

Charmaz, Kathy (1991) *Good Days, Bad Days: the self in chronic illness and time*. New Brunswick, NJ: Rutgers University Press.

Chibnall, Marjorie (1975) 'Pliny's *Natural History* and the middle ages' in Thomas A. Dorey (ed.), *Empire and Aftermath: Silver Latin II*, London: Routledge and Kegan Paul, 57–78.

Churchill, Fleetwood (1864) *On the Diseases of Women*, 5th edition, Dublin: Fannin and Co. and London: Longman.

Clark, Gillian (1993) *Women in Late Antiquity: pagan and Christian lifestyles*, Oxford: Clarendon Press.

Clark, Stephen R.L. (1975) *Aristotle's Man*, Oxford: Clarendon Press.

Clologe, Charles H.T. (1905) *Essai sur l'histoire de la gynécologie dans l'antiquité grecque jusqu'à la collection hippocratique*, Bordeaux: A. Arnaud.

Cohen, David (1991) *Law, Sexuality, and Society. The enforcement of morals in classical Athens*, Cambridge: Cambridge University Press.

Cole, Thomas (1967) *Democritus and the Sources of Greek Anthropology* (American Philological Association Monograph 25), Cleveland, OH: Western Reserve University Press.

Conway, George A. and Slocumb, John C. (1979) 'Plants used as abortifacients and emmenagogues by Spanish New Mexicans', *Journal of Ethnopharmacology* 1: 241–61.

Cornarius, Janus (1536) *Claudii Galeni libri novem, nunc primum Latini facti* (includes *Libri V iam primum in Latinam linguam conversi: De causis respirationis. De utilitate respirationis. De difficultate respirationis libri III* and *De uteri dissectione, de foetus formatione et de semine libri*), Basel: Froben.

—— (1546) *Hippocratis Coi medicorum omnium longe principis, opera quae ad nos extant omnia*, Basel: Froben.

Crawford, Patricia (1978) 'Attitudes to pregnancy from a woman's spiritual diary, 1687–8', *Local Population Studies* 21: 43–5.

—— (1981) 'Attitudes to menstruation in seventeenth-century England', *Past and Present* 91: 47–73.

—— (1994) 'Sexual knowledge in England, 1500–1750' in Porter and Teich 1994: 82–106.

Critchley, Edmund M.R. and Cantor, H.E. (1984) 'Charcot's hysteria renaissant', *British Medical Journal* 289: 1785–8.

Crosse, John Green (1851) *Cases in Midwifery*, London: Churchill and Norwich: Stevenson and Matchett.

Cullen, William (1803) *The Edinburgh Practice of Physic, Surgery and Midwifery*, London: G. Kearsley.

Cunningham, Andrew (1997) *The Anatomical Renaissance: the resurrection of the anatomical projects of the ancients*, Aldershot and Brookfield, VT: Scolar Press.

Cyrino, Monica Silveira (1995) *In Pandora's Jar: lovesickness in early Greek poetry*, Lanham, MD and London: University Press of America.

Dally, Ann (1991) *Women under the Knife: a history of surgery*, London: Hutchinson Radius.

Daremberg, Charles (1856) *Oeuvres anatomiques, physiologiques et médicales de Galien* II, Paris: Baillière.

Davies, Celia (ed.) (1980) *Rewriting Nursing History*, London: Croom Helm.

Davis, Patricia (1988) *Aromatherapy. An A–Z*, Saffron Walden: C.W. Daniel.

Dean, Peter D.G., Exley, D. and Goodwin, T.W. (1971) 'Steroid oestrogens in plants: re-estimation of oestrone in pomegranate seeds', *Phytochemistry* 10: 2215–16.

Dean-Jones, Lesley A. (1989) 'Menstrual bleeding according to the Hippocratics and Aristotle', *Transactions of the American Philological Association* 119: 177–92.

—— (1994) *Women's Bodies in Classical Greek Science*, Oxford: Clarendon Press.

de Baillou, Guillaume (1640) *Epidemiorum et Ephemeridum libri duo*, Paris: J. Quesnel.

—— (1643) *De Virginum et Mulierum Morbis liber, in quo multa ad mentem Hippocratis explicantur*, Paris: J. Quesnel.

Debru, Armelle (1992) 'La suffocation hystérique chez Galien et Aetius: Réécriture et emprunt de "je"', in Antonio Garzya (ed.), *Tradizione e ecdotica dei testi medici tardoantichi e bizantini*, Atti del Convegno Internazionale, Anacapri, 29–31 ottobre 1990, Napoli: M. D'Auria, 79–89.

—— (1996) *Le Corps respirant, la pensée physiologique chez Galien*, Leiden: E.J. Brill.

Deichgräber, Karl (1982) *Die Patienten des Hippokrates. Historisch-prosopographische Beiträge zu den Epidemien des Corpus Hippocraticum* (Abhandlungen der geistes- und socialwissenschaftlichen Klasse, Mainz, Jahrgang 1982, nr. 9), Wiesbaden: Franz Steiner.

de la Corde, Maurice (1574) *Hippocratis Coi libellus Peri Partheniôn, hoc est, De iis quae virginibus accidunt*, Paris: Gabriel Buon.

Delacoux, Alexis (1834) *Biographie des sages-femmes célebres, anciennes, modernes, et contemporaines*, Paris: Trinquart.

De Laszlo, Henry and Henshaw, Paul S. (1954) 'Plant materials used by primitive peoples to affect fertility', *Science* 119: 626–30.

Deloughery, Grace L. (1977) *History and Trends of Professional Nursing*, 8th edition, St Louis, MO: C.V. Mosby.

Demand, Nancy (1994) *Birth, Death, and Motherhood in Classical Greece*, Baltimore, MD and London: Johns Hopkins University Press.

Denman, Thomas (1788) *An Introduction to the Practice of Midwifery*, London: J. Johnson.

—— (1832) *An Introduction to the Practice of Midwifery*, 7th edition, London: E. Cox.

Des Roches, Catherine and Des Roches, Madeleine (1578) *Les Oeuvres des Mes-Dames des Roches de Poetiers mere et fille*, Paris: L'Angelier.

Detienne, Marcel (1967) *Les maîtres de verité dans la grèce archaïque*, Paris: Maspero; English trans. by Janet Lloyd, *The Masters of Truth in Ancient Greece*, New York: Zone Books, 1996.

—— (1972) *Les Jardins d'Adonis*, Paris: Gallimard; English trans. by Janet Lloyd, *The Gardens of Adonis: spices in Greek mythology*, Hassocks: Harvester Press, 1977.

—— (1976) 'Potagerie de femme, ou comment engendrer seule', *Traverses* 5–6: 75–81.

—— (1977) *Dionysos mis à mort*, Paris: Gallimard; English trans. by Mireille and Leonard Müllner, *Dionysos Slain*, Baltimore, MD: Johns Hopkins University Press, 1979.

—— (1979) 'Violentes "eugénies". En pleines Thesmophories: des femmes couvertes de sang' in Detienne and Vernant 1979: 183–214; English trans. by Paula Wissing, 1989, 'The violence of well-born ladies: women in the Thesmophoria', 129–47.

—— and Vernant, Jean-Pierre (1974) *Les Ruses de l'intelligence: la mêtis des grecs*, Paris: Flammarion; English trans. by Janet Lloyd, *Cunning Intelligence in Greek Culture and Society*, Hassocks: Harvester Press, 1978.

—— (1979) *La Cuisine du sacrifice en pays grec*, Paris: Gallimard; English trans. by Paula Wissing, *The Cuisine of Sacrifice among the Greeks*, Chicago: Chicago University Press, 1989.

Di Benedetto, Vincenzo (1986) *Il medico e la malattia: la scienza di Ippocrate*, Turin: G. Einaudi.

Diepgen, Paul (1911) *Gualteri Agilonis, Summa medicinalis: Nach den Münchener Cod. Lat. Nr. 325 und 13124 erstmalig ediert: mit einer vergleichenden Betrachtung älterer medizinischer Kompendien des Mittelalters*, Leipzig: Johann Ambrosius Barth.

—— (1933) 'Reste antiker Gynäkologie im frühen Mittelalter', *Quellen und Studien zur Geschichte der Naturwissenschaften* 3: 226–42.

—— (1937) *Die Frauenheilkunde der alten Welt: Handbuch der Gynäkologie XII, 1*, Munich: J.F. Bergmann.

Diller, Anthony (1980) 'Cross-cultural pain semantics', *Pain* 9: 9–26.

Dillon, Matthew P.J. (1994) 'The didactic nature of the Epidaurian *iamata*', *Zeitschrift für Papyrologie und Epigraphik*, 101: 239–60.

—— (1997) *Pilgrims and Pilgrimage in Ancient Greece*, London and New York: Routledge.

Dionis, Pierre (1710) *A Course of Chirurgical Operations, demonstrated in the Royal Garden at Paris*, London: Jacob Tonson.

Dixon, Laurinda S. (1995) *Perilous Chastity: women and illness in pre-Enlightenment art and medicine*, Ithaca, NY and London: Cornell University Press.

Dock, Lavinia Lloyd and Stewart, I.M. (1938) *A Short History of Nursing*, 4th edition; first published 1920, New York: Putnam's.

Dodds, E.R. (1951) *The Greeks and the Irrational*, Berkeley: University of California Press.

Dolan, Josephine A. (1978) *Nursing in Society: an historical perspective*, 14th edition, Philadelphia: W.B. Saunders.

Dols, Michael W. (1973) *Medieval Islamic Medicine: Ibn Ridwan's treatise 'On the Prevention of Bodily Ills in Egypt'*, Berkeley, Los Angeles and London: University of California Press.

Donahue, M. Patricia (1985) *Nursing: The Finest Art. An illustrated history*, St Louis, MO: C.V. Mosby.

Donati, Giovanni Battista (1582) *Commentarius in magni Hippocratis Coi librum de morbis virginum*, Lucca: J. Guidobonius.

Douglas, John (1736) *A Short Account of the State of Midwifery in London, Westminster, &c.*, London: the author.

Drabkin, Miriam F. and Drabkin, Israel, E. (1951) *Caelius Aurelianus: Gynaecia. Fragments of a Latin version of Soranus' Gynaecia from a thirteenth-century manuscript*, *Bulletin of the History of Medicine* Supplement 13, Baltimore, MD: Johns Hopkins University Press.

DuBois, Page (1988) *Sowing the Body: psychoanalysis and ancient representations of women*, Chicago: University of Chicago Press.

—— (1991) *Torture and Truth*, New York and London: Routledge.

Duckworth, Wynfrid L.H., Lyons, Malcolm C. and Towers, Bernard (eds) (1962) *Galen, On Anatomical Procedures*, translated by the editors, Cambridge: Cambridge University Press.

Duden, Barbara (1991) *The Woman Beneath the Skin: a doctor's patients in eighteenth-century Germany*, Cambridge, MA: Harvard University Press.

Duffy, John (1963) 'Masturbation and clitoridectomy: a nineteenth-century view', *Journal of the American Medical Association* 186: 246–8.

Duffy, John (1984) 'Byzantine medicine in the sixth and seventh centuries: aspects of teaching and practice' in John Scarborough (ed.), *Symposium on Byzantine Medicine*, *Dumbarton Oaks Papers* 38: 21–7.

Duminil, Marie-Paule (1979) 'La recherche hippocratique aujourd'hui', *History and Philosophy of the Life Sciences* 1: 153–81.

—— (1983) *Le Sang, les vaisseaux, le coeur dans la collection hippocratique: anatomie et physiologie*, Paris: Éds Belles Lettres.

Dumont, Martial (1971) 'La délirante "Luciniade" de l'anti-césarien Jean-François Sacombe', *Revue Française de Gynécologie et d'Obstétrique* 66: 199–204.

Durand, Jean-Louis (1979a) 'Bêtes grecques. Propositions pour une topologie des corps à manger' in Detienne and Vernant 1979: 133–65; English trans. by Paula Wissing, 1989, 'Greek animals: towards a topology of edible bodies', 87–118.

—— (1979b) 'Du rituel comme instrumental' in Detienne and Vernant 1979:

167–81; English trans. by Paula Wissing, 1989, 'Ritual as instrumentality', 119–28.

Durling, Richard J. (1961) 'A chronological census of Renaissance editions and translations of Galen', *Journal of the Warburg and Courtauld Institutes* 24: 230–305.

Edelstein, Emma J. and Edelstein, Ludwig (1945) *Asclepius: a collection and interpretation of the testimonies*, 2 vols, Baltimore, MD: Johns Hopkins University Press.

Edelstein, Ludwig (1931) 'The Hippocratic physician', reprinted in O. and C.L. Temkin (eds), *Ancient Medicine: selected papers of Ludwig Edelstein*, Baltimore, MD: Johns Hopkins University Press, 1967, 87–110.

—— (1939) 'The genuine works of Hippocrates', *Bulletin of the History of Medicine* 7: 236–48, reprinted in O. and C.L. Temkin (eds), *Ancient Medicine: selected papers of Ludwig Edelstein*, Baltimore, MD: Johns Hopkins University Press, 1967, 133–44.

Egert, Ferdinand P. (1936) *Gynäkologische Fragmente aus dem frühen Mittelalter. Nach einer Petersburger Handschrift aus dem VIII–IX Jahrhundert, Abhandlung zur Geschichte der Medizin und der Naturwissenschaften* 11, Berlin: E. Ebering.

Eisenberg, Leon (1977) 'Disease and illness: distinctions between professional and popular ideas of sickness', *Culture, Medicine and Psychiatry* 1: 9–23.

Estienne, Charles (1590) *Dictionarium historicum, geographicum, poeticum* . . . , Geneva: Jacob Stoer.

Étienne, Roland and Le Dinahet, Marie-Thérèse (eds) (1991) *L'Espace sacrificiel dans les civilisations méditerranéennes de l'antiquité*, actes du colloque tenu à la Maison de l'Orient, 4–7 juin 1988, Paris: de Boccard.

Evenden, Doreen (1991) 'Seventeenth-century London midwives: their training, licensing and social profile', PhD dissertation, McMaster University, Canada.

Ey, Henri (1964) 'Hysteria: history and analysis of the concept' in Roy 1982: 3–19.

Fabrega, Horacio F. and Silver, Daniel B. (1973) *Illness and Shamanistic Curing in Zinacantan: an ethnomedical analysis*, Stanford, CA: Stanford University Press.

Fabrega, Horacio F. and Tyma, Stephen (1976) 'Culture, language and the shaping of illness: an illustration based on pain', *Journal of Psychosomatic Research* 20: 323–37.

Farnell, Lewis R. (1896–1909) *Cults of the Greek States*, 5 vols, Oxford: Clarendon Press.

Farnsworth, Norman R., Bingel, Audrey S., Cordell, Geoffrey A., Crane, Frank A. and Fong, Harry H. S. (1975a) 'Review article: potential value of plants as sources of new antifertility agents I', *Journal of Pharmaceutical Sciences* 64(4): 535–98.

—— (1975b) 'Review article: potential value of plants as sources of new antifertility agents II', *Journal of Pharmaceutical Sciences* 64(5): 717–54.

Farrell-Beck, Jane and Kidd, Laura Klosterman (1996) 'The roles of health professionals in the development and dissemination of women's sanitary products, 1880–1940', *Journal of the History of Medicine and Allied Sciences* 51: 325–52.

Fasbender, Heinrich (1897) *Entwickelungslehre, Geburtshülfe und Gynäkologie in den hippokratischen Schriften*, Stuttgart: F. Enke.

Feeny, Patrick (1964) *The Fight against Leprosy*, London: Elek Books.

Ferckel, Christoph (1912) *Die Gynäkologie des Thomas von Brabant: Ein Beitrag zur Kenntnis der mittelalterlichen Gynäkologie und ihrer Quellen, Alte Meister der Medizin und Naturkunde in Facsimile – Ausgaben und Neudrucken* 5, Munich: Carl Kühn.

Ferrante, Joan (1988) 'Biomedical versus cultural constructions of abnormality: the case of idiopathic hirsutism in the United States', *Culture, Medicine and Psychiatry* 12: 219–38.

Ferrari, Gian A. and Vegetti, Mario (1983) 'Science, technology and medicine in the classical tradition' in Pietro Corsi and Paul Weindling (eds) (1983) *Information Sources in the History of Science and Medicine*, London and Boston: Butterworth Scientific, 197–220.

Festugière, André-Jean (1948) *Hippocrate, l'ancienne médecine*, Paris: C. Klincksieck.

Figlio, Karl (1978) 'Chlorosis and chronic disease in nineteenth-century Britain: the social constitution of somatic illness in a capitalist society', *Social History* 3: 167–97.

Finkler, Kaja (1994) 'Sacred healing and biomedicine compared', *Medical Anthropology Quarterly* 8: 178–97.

Fissell, Mary E. (1992) 'Readers, texts, and contexts: vernacular medical works in early modern England', in Roy Porter (ed.), *The Popularization of Medicine 1650–1850*, London: Routledge, 72–96.

Fitzpatrick, M. Louise (1977) 'Review essay: nursing', *Signs* 2: 818–34.

Flashar, Hellmut and Jouanna, Jacques (1997) *Médecine et morale dans l'antiquité*, Entretiens sur l'antiquité classique XXXVII, Geneva: Fondation Hardt.

Flemming, Rebecca and Hanson, Ann Ellis (forthcoming) 'Hippocrates *Peri Partheniôn*: *Diseases of Young Girls*', *Early Science and Medicine.*

Fogo, Andrew (1803) *Observations on the Opinions of Ancient and Modern Physicians, including those of the late Dr Cullen on Amenorrhea, or Green-sickness*, Newcastle: D. Akenhead.

Foley, Helene P. (1982) 'Marriage and sacrifice in Euripides' *Iphigeneia in Aulis*', *Arethusa* 15: 159–80.

Föllinger, Sabine (1996) *Differenz und Gleichheit. Das Geschlechterverhältnis in der Sicht griechischer Philosophen des 4. bis 1. Jahrhunderts v. Chr.*, Stuttgart: F. Steiner (= *Hermes* Einzelschriften, Heft 74).

Fontanus, Nicolaus (1652) *The Womans Doctour*, London: J. Blague and S. Howes.

Fossel, Viktor (1914) 'Aus den medizinischen Briefen des pfalzgräflichen Leibarztes Johannes Lange (1485–1565)', *Sudhoffs Archiv für Geschichte der Medizin* 7: 238–52.

Foucault, Michel (1970) *The Order of Things*, section repr. in Richard T. and Fernande M. de George (eds) (1972), *The Structuralists: from Marx to Lévi-Strauss*, New York: Anchor Books, 256–85.

—— (1985) *The History of Sexuality, II. The Use of Pleasure*, trans. Robert Hurley, New York: Random House; French *L'Usage des plaisirs*, Paris: Gallimard, 1984.

—— (1986) *The History of Sexuality, III. The care of the self*, trans. Robert Hurley, New York: Pantheon Books.

Fox, Samuel (1839) *Observations on the Disorder of the General Health of Females called Chlorosis: shewing the true cause to be entirely independent of peculiarities of sex*, London: S. Highley.

Frede, Michael (1982) 'The method of the so-called methodical school of medicine' in Jonathan Barnes, Jacques Brunschwig, Myles Burnyeat and Malcolm Schofield (eds), *Science and Speculation: studies in Hellenistic theory and practice*, Cambridge and New York: Cambridge University Press, 1–23.

Friedman, Alice (1987) 'Midwifery: legal or illegal? A case study of an accused, 1905' in Maggs 1987: 74–87.

Frier, Bruce W. (1994) 'Natural fertility and family limitation in Roman marriage', *Classical Philology* 89: 318–33.

Frisk, Hjalmar (1960–72) *Griechisches Etymologisches Wörterbuch* (3 vols), Heidelberg: C. Winter.

Frontisi-Ducroux, Françoise (1975) *Dédale: mythologie de l'artisan en Grèce ancienne*, Paris: Maspero.

Furley, David J. and Wilkie, J.S. (1984) *Galen on Respiration and the Arteries*, Princeton, NJ: Princeton University Press.

Furth, Charlotte (1986) 'Blood, body and gender: medical images of the female condition in China, 1600–1850', *Chinese Science* 7: 43–66.

Gabbay, John (1982) 'Asthma attacked? Tactics for the reconstruction of a disease concept' in Peter Wright and Andrew Treacher (eds), *The Problem of Medical Knowledge: Examining the Social Construction of Medicine*, Edinburgh: Edinburgh University Press, 23–48.

Gadow, Sally (1980) 'Body and self: a dialectic', *Journal of Medicine and Philosophy* 5: 172–85.

Gaisser, Julia Haig (1993) *Catullus and his Renaissance Readers*, Oxford: Clarendon Press.

Gamarnikow, Eva (1978) 'Sexual division of labour: the case of nursing' in A. Kuhn and A.M. Wolpe (eds) *Feminism and Materialism: women and modes of production*, London: Routledge and Kegan Paul.

—— (1991) 'Nurse or woman: gender and professionalism in reformed nursing 1860–1923' in Pat Holden and Jenny Littlewood (eds) *Anthropology and Nursing*, London: Routledge, 110–29.

García-Ballester, Luis (1994) 'Galen as a clinician: his methods in diagnosis' in *Aufstieg und Niedergang der Römischen Welt* II 37.2, Berlin and New York: Walter de Gruyter, 1636–71.

Gardner, Augustus K. (1852) *A History of the Art of Midwifery, a Lecture Delivered at the College of Physicians and Surgeons, November 11th, 1851*, New York: Stringer and Townsend.

Gardner, Jane F. (1986) *Women in Roman Law and Society*, London: Croom Helm.

Garland, Robert (1992) *Introducing New Gods: the politics of Athenian religion*, London: Duckworth.

Garro, Linda C. (1992) 'Chronic illness and the construction of narratives' in Mary-Jo DelVecchio Good *et al.* 1992, 100–37.

Garzya, Antonio (1984) 'Problèmes relatifs à l'édition des livres IX–XVI du *Tétrabiblon* d'Aétios d'Amida', *Revue des Etudes Anciennes* 86: 245–57.

Gay, Peter (1984) *The Bourgeois Experience: Victoria to Freud.* Vol. 1: *Education of the Senses*, New York and Oxford: Oxford University Press.

Geertz, Clifford (1983) 'Common sense as a cultural system', in *Local Knowledge: further essays in interpretive anthropology*, New York: Basic Books, 73–93.

Gelbart, Nina (1993) 'Midwife to a nation: Mme du Coudray serves France' in Marland 1993a: 131–51.

Gellner, Ernest (1964) *Thought and Change*, London: Weidenfeld and Nicholson.

Gewargis, Albert A. (1980) 'Gynäkologisches aus dem 'Kamil as-Sina'a at-Tibbiya' des 'Ali ibn al-'Abbas al-Magusi', Inaugural dissertation, Friedrich-Alexander-Universität, Erlangen-Nürnberg.

Girard, Marie-Christine (1983) 'La femme dans le *corpus* hippocratique', *Cahiers des Études Anciennes* 15: 69–80.

Gleason, Maud (1990) 'The semiotics of gender: physiognomy and self-fashioning in the second century CE' in Halperin *et al.* 1990: 389–415.

—— (1995) *Making Men. Sophists and self-presentation in ancient Rome*, Princeton, NJ: Princeton University Press.

Goldhill, Simon (1995) *Foucault's Virginity: ancient erotic fiction and the history of sexuality*, Cambridge: Cambridge University Press.

Good, Byron J. (1992) 'A body in pain – the making of a world of chronic pain' in Mary-Jo DelVecchio Good *et al.* 1992, 29–48.

—— (1994) *Medicine, Rationality, and Experience: an anthropological perspective*, Cambridge: Cambridge University Press.

Good, Byron J. and Good, Mary-Jo DelVecchio (1981) 'The meaning of symptoms: a cultural hermeneutic model for clinical practice' in Leon Eisenberg and Arthur Kleinman (eds), *The Relevance of Social Science for Medicine*, Dordrecht: D. Reidel, 165–96.

—— (1993) '"Learning medicine": the construction of medical knowledge at Harvard Medical School' in Shirley Lindenbaum and Margaret Lock (eds), *Knowledge, Power and Practice. The anthropology of medicine and everyday life*, Berkeley: University of California Press, 81–107.

Good, Mary-Jo DelVecchio, Brodwin, Paul E., Good, Byron J. and Kleinman, Arthur (eds) (1992) *Pain as Human Experience: an anthropological perspective*, Berkeley, Los Angeles and London: University of California Press.

Goode, William J. (1960) 'Encroachment, charlatanism, and the emerging profession: psychology, sociology, and medicine', *American Sociological Review* 25: 902–14.

Goodnow, Minnie (1961) *Nursing History*, Philadelphia: W.B. Saunders (first published 1919).

Goody, Jack (ed.) (1968) *Literacy in Traditional Societies*, Cambridge: Cambridge University Press.

—— (1986) *The Logic of Writing and the Organization of Society*, Cambridge: Cambridge University Press.

Gourevitch, Danielle (1984) *Le Mal d'être femme: La femme et la médecine dans la Rome antique*, Paris: Éds Belles Lettres.

—— (1988) 'Situation de Soranos dans la médecine antique' in *Soranos d'Éphèse: Maladies des femmes 1.1*, Paris: Les Belles Lettres, vii–xlvi.

—— (1994) 'Review of Lesley-Ann Dean-Jones, *Women's Bodies in Classical Greek Science*', *History and Philosophy of the Life Sciences* 16: 498–500.

Graf, Fritz (1992) 'Heiligtum und Ritual: das Beispiel der Griechisch-Römischen Asklepieia' in O. Reverdin and B. Grange (eds), *Le Sanctuaire grec*, Entretiens sur l'antiquité classique XXXVII, Geneva: Fondation Hardt, 152–99.

Grant, Mary (1960) *The Myths of Hyginus*, Lawrence: University of Kansas Press.

Green, Monica H. (1985) 'The transmission of ancient theories of female physiology and disease through the early Middle Ages', PhD dissertation, Princeton University.

—— (1987) 'The *De Genecia* attributed to Constantine the African', *Speculum* 62: 299–323.

—— (1990) 'Constantinus Africanus and the conflict between religion and science' in G.R. Dunstan (ed.), *The Human Embryo: Aristotle and the Arabic and European traditions*, Exeter: University of Exeter Press, 47–69.

—— (1996a) 'The development of the *Trotula*', *Revue d'Histoire des Textes* 26: 119–203.

—— (1996b) 'A handlist of Latin and vernacular manuscripts of the so-called *Trotula* texts', *Scriptorium* 50: 137–75.

—— (forthcoming) *'The Diseases of Women According to Trotula': a medieval compendium of women's medicine.*

—— (forthcoming) *Women and Literate Medicine in Medieval Europe: Trota and the 'Trotula'*, Cambridge: Cambridge University Press.

Grensemann, Hermann (1975a) 'Eine jüngere Schicht in den gynäkologischen Schriften' in Louis Bourgey and Jacques Jouanna (eds), *La Collection hippocratique et son rôle dans l'histoire de la médecine, Colloque de Strasbourg, 23–27 octobre 1972*, Leiden: Brill, 151–69.

—— (1975b) *Knidische Medizin I*, Berlin and New York: de Gruyter.

—— (1982) *Hippokratische Gynäkologie. Die gynäkologischen Texte des Autors C nach den pseudohippokratischen Schriften De muliebribus I, II und De Sterilibus*, Wiesbaden: Franz Steiner.

Grmek, Mirko (1987) 'Les *indicia mortis* dans la médecine gréco-romaine' in François Hinard (ed.), *La Mort, les morts et l'au-delà dans le monde romain*, Actes du Colloque de Caen, 20–22 novembre, 1985, Caen: Centre des Publications de l'Université, 129–44.

—— and Robert, Fernand (1977) 'Dialogue d'un médecin et d'un philologue sur quelques passages des Epidémies VII' in Robert Joly (ed.), *Corpus Hippocraticum. Actes du Colloque hippocratique de Mons, septembre 1975*, Mons: Université de Mons, 275–90.

Gubb, Alfred S. (1879) *Aids to Gynaecology*, London: Baillière Tindall and Cox; New York: Putnam and Sons.

Guerra, Giorgio del (1953) *Il libro di Metrodora sulle malattie delle donne e Il ricettario di cosmetica e terapia*, Milan: Ceschina.

—— (1968) 'La medicina bizantina e il codice medico-ginecologia di Metrodora', *Scientia Veterum* 118: 67–94.

—— (1994) *Metrodora. Medicina e Cosmesi ad Uso delle Donne. La antica sapienza femminile e la cura di sé*, Milan: Mimesis.

Guillemeau, Jacques (1612) *Child-Birth or, the Happy Deliverie of Women*, London: A. Hatfield.

Gujral, M.L., Varma, D.R. and Sareen, K.N. (1960) 'Oral contraceptives. Part I. Preliminary observations on the antifertility effect of some indigenous drugs', *Indian Journal of Medical Research* 48: 46–51.

Guthrie, Douglas (1953) 'Nursing through the ages: from earliest times to medieval era', *Nursing Mirror* 17 July: x–xii.

Guze, Samuel B. (1967) 'The diagnosis of hysteria: what are we trying to do?' *American Journal of Psychiatry* 124: 491–8.

Hall, G. Stanley (1904) *Adolescence: Its psychology and its relations to physiology, anthropology, sociology, sex, crime, religion and education*, Vol. 1, London: Sidney Appleton; New York: D. Appleton and Co.

Hall, Marshall (1850) 'On a new and lamentable form of hysteria', *The Lancet*, 1 June: 660–1.

Halperin, David M. (1990) 'Why is Diotima a woman? Platonic *erôs* and the figuration of gender' in Halperin *et al.* 1990, 257–308.

Halperin, David M., Winkler, John J. and Zeitlin, Froma I. (eds) (1990) *Before Sexuality: the construction of erotic experience in the ancient Greek world*, Princeton, NJ: Princeton University Press.

Hansen, Axel (1931) 'Die Chlorose im Altertum', *Sudhoffs Archiv für Geschichte der Medizin* 24: 175–84.

Hanson, Ann Ellis (1975) 'Hippocrates: *Diseases of Women* I: archives', *Signs* 1: 567–84.

—— (1981) 'Anatomical assumptions in Hippocrates, *Diseases of Women I.1: my mother the earth*', paper delivered at the American Philological Association, summary in *Society for Ancient Medicine Newsletter* 8: 4–5.

—— (1985) 'Papyri of medical content', *Yale Classical Studies* 28: 25–47.

—— (1987) 'The eight months' child and the etiquette of birth: *Obsit omen!*', *Bulletin of the History of Medicine* 61: 589–602.

—— (1989) 'Diseases of women in the *Epidemics*' in Baader and Winau 1989: 38–51.

—— (1990) 'The medical writers' woman' in Halperin *et al.* 1990: 309–37.

—— (1991) 'Continuity and change: three case studies in Hippocratic gynecological therapy and theory' in Pomeroy 1991: 73–110.

—— (1992a) 'The logic of the gynecological prescriptions' in Juan Antonio López Férez (ed.), *Tratados Hipocráticos: Actas del VIIe colloque international hippocratique*, Madrid, 24–29 de Septiembre de 1990, Madrid: Universidad Nacional de educación a distancia, 235–50.

—— (1992b) 'The origin of female nature', *Helios* 19: 31–71.

—— (1994) 'A division of labor: roles for men in Greek and Roman births', *Thamyris* 1: 157–202.

—— (1996a) 'Phaenarete: mother and *maia*', in Wittern and Pellegrin 1996: 159–82.

—— (1996b) 'Fragmentation and the Greek medical writers' in Glenn W. Most (ed.), *Collecting Fragments*, Göttingen: Vandenhoeck and Ruprecht, 289–314.

—— (forthcoming) 'Talking recipes in the gynecological texts of the *Hippocratic Corpus*' in Maria Wyke (ed.), *Parchments of Gender: reading the bodies of antiquity*, Oxford and New York: Oxford University Press.

—— and Armstrong, David (1986) 'Vox virginis', *Bulletin of the Institute of Classical Studies* 33: 97–100.

—— and Green, Monica H. (1994) 'Soranus of Ephesus: *Methodicorum princeps*' in *Aufstieg und Niedergang der Römischen Welt* II 37.2, Berlin: de Gruyter, 968–1075.

Harborne, Jeffrey B. (1982) *Introduction to Ecological Biochemistry*, 2nd edition, London and New York: Academic Press.

—— (1993) *Introduction to Ecological Biochemistry*, 4th edition, London and New York: Academic Press.

Hare, Evan H. (1962) 'Masturbatory insanity: the history of an idea', *Journal of Mental Science* 108: 1–25.

Harley, David N. (1981) 'Ignorant midwives – a persistent stereotype', *Bulletin of the Society for the Social History of Medicine* 28: 6–9.

—— (1990) 'Historians as demonologists: the myth of the midwife-witch', *Social History of Medicine* 3: 1–26.

Hartog, François (1980) *Le Miroir d'Hérodote: essai sur la répresentation de l'autre*, Paris: Gallimard; English trans. by Janet Lloyd, *The Mirror of Herodotus: the representation of the Other in the writing of history*, Berkeley, Los Angeles and London: University of California Press, 1988.

Hayes, Rose Oldfield (1975) 'Female genital mutilation, fertility control, women's roles, and the patrilineage in modern Sudan: a functional analysis', *American Ethnologist* 2: 617–33.

Heckenbach, Joseph (1911) *De nuditate sacra sacrisque vinculis* in Albrecht Dieterich and Richard Wünsch, *Religionsgeschichtliche Versuche und Vorarbeiten* 9.3.

Heftmann, Erich, Ko, Shui-Tze and Bennett, Raymond D. (1966) 'Identification of estrone in pomegranate seeds', *Phytochemistry* 5: 1337–9.

Heiberg, Johan L. (1912) *Pauli Aeginetae libri tertii interpretatio Latina antiqua*, Leipzig: Teubner.

Heidel, William A. (1941) *Hippocratic Medicine: its spirit and method*, New York: Columbia University Press.

Helman, Cecil G. (1978) '"Feed a cold, starve a fever" – folk models of infection in an English suburban community, and their relation to medical treatment', *Culture, Medicine and Psychiatry* 2: 107–37.

—— (1984) *Culture, Health and Illness: an introduction for health professionals*, Bristol: Wright.

—— (1985) 'Disease and pseudo-disease: a case history of pseudo-angina' in Robert A. Hahn and Attwood D. Gaines (eds), *Physicians of Western Medicine: anthropological approaches to theory and practice*, Dordrecht: D. Reidel, 293–331.

Henderson, Jeffrey (1975) *The Maculate Muse: obscene language in Attic comedy*, New Haven, CT: Yale University Press.

Herfst, Pieter (1922) *Le Travail de la femme dans la Grèce ancienne*, Utrecht: A. Oosthoek (reprinted 1979).

Héritier, Françoise (1978) 'Fécondité et stérilité: la traduction de ces notions dans le champ idéologique au stade préscientifique' in Evelyne Sullerot (ed.), *Le Fait féminin*, Paris: Fayard, 387–96.

Herzog, Rudolf (1931) *Die Wunderheilungen von Epidauros: ein Beitrag zur Geschichte der Medizin und der Religion*, *Philologus* supplement 22(3), Leipzig: Dieterich.

Hess, Ann Giardina (1993) 'Midwifery practice among the Quakers in southern rural England in the late seventeenth century' in Marland 1993a: 49–76.

Hodges, Nathaniel (1672) *Loimologia: sive, Pestis nuperae apud populum Londinensem grassantis narratio historica*, London: Godbid.

Hoekelman, Robert A. (1975) 'Nurse–physician relationships', *American Journal of Nursing* 75: 1150–2.

Hoffmann, Geneviève (1992) *La Jeune Fille, le pouvoir et la mort dans l'Athènes classique*, Paris: de Boccard.

Holden, Ward A. (1907) 'Aelius Aristides: a hypochondriac in the time of the Antonines', *Medical Library and Historical Journal* 5: 18–23.

Holzworth, Jean (1943) 'Light from a medieval commentary on the text of the *Fabulae* and *Astronomica* of Hyginus', *Classical Philology* 38: 126–31.

Honwana, Alcinda (1998) 'Healing for peace: traditional healers and post-war reconstruction in Southern Mozambique' in John Hinnells and Roy Porter (eds), *Religion, Health and Suffering*, London: Kegan Paul.

Hopkins, Keith (1965) 'Contraception in the Roman Empire', *Comparative Studies in Society and History* 8: 124–51.

Horowitz, Maryanne Cline (1976) 'Aristotle and woman', *Journal of the History of Biology* 9: 183–213.

Horstmanshoff, Hermann F.J. (1990) 'The ancient physician: craftsman or scientist?', *Journal of the History of Medicine and Allied Sciences* 45: 176–97.

Hudson, Robert P. (1977) 'The biography of disease: lessons from chlorosis', *Bulletin of the History of Medicine* 51: 448–63.

Hugh-Jones, Christine (1979) *From the Milk River: spatial and temporal processes in Northwest Amazonia*, Cambridge: Cambridge University Press.

Hugh-Jones, Stephen (1979) *The Palm and the Pleiades. Initiation and cosmology in Northwest Amazonia*, Cambridge: Cambridge University Press.

Hughes, John S. (1994) '"Country boys make the best nurses": nursing the insane in Alabama, 1861–1910', *Journal of the History of Medicine and Allied Sciences* 49: 79–106.

Hurd-Mead, Kate Campbell (1938) *A History of Women in Medicine*, Haddam, CT: The Haddam Press.

Ibn al-Jazzar (1515) *Viaticum*, in *Opera Ysaac*, Lyons: B. Trot and J. de Platea.

Irigoin, Jean (1973) 'Tradition manuscrite et histoire du texte: quelques problèmes relatifs à la Collection hippocratique', *Revue d'Histoire des Textes* 3: 1–13.

Irwin, Eleanor (1974) *Colour Terms in Greek Poetry*, Toronto: Hakkert.

Jackson, Jean E. (1992) '"After a while no one believes you": real and unreal pain' in Mary-Jo DelVecchio Good *et al.* 1992, 138–68.

Jacquart, Danielle (1994) 'Note sur la traduction latine du *Kitab al-Mansuri* de Rhazès', *Revue d'Histoire des Textes* 24: 359–74.

—— and Thomasset, Claude (1988) *Sexuality and Medicine in the Middle Ages*, trans. Matthew Adamson, Cambridge: Polity Press in association with Basil Blackwell (French edition *Sexualité et savoir médical au Moyen Age*, Paris: Presses Universitaires de France, 1985).

Jaeger, Werner (1957) 'Aristotle's use of medicine as a model of method in his *Ethics*', *Journal of Hellenic Studies* 77: 54–61.

James, Robert (1743–5) *A Medical Dictionary*, London: T. Osborne.

Jardine, Lisa and Grafton, Anthony (1990) '"Studied for action": how Gabriel Harvey read his Livy', *Past and Present* 129: 30–78.

Jazi, Radhi (1986) 'Millénaire d'Ibn al-Jazzar, pharmacien maghrébin, médecin des pauvres et des déshérités', *Revue d'Histoire de la Pharmacie* 33: 5–12, 108–20.

—— (1987) 'Aphrodisiaques et médicaments de la reproduction chez ibn al-Jazzar, médecin et pharmacien maghrébin du Xᵉ siècle', *Revue d'Histoire de la Pharmacie* 34: 155–70, 243–59.

Jenkins, Ian (1983) 'Is there life after marriage? A study of the abduction motif in vase paintings of the Athenian wedding ceremony', *Bulletin of the Institute of Classical Studies* 30: 137–45.

Jensen, Deborah MacLurg (1943) *A History of Nursing*, St Louis, MO: C.V. Mosby.

Johns, Catherine (1995) 'Poison and witchcraft in the ancient world', MA dissertation, University of Newcastle upon Tyne.

Joly, Robert (1966) *Le Niveau de la science hippocratique, contribution à la psychologie de l'histoire des sciences*, Paris: Éds Belles Lettres.

—— (1977) 'Indices léxicaux pour la datation de Génération-Nature de l'enfant-Maladies IV' in Robert Joly (ed.), *Corpus Hippocraticum. Actes du Colloque hippocratique de Mons, septembre 1975*, Mons: Université de Mons, 136-47.

—— (1983) 'Hippocrates and the school of Cos' in Ruse 1983: 29–47.

Jones, Anne Hudson (ed.) (1988) *Images of Nurses: perspectives from history, art, and literature*, Philadelphia: University of Pennsylvania Press.

Jones, Ernest Lloyd (1897) *Chlorosis: the special anaemia of young women*, London: Baillière Tindall and Cox.

Jones, William H.S. (1923) 'Ancient nursing', in *Hippocrates*, vol. II (Loeb edition), London: Heinemann, xxx–xxxii.

—— (1931) 'Introduction', in *Hippocrates*, vol. IV (Loeb edition): London: Heinemann, ix–lviii.

—— (1947) *The Medical Writings of Anonymus Londinensis*, Cambridge: Cambridge University Press.

Jorden, Edward (1603) *A Brief Discourse of a Disease Called the Suffocation of the Mother*, London: John Windet.

Joshel, Sandra R. (1986) 'Nurturing the master's child: slavery and the Roman child-nurse', *Signs* 12: 3–22.

Jouanna, Jacques (1961) 'Présence d'Empédocle dans la collection hippocratique', *Bulletin de l'Association Guillaume Budé*, 452–63.

—— (1977) 'La *collection hippocratique* et Platon (*Phèdre, 269c–272a*)', *Revue des Études Grecques* 90: 15–28.

—— (1983) 'Littré, éditeur et traducteur d'Hippocrate', in *Actes du Colloque Émile Littré, 1801–1881, Paris, 7–9 octobre 1981*, Centre international de Synthèse, Paris: Albin Michel, 285–301.

—— (1984) 'Rhétorique et médecine dans la collection hippocratique: contribution à l'histoire de la rhétorique au Ve siècle', *Revue des Études grecques* 97: 26–44.

—— (1992) *Hippocrate*, Paris: Fayard.

Kahn, Laurence (1973) 'Le récit d'un passage et ses points nodaux: le vol et le sacrifice des boeufs d'Apollon par Hermès' in Bruno Gentili and Giuseppe Paioni (eds), *Il mito greco: atti del convegno internazionale Urbino, 7–12 maggio 1973*, Rome: Eds dell'Ateneo e Bizzarri, 107–17.

—— (1978) *Hermès passe; ou, les ambiguïtés de la communication*, Paris: Maspero.

Kamat, Vinay R. (1995) 'Reconsidering the popularity of primary health centers in India: a case study from rural Maharashtra', *Social Science and Medicine* 41: 87–98.

Kampen, Natalie Boymel (1988) 'Before Florence Nightingale: a prehistory of nursing in painting and sculpture' in A.H. Jones 1988: 6–39.

Kass, Amalie M. (1995) '"Called to her at three o'clock a.m.": obstetrical practice in physician case notes', *Journal of the History of Medicine and Allied Sciences* 50: 194–229.

Kee, Howard C. (1982) 'Self-definition in the Asklepios cult', in Ben F. Meyer and E.P. Sanders (eds), *Jewish and Christian Self-Definition*, vol. 3: *Self-Definition in the Graeco–Roman World*, London: SCM Press, 118–36.

Kelly, Emerson Crosby (1939) 'Introduction', in Francis Adams, *The Genuine Works of Hippocrates*, London: Baillière, Tindall and Cox; Baltimore, MD: Williams and Wilkins, v–viii.

Kibre, Pearl (1945) 'Hippocratic writings in the Middle Ages', *Bulletin of the History of Medicine* 18: 371–412.

—— (1976) 'Hippocrates latinus: repertorium of Hippocratic writings in the Latin Middle Ages: II', *Traditio* 32: 257–92.

—— (1980) 'Hippocrates latinus: repertorium of Hippocratic writings in the Latin Middle Ages: VI', *Traditio* 36: 347–72.

King, Helen (1985) 'From parthenos to gynê: the dynamics of category', PhD thesis, University of London.

—— (1986a) 'Tithonos and the *tettix*', *Arethusa* 19: 15–35.

—— (1986b) 'Agnodike and the profession of medicine,' *Proceedings of the Cambridge Philological Society* 32: 53–77.

—— (1993a) 'Once upon a text: the Hippocratic origins of hysteria,' in Sander L. Gilman, Helen King, Roy Porter, G.S. Rousseau and Elaine Showalter, *Hysteria Beyond Freud*, Berkeley and Los Angeles: University of California Press, 3–90.

—— (1993b) 'The politick midwife: models of midwifery in the work of Elizabeth Cellier' in Marland 1993a: 115–30.

—— (1994) 'Sowing the field: Greek and Roman sexology' in Porter and Teich 1994: 29–46.

—— (1995a) 'Medical texts as a source for women's history' in Anton Powell (ed.), *The Greek World*, London: Routledge, 199–218.

—— (1995b) '"As if none understood the Art that cannot understand Greek": the education of midwives in seventeenth-century England' in Vivian Nutton and Roy Porter (eds), *The History of Medical Education in Britain*, Amsterdam: Rodopi, 184–98.

—— (1995c) 'Food and blood in Hippocratic gynaecology' in John Wilkins, David Harvey and Mike Dobson (eds), *Food in Antiquity*, Exeter: University of Exeter Press, 351–8.

Kleinman, Arthur (1988) *The Illness Narratives. Suffering, healing and the human condition*, New York: Basic Books.

—— (1992) 'Pain and resistance: the delegitimation and relegitimation of local worlds' in Mary-Jo DelVecchio Good *et al.* 1992: 169–97.

Kollesch, Jutta (1973) *Untersuchungen zu den pseudogalenischen Definitiones Medicae*, Berlin: Akademie-Verlag.

Krell, David Farrell (1975) 'Female parts in *Timaeus*', *Arion* 2: 400–21.

Kristeller, Paul Oskar (1945) 'The school of Salerno: its development and its contribution to the history of learning', *Bulletin of the History of Medicine* 17: 138–94.

—— (1976) 'Bartholomaeus, Musandinus and Maurus of Salerno and other early commentators of the "Articella", with a tentative list of texts and manuscripts', *Italia Medioevale e Umanistica* 19: 57–87.

Kucharski, P. (1939) 'La "Méthode d'Hippocrate" dans le *Phèdre*', *Revue des Études Grecques* 52: 301–57.

Kudlien, Fridolf (1968) 'Early Greek primitive medicine', *Clio Medica* 3: 305–36.

Lacey, Walter K. (1968) *The Family in Classical Greece*, London: Thames and Hudson.

Laget, Mireille (1979) 'Le Césarienne ou la tentation de l'impossible, XVIIe et XVIIIe siècle', *Annales de Bretagne et des Pays de l'Ouest* 86: 177–89.

—— (1980) 'Childbirth in seventeenth- and eighteenth-century France: obstetrical practices and collective attitudes' in Robert Forster and Orest Ranum (eds), *Medicine and Society in France: selections from Annales E.S.C. vol. 6*, Baltimore, MD: Johns Hopkins University Press, 137–76.

Laín Entralgo, Pedro (1970) *The Therapy of the Word in Classical Antiquity*, ed. and trans. Lelland J. Rather and John M. Sharp, New Haven, CT: Yale University Press.

Lakatos, Imre (1978) 'Falsification and the methodology of scientific research' in John Worrall and Gregory Currie (eds), *Imre Lakatos: the methodology of scientific research programmes. Philosophical papers, vol. I*, Cambridge: Cambridge University Press, 8–101.

Landouzy, Marc Hector (1846) *Traité complet de l'hystérie*, Paris and London: Baillière.

Lange, Johannes (1554) *Medicinalium epistolarum miscellanea*, Basel: J. Oporinus.

Langholf, Volker (1986) 'Kallimachos, Komödie und hippokratische Frage', *Medizinhistorisches Journal* 21: 3–30.

—— (1990) *Medical Theories in Hippocrates. Early texts and the 'Epidemics'*, Berlin and New York: de Gruyter.

—— (1996) 'Nachrichten bei Platon über die Kommunikation zwischen Ärtzen und Patienten' in Wittern and Pellegrin 1996: 113–42.

Laplantine, François (1986) *Anthropologie de la maladie*, Paris: Éds Payot.

Laqueur, Thomas (1990) *Making Sex: body and gender from the Greeks to Freud*, Cambridge, MA: Harvard University Press.

Lasserre, François and Mudry, Philippe (eds) (1983) *Formes de pensée dans la collection hippocratique. Actes du Colloque hippocratique de Lausanne 1981*, Geneva: Droz.

Lawrence, Susan C. and Bendixen, Kae (1992) 'His and hers: female anatomy in anatomy texts for US medical students, 1890–1989', *Social Science and Medicine* 35: 925–34.

Laws, Sophie (1990) *Issues of Blood: the politics of menstruation*, London: Macmillan.

Laycock, Thomas (1840) *A Treatise on the Nervous Diseases of Women*, London: Longman, Orme, Brown, Green and Longmans.

Le Clerc, Daniel (1696) *Histoire de la médecine*, Geneva: J.A. Chouet and D. Ritter.

—— (1699) *The History of Physick*, London: D. Brown, A. Roper and J. Leigh.

—— (1702) *Histoire de la médecine*, Amsterdam: George Gallet.

Lefkowitz, Mary R. (1981) *Heroines and Hysterics*, London: Duckworth.

Le Loyer, Pierre (1586) *IIII Livres des Spectres ou Apparitions et visions d'esprits, anges et demons . . .* , Angers: G. Nepueu.

—— (1605) *A Treatise of Specters or Strange Sights, Visions and Apparitions . . .* , London: M. Lownes.

Lemerle, Paul (1986) *Byzantine Humanism: the first phase*, trans. Helen Lindsay and Ann Moffatt, Canberra: Australian Association for Byzantine Studies, *Byzantina Australiensa* 3.

Leoniceno, Niccolò (1497) *Libellus de Epidemia, quam vulgo morbum Gallicum vocant*, Venice: Aldus Manutius.

Lettsom, John Coakley (1795) *Hints respecting the Chlorosis of Boarding-schools*, London: C. Dilly.

Levine, Jon D., Gordon, Newton C. and Fields, Howard C. (1978) 'The mechanism of placebo analgesia', *Lancet* 2: 654–7.

Lewis, Gilbert (1976) 'A view of sickness in New Guinea' in J.B. Loudon (ed.), *Social Anthropology and Medicine* (ASA Monograph 13), London: Academic Press, 49–103.

—— (1980) *Day of Shining Red: an essay in understanding ritual*, Cambridge: Cambridge University Press.

—— (1993) 'Double standards of treatment evaluation' in Shirley Lindenbaum and Margaret Lock (eds), *Knowledge, Power and Practice. The anthropology of medicine and everyday life*, Berkeley: University of California Press, 189–218.

Lewis, Ioan M. (1971) *Ecstatic Religion: an anthropological study*, Harmondsworth: Penguin Books.

Lichtenthaeler, Charles (1963) *Études Hippocratiques VII–X: Étude VIII: De l'économie du Pronostic d'Hippocrate* (Collection de l'École Française de Rome 79), Geneva: Droz.

Liénard, Édm. (1938) 'Pro Hygini Argonautarum Catalogo', *Latomus* 2: 240–55.

Lilja, Saara (1976) *Dogs in Ancient Greek Poetry*, Helsinki: Societas Scientiarum Fennica.

Linders, Tullia (1972) *Studies in the Treasure Records of Artemis Brauronia found in Athens*, Stockholm: Svenska Institutet i Athen, 4.19.

Lingo, Alison Klairmont (1986) 'Empirics and charlatans in early modern France: the genesis of the classification of the "Other" in medical practice', *Journal of Social History* 19: 583–603.

Lippi, Donatella and Arieti, Stefano (1985) 'La ricezione del *Corpus hippocraticum* nell'Islam' in Mazzini and Fusco 1985: 399–402.

Littré, Émile (1863–77) *Dictionnaire de la langue française*, Paris: Hachette.

Lloyd, Geoffrey E.R. (1966) *Polarity and Analogy: two types of argumentation in early Greek thought*, Cambridge: Cambridge University Press.

—— (1975) 'The Hippocratic question', *Classical Quarterly* 25: 171–92; reprinted in *Methods and Problems in Greek Science*, Cambridge: Cambridge University Press, 1991, 194–223.

—— (1979) *Magic, Reason and Experience: studies in the origin and development of Greek science*, Cambridge: Cambridge University Press.

—— (1983) *Science, Folklore and Ideology: studies in the life sciences in ancient Greece*, Cambridge: Cambridge University Press.

—— (1987) *The Revolutions of Wisdom: studies in the claims and practice of ancient Greek science*, Berkeley: University of California Press.

Lloyd-Jones, Hugh (1983) 'Artemis and Iphigeneia', *Journal of Hellenic Studies* 103: 87–102.

Logan, Michael H. (1977) 'Humoral medicine in Guatemala and peasant acceptance of modern medicine', in David Landy (ed.), *Culture, Disease and Healing*, New York: Macmillan, 487–95 (also in Michael H. Logan and Edward E. Hunt (eds), *Health and the Human Condition: perspectives on medical anthropology*, Belmont, CA: Wadsworth, 1978, 363–75).

Longfield-Jones, Gwen M. (1986) 'A Graeco-Roman speculum in the Wellcome Museum', *Medical History* 30: 81–9.

Longrigg, James (1985) 'A "seminal" debate in the fifth century BC?' in Allan Gotthelf (ed.), *Aristotle on Nature and Living Things: philosophical and historical studies presented to David M. Balme*, Pittsburgh, PA: Mathesis Publications; Bristol: Bristol Classical Press, 277–87.

—— (1993) *Greek Rational Medicine: philosophy and medicine from Alcmaeon to the Alexandrians*, London: Routledge.

Lonie, Iain M. (1978) 'Cos versus Cnidus and the historians: Part I', *History of Science* 16: 42–75.

—— (1981) *The Hippocratic Treatises 'On Generation', 'On the Nature of the Child', 'Diseases IV'*, Berlin and New York: de Gruyter.

—— (1983) 'Literacy and the development of Hippocratic medicine', in Lasserre and Mudry 1983: 145–61.

—— (1985) 'The "Paris Hippocratics": teaching and research in Paris in the second half of the sixteenth century' in Andrew Wear, Roger K. French and Iain M. Lonie (eds), *The Medical Renaissance of the Sixteenth Century*, Cambridge and New York: Cambridge University Press, 155–74.

Loraux, Nicole (1978) 'Sur la Race des femmes et quelques-unes de ses tribus', *Arethusa* 11: 43–87; trans. in Loraux 1993: 72–110.

—— (1981a) 'La Cité comme cuisine et comme partage', *Annales Économies, Sociétés, Civilisations* 36: 614–22.

—— (1981b) 'Le Lit, la guerre', *L'Homme* 21: 37–67.

—— (1982) 'Ponos. Sur quelques difficultés de la peine comme nom du travail', *Annali dell'Instituto Orientale di Napoli* 4: 171–92.

—— (1984) 'Le Corps étranglé: quelques faits et beaucoup de répresentations' in Yan Thomas (ed.), *Du Châtiment dans la cité: supplices corporels et peine de mort dans le monde antique*, Rome: L'École française de Rome; Paris: Éds de Boccard, 195–218; trans. as Loraux 1995: 101–15.

—— (1987) *Tragic Ways of Killing a Woman*, trans. Anthony Forster, Cambridge, MA and London: Harvard University Press; French original, *Façons tragiques de tuer une femme*, Paris: Hachette, 1985.

—— (1993) *The Children of Athena: Athenian ideas about citizenship and the division between the sexes*, trans. by Caroline Levine, Princeton, NJ: Princeton University Press; French original, *Les Enfants d'Athéna: idées athéniennes sur la citoyenneté et la division des sexes*, Paris: Maspero, 1981 and Éds La Découverte, 1984.

—— (1995) *The Experiences of Tiresias: the feminine and the Greek man*, trans. Paula Wissing, Princeton, NJ: Princeton University Press.

Loudon, Irvine S.L. (1980) 'Chlorosis, anaemia, and anorexia nervosa', *British Medical Journal* 281: 1669–75.

—— (1984) 'The diseases called chlorosis', *Psychological Medicine* 14: 27–36.

—— (1986) *Medical Care and the General Practitioner, 1750–1850*, Oxford: Clarendon Press.

MacCormack, Carol P. (1977) 'Women and symbolic systems: biological events and cultural control', *Signs* 3: 93–100.

MacDonnel, David Evans (1809) *A Dictionary of Quotations in Most Frequent Use*, 5th edition, London: G. Wilkie and J. Robinson.

MacEoin, Beth (1992) *Homoeopathy*, Sevenoaks: Headway Lifeguides, Hodder and Stoughton.

McFarland, Ronald E. (1975) 'The rhetoric of medicine: Lord Herbert's and Thomas Carew's poems of green-sickness', *Journal of the History of Medicine and Allied Sciences* 30: 250–8.

McLaren, Angus (1984) *Reproductive Rituals: the perception of fertility in England from the sixteenth to the nineteenth century*, London and New York: Methuen.

—— (1990) *A History of Contraception from Antiquity to the Present Day*, Oxford and Cambridge, MA: Basil Blackwell.

—— (1993) 'Privileged communications: medical confidentiality in late Victorian Britain', *Medical History* 37: 127–47.

—— (1994) '"Not a stranger: a doctor": medical men and sexual matters in the late nineteenth century' in Porter and Teich 1994: 267–83.

McLaren, Dorothy (1975) 'Emmenologia: a curse or a blessing?', *Bulletin of the Society for the Social History of Medicine* 25: 65–7.

McMurtrie, Henry (1871) *The Woman's Medical Companion, and Nursery-Adviser*, Philadelphia: T. Elwood Zell.

Maggs, Christopher J. (1985) *The Origins of General Nursing*, London: Croom Helm.

—— (ed.) (1987) *Nursing History: the state of the art*, London: Croom Helm.

Mai, François M. and Merskey, Harold (1981) 'Briquet's concept of hysteria: an historical perspective', *Canadian Journal of Psychiatry* 26: 57–63.

Manetti, Daniela (1990) 'Data-recording in *Epid.* II 2-3: some considerations' in Potter *et al.* 1990: 143–58.

—— and Roselli, Amneris (1982) *Ippocrate: Epidemie, libro sesto*, Florence: La nuova Italia.

Mansfeld, Jaap (1980) 'Plato and the method of Hippocrates', *Greek, Roman and Byzantine Studies* 21: 341–62.

—— (1983) 'The historical Hippocrates and the origins of scientific medicine' in Ruse 1983: 49–76.

Manuli, Paola (1980) 'Fisiologia e patologia del femminile negli scritti ippocratici dell'antica ginecologia greca' in Mirko D. Grmek (ed.), *Hippocratica. Actes du Colloque hippocratique de Paris 1978*, Paris: Éds de CNRS, 393–408.

—— (1982) 'Elogia della castità: La *Ginecologia* di Sorano', *Memoria* 3: 39–49.

—— (1983) 'Donne mascoline, femmine sterili, vergini perpetue. La ginecologia greca tra Ippocrate e Sorano' in Campese *et al.* 1983: 147–92.

Marcovich, M. (1972) 'Sappho fr. 31: anxiety attack or love declaration?' *Classical Quarterly* 22: 19–32.

Marganne, Marie-Hélène (1981) *Inventaire analytique des papyrus grecs de médecine*, Geneva: Droz.

Marland, Hilary (ed.) (1993a) *The Art of Midwifery: early modern midwives in Europe*, London and New York: Routledge.

—— (1993b) 'The *'burgerlijke'* midwife: the *stadsvroedvrouw* of eighteenth-century Holland' in Marland 1993a: 192–213.

Marland, Hilary, van Lieburg, M.J. and Kloosterman, G.J. (1987) *'Mother and Child were Saved'. The memoirs (1693–1740) of the Frisian midwife Catharina Schrader*, Amsterdam: Rodopi.

Marsden, C. David (1986) 'Hysteria – a neurologist's view', *Psychological Medicine* 16: 277–88.

Masterpiece (Anon.) (1694) *Aristotle's Masterpiece, or, the secrets of generation displayed in all the parts thereof*, London: printed for W.B..

Matakiewicz, Helena (1932–3) 'De Hygino Mythographo', *Eos* 34: 93–110.

Mayou, Richard (1975) 'The social setting of hysteria', *British Journal of Psychiatry* 127: 466–9.

Mazzini, Innocenzo (1985) 'Ippocrate latino dei secolo V–VI; tecnica di traduzione' in Mazzini and Fusco 1985: 383–7.

—— and Flammini, Giuseppe (1983) *De conceptu. Estratti di un'antica traduzione latina del Peri gynaikeiôn pseudippocratico I*, Bologna: Pàtron.

—— and Fusco, Franca (1985) *I testi di medicina latini antichi: problemi filologici e storici*, Atti del I Convegno Internazionale, 26–28 aprile, Università di Macerata: G. Bretschneider.

Mellish, Joyce Mary (1984) *A Basic History of Nursing*, Durban and Pretoria: Butterworths.

Mercado, Luis (1587) *De mulierum affectionibus libri IIII*, Venice: F. Valgrisi.

Merskey, Harold (1979) *The Analysis of Hysteria*, London: Baillière Tindall.
—— (1985) 'Hysteria: the history of a disease: Ilza Veith', *British Journal of Psychiatry* 147: 576–9.
—— (1986) 'The importance of hysteria', *British Journal of Psychiatry* 149: 23–8.
—— and Potter, Paul (1989) 'The womb lay still in ancient Egypt', *British Journal of Psychiatry* 154: 751–3.
Meuli, Karl (1975) 'Die gefesselten Götter' in *Gesammelte Schriften* II, Basel: Schwabe, 1035–81.
Meyerhof, Max (1926) 'New light on Hunain ibn Ishaq and his period', *Isis* 8: 685–724.
—— (1931) '"Ali at-Tabari's "Paradise of Wisdom", one of the oldest Arabic compilations of medicine', *Isis* 16: 6–54.
—— and Joannides, D. (1938) *La Gynécologie et l'obstétrique chez Avicenne (Ibn Sina) et leurs rapports avec celles des Grecs*, Cairo: E. and R. Schindler.
Micale, Mark (1989) 'Hysteria and its historiography: a review of past and present writings, I and II', *History of Science* 27: 223–61, 319–51.
Mikalson, Jon D. (1983) *Athenian Popular Religion*, Chapel Hill and London: University of North Carolina Press.
Mills, Simon (1992) *Woman Medicine. Vitex Agnus-Castus*, Christchurch, Dorset: Amberwood Publishing.
Mitchinson, Wendy (1986) 'Hysteria and insanity in women: a nineteenth-century Canadian perspective', *Journal of Canadian Studies* 21: 87–105.
Moerman, Daniel E. (1992) 'Minding the body: the placebo effect unmasked' in Maxine Sheets-Johnstone (ed.), *Giving the Body Its Due*, Albany, NY: SUNY Press, 69–84.
Moisan, Monique (1990) 'Les Plantes narcotiques dans le *Corpus hippocratique*' in Potter *et al.* 1990: 381–92.
Moïssidés, M. (1922) 'Contribution à l'étude de l'avortement dans l'antiquité grecque', *Janus* 26: 59–85, 129–45.
Mol, Annemarie and Berg, Marc (1994) 'Principles and practice of medicine: the co-existence of various anemias', *Culture, Medicine and Psychiatry* 18: 247–65.
Moore, Lisa Jean and Clarke, Adele E. (1995) 'Clitoral conventions and transgressions: graphic representations in anatomy texts, *c.*1900–1991', *Feminist Studies* 21: 255–301.
Moore, Susan (1988) *A Guide to Chiropractic*, London: Hamlyn.
Morris, David B. (1991) *The Culture of Pain*, Berkeley: University of California Press.
Moscucci, Ornella (1990) *The Science of Woman: gynaecology and gender in England, 1800–1929*, Cambridge: Cambridge University Press.
Motte, André (1973) *Prairies et jardins de la Grèce antique: de la religion à la philosophie*, Brussels: Palais des Académies.
Mudry, Philippe (1982) *La préface du 'De medicina' de Celse*, Rome: Institut Suisse.
—— (1997) 'Éthique et médecine à Rome: La *Préface* de Scribonius Largus ou l'affirmation d'une singularité' in Flashar and Jouanna 1997: 297–322.
Muff, Janet (1988) 'Of images and ideals: a look at socialization and sexism in nursing' in A.H. Jones 1988: 197–220.
Müller-Rohlfsen, Inge (1980) *Die lateinische Ravennatische Übersetzung der hippokratischen Aphorismen aus dem 5./6. Jahrhundert n. chr.*, Geistes- und social-wissenschaftliche Dissertationen 55, Hamburg: Hartmut Lüdke.

Muret, Marc Antoine de (1554) *Catullus. Et in eum commentarius M.A. Mureti*, Venice: Aldine.

Murphy, Yolanda and Murphy, Robert F. (1974) *Women of the Forest*, New York: Columbia University Press.

Nath, D., Sethi, N., Singh, R.K. and Jain, A.K. (1992) 'Commonly used Indian abortifacient plants with special reference to their teratologic effects in rats', *Journal of Ethnopharmacology* 36: 147–54.

Nathanson, Constance A. (1975) 'Illness and the feminine role: a theoretical overview', *Social Science and Medicine* 9: 57–62.

—— (1991) *Dangerous Passage: the social control of sexuality in women's adolescence*, Philadelphia: Temple University Press.

Nichol, Guy (1969) 'The clitoris martyr', *World Medicine* 4 (16): 59–65.

Nichter, Mark (1978) 'Patterns of resort in the use of therapy systems and their significance for health planning in South Asia', *Medical Anthropology* 2 (2): 29–58.

Nickel, Diethard (1979) 'Berufsvorstellungen über weibliche Medizinalpersonen in der Antike', *Klio* 61: 515–18.

—— (1981) 'Medizingeschichtliches in den "Fabulae" des Hyginus', *International Congress for the History of Medicine* 26, II: 170–3.

Nilsson, Martin P. (1961–7) *Geschichte der griechischen Religion*, 2 vols (*Handbuch der Altertumswissenschaft* 5.2), Munich: Beck.

Norri, Juhani (1992) *Names of Sicknesses in English, 1400–1550: an exploration of the lexical field*, Helsinki: Suomalainen tiedeakatemia.

Nutting, M. Adelaide and Dock, Lavinia Lloyd (1907) *A History of Nursing*, 2 vols, New York and London: G.P. Putnam's Sons.

Nutton, Vivian (ed.) (1979) *Galen, On Prognosis*, CMG V.8.1, Berlin: Akademie-Verlag.

—— (1984a) 'John Caius und Johannes Lange: medizinischer Humanismus zur Zeit Vesals', *NTM – Schriftenreihe für Geschichte der Naturwissenschafte, Technik und Medizin* 21: 81–7.

—— (1984b) 'From Galen to Alexander: aspects of medicine and medical practice in late antiquity' in John Scarborough (ed.), *Symposium on Byzantine Medicine, Dumbarton Oaks Papers* 38: 1–14; reprinted in Nutton 1988: ch.10.

—— (1985a) 'The drug trade in antiquity', *Journal of the Royal Society of Medicine* 78: 138–45.

—— (1985b) 'Humanist surgery' in Andrew Wear, Roger K. French and Iain M. Lonie (eds), *The Medical Renaissance of the Sixteenth Century*, Cambridge and New York: Cambridge University Press, 75–99.

—— (1985c) 'Murders and miracles: lay attitudes towards medicine in classical antiquity', in Roy Porter (ed.), *Patients and Practitioners: lay perceptions of medicine in pre-industrial society*, Cambridge: Cambridge University Press, 23–53; reprinted in Nutton 1988: ch.8.

—— (1988) *From Democedes to Harvey*, London: Variorum Reprints.

—— (1989) 'Hippocrates in the Renaissance', in Baader and Winau 1989: 420–39.

—— (1991) 'Style and context in the *Method of Healing*' in Fridolf Kudlien and Richard J. Durling (eds), *Galen's Method of Healing: proceedings of the 1982 Galen Symposium*, Leiden: Brill, 1–25.

—— (1992) 'Healers in the medical market place: towards a social history of Graeco-

Roman medicine' in Andrew Wear (ed.), *Medicine and Society: historical essays*, Cambridge: Cambridge University Press, 15–58.

—— (1993) 'Roman medicine: tradition, confrontation, assimilation', *Aufstieg und Niedergang der Römischen Welt* II 37.1, Berlin and New York: Walter de Gruyter, 49–78.

—— (1994) 'Greek science in the sixteenth-century Renaissance' in Judith V. Field and Frank A.J.L. James (eds), *Renaissance and Revolution: humanists, scholars, craftsmen and natural philosophers in early modern Europe*, Cambridge: Cambridge University Press, 15–28.

—— (1995a) 'The medical meeting place' in van der Eijk *et al.* 1995: 3–25.

—— (1995b) 'What's in an oath?', *Journal of the Royal College of Physicians of London* 29, 518–24.

—— (1997) 'Hippocratic morality and modern medicine' in Flashar and Jouanna 1997: 31–56.

Oberhelman, Steven M. (1993) 'Dreams in Graeco-Roman medicine', *Aufstieg und Niedergang der Römischen Welt* II 37.1, Berlin and New York: Walter de Gruyter, 121–56.

Olasky, Marvin (1988) *The Press and Abortion, 1838–1988*, Hillsdale, NJ: Lawrence Erlbaum Associates.

Osborne, Robin (1985) *Demos: The Discovery of Classical Attika*, Cambridge: Cambridge University Press.

—— (1993) 'Women and sacrifice in classical Greece', *Classical Quarterly* 43: 392–405.

Padel, Ruth (1983) 'Women: model for possession by Greek daemons' in Averil Cameron and Amelie Kuhrt (eds), *Images of Women in Antiquity*, London: Croom Helm, 3–19.

—— (1992) *In and Out of the Mind: Greek images of the tragic self*, Princeton, NJ: Princeton University Press.

Paget, James (1873) 'Nervous mimicry' in Stephen Paget (ed.) (1902), *Selected Essays and Addresses by Sir James Paget*, London: Longmans, Green and Co., 73–144.

Palis, James, Rossopoulos, Evangelos and Triarhou, Lazaros C. (1985) 'The Hippocratic concept of hysteria: a translation of the original texts', *Integrative Psychiatry* 3: 226–8.

Palmieri, Nicoletta (1981) 'Un antico commento a Galeno della scuola medica di Ravenna', *Physis* 23: 197–296.

Panofsky, Dora and Panofsky, Erwin (1956) *Pandora's Box: the changing aspects of a mythical symbol*, London: Routledge and Kegan Paul (reprinted in German, 1991, Princeton University Press).

Parker, Robert (1983) *Miasma: pollution and purification in early Greek religion*, Oxford: Oxford University Press.

—— (1996) *Athenian Religion: a history*, Oxford: Clarendon Press.

Parkin, Tim G. (1992) *Demography and Roman Society*, Baltimore, MD and London: Johns Hopkins University Press.

Pattison, John (1866) *Diseases Peculiar to Women*, London: Henry Turner.

Pavey, Agnes E. (1938) *The Story of the Growth of Nursing: as an Art, a Vocation, and a Profession*, London: Faber and Faber.

Pearce, Tola Olu (1993) 'Lay medical knowledge in an African context' in Shirley Lindenbaum and Margaret Lock (eds), *Knowledge, Power and Practice. The anthropology of medicine and everyday life*, Berkeley: University of California Press, 150–65.

Pearcy, Lee T. (1988) 'Theme, dream, and narrative: reading the *Sacred Tales* of Aelius Aristides', *Transactions of the American Philological Association* 118: 377–91.

—— (1992) 'Diagnosis as narrative in ancient literature', *American Journal of Philology* 113: 595–616.

Pechey, John (1694) *Some Observations Made upon the Bermudas Berries Imported from the Indies: Shewing their Admirable Virtues in Curing the Green-sickness*, London.

Pelling, Margaret and Webster, Charles (1979) 'Medical practitioners' in Webster 1979: 165–235.

Perkins, Judith (1992) 'The "self" as sufferer', *Harvard Theological Review* 85: 245–72.

—— (1995) *The Suffering Self: pain and narrative representation in the early Christian era*. London and New York: Routledge.

Perlman, Paula (1983) 'Plato *Laws* 833C–834D and the bears of Brauron', *Greek, Roman and Byzantine Studies* 24: 115–30.

—— (1989) 'Acting the she-bear for Artemis', *Arethusa* 22: 111–33.

Peterson, Donald W. (1977) 'Observations on the chronology of the Galenic corpus', *Bulletin of the History of Medicine* 51: 484–95.

Peterson, M. Jeanne (1978) *The Medical Profession in Mid-Victorian London*, Berkeley and London: University of California Press.

—— (1984) 'Gentlemen and medical men: the problem of professional recruitment', *Bulletin of the History of Medicine* 58: 457–73.

—— (1986) 'Dr Acton's enemy: medicine, sex and society in Victorian England', *Victorian Studies* 29: 569–90.

Phillippo, J.C. (1890) 'On the arrest and cure of leprosy by the external and internal use of the gurjun and chaulmoogra oils', *Transactions of the Epidemiological Society of London* 9: 70–5.

Pigeaud, Jackie (1982) 'Pro Caelio Aureliano', Mémoires du Centre Jean Palerne 3: *Médecins et Médecine dans l'Antiquité*, Université de Saint-Etienne, 105–17.

—— (1988) 'Le style d'Hippocrate ou l'écriture fondatrice de la médecine' in Marcel Detienne (ed.), *Les Savoirs de l'écriture en Grèce ancienne*, Lille: Presses Universitaires, 305–29.

—— (1990) 'La Maladie a-t-elle un sens chez Hippocrate?' in Potter *et al.* 1990: 17–38.

Pinault, Jody Rubin (1992) 'The medical case for virginity in the early second century CE: Soranus of Ephesus, *Gynecology* 1.32,' *Helios* 19: 123–39.

Plarr, Victor G. (1930) *Plarr's Lives of the Fellows of the Royal College of Surgeons of England* (revised by Sir D'Arcy Power), Bristol: J. Wright and Son; London: Simpkin, Marshall.

Pomeroy, Sarah B. (1977) '*Technikai kai mousikai*: the education of women in the fourth century and in the Hellenistic period', *American Journal of Ancient History* 2: 51–68.

—— (ed.) (1991) *Women's History and Ancient History*, Chapel Hill and London: University of North Carolina Press.

Porta, Giovan Battista della (1601) *De humana physiognomonia libri IV*, Ursellis: Cornelii Sutorii.

Porter, Roy (1985) '"The Secrets of generation display'd": *Aristotle's Masterpiece* in eighteenth century England', *Eighteenth Century Life* 9: 1–21; special issue, Robert

P. Maccubbin (ed.), *Unauthorized Sexual Behaviour during the Enlightenment*, Williamsburg, VA: College of William and Mary.

—— (1987) 'A touch of danger: the man-midwife as sexual predator' in George S. Rousseau and Roy Porter (eds), *Sexual Underworlds of the Enlightenment*, Manchester: Manchester University Press, 206–32.

—— (1989) *Health for Sale. Quackery in England 1660–1850*, Manchester and New York: Manchester University Press.

—— (1990) 'Female quacks in the consumer society', *History of Nursing Society Journal* 3: 1–25.

—— (1991) 'History of the body' in Peter Burke (ed.), *New Perspectives on Historical Writing*, Philadelphia: Pennsylvania State University Press, 206–32.

—— (1994) 'The literature of sexual advice before 1800' in Porter and Teich 1994: 134–57.

—— and Porter, Dorothy (1989) *Patient's Progress. Doctors and doctoring in eighteenth-century England*, Stanford, CA: Stanford University Press.

—— and Teich, Mikuláš (1994) *Sexual Knowledge, Sexual Science: the history of attitudes to sexuality*, Cambridge: Cambridge University Press.

Potter, John (1728) *Archaeologia Graeca: or, The antiquities of Greece*, 5th edition, vol. 2, London: J. and J. Knapton.

—— (1764) *Archaeologia Graeca: or, The antiquities of Greece*, 8th edition, vol. 2, London: J. and J. Knapton.

Potter, Paul (1976) 'Herophilus of Chalcedon: an assessment of his place in the history of anatomy', *Bulletin of the History of Medicine* 50: 45–60.

—— (1989) 'Epidemien I/III: Form und Absicht der zweiundvierzig Fallbeschreibungen', in Baader and Winau 1989: 9–19.

Potter, Paul, Maloney, Gilles and Desautels, Jacques (eds) (1990), *La Maladie et les maladies dans la Collection hippocratique: Actes des VIe Colloque international hippocratique, Québec, 28 septembre–3 octobre 1987*, Quebec: Eds du Sphinx.

Price, Simon R.F. (1990) 'The future of dreams: from Freud to Artemidoros' in Halperin *et al.* 1990: 365–87.

Price, Theodora H. (1978) *Kourotrophos: cults and representations of the Greek nursing deities*, Leiden: Brill.

Prince, Raymond and Tcheng-Laroche, Françoise (1987) 'Culture-bound syndromes and international disease classifications', *Culture, Medicine and Psychiatry* 11: 3–19.

Proceedings of the Seventh Annual Meeting of the London Surgical Home for the Reception of Gentlewomen and Females of Respectability suffering from Curable Surgical Diseases, July 25th 1865 (1865), London: Savill and Edwards.

Pucci, Pietro (1977) *Hesiod and the Language of Poetry*, Baltimore, MD: Johns Hopkins University Press.

Purkiss, Diane (1996) *The Witch in History: early modern and twentieth-century representations*, London: Routledge.

Radicchi, Rino (1970) *La Gynaecia di Muscione*, Pisa: Giardini.

Redfield, James M. (1975) *Nature and Culture in the Iliad: the tragedy of Hector*, Chicago and London: University of Chicago Press.

—— (1982) 'Notes on the Greek wedding', *Arethusa* 15: 181–201.

Reinach, Salomon (1904) 'Medicus' in Charles Daremberg and Edm. Saglio (eds), *Dictionnaire des Antiquités grecques et romaines* 3.2, Paris: Hachette, 1669–1700.

Renzi, Salvatore de (1853) *Collectio Salernitana II*, Naples: Filiatre-Sebezio.

Rey, Roselyne (1993) *History of Pain*, trans. Louise Elliott Wallace, J.A. Cadden and S.W. Cadden, Cambridge MA: Harvard University Press; French original, *Histoire de la douleur* Paris: Éds de la Découverte, 1993.

Reynolds, John Russell (1880) *A System of Medicine*, 3 vols, Philadelphia: H.C. Lea's Sons.

Reynolds, Leighton Durham (ed.) (1983) *Texts and Transmission: a survey of the Latin classics*, Oxford: Clarendon Press.

Rhazes (1505) *Continens Rasis ordinatus et correctus . . .* (al-Hawi), Venice: Bon. Locatellum.

—— (1534) *Rhases Philosophi Tractatus nonus ad regem Almansorem, de curatione morborum particularium*, Paris: Simon de Colines.

Ricci, J.V. (1950) *Aetios of Amida: the gynecology and obstetrics of the sixth century* AD, Philadelphia: Blakiston.

Richards, Audrey I. (1956) *Chisungu: a girls' initiation ceremony among the Bemba of Zambia*, London: Tavistock Publications.

Richlin, Amy (1991) 'Zeus and Metis: Foucault, feminism, classics', *Helios* 18: 160–80.

Riddle, John M. (1984) 'Gargilius Martialis as a medical writer', *Journal of the History of Medicine and Allied Sciences* 39: 408–29.

—— (1985) *Dioscorides on Pharmacy and Medicine* (History of Science series, 3), Austin: University of Texas Press.

—— (1987) 'Folk tradition and folk medicine: recognition of drugs in classical antiquity', in J. Scarborough (ed.), *Folklore and Folk Medicines*, Wisconsin: American Institute of the History of Pharmacy, 33–61.

—— (1992) *Contraception and Abortion from the Ancient World to the Renaissance*, Cambridge, MA: Harvard University Press.

—— (1993) 'High medicine and low medicine in the Roman Empire' in *Aufstieg und Niedergang der Römischen Welt* II 37.1, Berlin and New York: Walter de Gruyter, 102–20.

—— (1997) *Eve's Herbs: a history of contraception and abortion in the West*, Cambridge, MA: Harvard University Press.

Riley, H.T. (1856) *Dictionary of Latin Quotations, Proverbs, Maxims and Mottos*, London: Henry G. Bohn.

Risse, Guenter B. (1988) 'Hysteria at the Edinburgh Infirmary: the construction and treatment of a disease, 1770–1800', *Medical History* 32: 1–22.

Robb, Hunter (1892) 'Hippocrates on hysteria', *Johns Hopkins Hospital Bulletin* 3: 78–9.

Robert, Louis (1964) 'Femmes médecins' (s.v. *Mousa Agathokleous iatreinê*) in Nezih Firatli and Louis Robert, *Les stèles funéraires de Byzance gréco-romaine*, Paris: Adrien Maisonneuve, 175–8.

Roberts, Joan I. and Group, Thetis M. (1995) *Feminism and Nursing: an historical perspective on power, status, and political activism in the nursing profession*, Westport, CT and London: Praeger.

Robinson, Victor (1946) *White Caps: the story of nursing*, Philadelphia: Lippincott.

Roche, Nicolas de la (1542) *De morbis mulierum curandis*, Paris: V. Gaultherot.

Roesch, Paul (1984) 'Médecins publics dans les cités grecques', *Histoire des sciences médicales* 18: 279–93.

Rosaldo, Michelle Zimbalist and Atkinson, Jane Monnig (1975) 'Man the hunter and woman: metaphors for the sexes in Ilongot magical spells' in Roy Willis (ed.), *The*

Interpretation of Symbolism (Association of Social Anthropologists Studies 3), London: Malaby Press, 43–75.

Rose, Valentin (1879) *Cassii Felicis De Medicina: ex Graecis Logicae Sectae Auctoribus Liber Translatus*, Leipzig: Teubner.

—— (1882) *Sorani Gynaeciorum vetus translatio Latina*, Leipzig: Teubner.

—— (1894) *Theodori Prisciani: Euporiston Libri III*, Leipzig: Teubner.

Rousselle, Aline (1980) 'Images médicales du corps. Observation féminine et idéologie masculine: le corps de la femme d'après les médecins grecs', *Annales. Économies, Sociétés, Civilisations*, 35: 1089–1115.

—— (1988) *Porneia: On desire and the body in antiquity*, trans. Felicia Pheasant, Oxford: Basil Blackwell; first published as *Porneia*, Paris: Presses Universitaires de France, 1983.

Rousset, François (1588) *Hysterotomotokia*, trans. Caspar Bauhin, Basel: Conrad Waldkirch. (First published 1581, in French.)

Roy, Alec (ed.) (1982) *Hysteria*, Chichester: John Wiley.

Rudhardt, Jean (1958) *Notions fondamentales de la pensée religieuse et actes constitutifs du culte dans la Grèce classique*, Geneva: E. Droz.

Ruse, Michael (ed.) (1983) *Nature Animated: papers of the Third International Conference on the History and Philosophy of Science, Montreal, Canada 1980*, vol. 2, Dordrecht: Reidel.

Russell, C. Scott (1968) *The World of a Gynaecologist*, Edinburgh and London: Oliver and Boyd.

Rutherford, Ian (1995) "The Poetics of the *Paraphthegma*: Aelius Aristides and the *Decorum* of self-praise" in Doreen Innes, Harry Hine and Christopher Pelling (eds), *Ethics and Rhetoric: classical essays for Donald Russell on his seventy-fifth birthday*. Oxford: Clarendon Press, 193–204.

Sacombe, Jean-François (1792) 'La Luciniade ou l'art des accouchements, poème didactique', Paris.

Saha, J.C. and Kasinathan, S. (1961) 'Ecbolic properties of Indian medicinal plants, Part II', *Indian Journal of Medical Research* 49(6): 1094–8.

Saha, J.C., Savini, E.C. and Kasinathan, S. (1961) 'Ecbolic properties of Indian medicinal plants, Part I', *Indian Journal of Medical Research* 49(1): 130–51.

Sale, William (1965) 'Callisto and the virginity of Artemis', *Rheinisches Museum für Philologie* 108: 11–35.

Sankovich, Tilde A. (1988) *French Women Writers and the Book: myths of access and desire*, Syracuse, NY: Syracuse University Press.

Santow, Gigi (1995) '*Coitus interruptus* and the control of natural fertility', *Population Studies* 49: 19–43.

Sarrazin, Pierre (1921) *La Gynécologie dans les écrits hippocratiques*, Paris: L. Arnette.

Satow, R. (1979–80) 'Where has all the hysteria gone?', *Psychoanalytic Review* 66: 463–77.

Sauri, J. (1973) 'La concepcion Hipocratica de la histeria', *Actas Luso-Espanolas de Neurologia Psiquitria y Ciencias Afinas* 1(4): 539–46.

Sawyer, Ronald C. (1986) 'Patients, healers, and disease in the southeast Midlands, 1597–1634', PhD thesis, University of Wisconsin-Madison.

Scarborough, John (1976) 'Celsus on human vivisection at Ptolemaic Alexandria', *Clio Medica* 11: 25–38.

—— (1991) 'The pharmacology of sacred plants, herbs, and roots' in Chris A. Faraone

and Dirk Obbink (eds), *Magika Hiera. Ancient Greek magic and religion*, New York and Oxford: Oxford University Press, 138–74.
—— (1995) 'The opium poppy in Hellenistic and Roman medicine' in Roy Porter and Mikuláš Teich (eds), *Drugs and Narcotics in History*, Cambridge and New York: Cambridge University Press, 4–23.
—— and Nutton, Vivian (1982) 'The Preface of Dioscorides' *Materia Medica*: introduction, translation, and commentary', *Transactions and Studies of the College of Physicians of Philadelphia* 4: 187–227.
Scarry, Elaine (1985) *The Body in Pain: the making and unmaking of the world*, New York and Oxford: Oxford University Press.
Schaps, David (1977) 'The woman least mentioned: etiquette and women's names', *Classical Quarterly* 27: 323–30.
Schenck von Grafenberg, Joannes (1600) *Observationum medicarum, rararum, novarum, admirabilium, et monstrosarum libri*, Frankfurt: E. Paltheniana, sumtibus J. Rhodius.
Scheper-Hughes, Nancy and Lock, Margaret M. (1987) 'The mindful body: a prolegomenon to future work in medical anthropology', *Medical Anthropology Quarterly* 1: 6–41.
Schiebinger, Londa (1989) *The Mind Has No Sex? Women in the origins of modern science*, Cambridge, MA and London: Harvard University Press.
Schipperges, Heinrich (1964) 'Die Assimilation der arabischen Medizin durch das lateinische Mittelalter', *Sudhoffs Archiv* Beiheft 3, Wiesbaden: Franz Steiner.
Schmitt, Pauline (1977) 'Athéna Apatouria et la ceinture: les aspects féminins des Apatouries à Athènes', *Annales. Économies, Sociétés, Civilisations*, 32: 1059–73.
Schöne, Hermann I. (1924) 'Hippokrates Peri Pharmakon', *Rheinisches Museum* 73: 434–48.
Schönfeld, Jutta (1974) 'Die Zahnheilkunde im "Kitab Zad al-musafir" des al-Gazzar', *Sudhoffs Archiv für Geschichte der Medizin* 58: 380–403.
Schultz, James A. (1991) 'Medieval adolescence: the claims of history and the silence of German narrative', *Speculum* 66: 519–39.
Schurig, Martin (1729) *Parthenologia Historico-Medica, hoc est, Virginitatis Consideratio*, Dresden and Leipzig: C. Hekel.
Schwartz, Jacques (1957) 'Une source papyrologique d'Hygin le mythographe', *Studi in onore di Aristide Calderini e Roberto Paribeni* vol. 2, Milan: Editrice Ceschina, 151–6.
Schwarz, Emil (1951) *Chlorosis: a retrospective investigation*, Supplementum *Acta Medica Belgica*, Brussels: Presses imprimerie médicale et scientifique.
Scoffern, John (1867) *The London Surgical Home; or, Modern Surgical Psychology*, London: published by the author.
Scull, Andrew and Favreau, Diane (1986) 'The clitoridectomy craze', *Social Research* 53: 243–60.
Segal, Charles (1975) 'Mariage et sacrifice dans les *Trachiniennes* de Sophocle', *L'Antiquité classique* 44: 30–53.
Sermon, William (1671) *The Ladies Companion, or the English Midwife*, London: E. Thomas.
Seymer, Lucy Ridgely (1932) *A General History of Nursing*, New York: Macmillan; London: Faber and Faber.
Sezgin, Fuat (1971) *Geschichte des arabischen Schriftums*, Band 3, Leiden: E.J. Brill.
Sharp, Jane (1671) *The Midwives Book*, London: S. Miller.

Shorter, Edward (1983) *A History of Women's Bodies*, London: Allen Lane.
—— (1984) 'Les désordres psychosomatiques sont-ils "hystériques"? Notes pour une recherche historique', *Cahiers internationaux de sociologie* 76: 201–24.
—— (1986) 'Paralysis: the rise and fall of a "hysterical" symptom', *Journal of Social History* 19: 549–82.
Showalter, Elaine (1993) 'Hysteria, feminism, and gender' in Sander L. Gilman, Helen King, Roy Porter, G.S. Rousseau and Elaine Showalter, *Hysteria Beyond Freud*, Berkeley and Los Angeles: University of California Press, 286–344.
—— (1997) *Hystories: hysterical epidemics and modern culture*, New York: Columbia University Press.
Siddall, A. Clair (1982) 'Chlorosis – etiology reconsidered', *Bulletin of the History of Medicine* 56: 254–60.
Siegel, Rudolph E. (1970) *Galen on Sense Perception: his doctrines, observations and experiments on vision, hearing, smell, taste, touch and pain, and their historical sources*, New York and Basel: S. Karger.
—— (1976) *Galen on the Affected Parts*, New York and Basel: S. Karger.
Siggel, Alfred (1941) 'Gynäkologie, Embryologie und Frauenhygiene aus dem "Paradies der Weisheit über die Medizin" des Abu Hasan 'Ali b. Sahl Rabban at-Tabari nach der Ausgabe von Dr M. Zubair as-Siddiqi, 1928', *Quellen und Studien zur Geschichte der Naturwissenschaften und der Medizin* 8: 216–72.
Simon, Bennett (1978) *Mind and Madness in Ancient Greece: the classical roots of modern psychiatry*, Ithaca, NY: Cornell University Press.
Simmer, Hans H. (1977) 'Pflüger's nerve reflex theory of menstruation: the product of analogy, teleology and neurophysiology', *Clio Medica* 12: 57–90.
Singer, Charles (1922) *Greek Biology and Greek Medicine*, Oxford: Clarendon Press.
—— (1923) 'Medicine' in R.W. Livingstone (ed.), *The Legacy of Greece*, Oxford: Clarendon Press, 201–48.
—— (1959) 'The strange histories of some anatomical terms', *Medical History* 3: 1–7.
Singer, Peter N. (1997) (trans.) *Galen: Selected Works*, Oxford and New York: Oxford University Press World's Classics.
Siraisi, Nancy G. (1987) *Avicenna in Renaissance Italy: the canon and medical teaching in Italian universities after 1500*, Princeton, NJ: Princeton University Press.
Sissa, Giulia (1983) 'Il corpo della donna. Lineamenti di una ginecologia filosofica' in Campese *et al.* 1983: 81–145.
—— (1990) *Greek Virginity*, trans. Arthur Goldhammer, Cambridge, MA; Harvard University Press; French original, *Le Corps virginal*, Paris: Hachette, 1989.
Skarzynski, Boleslaw (1933) 'An oestrogenic substance from plant material', *Nature* 27 May: 766.
Skultans, Vieda (1970) 'The symbolic significance of menstruation and the menopause', *Man* 5: 639–51.
—— (1987) 'The management of mental illness among Maharashtrian families: a case study of a Mahanubhav healing temple', *Man* 22: 661–79.
—— (1991) 'Women and affliction in Maharashtra: a hydraulic model of health and illness', *Culture, Medicine and Psychiatry* 15: 321–59.
Slater, Eliot (1965) 'Diagnosis of "hysteria"', *British Medical Journal* 1: 1395–9.
—— (1976) 'What is hysteria?' in Roy 1982: 37–40.
Smith, Wesley D. (1979) *The Hippocratic Tradition*, Ithaca, NY: Cornell University Press.

—— (1989) 'Notes on ancient medical historiography', *Bulletin of the History of Medicine* 63: 73–109.

—— (1990) (ed. and trans.) *Hippocrates. Pseudepigraphic Writings* (Studies in Ancient Medicine, 2), Leiden and New York: E.J. Brill.

Snowden, Robert and Christian, Barbara (eds) (1983) *Patterns and Perceptions of Menstruation: a World Health Organisation international collaborative study*, London: Croom Helm; New York: St Martin's Press.

Snyder, Jane McIntosh (1991) 'Public occasion and private passion in the lyrics of Sappho of Lesbos', in Pomeroy 1991: 1–19.

Sournia, Jean-Charles (1983) 'Littré, historien de la médecine' in *Actes du Colloque Littré, Paris, 7–9 octobre 1981*, Centre international de Synthèse, Paris: Albin Michel, 263–9.

Sperber, Dan (1975) *Rethinking Symbolism*, trans. Alice L. Morton, Cambridge: Cambridge University Press.

—— (1985) *On Anthropological Knowledge: three essays*, first published as *Le Savoir des anthropologues*, Paris: Hermann, 1982, Cambridge Studies in Social Anthropology 54, Maison des Sciences de l'Homme and Cambridge: Cambridge University Press.

Starobinski, Jean (1981) 'Chlorosis – the "green sickness"', *Psychological Medicine* 11: 459–68.

Stengel, Alfred (1896) 'Diseases of the blood' in Thomas L. Stedman (ed.), *Twentieth Century Practice*, vol. 7, London: Sampson Low, Marston and Co., 231–525.

Stephanus, Joannes (1635) *In Hippocratis Coi libellum De virginum morbis commentarius*, Venice: Brogiollus.

Stevens, John (1849–66?) *Man-Midwifery exposed*, 2nd edition, London: William Horsell.

Stevenson, Lloyd G. (1965) '"New diseases" in the seventeenth century', *Bulletin of the History of Medicine* 39: 1–21.

Strathern, Marilyn (1972) *Women in Between. Female roles in a male world: Mount Hagen, New Guinea*, London: Seminar Press.

Sullivan, Mark D. (1993) 'Placebo controls and epistemic control in orthodox medicine', *Journal of Medicine and Philosophy* 18: 213–31.

Summers, Anne (1988) *Angels and Citizens: British women as military nurses 1854–1914*, London: Routledge and Kegan Paul.

Sydenham, Thomas (1753) *The Entire Works of Dr. Thomas Sydenham*, 3rd edition, trans. John Swan, London: E. Cave.

Tait, R. Lawson (1889) *Diseases of Women and Abdominal Surgery*, vol.1, Philadelphia: Lea.

Tambiah, Stanley J. (1990) *Magic, Science, Religion, and the Scope of Rationality*, Cambridge: Cambridge University Press.

Tanner, Thomas Hawkes (1867) 'On excision of the clitoris as a cure for hysteria, &c.', *Transactions of the Obstetrical Society of London for the Year 1866* 8: 360–84.

Tansey, Tilli (E.M.) and Milligan, Rosemary C.E. (1990) 'The early history of the Wellcome Research Laboratories, 1894–1914' in Jonathan Liebenau, Gregory J. Higby and Elaine C. Stround (eds), *Pill Peddlers: essays on the history of the pharmaceutical industry*, Madison, WI: American Institute of the History of Pharmacy, 91–106.

Tardy, Claude (1648) *In libellum Hippocratis de virginum morbis: commentario paraphrastica*, Paris: apud Jacobum de Senlecque, et apud Carolum du Mesnil.

Taylor, David C. (1986) 'Hysteria, play-acting and courage', *British Journal of Psychiatry* 149: 37–41.

Taylor, Frederick (1896) 'A discussion on anaemia: its causation, varieties, assorted pathology, and treatment', *British Medical Journal* 2, 19 September: 719–25.

Temkin, Owsei (1932) 'History of Hippocratism in late antiquity: the third century and the Latin West', reprinted in *The Double Face of Janus and Other Essays in the History of Medicine*, Baltimore, MD: Johns Hopkins University Press, 1977, 167–77.

—— (1935) 'Celsus' "On medicine" and the ancient medical sects', *Bulletin of the Institute of the History of Medicine* 3: 249–64.

—— (1953) 'Greek medicine as science and craft', *Isis* 44: 213–25.

Thivel, Antoine (1981) *Cnide et Cos? Essai sur les doctrines médicales dans la collection hippocratique*, Paris: Éds Belles Lettres.

—— (1983) 'Médecine hippocratique et pensée ionienne, réponse aux objections et essai de synthèse', in Lasserre and Mudry 1983: 211–32.

Thorndike, Lynn (1957) 'Newness and novelty in seventeenth century medicine' in Philip P. Wiener and Aaron Noland (eds), *Roots of Scientific Thought: a cultural perspective*, New York: Basic Books, 443–57.

Thornton, Bruce (1991) 'Constructionism and ancient Greek sex', *Helios* 18: 181–93.

Thornton, John L. (1982) *Jan van Rymsdyk, Medical Artist of the Eighteenth Century*, Cambridge and New York: Oleander Press.

Tiraqueau, Andreas (1566) *Commentarii de nobilitate et iure primigeniorum*, Lugduni: Guliel. Rouillius.

—— (1576) *De legibus connubialibus et iure maritali*, Venice.

Tone, Andrea (1996) 'Contraceptive consumers: gender and the political economy of birth control in the 1930s', *Journal of Social History* 29: 485–506.

Towler, Jean and Bramall, Joan (1986) *Midwives in History and Society*, London: Croom Helm.

Traister, Barbara H. (1991) '"Matrix and the pain thereof": a sixteenth-century gynaecological essay', *Medical History* 35: 436–51.

Trillat, Étienne (1986) *Histoire de l'hystérie*, Paris: Éditions Seghers.

—— (1987) 'Trois itinéraires à travers l'histoire de l'hystérie', *Histoire des Sciences médicales* 21: 27–31.

Turbayne, Colin M. (1976) 'Plato's "fantastic" appendix: the procreation model of the *Timaeus*', *Paideia* special issue: 125–40.

Turner, Bryan S. (1990) 'Recent developments in the theory of the body' in Mike Featherstone, Mike Hepworth and Bryan S. Turner (eds), *The Body: social process and cultural theory*, London: Sage Publications, 1–35.

Ullmann, Manfred (1977) 'Zwei spätantike Kommentare zu der hippokratischen Schrift *De morbis muliebribus*', *Medizinhistorisches Journal* 12: 245–62.

—— (1978) *Islamic Medicine*, trans. Jean Watt, Edinburgh: Edinburgh University Press; first published as *Die Medizin im Islam*, Leiden: Brill, 1970.

Van Brock, Nadia (1961) *Recherches sur le vocabulaire médical du grec ancien: soins et guérison*, Paris: Klincksieck.

van der Eijk, Philip J., Horstmanshoff, Hermann F.J. and Schrijvers, P.I. (eds) (1995) *Ancient Medicine in its Socio-Cultural Context*, 2 vols, Amsterdam: Rodopi.

van der Geest, Sjaak (1991) 'Marketplace conversations in Cameroon: how and why popular medical knowledge comes into being', *Culture, Medicine and Psychiatry* 15: 69–90.

van der Geest, Sjaak, Whyte, Susan Reynolds and Hardon, Anita (1996) 'The anthropology of pharmaceuticals: a biographical approach', *Annual Review of Anthropology* 25: 153–78.

van der Kwaak, Anke (1992) 'Female circumcision and gender identity: a questionable alliance?', *Social Science and Medicine* 35: 777–87.

van Foreest, Pieter (1599) *Observationum et curationum medicinalium, liber vigesimus-octavus, de mulierum morbis*, Leyden: Plantin.

van Straten, Folkert T. (1981) 'Gifts for the gods' in H.S. Versnel (ed.), *Faith, Hope and Worship. Aspects of religious mentality in the ancient world*, Leiden: Brill, 65–151.

—— (1992) 'Votives and votaries in Greek sanctuaries' in O. Reverdin and B. Grange (eds), *Le Sanctuaire grec*, Geneva: Fondation Hardt, 247–84.

Varandal, Joannes (1619) *De morbis et affectibus mulierum*, Lyons: B. Vincent.

Vassès, Jean (1533) *De causis respirationis libellus. De usu respirationis liber unus. De spirandi difficultate libri tres*, Paris: Simon de Colines.

Vázquez Buján, Manuel E. (1982) 'Vindiciano y el tratado *De natura generis humani*', *Dynamis* 2: 25–56.

—— (1986) *El De mulierum affectibus del Corpus Hippocraticum*, Santiago del Compostela: Universidad de Santiago del Compostela.

Vegetti, Mario (1979) *Il coltello e lo stilo. Animali, schiavi, barbari e donne alle origini della razionalità scientifica*, Milan: Il Saggiatore.

Veith, Ilza (1965) *Hysteria: the history of a disease*, Chicago and London: University of Chicago Press.

Vernant, Jean-Pierre (1968) Introduction to *Problèmes de la guerre en Grèce ancienne*, Paris: Mouton/École Pratique des Hautes Études, 9–30.

—— (1974) 'Le mythe prométhéen chez Hésiode' in *Mythe et société en Grèce ancienne*, Paris: Maspero, 177–94; English trans. by Janet Lloyd, *Myth and Society in Ancient Greece*, New York, 1990.

—— (1979) 'À la table des hommes: Mythe de fondation du sacrifice chez Hésiode' in Detienne and Vernant 1979: 37–132; English trans. by Paula Wissing, 1989, 'At man's table: Hesiod's foundation myth of sacrifice', 21–86 (see Detienne and Vernant 1979).

—— (1979–80) 'Étude comparée des religions antiques. Resumé des cours et travaux de l'année scolaire 1979/80', *Extrait de l'annuaire du Collège de France*, 453–66.

—— (1980–1) 'Étude comparée des religions antiques. Resumé des cours et travaux de l'année scolaire 1980/81', *Extrait de l'annuaire du Collège de France*, 391–406.

—— (1982–3) 'Étude comparée des religions antiques. Resumé des cours et travaux de l'année scolaire 1982/83', *Extrait de l'annuaire du Collège de France*, 443–58.

Versluysen, Margaret Connor (1980) 'Old wives' tales? Women healers in English history' in Celia Davies (ed.) *Rewriting Nursing History*, London: Croom Helm, 175–99.

Vertue, H. St. H. (1955) 'Chlorosis and stenosis', *Guy's Hospital Reports* 104: 329–48.

Vial, Claude (1985) 'La femme athénienne vue par les orateurs' in Anne-Marie Vérilhac (ed.) *La Femme dans le monde méditerranéen I, L'Antiquité*, Lyon: Travaux de la Maison de l'Orient 10, 47–60.

von Noorden, Karl (1905) 'Chlorosis' in Alfred Stengel (ed.), *Diseases of the Blood*, Philadelphia and London: W.B. Saunders, 339–536.

von Staden, Heinrich (1989) *Herophilus. The Art of Medicine in Early Alexandria*, Cambridge: Cambridge University Press.

—— (1991a) '*Apud nos foediora verba*: Celsus' reluctant construction of the female body' in Guy Sabbah (ed.), *Le Latin médical: la constitution d'un langage scientifique*, Saint-Étienne: Publications de l'Université de Saint-Étienne, 271–96.

—— (1991b) 'Matière et signification: rituel, sexe et pharmacologie dans le corpus hippocratique', *L'Antiquité classique* 60: 42–61.

—— (1992a) 'Women and dirt', *Helios* 19: 7–30.

—— (1992b) 'Spiderwoman and the chaste tree: the semantics of matter', *Configurations* 1: 23–56.

—— (1992c) 'The mind and skin of Heracles: heroic diseases' in Danielle Gourevitch (ed.), *Maladie et maladies: histoire et conceptualisation, Mélanges en l'honneur de Mirko Grmek*, École Pratique des Hautes Études, IVe section: Hautes Études Médiévales et Modernes 70, Geneva: Librairie Droz, 131–50.

—— (1992d) 'The discovery of the body: human dissection and its cultural contexts in ancient Greece', *Yale Journal of Biology and Medicine* 65: 223–41.

—— (1992e) 'Affinities and elisions: Helen and Hellenocentrism', *Isis* 83: 578–95.

—— (1994) 'Anatomy as rhetoric: Galen on dissection and persuasion', *Journal of the History of Medicine and Allied Sciences* 50: 47–66.

—— (1996) '"In a pure and holy way": personal and professional conduct in the Hippocratic Oath?', *Journal of the History of Medicine and Allied Sciences* 51: 404–37.

Wack, Mary F. (1990) *Lovesickness in the Middle Ages: the Viaticum and its commentaries*, Philadelphia: University of Pennsylvania Press.

Walshe, Sir Francis (1965) 'Diagnosis of hysteria', *British Medical Journal* 2: 1451–4.

Walter, George (1935) 'Peri Gynaikeion A of the Corpus Hippocraticum in a medieval translation', *Bulletin of the Institute of the History of Medicine* 3: 599–606.

Wear, Andrew (1992) 'The popularization of medicine in early modern England' in Roy Porter (ed.), *The Popularization of Medicine 1650–1850*, London: Routledge, 17–41.

Webster, Charles (ed.) (1979) *Health, Medicine and Mortality in the Sixteenth Century*, Cambridge: Cambridge University Press.

Wehrli, Fritz (1953) *Die Schule des Aristoteles: Heft VII, Herakleides Pontikos*, Basel: Schwabe.

Weinberg, Bernard (1950) 'Translations and commentaries of Longinus, *On the Sublime*, to 1600: a bibliography', *Modern Philology* 47: 145–51.

Weisensee, Mary (1986) 'Women's health perceptions in a male-dominated world' in Diane K. Kjervik and Ida M. Martinson (eds), *Women in Health and Illness: life experiences and crises*, Philadelphia: W.B. Saunders, 19–33.

Weisser, Ursula (1983) *Zeugung, Vererbung und Pränatale Entwicklung in der Medizin des arabisch-islamischen Mittelalters*, Erlangen: Hannelore Lülung.

—— (1989) 'Das Corpus Hippocraticum in der arabischen Medizin' in Baader and Winau 1989: 377–408.

Wellmann, Max (1922) 'Der Verfasser des Anonymus Londinensis', *Hermes* 57: 396–429.

Wendell, Susan (1996) *The Rejected Body: feminist philosophical reflections on disability*, New York and London: Routledge.

Wesley, George R. (1979) *A History of Hysteria*, Washington, DC: University Press of America.

West, Charles (1864) *Lectures on the Diseases of Women*, 3rd edition, London: J. and A. Churchill.

West, Martin L. (1978) *Hesiod: Works and Days*, Oxford: Oxford University Press.

White, Suzanne (1985) 'Medicine's humble humbug: four periods in the understanding of the placebo', *Pharmacy in History* 27: 51–60.

Whitteridge, Gweneth (1971) *William Harvey and the Circulation of the Blood*, London: Macdonald; New York: American Elsevier.

Willetts, R.F. (1958) 'Cretan Eileithyia', *Classical Quarterly* 8: 221–3.

Williams, Katherine E. (1990) 'Hysteria in seventeenth-century case records and unpublished manuscripts', *History of Psychiatry* 1: 383–401.

Willughby, Percival (1863) *Observations in Midwifery*, ed. Henry Blenkinsop, Warwick: Cooke; reprinted Wakefield: S.R. Publishing, 1972.

Wilson, Adrian (1985) 'William Hunter and the varieties of man-midwifery', in William F. Bynum and Roy Porter (eds), *William Hunter and the Eighteenth-Century Medical World*, Cambridge: Cambridge University Press, 343–69.

—— (1995) *The Making of Man-Midwifery: childbirth in England, 1660–1770*, Cambridge, MA: Harvard University Press.

Wilson, Bryan R. (ed.) (1979) *Rationality*, Oxford: Basil Blackwell.

Wilson, Nigel G. (1983) *Scholars of Byzantium*, London: Duckworth.

Winkler, John J. (1990) *The Constraints of Desire: the anthropology of sex and gender in ancient Greece*, New York: Routledge.

Winslow, Deborah (1980) 'Rituals of first menstruation in Sri Lanka', *Man* 15: 603–25.

Withering, William (1785) *An Account of the Foxglove and some of its Medical Uses*, London: C.G.J. and J. Robinson.

Withers, Maurine (1979) 'Agnodike: the first midwife/obstetrician', *Journal of Nurse-Midwifery* 24: 4.

Withington, Edward T. (1921) 'The Asclepiadae and the priests of Asklepios' in Charles Singer (ed.), *Studies in the History and Method of Science*, vol. 2, Oxford: Clarendon Press, 192–205.

Wittern, Renate and Pellegrin, Pierre (eds) (1996) *Hippokratische Medizin und antike Philosophie. Verhandlung des VIII. Internationalen Hippokrates-Kolloquiums, 23–28 Sept. 1995*, Hildesheim: Olms-Weidmann.

Wolf, Caspar (1564) *Harmonia Gynaeciorum* in *Gynaeciorum, hoc est, de mulierum tum aliis, tum gravidarum, parientium et puerperarum affectibus et morbis, libri veterum ac recentiorum . . .* (1566), Basel: Thomas Guarinus, 5–186.

Wolff, B. Berthold and Langley, Sarah (1968) 'Cultural factors and the response to pain: a review', *American Anthropologist* 70: 494–501.

Wolveridge, James (1671) *Speculum Matricis; or, the expert midwives handmaid*, London.

Woodruff, Robert A. (1967) 'Hysteria: an evaluation of objective diagnostic criteria by the study of women with chronic mental illnesses', *British Journal of Psychiatry* 114: 1115–19.

Woodruff, Robert A., Goodwin, Donald W. and Guze, Samuel B. (1974) 'Hysteria (Briquet's Syndrome)' in Roy 1982: 117–29.

Wright, John P. (1980) 'Hysteria and mechanical man', *Journal of the History of Ideas* 41: 233–47.

Wujastyk, Dominic (1998) 'Miscarriages of justice' in John Hinnells and Roy Porter (eds), *Religion, Health and Suffering*, London: Kegan Paul.

Young, Allan (1980) 'An anthropological perspective on medical knowledge', *Journal of Medicine and Philosophy* 5: 102–16.

Young, M.J.L., Latham, J.D. and Serjeant, R.B. (eds) (1990) *Religion, Learning and Science in the Abbasid Period* (Cambridge History of Arabic Literature), Cambridge: Cambridge University Press.

Zafiropulo, Jean (1953) *Empédocle d'Agrigente*, Paris: Éds Belles Lettres.

Zborowski, Mark (1952) 'Cultural components in responses to pain', *Journal of Social Issues* 8: 16–30.

Zeitlin, Froma I. (1996) 'Signifying difference: the case of Hesiod's Pandora' in *Playing the Other: Gender and Society in Classical Greek Literature*, Chicago and London: University of Chicago Press, 53–86.

Zervos, Skeuos (ed.) (1901) *Aetii sermo sextidecimus et ultimus*, Leipzig: Mangkos.

INDEX